THE

HOUSE

OF

KENNEDY

For a preview of upcoming books and information about the author, visit JamesPatterson.com or find him on Facebook, Twitter, or Instagram.

THE
HOUSE
OF
KENNEDY

JAMES PATTERSON
AND CYNTHIA FAGEN

BACK BAY BOOKS

Little, Brown and Company

New York Boston London

Back Bay Books / Little, Brown and Company
Hachette Book Group
1290 Avenue of the Americas, New York, NY 10104
littlebrown.com

Originally published in hardcover by Little, Brown and Company, April 2020

First Back Bay trade paperback edition, March 2021

Back Bay Books is an imprint of Little, Brown and Company, a division of Hachette Book Group, Inc. The Back Bay Books name and logo are trademarks of Hachette Book Group, Inc.

The publisher is not responsible for websites (or their content) that are not owned by the publisher.

The Hachette Speakers Bureau provides a wide range of authors for speaking events. To find out more, go to hachettespeakersbureau.com or call (866) 376-6591.

Part Title photographs courtesy of the following: One—Morgan Collection/Getty Images; Two—Imagno/Getty Images; Three—Bettmann Archive//Getty Images (both images); Four—Walter Sanders/The LIFE Picture Collection via Getty Images; Five—Bill Eppridge/The LIFE Picture Collection via Getty Images; Six—Ron Galella, Ltd./Ron Galella Collection via Getty Images; Seven—Everett/Shutterstock; Eight—Ron Galella/Ron Galella Collection via Getty Images.

ISBN 978-0-316-45448-3 (hc) / 978-0-316-494861 (large print) / 978-0-316-70283-6 (pb)
Library of Congress Control Number: 2019956555

Printing1,2020

LSC-C

Printed in the United States of America

PROLOGUE

The frail old man wakes screaming, tangled in an American flag—the same one that draped the coffin of his slain son, President John Fitzgerald Kennedy, three days after his November 22, 1963, assassination.

Joseph Kennedy Sr., the seventy-five-year-old patriarch of the Kennedy dynasty, who once could sway prime ministers and presidents with his Irish charm, is suffering the lingering effects of a stroke, unable to communicate beyond moaning the words "yaaa" and "nooo." Trapped inside his nearly paralyzed body, he struggles to pull himself free from the flag.

The flag had sheathed the president's casket, borne by horse-drawn caisson to Arlington National Cemetery two days earlier. After the army bugler sounded taps, the military honor guard watching over the gravesite folded the flag thirteen times to form a triangle showing only a field of blue stars, as customary, then presented it to Jacqueline Bouvier Kennedy, the president's stoic widow.

And Jackie wants her beloved father-in-law to have it. The

man she calls "Grandpa" has been convalescing at the Kennedy compound in Hyannis Port, Massachusetts, too ill to attend the funeral. Before Jackie kisses Joe Sr. good-bye to return to her two small children, Caroline and John Jr., she leaves the flag near his bed—where, during the night, Joe's niece Ann Gargan has innocently unfolded the flag and placed it over him.

⸺ ◈ ⸺

Three days earlier, when the news of Jack's death had first broken and the world mourned the assassination of the dashing thirty-fifth president, private nurse Rita Dallas kept watch over his bedridden father.

"He was a helpless man who had lost a son," Dallas observed. "But even more he was a man yet to be comforted by his family, yet to be told anything except that his son had been murdered."

While Joe's wife, Rose Kennedy, paced in her room across the hall from her husband's, too distraught to talk, two of their children, Senator Ted Kennedy and his older sister Eunice Kennedy Shriver, rushed to Joe's bedside to perform the grim family duty.

Eunice grabbed her father's withered hand and kissed him. "Daddy, there's been an accident," she whispered. "Jack was in an accident, Daddy. Oh, Daddy. Jack's dead. He's dead. But he's in Heaven," she affirmed. "Jack's okay, isn't he, Daddy?"

Ted, his face tearstained, told him the awful news: "Dad, Jack was shot."

The man who taught his children that crying is a sign of weakness closed his eyes, and two teardrops fell down his cheeks.

"Nooo," he howled.

⸺ ◈ ⸺

Already, he has outlived his firstborn, Joe Jr., a World War II navy pilot killed while flying a secret combat mission, as well as his free-spirited daughter Kathleen, who died in a private plane crash. And his oldest daughter, Rosemary, who he subjected to a disastrous experimental lobotomy, is left permanently disabled. And now, his second-born son, Jack—killed, his gruesome death caught on film.

Joseph Kennedy Sr.'s life's ambition is to place a Kennedy in the White House, and he will see his two surviving sons pick up the baton and reach for the Oval Office. But Bobby is murdered before he can capture the Democratic presidential nomination, and Ted is caught in a scandal that leaves a woman dead, dooming his chances to attain the presidency.

In July 1969, Ted Kennedy wonders aloud if a "curse actually did hang over all the Kennedys." From Joe Sr.'s death in November that same year to nearly three decades later in July 1999, when Jack's son (and heir apparent to America's version of a royal family), John F. Kennedy Jr., meets his own terrible fate, tragedies continue to haunt the House of Kennedy.

"The Kennedy Curse" is an idea that endures.

PART ONE

The Patriarch

JOSEPH PATRICK KENNEDY SR.

CHAPTER 1

They are known as "coffin ships": overcrowded, disease-riddled, barely seaworthy sailing vessels that transport millions of impoverished Irish fleeing the mid-nineteenth-century Great Hunger, or potato famine, hoping to begin new lives in the US and Canada. Assuming they make it that far—some 30 percent of transatlantic passengers commonly die at sea during the treacherous three-thousand-mile crossings, which can take as long as four months.

Given the conditions, many travelers mark their departure from Ireland with an "American wake," evoking the finality of the voyage they are about to undertake. One such traveler is Patrick Joseph Kennedy, a twenty-seven-year-old cask and barrel maker from Dunganstown, County Wexford, and future great-grandfather of President John F. Kennedy. His name appears on the 1849 manifest of the SS *Washington Irving*, a ship with fewer than five years under sail.

Records of shipboard conditions indicate that they are universally harrowing, and the monthlong crossing from Liverpool to Boston is no exception. Overcrowding and unsanitary quarters propagate deadly cases of cholera, smallpox, and measles; the ship's crew toss scores of corpses to the sharks that incessantly circle the three-masted ship.

While Kennedy family lore tells of Patrick traveling in steerage with his bride-to-be, Bridget Murphy (as well as her parents, who'd toiled their whole lives as tenant farmers of absentee British landlords), practical evidence of that can't be found. Regardless, Patrick and Bridget did most likely meet in Ireland and plan to marry in America—which they'll do in September 1849, in Boston's Cathedral of the Holy Cross.

The ship docks in Boston, a city of seventeen thousand, on April 21, 1849.

Conditions on land are not always an improvement—the Boston Brahmins atop the city's entrenched class system scorn the new immigrants as "shanty Irish" (after the Dickensian squalor of their vermin- and disease-infested tenement quarters), and fruitless searches for jobs that pay a decent wage are underscored by sternly worded want ads declaring, "No Irish Need Apply."

For a time, Patrick Kennedy and his bride are among the lucky ones. He and Bridget have five children in nine years, and he steadily works his trade. More than a hundred years later, on a state visit to Ireland in 1963, President Kennedy states: "When my great-grandfather left here to become a cooper in East Boston, he carried nothing with him except two things: a strong religious faith and a strong desire for liberty. I am glad to say that all of his great-grandchildren have valued that inheritance."

Unfortunately, at age thirty-five, Patrick succumbs to cholera. The year of his death is 1858. The date is November 22. Exactly 105 years later, that same date will forever loom as the day his great-grandson loses his life.

With five children to support, widow Bridget can't mourn for long. Though barely literate, she proves to be a savvy businesswoman. She becomes a hairdresser at the upscale retailer Jordan Marsh, founded in 1851 as a dry-goods emporium. Then she buys a notions shop—and expands her wares to include whiskey.

The youngest of the five Kennedy children, Patrick Joseph Jr.—nicknamed P.J.—inherits his parents' ambition. He is in his mid-teens when he's hired on as a stevedore, loading and unloading ships' cargo, and by the time he's in his twenties, owns several saloons popular among the Irish Catholic working class. He marries Mary Augusta Hickey, daughter of another well-to-do Irish Catholic saloon keeper, in 1887.

The liquor business makes P.J. rich, but he has a thirst for politics. In a city where Protestants control commerce, industry, and education, P.J. finds another way to peddle influence. He starts giving out free drinks to those who can help him rise in the Democratic Party.

Among them is the future mayor of Boston, John "Honey Fitz" Fitzgerald. The two men forge what will become a powerful alliance. P.J. becomes a boss in East Boston's Ward Two, where the booming Irish population now accounts for a third of Boston's residents. As Irish Catholics swell the ranks of the police and fire departments, P.J.'s political clout soars. He is only twenty-seven when he's elected to the first of what will be five consecutive terms in the Massachusetts House of Representatives, followed by two terms in the state senate.

Soon, P.J.'s formidable negotiation skills and political savvy steer him out of the barroom and into the world of finance. He purchases shares in a local bank, the Columbia Trust Company. The Kennedy fortunes rise exponentially. The family has finally shed the derisive moniker of penniless "shanty Irish" and joined the ranks of the respectable, moneyed "lace curtain Irish."

On September 6, 1888, P.J. and Mary celebrate the arrival of their firstborn, a son. They don't stretch their choices for a name. P.J. simply reverses his own initials. The newborn is christened Joseph Patrick.

Unlike their impoverished Irish immigrant grandparents, Joe and his three younger sisters grow up with all perks of wealth. They live in a three-story redbrick mansion on exclusive Jeffries Point, with a view of bustling Boston Harbor.

As an enterprising teenager, Joe works in a haberdashery, and on Fridays he lights the coal stoves for Orthodox Jews forbidden to work on their Sabbath.

He attends the exclusive public Boston Latin School. Joe stands out for being Catholic among the overwhelmingly Protestant student body—and for an academic record poor enough to necessitate repeating the eleventh grade. But Joe is socially astute, always working an angle. Tall and lean with piercing blue eyes, he joins the school's baseball team, and the recognition helps get him elected class president.

Getting into WASPy Harvard in 1908 isn't as easy, especially with his less-than-stellar grades. But Joe isn't shy about using his father's connections. And whenever his grades tank, Joe plies teachers with the family currency: a bottle of Haig & Haig Scotch.

But it's P.J., a portly man with a handlebar mustache and years of service in Massachusetts state government, who teaches his son the biggest lesson of all: "Win at all costs." One of young Joe's earliest memories, biographer Edward Klein relates, is of two of P.J.'s campaign aides bragging, "We voted 128 times today."

Joe graduates from Harvard in 1912 envisioning a future in banking, despite it being a field long dominated by Brahmins. His father, a director of the small Boston bank Columbia Trust Company, secures Joe a position as assistant state bank examiner, conducting the exacting work of audits and financial regulatory compliance.

"Banking could lead a man anywhere," Joe boasts, then proves his claim by becoming the country's youngest bank president at age twenty-five.

"Joe Kennedy saw early," a friend observes, that "power came from money." For Joe, learning the rules of finance is also an education in how to break them—undetected.

Business associates are keenly aware of Joe's cutthroat—often amoral—tactics. As the Kennedy family interest in Columbia Trust comes under attack during a wave of hostile takeover attempts, Joe borrows heavily. His three sisters and their families endure heavy losses from risky stock investments Joe makes with their money. But despite being deeply in debt, Joe manages to turn his fortunes around, and in 1914 marries Mayor Honey Fitz's convent-educated daughter Rose Fitzgerald. The pair will go on to create what the December 1969 *Ladies' Home Journal* dubs "the century's most historic family."

Over the next seventeen years, Rose bears nine children: Joseph "Joe" Patrick Jr. in 1915, John "Jack" Fitzgerald in 1917, Rose "Rosemary" Marie in 1918, Kathleen "Kick" Agnes in 1920, Eunice Mary in 1921, Patricia "Pat" Helen in 1924, Robert "Bobby" Francis in 1925, Jean Ann in 1928, and Edward "Ted" Moore in 1932.

All of the Kennedy children grow up with their grandfather P.J.'s mantra—"win at all costs"—ringing in their ears. "The big thing we learned from Daddy," Eunice says, "was win. Don't come in second or third—that doesn't count—but win, win, win."

Even so, Rose and Joe make the children understand the imperative of devotion to public service. "To whom much is given, much is expected," from the Gospel of St. Luke, is often repeated in the Kennedy household.

Youngest daughter Jean Kennedy Smith, who would go on to

serve as ambassador to Ireland from 1993 to 1998, pinpoints her parents' motivations: "They were very conscious of the tremendous oppression their ancestors had overcome and were extremely thankful to be Americans. They felt a duty to give back to the country that had embraced their family."

⟩⟨⟩⟨⟩

Joe and Rose Kennedy begin their early family life in a nine-room Colonial house at 83 Beals Street in Brookline, Massachusetts. Joe is employed at the Boston brokerage Hayden, Stone & Company, under the mentorship of Galen Stone, until he goes into business for himself as "Joseph P. Kennedy, Banker." But by the late 1920s, Joe—by then a father of seven and already a multimillionaire—sours on the strictures of his hometown.

Boston is "no place to bring up children," he decides, ordering up a private railcar to transport the family to Riverdale, New York, where in 1927 the family takes up residence in relatively close proximity to Wall Street. A 1963 *Fortune* magazine profile of Joe quotes the banker and Bostonian Ralph Lowell: "This city was a small, clear puddle. New York was a big, muddy one, and that's what Joe wanted." Joe enhances his career as an independent financier, achieving further astonishing success as a speculator.

Exactly *how* wealthy he becomes is a little murky, even to Joe. When Rose reads that *Fortune* has estimated his wealth in the mid-1920s as two million dollars (around twenty-five million in today's dollars), she asks "if it was true, and if so, why he hadn't told her they were rich," biographer Ronald Kessler says. Joe's evasive reply is "How could I tell you, when I didn't know myself?"

Two years later, the family moves to Crownlands, a 1905 mansion situated on a multiacre property at 294 Pondfield Road in Bronxville. According to Patricia Kennedy Lawford, those were "very, very happy times particularly on weekends and holidays where Joe junior and John returned from school usually with houseguests."

Ted Kennedy recalls his father's adage "Home holds no fear for me." But the meaning could cut two ways. "Complaining was strictly forbidden. We were not allowed to sit around moaning because we could not go to the movies or received a poor mark in our geometry class," Jean Kennedy Smith says. "Dad's voice would clamp down in our ears. 'There's no whining in this house!'"

"Dinner at Uncle Joe's began promptly at 7:15 o'clock," Kennedy cousin Joe Gargan recalls, "and no one was to be late." Biographer Thomas Reeves further relates, "If one of the [children's] guests was tardy, Joe would often fly into a rage and administer a tongue-lashing. One such victim [was] a pal of Jack's who never returned" to the Kennedy table.

Meals are also a time for discussions of current events and politics, often kicked off with questions. "Where has Amelia Earhart gone?" Jean Kennedy Smith recalls being asked at age nine when the famous aviator went missing.

Inevitably, the talk turns to Joe Sr.'s aspiration to have his family run the country. Eunice Kennedy Shriver explains how Rose, the children's "greatest teacher," helped the young ones through. "She taught us to listen to Dad's dinner table conversations about politics, which seemed too boring to a small child but later become the basis for our life's work."

And Rose herself, Jean recalls, would arrive at the breakfast table "with newspaper articles she found interesting pinned to her dress."

For her part, Rose describes the household division of labor between her and Joe in business terms: "We were individuals with highly responsible roles in a partnership that yielded rewards which we shared. There was nothing that he could do to help me in bearing a child, just as there was nothing I could do directly in helping him bear the burdens of business."

Any motherly frustrations are carefully confined, even in her journal: "Took care of children. Miss Brooks, the governess, helped. Kathleen still has bronchitis and Joe sick in bed. Great life."

Frustrations aside, Rose harbors great nostalgia for precious childhood memorabilia, and keeps meticulous family records. "There's a memory of mine, and of all of us, growing up," Pat Kennedy later says, "that Mother was in the attic, putting things away."

"Mother kept all our vital statistics on index cards that became an absolute necessity as our numbers began to grow," recounts Jean. The international press, Rose remarks, lauded her card file as a "symbol of 'American efficiency.' Actually, it had just been a matter of 'Kennedy desperation.'"

Young Jack's poor health was a constant worry for Rose. "Jack had what Mother called an 'elfin quality,'" Jean explains of her elder brother, "because he was so sickly for most of his childhood. Whooping cough, measles, chicken pox, and the dreaded scarlet fever all found Jack and sent him to bed."

Yet Joe draws on a father's supreme confidence in the strength of his son Jack, a feeling that would endure throughout the Kennedy presidency. "I see him on TV," he tells presidential biographer William Manchester many years later, "in rain and cold, bareheaded, and I don't worry. I know nothing can happen to him. I tell you, something's watching out for him. I've stood by his deathbed four times. Each time I said good-bye to him, and he always came back.... When you've been through something like that and back, and the Pacific, what can hurt you? Who's going to scare you."

Joe dares to believe that nothing else bad could happen to Jack.

He is a Kennedy, after all.

CHAPTER 2

In 1926, before moving his growing brood from Boston to New York, a restless Joe Kennedy leaves his family on the East Coast to follow a twentieth-century California gold rush: Hollywood. There's money to be made and women to be had.

To maximize potential profit, Joe targets small film studios. He partners to buy the fledgling FBO, Film Booking Office of America, for one million dollars. It's the predecessor of Radio-Keith-Orpheum, RKO, later famous for greenlighting then-unknown director Orson Welles to make *Citizen Kane.* As studio head, Joe's aim is to make "American films for Americans." But it's much more profitable to make cheap pictures like *The Gorilla Hunt,* the kind of film that he "couldn't for the life of him understand why it made money, but it did," notes actress Gloria Swanson.

In clubby Hollywood, an outsider attracts outsize attention. *Who is Joe Kennedy? What interest does an East Coast banker have in the movie business?* rival studio heads want to know. The mutual distrust is inflamed by Joe's virulent anti-Semitism, a discordant echo of the discrimination his own Irish Catholic ancestors suffered at the hands of Boston Protestants. He tells friends of his intention to wipe out the Jewish movie producers he calls "pants pressers."

"Joe Kennedy operated just like Joe Stalin," associates remark, and gossip columnist Louella Parsons dubs Joe "the Napoleon of the movies." He is the only studio head in Hollywood history to run three of them simultaneously. He slashes jobs, turning each property into a streamlined model of fiscal austerity, a blueprint for future studio management and mergers. He's also instrumental in bringing talkies to the silver screen despite critics who are still convinced the new technology is a fad.

When his father, P.J. Kennedy, passes away, Joe is too busy to return to Boston for the funeral.

He's rarely too busy for a pretty girl, however. Indeed, Joe's appetite for bedding young women is known to be insatiable. He asks a New York theater manager to arrange introductions to "all the good-looking girls in your company," any aspiring actresses with Hollywood dreams. "I have a gang around me that must be fed on wild meat," he writes.

But unknown ingenues won't further Joe's business interests. For that, he needs movie stars. He tries and fails to convince Babe Ruth to appear in his movies. Then, in November 1927, he meets Gloria Swanson at a New York City luncheon in the hotel dining room at the Barclay, where she is a frequent guest. An instant attraction sparks between the six-foot, bespectacled, thirty-eight-year-old studio head and the twenty-eight-year-old screen siren who stands less than five feet tall.

At the table, Joe hands Swanson, whom the renowned director Cecil B. DeMille called "the movie star of all movie stars," a book he edited, *The Story of Films*. The gift marks the beginning of a three-year romance.

Though Swanson earns millions, her lavish lifestyle drains her coffers. In 1924, *Photoplay* magazine breathlessly reports on her extravagant expenditures—ten thousand dollars a year on lingerie and five hundred a month for perfume—in an era when the average American individual income is fifty-five hundred dollars annually.

The debonair Boston banker turned Hollywood producer promises to get her out of debt. He convinces her to let him manage her finances, filing a charter in Delaware for a new company, Gloria Productions, Inc., and instituting a complex system in which he'll write "a letter to the files saying one thing and then order the exact reverse on the phone." Though Swanson is grateful to Joe, who has "taken the business load off" of her, her finances show little sign of improvement, thanks in part to his underhanded habit of charging his own pricey personal expenses to her account. At least one newspaper cites Joe's transcontinental calls to Swanson as "the largest private telephone bill in the nation during the year 1929."

Joe is smitten with the blue-eyed screen goddess. Their intimate affair begins one afternoon at the Hotel Poinciana in Palm Beach. He slyly arranges to have his friend and business associate Edward Moore take Swanson's third husband, the French marquis Henri de Bailly de La Falaise, on a deep-sea fishing trip while Joe makes a surprise visit to Swanson's room.

"He moved so quickly that his mouth was on mine before either of us could speak," she recounts in her memoir, *Swanson on Swanson*.

"With one hand he held the back of my head, with the other he stroked my body and pulled at my kimono. He kept insisting in a drawn-out moan, 'No longer, no longer. Now.' He was like a roped horse, rough, arduous, racing to be free. After a hasty climax he lay beside me, stroking my hair. Apart from his guilty, passionate mutterings, he had still said nothing cogent."

The affair escalates in intensity, with the married Joe proclaiming his "fidelity" to the married Swanson. As she writes in her memoir, "He stunned me by telling me proudly that there had been no Kennedy baby that year"—though his wife, Rose, had been already five months pregnant with their eighth child, Jean Ann (born February 20, 1928), when Joe and Swanson met in November 1927. "What he wanted more than anything, he continued, was for us to have a child," Swanson writes. Swanson is not interested in this career-threatening idea, and flatly refuses.

Except when it comes to the children, Rose and Joe deliberately lead separate lives: "If he was in Europe, she would be here [in the States], and if she was in New York, he would be in Palm Beach. If he was in Palm Beach, she would be in New York," a family friend remembers.

In 1929, Joe books two sets of accommodations for a steamship Atlantic crossing—one stateroom suite for Rose and the eight kids, and, on a deck below, one for Swanson. The illicit pair strolls the ship deck arm in arm, shipboard gossip feeding tabloid headlines.

Biographer Doris Kearns Goodwin recounts an extended family argument over the affair, in which Rose's mother, Josie, chastises her daughter. "You see, you fool, your beloved husband is no different from your beloved father. Now you finally know what men are really like."

But Rose manages to maintain the upper hand over "poor little Gloria," as she calls Swanson. She knows Joe will never divorce her; nor does he have any inclination to marry any of his many mistresses. Swanson writes of Rose, "Was she a fool, I asked myself...or a saint? Or just a better actress than I was?"

"Kennedy is the first and only outsider to fleece Hollywood," says Betty Lasky, daughter of the Paramount cofounder Jesse Lasky. During his three-year reign, Joe's only major failure is the ill-fated *Queen Kelly* (originally titled *The Swamp*), a sexually explosive, uncensored 1929 silent movie. Gloria Swanson, then age thirty, plays the title role of poor Irish convent girl, Patricia "Kitty" Kelly. Joe hires the renowned Austrian film director Erich von Stroheim.

But the production is an utter failure. Stroheim insists on hundreds of retakes, busting the budget. Swanson quits. Joe shells out an additional six hundred thousand dollars to salvage the movie, but when it becomes clear that the film is a disaster, Joe is devastated. Swanson, in her autobiography, recalls how he once left a screening of the footage to burst into her bungalow on the Pathé lot. "He held his head in his hands, and little, high-pitched sounds escaped from his rigid body, like those of a wounded animal whimpering in a trap. He finally found his voice. It was quiet, controlled. 'I've never had a failure in my life' were his first words." The experience leads Joe to break his own family edict—"Kennedys don't cry."

Queen Kelly is shelved for decades, finally receiving a New York theatrical premiere in 1985, though movie trivia fans might recognize it from Billy Wilder's 1950 masterpiece, *Sunset Boulevard*. Swanson, then fifty-one, plays Norma Desmond, a delusional aging silent film star. In one scene, where she is watching a movie starring her younger self, the images are unreleased snippets from *Queen Kelly*. The second piece of trivia? In the film, *Queen Kelly* director Erich von Stroheim plays Desmond's devoted servant.

Joe doesn't allow the *Queen Kelly* debacle to slow his roughshod ride through Hollywood. He buys up theaters to showcase his films. Not everyone wishes to sell to him, but Joe has some strong-arm tactics. According to Ronald Kessler's biography, *The Sins of the Father,* in 1929 Greek-born Alexander Pantages refuses multiple offers to sell his sixty movie palaces to Joe Kennedy. Within months, Pantages is accused of raping seventeen-year-old Eunice Pringle in a broom closet in one of his LA theaters.

"There he is, the beast!" Pringle exclaims of Pantages, racing to the lobby in search of the police.

Pantages shouts, "She's trying to frame me!" but is promptly arrested.

At trial, Pringle is the star witness, testifying to a rapt courtroom full of newspaper reporters, "He was kissing me madly. Not only was he kissing me," she says, dramatically pointing to her breasts, "he was biting me."

Pantages is convicted and sentenced to fifty years behind bars—until his lawyer appeals the judge's denial of testimony about the underage accuser's "morals," especially Pringle's living with a man out of wedlock. The new trial introduces proof that the dimensions of the broom closet made the alleged details of the rape a physical impossibility. Pantages is acquitted in 1931, but at the cost of his multimillion-dollar fortune. Now broke, he is forced to sell his business to Joe for three and a half million dollars, less than half of the original eight-million-dollar offer.

By 1933, Eunice Pringle has a change of heart. As Ronald Kessler relates, she is preparing to publicly expose her true involvement in the case, and who put her up to it, when she suddenly dies, possibly from cyanide poisoning. The cause of death—murder or suicide—is undetermined. In a deathbed confession to her mother and a friend, Pringle names Joe Kennedy as the mastermind behind the Pantages setup, claiming that in exchange for false testimony, the producer paid Pringle's agent ten thousand dollars and guaranteed the young woman stardom. She dies without ever receiving the money or the fame.

Yet while Joe certainly profited from Pantages's crises, any nefarious involvement on his part remains unproven.

"He's a charmer," pronounces Frances Marion, a top screenwriter and memoirist. "A typical Irish charmer, but he's a rascal." The scribe—who was the highest-paid screenwriter of Hollywood's Golden Age, making three thousand dollars per week (more than forty thousand in today's dollars) at MGM in the 1920s—recognizes the illusion of power that Irish charm wields. "Frances rarely said anything negative about anyone," her daughter-in-law later recalls, "but she hated Joe Kennedy with a passion."

Joe's final act in Hollywood is to write himself out, having added prosperously to his already considerable fortune.

CHAPTER 3

When the time comes that a shoeshine boy knows as much as I do about what is going on in the stock market, it's time for me to get out." Even as Joe Kennedy Sr. turns from Hollywood and finance to politics, he's spinning yet another tale, this one tailored to Wall Streeters eager to pin him for short-selling on the largely unregulated stock market.

As the 1929 crash hits and the Great Depression takes hold, Joe demonstrates his support of Franklin Delano Roosevelt's efforts toward shoring up the capitalist system by becoming one of FDR's biggest campaign donors. And when in 1934, soon after his first inauguration, President Roosevelt creates the Securities and Exchange Commission—for the protection of investors from swindles, schemes, and insider trading—he has a surprise appointee for chairman of the SEC: Joe Kennedy Sr.

The president rates Joe's deep knowledge of financial trickery as an asset. He wryly observes, "It takes a thief to catch a thief."

And Joe does indeed go after them. During his yearlong tenure, the SEC mandates the registration of stock sales and financial disclosures and investigates some two thousand small securities fraud cases. On July 25, 1934, Chairman Kennedy addresses the National Press Club, positioning the SEC as "simple and honest," and says, "Only those who see things crookedly will find [the new rules] harsh."

Joe "had the sense to recognize the opportunity offered by the SEC," one financier says, and to revel in his power. "Joe could tell the moneymen in New York what they would do, and they damned well better do it, or he could sweep them into the sea."

Though some moguls continue to operate unchecked, Joe's new rules do ensnare at least one notable: John "Black Jack" Bouvier. Bouvier is a handsome Hamptons socialite who made his fortune on Wall Street, though he prefers gambling, drinking, and womanizing to boardroom duties.

In July 1929, when Bouvier's daughter Jacqueline (later to become one of America's most beloved First Ladies) is born, "Black Jack" is a wealthy man. But unlike Joe, who strategically divested himself of vulnerable stock holdings in advance of the October 1929 crash, Bouvier is financially decimated by it, and goes on to owe substantial back taxes and subsist on loans from his father-in-law.

Joe enjoys being a "Washington insider," with the accompanying political and social freedoms. He rents Marwood, a thirty-three-room, eleven-bathroom Italianate mansion in Maryland overlooking the Potomac River.

Kennedy and President Roosevelt enjoy a warm, if cautious, friendship. The two men smoke cigars together when the wheelchair-bound president visits the house, accessible via an elevator Joe has installed specifically to accommodate FDR.

On the weekends, Joe visits with Rose and the kids, either

at their home in Bronxville; the compound in Hyannis Port on Cape Cod, purchased in 1928; or the Palm Beach mansion, purchased in 1933. He devotedly writes weekly letters to each of his sons and daughters, though he reserves his sternest words for the boys. To Jack, in December 1934: "I am not expecting too much and I will not be disappointed if you don't turn out to be a real genius."

In September 1935, he steps down from the SEC to run the new US Maritime Commission, responsible for building modern merchant ships to replace World War I–era vessels.

Joe quietly plants stories about himself and his family in the press. One key contact is Henry Luce of *Time* magazine. Another is Arthur Krock, the *New York Times* Washington bureau chief, who enjoys vacations at the Kennedy mansion in Palm Beach and other luxury perks in exchange for favorable coverage.

All the while, Joe is deepening a friendship and business relationship with the president's son, James Roosevelt II, who finds himself caught between the interests of two powerful men he admires. In 1937 Joe writes, "You know as far as I am concerned...I am your foster-father."

As World War II looms in Europe, FDR knows that Joe is pining to be appointed the first Irish Catholic ambassador to Great Britain, but tells his son to instead offer him a consolation post. Arthur Krock, in his oral history interview for the John F. Kennedy Presidential Library and Museum, relates Joe's response: "He tried to get me to take the Secretaryship of Commerce and I knew it was only an attempt to shut me off from London, but London is where I want to go and it is the only place I intend to go and I told Jimmy so, and that's that."

Upon receiving word of his reaction to the offer, the president calls Joe to the Oval Office. In his memoir, *My Parents,* James Roosevelt recalls the fun his father unleashes at Joe's expense.

FDR makes two requests. "Would you mind stepping back a bit, by the fireplace perhaps, so I can get a good look at you?" Then, "Joe, would you mind taking your pants down?"

"I guess it was the power of the presidency," James Roosevelt theorizes as despite their mutual confusion, Joe complies, standing in front of the president in his underwear.

"Someone who saw you in a bathing suit once said something I now know to be true," FDR states. "Joe, just look at your legs. You are just about the most bowlegged man I have ever seen. Don't you know that the ambassador to the Court of Saint James's has to go through an induction ceremony in which he wears knee breeches and silk stockings? Can you imagine how you'll look? When photos of our new ambassador appear all over the world, we'll be a laughingstock. You're just not right for the job, Joe."

Still working the angles in spite of his embarrassment, Joe pleads, "Mr. President, if I can get the permission of His Majesty's government to wear a cutaway coat and striped pants to the ceremony, would you agree to appoint me?"

FDR won't relent. "Well, Joe, you know how the British are about tradition. There is no way you are going to get permission, and I must name a new ambassador soon."

Joe continues to bargain. "Will you give me two weeks?"

The president agrees—and how he laughs when Joe returns with official permission from the British government to wear trousers.

When Joe later presents his credentials to His Majesty King George VI, some observers credit his stubborn Irish moxie for bucking the traditional garb of breeches and silk stockings. They have no idea it was FDR who put him up to it.

CHAPTER 4

On February 23, 1938, Joe Kennedy Sr. sets sail on the SS *Manhattan* for Southhampton, England, as the new American ambassador to the Court of St. James. He travels alone that day, but his family continues to make news. "The Kennedy Family: Nine Children and Nine Million Dollars" trumpets *Life* magazine in advance of their transatlantic crossing, and "Jolly Joe, the Nine-Child Envoy" is widely celebrated in London. "The Kennedys were the royal family that England wanted to have," notes Will Swift, who writes about the Kennedys' "thousand days" in London.

The new ambassador, his wife, Rose, and their children settle in fashionable St. James Square, enjoying the diplomatic perks of chauffeured limos and a glittering social calendar. Rose delights in studying royal protocol in preparation for a May 11, 1938, presentation at Buckingham Palace for herself and her husband, along with their eldest daughters, eighteen-year-old Kathleen and nineteen-year-old Rosemary.

The Kennedys are popular guests among British high society.

At one 1938 dance, Lady Redesdale observes of Jack Kennedy, "I would not be surprised if that young man becomes President of the United States."

Jack's sister Kathleen—originally nicknamed "Kick" because her siblings stumbled over the full pronunciation, but it stuck for her spirited antics—also makes a heightened impression. At elite parties, she chews gum and, in her unmistakable American accent, calls the Duke of Marlborough "Dookie-Wookie." Lady Jean Ogilvy remembers Kick once starting a food fight, and how everyone at the table joined in. "If someone else had done that, it might have been rude or shocking…But she had this way about her that made it seem an absolute liberation," notes Paula Byrne, a Kick biographer.

Lem Billings, a family friend, recalls Kick's declaration that her days in England made her "a person in her own right, not just a Kennedy girl."

Around the same time, Joe and Charles Lindbergh, America's famous aviator, meet at the home of Lady Astor and form an instant friendship. Lindbergh is a Nazi sympathizer, and friendly with Hitler. Regarding the brewing war in Europe, Joe declares, "For the life of me I cannot see anything involved which could be remotely considered worth shedding blood for," and blames the Jews for instigating the Nazi persecution, bluntly stating to his aide Harvey Klemmer, "They brought it on themselves."

The British prime minister, Neville Chamberlain, also favors appeasement, and in September 1938 signs the Munich Agreement, which paves the way for Hitler to invade Czechoslovakia. "I believe it is peace for our time," Chamberlain optimistically declares.

But peace ends on September 3, 1939, when Hitler marches into Poland and England declares war on Germany.

When Joe calls FDR with the news, his voice is trembling.

"It's the end of the world. The end of everything," he says, and asks to come back to Washington. Roosevelt forbids any such acknowledgment of American fear.

Nevertheless, Joe surreptitiously sends his family home immediately—taking precaution to book them on separate travel accommodations. Rose, Kick (age nineteen), Eunice (eighteen), and Bobby (thirteen), set out on September 12, 1939, aboard the SS *Washington,* crowded with nearly fifteen hundred Americans fleeing Europe. Patricia (fifteen), Jean (eleven), and Ted (seven), board a second vessel, and Joe Jr. (twenty-four), a third. Jack (twenty-two), crosses the Atlantic by plane. Only Rosemary, who turns twenty-one that September 13, stays "out of duty to remain behind with [her] father" at a convent school in rural Hertfordshire.

With the bombing of London still a year off, and America's entrance into the war uncertain, Joe takes bold, even reckless, action. Without consulting the State Department, he arranges a meeting with Hitler to "bring about a better understanding between the United States and Germany." The attempt fails, effectively ending his ambassadorship, and perhaps his political career.

Yet a letter to a friend reveals how quickly Joe is able to redirect his ambitions: "I find myself more interested in what young Joe is going to do than in what I am going to do with the rest of my life."

On the eve of the 1940 presidential election, Joe returns home, his ties to FDR severely diminished. He leans away from the president in favor of the inexperienced Republican candidate Wendell Willkie, who'd been a Democrat until 1939. But Roosevelt, who is running for an extraordinary (then constitutional) third term, needs Joe to secure the Catholic vote.

With the election set for November 5, FDR extends Joe and

Rose an invitation. "Come to the White House tonight for a little family dinner," he offers, feeding Joe's lust for presidential power, and the promises of future endorsements.

Joe falls in line, agreeing to appear on a national radio broadcast in support of Roosevelt's candidacy. He writes the speech in secret, revealing his words to no one.

On October 29, 1940, Joe goes on the radio and speaks of America, of politics, and, finally, of his family. "After all, I have a great deal at stake in this country. My wife and I have given nine hostages to fortune. Our children and your children are more important than anything else in the world."

His popular ideas turn out the vote. Roosevelt is elected for a third term. At age fifty-six, Joe will see the president win a fourth term, too.

Nine hostages to fortune. How darkly prophetic a father's words would prove for his children.

PART TWO

The Two Roses

ROSE FITZGERALD KENNEDY AND ROSE MARIE "ROSEMARY" KENNEDY

CHAPTER 5

Public life starts early for the woman who will become the matriarch of the Kennedy political dynasty.

With her long black hair, petite figure, and perfect posture, Rose Elizabeth is a familiar sight at campaign events for her father, John "Honey Fitz" Fitzgerald. Young Rose has lost count how many times she's accompanied her gregarious father on the piano. At weddings, wakes, or before the first pitch at the new Fenway Park, "Honey Fitz" plays to the crowds with his signature song, "Sweet Adeline." By the time he is elected the first Irish American mayor of Boston in 1906, the year after Rose graduates from Dorchester High School, he has already served three terms in the US Congress.

Though devoutly Catholic, Rose rejects the domesticity of her shy mother, Mary Josephine, or "Josie." "I was crazy about traveling," Rose recalls. (Her son Jack will grow to deeply resent her frequent absences, though his youthful anger—"Gee, you're a great mother to go away and leave your children alone"—morphs into adult bitterness: "She was on her knees in churches all over the world.")

As a girl, what Rose prays for most ardently is handsome, charismatic Joseph Patrick Kennedy. She first set eyes on him at Old Orchard Beach, Maine, where Boston's wealthy "lace curtain Irish" spent their summers.

She was six and he was eight.

They start dating when she is sixteen, perhaps the happiest year of Rose's life. "I wish I was sixteen" again, she declares on her one hundredth birthday.

But although Rose invites Joe to a graduation dance at Dorchester High, theirs is a forbidden courtship. Her father, Honey Fitz, detests the mediocre—in academics and athletics—member of the Harvard class of 1912, and he bans Joe from his house.

"My father didn't think I should marry the first man who asked me, and still I was very much in love, and I still didn't want to offend my parents—so we used to have these rendezvous," Rose recalls in the BBC documentary *Rose Kennedy Remembers*.

Rose will have to part temporarily from Joe, however, and for an important reason. She's been accepted by Wellesley College, the prestigious liberal arts school less than twenty miles from her home in the Boston suburb of Dorchester.

She'll miss Joe of course, but this will be her first adventure all her own. She plans to learn French and German, get her degree in music, and become a teacher.

The evening before she's set to leave for Wellesley, Honey Fitz sits his seventeen-year-old daughter down and tells her to unpack. She won't be going. He and her mother, Josie, have decided that Rose is too young.

It's a selfish lie.

The mayor wants to save his own political skin. In the

midst of a challenging reelection campaign, the local bishop has warned Honey Fitz that his daughter's attendance at a "modernist" secular college might cost him the Catholic vote.

Honey Fitz nevertheless loses the 1908 election and breaks his daughter's trust in him.

"There was screaming and yelling and absolute madness," Rose recalls to her niece, the writer Kerry McCarthy. "I was furious at my parents for years. I was angry at my church. As much as I loved my father, I never really forgave him for not letting me go."

Instead she enrolls in the Convent of the Sacred Heart in Boston but refuses to stop seeing Joe.

Honey Fitz takes drastic measures. He sends Rose and her sister Agnes to a Sacred Heart convent in the Netherlands for the next school year.

But when the homesick sisters return to Boston, Rose secretly starts seeing Joe again.

When they go ice skating, she wears a veil to hide her face. She'll allow other men to sign her dance card, but as soon as she is out of her mother's chaperoning sight, Rose partners with Joe. When he invites Rose to his 1911 Harvard junior prom, the Fitzgerald family once again collapses into turmoil.

Honey Fitz may be serving his second term as mayor of Boston, but his daughter is a citizen lost. He reluctantly gives Rose permission to marry Joe.

On October 7, 1914, after seven years of clandestine courtship, Rose, then twenty-four, and Joe, twenty-six, have their wedding day in the private chapel adjoining the home of Cardinal O'Connell, who officiates the modest ceremony.

Dressed in tails and a top hat, the ambitious young bank president looks the perfect groom. But as a husband, Joe will fall woefully short.

Rose's expectations of marriage are quickly dashed, especially in terms of sex.

"Now listen, Rosie, this idea of yours that there is no romance outside of procreation is simply wrong. It was not part of our contract at the altar," Joe tells her. "And if you don't open your mind to this, I'm going to tell the priest on you."

Rose remains a dutiful wife. In the Brookline house on Beals Street, Joe Jr. is born in 1915, followed by Jack in 1917. Obstetrician Dr. Frederick L. Good delivers the eldest Kennedy sons, as he will all nine children in the family.

But the birth of their third child goes terribly wrong.

It's September 13, 1918. World War I rages on, and so does a pandemic of Spanish influenza, infecting approximately five hundred million people, and killing fifty million worldwide, including six hundred seventy-five thousand Americans. Nearly seven thousand Bostonians have already died. To prevent further contamination, movie houses, churches, and other public gathering places are closed.

Rose goes into labor at home, as planned. But Dr. Good is detained. All physicians have been pressed into service to treat the sick and dying.

As biographer Kate Clifford Larson recounts, Rose was willing to wait, but the baby is not. She is already in the birth canal.

The nurse orders Rose to squeeze her legs tightly together to delay the birth, and, incredibly, goes so far as to push the baby's partially exposed head back into the birth canal for two excruciating hours—depriving the baby's fragile system of oxygen—until Dr. Good arrives. When the doctor finally arrives, he delivers a baby girl and pronounces her healthy.

Rosemary was "a beautiful child," Eunice Kennedy Shriver later writes in an essay published in September 1962 by the *Saturday Evening Post,* "resembling my mother in physical appearance."

Rose will also share her own name, Rose Marie, with this newest arrival. The family calls her Rosemary.

Though Rose employs a full household staff—baby nurse, housekeeper, cook (she never learned how to feed a family)—she insists, "It's a good idea to be around quite often so that you know what's going on," and she soon observes that baby Rosemary lacks the coordination her two older brothers readily displayed as toddlers, struggling with tasks as basic as walking or holding objects.

Joe desperately consults doctors and psychologists for a "cure," but medicine has yet to make sufficient pharmacological or therapeutic advancements. "I had never heard of a retarded child," Rose confesses. Specialists advise that Rosemary be confined to a mental institution.

"What can they do for her that her family can't do better?" Eunice recalls her father saying. "We will keep her at home."

Eunice underscores Joe's words: "And we did."

Rosemary's delays are cause for much dismay, especially as a reflection on her parents.

"I would much rather be the mother of a great son or daughter than be the author of a great book or the painter of a great painting," Rose famously says.

Rosemary does not seem destined to meet the Kennedy standard of greatness.

CHAPTER 6

Rose can count on her husband, Joe Kennedy Sr., to provide for the family, but she cannot rely on his day-to-day presence. He travels frequently for business—and pleasure. She confides in her diary (today stored at the John F. Kennedy Presidential Library in Boston) a torrent of feeling. She is at once certain of her husband's infidelities ("I had heard that chorus girls were gay, but evil, and worst of all, husband snatchers")—and dismissive of the idea ("But nothing shocking happened").

In 1920, while pregnant with her fourth child, Kathleen, Rose makes a bold break. She flees Beals Street for her presumed safe haven, the Fitzgerald residence. But Honey Fitz turns his daughter away, insisting that a wife must stand by her husband—as Rose's mother, Josie, has done.

Though the incident is never discussed outside the family, Rose's youthful determination that her married life would be different, freer, than her mother's, has faltered.

While Rose extends her absence at a religious retreat, two-year-old Jack falls ill with scarlet fever. Though Boston City Hospital is already past capacity, Joe applies his negotiation skills to enlist the influence of Mayor Andrew Peters, and Jack is admitted for treatment. The worried father keeps a two-month bedside vigil. "During the darkest days," Joe would write to Jack's doctor once the rash and fever have subsided, "I felt that nothing mattered except his recovery."

In 1921, Rose is pregnant once again, this time with Eunice. Joe buys a new house for the family, at 131 Naples Road in Brookline. Rose describes the place as "bigger and better," much like the "special presents" Joe bestows on her after the birth of each child. For instance, to celebrate Jean's arrival in 1928, she has her choice among three diamond bracelets.

At some point along the way, Rose decides to change her perspective.

"I used to say, 'Why did I spend time learning to read Goethe or Voltaire if I have to spend my life telling children why they should drink their milk or why they should only eat one piece of candy each day and then after meals.' But then I thought raising a family is a new challenge and I am going to meet it."

Rose is a strict disciplinarian. She insists the children attend Sunday Mass (she attends daily), and as Proverbs 13:24 instructs, she does not spare the rod. Actually, she uses a ruler from her desk, or a wooden coat hanger, an object she reasons "didn't hurt any more—probably less—than a ruler" to administer spankings "just hard enough to receive the message."

Besides, the Kennedy children are a rough-and-tumble brood, prone to intense physical rivalries. When the siblings "would play, they would knock each other down and gouge each other's eyes out with toys."

Rose sets up safety gates to protect the younger kids from the older ones, but the sounds of their roughhousing cannot be contained. According to biographer Evan Thomas, young

Bobby "used to lie in [his] bed at night sometimes and hear the sound of Joe banging Jack's head against the wall."

The exception to such violence is Rosemary, a gentle child. "She loved music, and my mother used to play the piano and sing to her," younger sister Eunice recalls.

Throughout another full decade of dutiful procreation— Eunice, Patricia, Bobby, Jean, and Ted, all born between 1921 and 1932—Rose polishes her presentation on motherhood. In 1936, she records in her calendar, "I looked upon child rearing as a profession and decided it was just as interesting and just as challenging as anything else and that it did not have to keep a woman tied down and make her dull or out of touch. She did not have to become an emaciated, worn-out old hag."

She proves herself the antithesis of an "old hag" when prominent fashion designers name Rose one of the best dressed women of the 1930s. "Joe always wanted me to dress well," Rose writes in her memoir. "It pleased him, in fact it delighted him, to have me turn up in something quite special."

Rose holds her family to the same fashionable and elegant standards she herself maintains. Thus her frustration when Jack looks less than his best, as at his Harvard graduation, "in his black academic gown, with a suitably serious expression, but with his feet in a pair of worn brown-and-white saddle shoes."

As the Kennedy family's public profile begins to rise, Rose oversees the upkeep of appearances among her photogenic family. "Mother is a perfectionist," Ted Kennedy says. She monitors the children's food intake and weighs them regularly. She also invests in cosmetic dentistry, encouraging the display of the toothy trademark Kennedy smile in all family portraits. A Choate School classmate noting, "When Jack flashed his smile, he could charm a bird off a tree," rates Rose's regimen a success.

Each summer, the Kennedys gather at Hyannis Port, where the siblings share time and activities. Sailing is a family favorite.

In 1935, calculates biographer Laurence Leamer in *The Kennedy Women,* "the young Kennedys, led by Eunice, Kathleen, and Pat . . . plus Rosemary, Jack and Joe Jr., came away with fourteen first prizes, thirteen seconds and thirteen thirds in seventy-six starts" from the Hyannis Port Yacht Club.

The Kennedy children are largely educated at boarding schools—convents for the girls, secular schools for the boys. For a time, Rosemary is homeschooled, but when she is in her early teens, Joe and Rose decide that Rosemary, too, is ready to live and study away from home. She does well academically, but she writes to Joe, "I get lonesome everyday," asking him, "Come to see me very soon."

The physical act of writing is difficult for Rosemary, but she perseveres, penning in blocky print affectionate letters to her father. "I would do anything to make you so happy. I hate to Disapoint [sic] you in anyway." But Rose and Joe's feelings go deeper than disappointment in Rosemary. They are fearful of being shunned in elite social circles for having a "defective child."

Yet Rosemary is easy to please. "She loved compliments," Eunice recalls. "Every time I would say, 'Rosemary, you have the best teeth and smile in the family,' she would smile for hours. She liked to dress up, wear pretty clothes, have her hair fixed and her fingernails polished. When she was asked out by a friend of the family, she would be thrilled."

Rosemary's happiest years may be those the family spends in England during Joe's service as ambassador. On May 11, 1938, she is presented to King George VI and Queen Elizabeth at Buckingham Palace, looking radiant in a white gown embellished with silver piping alongside her parents and sister Kathleen.

But the timing of the family's return to America upon Joe's abrupt resignation and the eruption of World War II unfortu-

nately parallels an inner conflict in Rosemary, whose behavior
noticeably regresses at age twenty-one.

Back in the States by 1940, Rose and Joe are concerned
that a "neurological disturbance" is the cause of their daughter's
emotional state, depression punctuated by violent verbal and
physical outbursts. Eunice tells of the family being "terribly serious about the problem," yet at the same time her parents
continue to wonder whether Rosemary might simply try harder
to assimilate into mainstream society.

With Joe Jr. departing for naval training, "the summer of
1941 would be the last one our family would ever have together," Rose Kennedy poignantly recalls.

That autumn, Rosemary's two closest-in-age siblings, Jack and
Kick, are both living in Washington, DC. Kick is assisting an editor for the *Washington Times-Herald,* and Jack is a new ensign in
the Naval Reserve, assigned to stateside intelligence work.

Rosemary is enrolled at Saint Gertrude's School of Arts and
Crafts, a convent school in DC catering to girls with develop-
mental delays. She is known to sneak out at night, often for
hours.

"I was always worried," Rose explains, "that she would run
away from home someday or that she would go off with someone who would flatter her or kidnap her." Though past the
typical pubescent age range, some doctors attribute Rosemary's
behavior to delayed hormonal changes. The real, unspoken fear
is that she may have a sexual encounter with a man and become
unwittingly pregnant.

"My great ambition was to have my children morally, physically, and mentally as perfect as possible," Rose states. But
Rosemary's uncontrolled behavior could publicly topple that
lofty standard.

Joe Sr. learns of a treatment he thinks can cure Rosemary: a
lobotomy.

On June 5, 1941, the American Medical Association holds its annual session in Cleveland, Ohio. A panel discussion by the Section on Nervous and Mental Diseases examines lobotomy, warning against the imprecise surgical procedure intended to treat disruptive behavior. Separating the frontal lobe from the rest of the brain, in effect destroying it, cannot "restore the person to a wholly normal state."

Through her connections at the *Washington Times-Herald*, Kick investigates the procedure and alerts her parents to its dangers. "Oh, Mother, no, it's nothing we want done for Rosie," Kick reports.

Even so, in the fall of 1941, as Ronald Kessler recounts in *The Sins of the Father*, Joe authorizes twenty-three-year-old Rosemary's admission to George Washington University Hospital, where Dr. Walter J. Freeman is a professor of neurology.

Freeman and his partner, neurosurgeon Dr. James Watts, are American pioneers of lobotomy.

Rosemary will be strapped to the operating table and anesthetized—just enough to numb the entry site at her temples, where her skull will be pierced by two holes, through which a blunt metal rod will be inserted.

As Dr. Watts performs the surgery, the supervising Dr. Freeman interacts with their patient to chart the changes in her condition. Rosemary performs simple recitations of prayers and songs. "We went through the top of the head. I think she was awake. She had a mild tranquilizer," Watts recounts to Kessler. "We made an estimate on how far to cut based on how she responded," he explains.

When she stops talking, the operation is complete.

"They knew right away that it wasn't successful. You could see by looking at her that something was wrong, for her head was tilted and her capacity to speak was almost entirely gone," Kennedy cousin Ann Gargan tells Doris Kearns Goodwin.

From that point on, Rosemary's mental capacity is irreversibly reduced to that of a preschooler. She will live out most of her life watched over by the nuns at St. Coletta's School for Exceptional Children in Wisconsin.

"I don't know what it is that makes eight children shine like a dollar [coin] and another one dull," Joe later tells John Siegenthaler, a journalist who joins the presidential campaign of 1960. "I guess it's the hand of God."

Rose would never forget the preventable tragedy that Joe brings on their eldest daughter. She dedicates her memoir, "To my daughter Rosemary and others like her—retarded in mind but blessed in spirit."

There are two Roses, but only one continues to bloom.

PART THREE

The Favorites

JOSEPH PATRICK KENNEDY JR. AND KATHLEEN "KICK" AGNES KENNEDY

CHAPTER 7

On August 12, 1944, the roar of propellers cuts through the silence in the English countryside surrounding Royal Air Force (RAF) Fersfield air base in Norwich. The airfield is newly constructed to Class-A bomber specifications for the Eighth US Army Air Force, commanded by Lieutenant General James Doolittle. It's a remote site intended to shield the operations of highly secret missions.

This one is just days old. On August 4, the combined operations "Aphrodite" (Army Air Force) and "Anvil" (Navy) had begun a series of planned attacks on German-controlled weapon complexes. With the program's reliance on the earliest stages of autopilot technology, the risk factor is high and the pressure to succeed higher still.

The first six Aphrodite missions have already failed.

Now Anvil makes its first attempt.

Navy lieutenant Joseph Patrick Kennedy Jr. looks through the caged cockpit of his battle-weary PB4Y-1—the navy designation of the Army Air Force's B-24 Liberator. The cargo load totals 374 fifty-five-pound boxes distributed throughout the plane. Together, they contain eleven tons of Torpex, or "torpedo explosive," a powerful combination of RDX, TNT, and powdered aluminum.

On board with the twenty-nine-year-old pilot is radio operator and copilot Lieutenant Wilford John "Bud" Willy. He is new to Joe Jr.'s second seat, outranking and replacing Ensign James Simpson, who sends Joe off with a handshake and parting words, "So long and good luck, Joe. I only wish I were going with you."

Surrounded by a unique protective formation of a dozen aircraft, the unmanned bomber is to be flown like a modern-day drone, continuing on a crash course over France to its target, the Fortress of Mimoyecques.

The fortress is an underground military complex that houses two dozen German V-3 superguns, long-range cannons known as the "London gun," primed to inflict even more damage than the thirty-six thousand bomb strikes of *Unternehmen Loge,* the German code name for the fifty-seven-day Blitz of 1940.

The plane takes off from the airfield's six-thousand-foot runway, leveling at an altitude of two thousand feet. The crew then must perform two crucial tasks: arm the detonators, then turn over radio navigation control to a mother PV-1 aircraft flying at twenty thousand feet. Over the English Channel, the men will bail out and await a rescue boat.

At least, that's the plan.

The "star of our family," is what Joe Sr. calls his eldest son. It's no surprise that the slender, handsome, athletic, blue-eyed Harvard student—accustomed to elite education and international travel—boasts among friends about the certainty of his destiny. After graduation from Harvard College in 1938, but before starting at Harvard Law School, Joe Jr. (and later Jack) undertakes an intensive tutorial with London School of Economics professor Harold Laski.

Laski, a socialist and a Jew who instructs via the exacting Socratic method, is a seemingly unconventional mentor for Joe Sr. to choose, but when questioned on it, he says, "My opinion has always been that you don't have to worry about the other side. We've got all the arguments on our side." It's also a test of his sons' mettle.

Together, Joe Jr. and Laski travel to Moscow to observe in person the regime of Joseph Stalin, general secretary of the Communist Party, whose name means "man of steel." While there, Laski poses intricate questions to his pupil on world leaders and their philosophies, demanding, "What will you do about this when you are president?"

Joe Jr. had already encountered the powerful and persistent leadership style of Adolf Hitler on a 1934 trip to Munich, after which the impressionable eighteen-year-old interprets for his father a rationale for inverse power dynamics: "Hitler is building a spirit in his men that would be envied in any country... This spirit would very quickly be turned into a war spirit, but Hitler has things well under control." Joe Jr. went on to describe the "excellent psychology"—perhaps intuited from Joe Sr.'s own anti-Semitic stance—of Hitler's vision for "the need of the common enemy... the Jews," though he added, "It is extremely sad, that noted professors, scientists, artists, etc. should have to suffer, but as you can see, it would be practically impossible to throw out only a part of them, from both the practical and psychological point of view."

Six years later, however, as Joe Jr. begins his second year at Harvard Law in September 1940, America seems on the brink of war with Hitler. On the fourteenth of that month, President

Roosevelt signs into law the Selective Service and Training Act, a peacetime measure to provide military instruction for up to nine hundred thousand male citizens between the ages of twenty-one and thirty-six.

Joe Jr., who is ranked near the middle of his law school class of five hundred, writes to a friend about his enlistment as "one of Roosevelt's several million numbers," adding, "I've always fancied the idea of flying and I've never fancied the idea of crawling with rifle and bayonet through European mud."

Concerned about the risks of airborne warfare, Joe Sr. pressures his typically obedient son to accept a desk assignment arranged through his government connections.

Joe Jr. refuses. The rebellious streak that inspires him to seek his aviator's wings in the Navy Air Corps rather than sit safely behind a desk alarms his father, who has spent years—including while ambassador to Great Britain—railing against America joining the war.

Now Joe Jr. is on the other side.

In his seventeenth fireside chat, recorded on May 27, 1941, Roosevelt makes his case for the impending necessity of war. "It is unmistakably apparent to all of us, unless the advance of Hitlerism is forcibly checked now, the Western Hemisphere will be within range of the Nazi weapons of destruction."

In May 1942, Joe Jr. is awarded his wings.

In September 1943, he travels with his squadron to England, where they serve alongside the British Naval Command.

"Kennedy was such a good pilot that we would have flown with him anywhere," states Alvin T. Jones, an aviation machinist's mate who performed many of Joe Jr.'s preflight inspections.

By that summer of 1944, Joe Jr. has successfully completed well over the twenty-five bombing missions required to complete his tour. He pushes on through D-Day, then seeks out a special assignment requiring what his brother Jack would later describe as "the most dangerous type of flying."

Joe Jr. has been preparing for this daring flight all his life.

In the last week of July 1944, Joe pens a cryptic letter to his father. "I am going to do something different for the next three weeks," he writes. "It is a secret and I am not allowed to say what it is, but it isn't dangerous so don't worry."

"Joe, don't tempt the fates," his father replies. "Just come home."

CHAPTER 8

Ensign John Demlein, pilot of the PV-1 mother ship, tries for a light moment on the tarmac, asking Joe if he's all caught up with his life insurance payments.

Joe flashes a toothy Kennedy grin. "I've got twice as much as I need," he says.

The day before, the lieutenant had a completely different conversation with electronics officer Lieutenant Earl Olsen. Olsen warns that faulty detonator wiring may spark an airborne explosion—and pleads with Joe to abort the mission.

"There was never an occasion for a mission that meant extra hazard that Joe did not volunteer [for]," recalls Joe Jr.'s squadron roommate, Louis Papas. "He had everyone's unlimited admiration and respect for his courage, zeal and willingness to undertake the most dangerous missions."

By his brother Jack's calculations, Joe Jr. has flown "probably more combat missions in heavy bombers than any other pilot of his rank in the Navy." Yet he's fighting an internal war on two fronts.

Jack, who joined the navy himself in September 1941, proudly declares, "Any man who may be asked in this century what he did to make his life worthwhile, I think can respond with a good deal of pride and satisfaction, 'I served in the United States Navy.'"

Though his first duty is deskside in a Washington, DC, intelligence post arranged by his sister Kathleen, by August 1943 Jack Kennedy is a naval war hero.

In a sibling rivalry marked by one-upmanship, by Joe's calculations, he has fallen behind. "My congrats on the [navy and marine] medal," he writes his younger brother after Jack is honored for facing down enemy combatants. Joe can't resist taking a dig at the same time, adding, "To get anything out of the Navy is deserving of a campaign medal in itself."

"It was involuntary. They sank my boat," Jack says self-deprecatingly of his heroics in saving the surviving crew after his gunship *PT-109* was rammed by Japanese destroyer *Amagiri* in the South Pacific.

Yet despite all of Joe Jr.'s heroic airborne missions, not once has he ever directly engaged the German foe. He'll have little to show for his risk-taking, Joe concludes. "It looks like I shall return home with the European campaign medal if I'm lucky."

———— ∞∞∞ ————

The August 12, 1944, mission proceeds according to plan. Eighteen minutes in, the autopilot is set and the plane makes its first remote-controlled turn. Willy removes the safety, and the explosive goes live. Joe radios the code phrase "Spade Flush," signaling that the final task before bailout is complete. The aircraft formation passes over New Delight Wood, near the town of Blythburgh, a hundred miles north of London and four miles from the North Sea.

Two loud booms shatter the airspace. The sky erupts in flames and swirling black smoke. Aircraft debris plunges toward earth, scattering for more than a mile and a half in each direction.

"Spade Flush" prove to be Joe's last words. He and Bud are killed instantly. "Nothing larger than a basketball could have survived the blast," Commander James Smith observes, based on his vantage point in an observation aircraft.

Lieutenant David McCarthy of the Eighth Combat Camera Unit witnesses the horror through his airborne camera.

"[The plane] just exploded in mid-air as we neared it and I was knocked halfway back to the cockpit. A few pieces of the Baby [drone] came through the plexiglass nose and I got hit in the head and caught a lot of fragments in my right arm. I crawled back to the cockpit and lowered the wheels so that [we] could make a quick emergency landing."

Another eyewitness, Mick Muttitt, then a local schoolboy, shares his memories with ITV News: "As it passed there was a trail of smoke coming from the weapons bay and then it exploded in an enormous fireball. And I vividly remember the engines continuing in the line of flight with the propellers still turning with trails of smoke from each one. It happened more than a mile and a half away but it still knocked the plaster off our ceiling. The next day my brother and I biked to Five Fingers heath and collected bits of wreckage."

The faulty wiring that Lieutenant Olsen detected proves to be the cause of the disaster. Subsequent investigations suggest a camera lacking an electrical shield may have set off an electromagnetic relay that tripped the detonator. One officer who saw the circuit board before the flight describes it as "something you'd make with a number two Erector set and Lincoln Logs."

Colonel Elliott Roosevelt—one of FDR's sons, and younger brother to James Roosevelt—was on board a Mosquito plane in the supporting formation and narrowly escaped the deadly explosion that killed Lieutenants Kennedy and Willy.

Decades later, in 1986, Elliott Roosevelt's son gives an interview to the *Boston Herald,* refuting a German newspaper's alternate version of Joe's death. According to *Bild am Sonntag,* antiaircraft officer Karl Heinz Wehn witnessed Joe Jr. survive the crash and parachute into woods, then be captured by soldiers of the 12th German Panzer Division and shot by SS troopers. During the interrogation, Wehn claims, one of the two captured aviators identified himself as "Joe Kennedy."

"If he [Wehn] says he interrogated Joe Kennedy Jr., I think he's dreaming," Elliott Roosevelt Jr. says. "He was never shot down. The plane exploded before it left the English coast."

Unfortunately for the Allies, not one of the fourteen Aphrodite or Anvil missions ever hit its intended target, and the "program killed more American airmen than it did Nazis." According to the author and US Air Force veteran Jack Olsen, Joe Jr.'s target in France wouldn't even have mattered, as it "had been abandoned by Hitler's missile men three months earlier." In January 1945, General Carl "Tooey" Spaatz, US commander of Strategic Air Forces in Europe, orders the operation scrapped.

Joe Jr. and Lieutenant Willy are posthumously honored for their valor with the Air Medal, the Distinguished Flying Cross, and the Navy Cross.

The Cross, with its combat distinction, is a higher honor than the non-combat Navy Marine Corps Medal awarded to Jack.

Even in death, Joe Jr.'s military accomplishments outshine his brother's. And Joe Sr. makes sure everyone knows it.

CHAPTER 9

On a Sunday afternoon in August 1944, two priests from the local parish knock on the door of the Kennedy home in Hyannis Port.

"[My] son was missing in action and presumed lost," Rose remembers them telling her. Joe Jr.'s plane had gone down the day before.

Reeling in shock, she runs upstairs to wake Joe Sr. from a nap.

"We sat with the priests in the smaller room off the living room, and from what they told us we realized there could be no hope . . . our son was dead."

"Joe went out on the porch and told the children. They were stunned. He said they must be brave: that's what their brother would want from them."

Jack corroborates his father's attitude. "Joe would not want us to stay around here crying, so let's go sailing," Rose's nephew Joe Gargan recalls Jack telling his younger siblings. According to the historian and sailor James W. Graham, they venture out on the family sailboat, *Victura*.

Joe Sr. retreats to his bedroom. He plays Beethoven on the turntable, despite his longtime concerns that love of classical music is a sign of weakness in a man. Not now, not at this moment.

Rose's only consolation is her Catholic faith. For many weeks, she retreats to her room, with only a rosary for solace.

Weeks later, a final letter from Joe Jr. arrives at Hyannis Port. The sight of the familiar handwriting plunges his father into the depths of sorrow.

Then another letter arrives. A naval lieutenant who attended Harvard with Joe Jr. offers comfort and consolation. "Through Joe's courage and devotion to what he thought was right, a great many lives have been saved."

Joe Sr. vows not to let his dream of a Kennedy son rising to the Oval Office die along with Joe Jr.

Kathleen channels her family identity into coping with the loss of her big brother, best friend, and champion. "Luckily, I am a Kennedy," she writes. "I have a very strong feeling that that makes a big difference about how to take things. I saw Daddy and Mother about Joe and I know that we've all got the ability not to be got down. There are lots of years ahead and lots of happiness left in the world though sometimes nowadays that's hard to believe."

Six years earlier, when the Kennedys had landed in England, the government called Joe Sr. "Ambassador" and tall Joe Jr. was known to British debutantes as "the Big One." In that first whirl of the London social season, Kathleen, known as Kick, set her sights on William John Robert Cavendish, the future Duke of Devonshire.

The outbreak of World War II would eventually separate the

pair, as Billy explores a career in politics and Kick works at the *Washington Times-Herald.* But by 1943, Kick has negotiated a return to London through service in the Red Cross. She makes a late-June crossing to reunite with Billy in early July.

The pair is in love and determined to marry. Yet despite Billy's impressive wealth and pedigree—assets Rose's father once insisted Joe was lacking—Joe and Rose withhold their blessing. Kick's parents hold hard and fast to the Catholic teaching that marrying outside the Church is a mortal sin. And Billy, a handsome, six-foot-four soldier who would rise to the rank of major in the Cold Stream Guards, is not only an Englishman, but also of Anglican faith.

Rose dismisses any possibility of compromise. "When both people have been handed something all their lives," she tells Kick, "how ironic it is that they can not have what they want most."

Only one Kennedy supports her decision: Joe Jr. Breaking from his role as one of the like-minded "two Joes," as Kick and Eunice call father and son, Joe Jr. chastises his hard-hearted parents. Joe says of their condemnation of her so-called sinful marriage, "As far as Kick's soul is concerned, I wish I had half her chance of seeing the Pearly Gates. As far as what people will say, the hell with them. I think we can all take it."

On May 6, 1944, in the midst of the privations of wartime London, the couple forgoes the kind of lavish, formal wedding that could have topped the society pages of every newspaper around the world for a modest civil ceremony at a registrar's office in Chelsea. Not only is Joe Jr. the sole Kennedy in attendance, but he gives the bride away. Kick loves him even more for that fraternal gesture.

"MISS KENNEDY A MARCHIONESS" a London paper announces. "THURSDAY—ENGAGED: TO-DAY—MARRIED," the headline continues somewhat snidely, noting that although the "engagement was announced only on Thursday," the couple had "a quiet wedding" that Saturday. "The bride's naval brother, Lieutenant J.P. Kennedy, brought her in, and the ceremony took place in a bare room, brightened only by three vases of carnations."

"MARRIED LIFE AGREES WITH ME!" Kick jubilantly reports to her family. But barely five weeks later, on June 13, Billy is ordered to active duty in France.

He leaves his beloved bride in a flurry of romantic longing. "This love," Billy writes, "seems to cause nothing but goodbyes."

———— ∽∞∾ ————

Even at twenty-nine, Joe Jr. seems not to be in any rush to marry himself, though there are rumors of a broken engagement to the Broadway actress Athalia Ponsell. (Ponsell is best known in later years for her grisly—and as yet unsolved—murder in January 1974, when she is found decapitated by machete outside her home in St. Augustine, Florida. She later becomes the subject of two true-crime books, as well as lingering questions of the cost of romancing a Kennedy.)

In the summer of 1944, Alvin Jones Jr. recalls, "Kennedy usually borrowed a quarter from his mechanic, so he could call a girlfriend before takeoff."

Those calls are likely to Patricia Wilson, whom he met in 1943 through Kick's social circles. The twice-divorced, Protestant daughter of a wealthy Australian sheep farmer would likely not have pleased Rose and Joe any more than Billy Cavendish has, and while Joe confides in Kick his growing love for Wilson, no other Kennedy ever knew that she was more than a passing acquaintance. "I had better get a gal while there is some life left in the old boy," Joe Jr. writes his mother in the last week of July. The family believes that he dies a lonely bachelor.

Kick flies home to Hyannis Port from London to attend Joe Jr.'s memorial mass. As the designated recipient of her brother's possessions, she then travels on to New York City to receive them via the Personal Effects Distribution Center in Scotia, New York.

In the city, her sister Eunice plays messenger, summoning Kick to Joe Sr.'s hotel room to receive yet another grim communication. It's been weeks since Kick has heard from her new husband, Billy. Now she learns that in the German-occupied town of Heppen, Belgium, Billy has been killed by a sniper's bullet. His sacrifice comes only weeks after Joe Jr. gave his life for his country. Within a month, Kick has lost her beloved brother and her husband.

For the next several years, Kick's search for happiness is unfulfilled—until she takes up with the married Earl Peter Wentworth Fitzwilliam, some years her senior, who has a reputation for being a womanizing gambler.

Kick confides in her brother Jack about this latest Kennedy dalliance with a Protestant, down to the cinematic detail that the man looks like Rhett Butler in *Gone with the Wind*. When Fitzwilliam promises to divorce his wife, Obby, and marry Kick, she once again summons up the courage to tell her estranged parents. Over the scandalous specter of divorce, Rose vows to disown her daughter.

Despite her mother's attitude, Kick reaches out to her "Darling Daddy," and arranges for the two of them to meet Joe Sr. at the Paris Ritz.

"I'd like to get Dad's consent," she tells Joe Jr.'s old friend Tom Schriber before she leaves New York. "He matters. But I'm getting married whether he consents or not."

On Thursday, May 13, 1948, Kick and Fitzwilliam fly out of London, stopping outside Paris to refuel their chartered ten-seater de Havilland Dove aircraft en route to the French Riviera before meeting with Joe Sr. During the layover—which includes a boozy lunch with friends—a terrible storm sets in, and the next leg of their route is to cross the storm center. The pilot and the navigator say the flight is too dangerous. But the couple won't wait.

They never make it to to their romantic weekend in Cannes. Friday morning, rescuers traverse the mountainous Rhône-Alpes region, some two hundred miles from Cannes, to reach the wreckage of the plane. There are no survivors. Kick's shoeless corpse is transported in an oxcart to the tiny town center of Privas.

A heartbroken Joe Sr. identifies Kick, who, in the words of Rose, was his "favorite of all the children."

The family decides not to bring Kick's body home, preferring to remember her in Hyannis Port at the same church where they mourned Joe Jr. four years earlier.

Billy's family arranges a memorial service. Rose refuses to fly to England. Jack promises, then fails, to represent the Kennedys.

Kick is interred in the small Derbyshire cemetery alongside members of the Cavendish family. The last line of her epitaph captures the essence of the vibrant young woman who touched so many lives: "Joy she gave—joy she has found."

Joe Sr. later attends a Requiem Mass in Kick's honor. He stands at her grave, a shattered man in a rumpled blue suit.

Unlike his sister Kick, Joe Jr. has no grave for his family to visit. Since losing his son, Joe Sr. has been focused on mounting a fitting tribute. On July 26, 1945, at a shipyard in Quincy, Massachusetts, Jean Kennedy christens the Navy destroyer USS

Joseph P. Kennedy Jr. (now part of the Battleship Cove Maritime Museum in Fall River, Massachusetts). But no memorial to his heroic final mission exists in Blythburgh, in spite of calls by local military groups to establish a tribute.

Huby Fairfield, curator of the Norfolk and Suffolk Aviation Museum at Flixton, tells the *Times* of London, "If someone doesn't do something soon, he will be forgotten. He gave his life for his country and ours—he didn't have to take part in the operation. He volunteered."

In January 1946, according to historian Edward J. Renehan Jr., Joe Sr. has a chance meeting with the former prime minister Winston Churchill at the Hialeah Park Race Track, where Joe has an ownership interest.

Churchill and Joe were frequently in conflict over Joe's certainty of Hitler's invincibility. Yet the former prime minister seems glad to reminisce. "I remember that one of the last times we met we were having dinner during an air raid. It didn't bother us very much, though, did it?"

Joe refuses to engage his onetime nemesis.

"You had a terrible time during the war; your losses were very great." Churchill continues. "I felt so sad for you and hope you received my messages."

"The world seems to be in a frightful condition," Churchill laments, sipping whiskey and smoking a large cigar.

"Yes," Joe at first agrees, then demands, "After all what did we accomplish by this war?"

"Well, at least, we have our lives," Churchill answers.

Joe can no longer contain his fury. "Not all of us."

PART FOUR

The President

JOHN FITZGERALD KENNEDY

CHAPTER 10

The little girl is staring at the man standing in her parents' living room in Boston. She points at his backside and giggles, "Jack, Jack, your blue underwear is showing through the seat of your pants."

Jack Kennedy looks over his shoulder and sees a blue strip of fabric through a split in the seam of his trousers. Jack and the little girl's father—his and Joe Jr.'s Harvard buddy Tom Bilodeau—break out in laughter over her discovery. In a day of speeches around the city, no one else has dared confront the young Massachusetts politician about his sartorial mishap.

Their banter draws Bilodeau's Irish mother-in-law into the room. Treating Jack like her own son, she says, "Jack, take your pants right off and I'll fix them," Bilodeau recalls in an interview for the JFK Presidential Library. "And right there in the living room, Jack took his pants off. My mother-in-law got out a needle and thread and sewed them and off he went to his next speaking engagement."

When Jack is later elected president, he invites the Bilodeau family to attend the inauguration in January 1961. Jack definitely remembered the ripped pants incident, Bilodeau chuckles, since "an invitation to my mother-in-law [was] addressed to his 'seamstress.'"

Jack Kennedy enters the Eightieth Congress as a Democratic Representative of the Eleventh District of Massachusetts in January 1947 at the age of twenty-nine, but is often mistaken for a staffer, given his youthful looks and informal, somewhat disheveled attire. "He wore the most godawful suits," Mary Davis, his secretary during congressional years 1947–52, would say. "Horrible looking, hanging from his frame."

As his mother, Rose, would so often lament, Jack cares nothing for his appearance. But he "had the best sense of humor of anybody I had ever met," Kirk Le Moyne "Lem" Billings, who first befriended Jack at Choate School, says. "If we were at a show together, he'd somehow manage to sneak backstage to see the leading singer," Lem recalls. "If we were eating out, he'd be so charming to the waitress that we'd end up with an extra dessert."

That charisma may be part natural, part reactive. Joe Sr.'s assessment of his two eldest sons has always been unfavorable to Jack. "Joe never thought Jack would do anything," Chuck Spalding, who also knew both brothers at Harvard, recalls Joe Sr. "didn't realize that by all odds, Jack was the most gifted. He thought Joe Jr. was."

Even after Joe Jr.'s death, Jack still futilely competes with his older brother. "I am now shadowboxing in a match the shadow is always going to win," Jack tells Lem.

Underscoring the strong correlation the Kennedys assumed

between mental ability and physical health is Rose's belief that Jack had a lower IQ than Joe Jr.—something she insists upon until after Jack's presidency.

"Jack never wanted us to talk about this," Lem Billings says in an oral history for the JFK Library in Boston, but "Jack Kennedy all during his life had few days when he wasn't in pain or sick in some way."

As Jack later tells his wife, Jackie, his was a childhood in confinement, "sick so much of the time, reading in bed, reading history . . . reading the Knights of the Round Table."

And while Jack tests at a "superior" IQ of 116 (today's assessments might rate it as high as 158) it takes three attempts—and a generous donation from Joe Sr., including two movie projectors—to get Jack through his entrance exams for the exclusive preparatory Choate School in Wallingford, Connecticut, where his older brother Joe Jr. is achieving academic and athletic success.

In Jack's junior year, with Joe Jr. now enrolled at Harvard, Jack is the only Kennedy at Choate. He's also the only student on campus to subscribe to the *New York Times*. Jack's English teacher spots "a very definite flair for writing" and encourages him to pursue it professionally. But a bout of hepatitis and various mysterious ailments end Jack's school term and his participation in athletics early.

While recuperating in New Haven Hospital, the indignant teenager writes his classmate Lem a humorously crass account of the invasive medical procedures he's forced to undergo. "No one is able to figure out what's wrong with me. They give me enemas until it comes out like drinking water which they all take a sip of. Then surrounded by nurses the doctor first stuck his finger up my ass. I just blushed because you know how it is. He wiggled suggestively and I rolled 'em in the aisles by saying 'you have good motion'!"

When Jack returns to Choate in winter 1935, his mischievous streak erupts. "What makes the whole problem more difficult," says the Choate housemaster Earl Leinbach, who has to contend with nuisances such as pillows bursting from dorm rooms, "is Jack's winning smile and charming personality." (Years later, in 1942, his eventual bride Jackie's own gifts as a mimic also land her in trouble at the exclusive Holton-Arms School in Washington, DC, when she is caught mid-parody by the teacher she is mocking, though nothing on the level of mayhem that Jack and Lem wreak with "the Muckers," their secret society of pranksters.)

But when Jack goes too far and sets off contraband firecrackers in the bathroom, destroying a toilet seat, he faces expulsion. Headmaster George St. John fumes, "I couldn't see how two boys from the same family as were Joe and Jack could be so different."

Joe Sr. is called to St. John's office, saving Jack from expulsion, but not from judgment. "Don't let me lose confidence in you again," he writes in a letter following the incident, "because it will be a nearly impossible task to restore it."

Jack graduates sixty-fifth in a class of 110. And he pulls off one last prank, persuading classmates to trade votes so that he's named "Most Likely to Succeed"—in a rigged election.

CHAPTER 11

In 1934, Jack Kennedy and Lem Billings, both seventeen years old, dress in formalwear for a night in Harlem, New York City. They tell their cabdriver to bypass the famous Cotton Club where the great Cab Calloway performs. On this night, the boys have in mind only one experience they want to enjoy: losing their virginity.

Ralph Horton, another school friend, escorts them to a brothel. First, they watch a pornographic movie for a pricey three dollars. Then Jack accompanies a prostitute into a room, where the deed is quickly done.

"They were frightened to death they'd get VD," says Horton. "So, I went with them to the hospital...where they got these salves and creams and a thing to shove up their penis to clean it out."

Sex is always on Jack's mind. Throughout his life, Jack will follow the Kennedy male tradition of coming on to any attractive woman—and succeeding. "Every woman either wants to mother him or marry him," the *New York Times* columnist James Reston would write of Jack as a presidential candidate.

Attendance at Harvard is another rite of passage for Kennedy men. Joe Sr. is class of 1912; Joe Jr. graduates cum laude in the class of 1938, and Jack joins the class of 1940. Younger brothers Bobby and Ted will follow.

In college, Jack earns the same middling grades as he did at Choate. "He could do what he wanted," the *Harvard Crimson* reports one of his professors as saying, "but he did not waste time on what did not interest him."

Instead, he pursues athletics, excelling at swimming, tennis, and football. Even though the six-footer is underweight at 156 pounds, he's a standout end for the freshman and junior varsity football teams, playing through the pain of a serious spinal injury he sustains in a game during his sophomore season.

Jack is a junior when FDR names his father ambassador to Great Britain in 1938. Though he remains at Harvard, he visits his expat family often during school breaks—he's even there in Britain when they declare war on Germany on September 3, 1939.

That same day, the German submarine U-30 commits a war crime—torpedoing the SS *Athenia*, an unarmed transatlantic passenger liner bound for Canada, killing more than a hundred of the nearly fourteen hundred on board, including twenty-eight Americans.

Jack travels to Scotland as an impromptu junior ambassador to visit with American survivors of the sunken ship.

"Young John Kennedy came up from London and assured us that we were all the nearest things to the [American] nation's heart and would be looked after," Mildred Finley, a teacher who boarded a lifeboat and then a British destroyer on her way to safety in Glasgow, tells Scotland's *Daily Record*.

"I, and several other of the most battered-looking survivors and children had pictures taken with him."

Some Americans demand an immediate escort home, telling "young Kennedy that [if] the whole American Navy had gone after Amelia Earhart, why couldn't a destroyer or two come for us. He smiled patiently and said he would tell his father. The group, of course, was somewhat hysterical: most of us were thankful for one ship."

A report in the *London Evening News* lauds his efforts, "Mr. Kennedy displayed a wisdom and sympathy of a man twice his age."

Citing to school officials the same "lack of transportation" that the *Athenia* survivors experience, Jack is late returning to Harvard to join his senior class. But the experience abroad cements a thesis he goes on to write called "Appeasement at Munich," a firsthand critique of England's inaction against Hitler and those (like Joe Sr.) who felt remaining neutral was an option. It goes on to be published in the United States in 1940, as the bestselling—due in part to Joe Sr. buying copies in bulk—*Why England Slept,* an allusion to Churchill's own 1938 book, *While England Slept.*

Kennedy graduates cum laude from Harvard in the spring of 1940 with a BA in government and international affairs. That fall he's back on campus—in California—auditing classes at the Stanford Graduate School of Business.

In 1941, after Joe Jr. enlists as one of "Roosevelt's Millions," Jack changes course.

At a dock in Edgartown, Martha's Vineyard, he tours a navy display of a PT—torpedo patrol—and becomes transfixed by the vessel. As America inches closer to war, he decides to follow his older brother's example and enlist.

But his dubious medical history disqualifies him for service. He is rejected, twice, by both the army and the navy.

Eventually, Joe Sr.'s powerful connections override Jack's poor health records, and he's given a place as an ensign in the Naval Reserve, writing weekly reports for the Office of Naval Intelligence out of Washington, DC.

Joe Sr. hopes to keep him out of trouble at home, but Jack keeps finding ways to wreak havoc.

CHAPTER 12

In wartime Washington, DC, Jack Kennedy falls in love—with a twice-married Danish journalist suspected of being a Nazi spy.

Inga Arvad—a former film actress and Miss Denmark whom Hitler once called "the most perfect example of Nordic beauty"—is hired by the *Washington Times-Herald* as a columnist. Jack's sister Kick also works for the *Times-Herald,* although she pines for England and her future husband Billy Cavendish, the Marquess of Hartington.

At Kick's suggestion, Arvad interviews Jack for her weekly social column, "Did You Happen to See?" touting him to Washington in November 1941 as "a boy with a future."

The blond, blue-eyed international sophisticate beguiles the younger man—twenty-four to her twenty-eight—who cuts a handsome figure in his navy dress whites.

Inga Arvad's already on J. Edgar Hoover's radar as a possible Nazi spy. Her FBI file would eventually grow to over twelve hundred pages. But although in the 1930s the columnist had written flattering pieces about Nazi leaders—like Hermann Goering, whose 1935 wedding she attended, and Hitler, who invited her to his private box at the 1936 Olympic Games in Berlin and gave her an autographed photo signed "To Inga Arvad, in friendly memory of Adolf Hitler"—the only secrets she reveals to her willing young lover involve pleasing a woman in bed. She has "gooey eyes" for Jack, and he calls her "Inga Binga." "He had the charm that makes the birds come out of their trees," she writes in a private letter. "When he walked into a room you knew he was there, not pushing, not domineering, but exuding animal magnetism."

They spend hours making love in her Washington apartment, which the FBI has bugged, and Hoover documents the encounters. The bugs make it a threesome of sorts. If the espionage accusations against Arvad hold true, Inga Arvad could be the Mata Hari of the Second World War.

As FBI investigations into Inga's background continue, with even her *Washington Times-Herald* colleagues questioning her loyalties (one approaching Jack's sister to ask, "Kick, do you think it is possible Inga could be a spy?"), Hoover warns Joe Sr. that Jack is "in big trouble and that he should get his son out of Washington immediately." He orders his agents to break in to Arvad's apartment, where no evidence discrediting Arvad is found—but plenty of salacious material regarding Jack comes to light.

As Kick would tell her journalist suitor, John White, when Jack informs Joe Sr. of his plans to marry the Protestant Arvad—once she is officially divorced from her jealous second husband, the Hungarian film director Paul Fejos—Joe was "getting ready to drag up the big guns" to end the affair.

But the navy is a step ahead, ordering a precautionary transfer to the Charleston Naval Shipyard, where Jack lectures factory munitions workers on safety procedures. The FBI comes, too, all the way to South Carolina.

Bugs in a Charleston hotel room reveal Arvad was never a spy, and Hoover closes his file on her. In March 1942, Jack does the same. (But the wartime confidences Jack exchanged with Arvad would never leave him. When Jack is elected president, Hoover reveals that he's preserved the intimate wiretap recordings. The master spy's hint at blackmail keeps him atop the ranks of the FBI.)

The breakup, in the end, is mutual, as their relationship seems doomed. As Arvad writes, her love for Jack overshadows her "reason. It took the FBI, the US Navy, nasty gossip, envy, hatred and big Joe" before she could see past it. "There is one thing I don't want to do, and that is harm you," she tells Jack. "You belong so whole-heartedly to the Kennedy clan, and I don't want you to ever get into an argument with your father on account of me."

Jack's friend Torbert MacDonald observes, "The breakup with Inga helped install a certain, 'I don't give a damn' mentality that made Jack want to go to the Pacific." It was the kind of attitude that could end in a serviceman sacrificing his life for his country.

Jack enrolls in an officer training course in Chicago. Having spent his childhood racing sailboats for the Kennedy "Cape Cod Navy," Jack honed his competitive instincts on the water.

Thomas Bilodeau, a frequent guest at the three-acre Kennedy compound in Hyannis Port, recalls the extreme measures Jack would take to win a race. "We were coming down to the finish line, and the winds let up…the boat was slowing down with my weight [215 pounds]," Bilodeau says, "and Jack turned to me and said, 'Over the side, boy. We've got to relieve ourselves of some weight.' So right out there in open water, I proceeded to just go over the side and he ran on to win the race."

Lem Billings also commented about his old friend, "Jack always had something to prove, physically." Given his lifelong poor health, he would "overcompensate and prove he was fit when he really wasn't. So, he turns into this killer football player and he turns into a voracious womanizer, a stud. Then what's next? Well, of course he turns into a voracious warrior, hungry for a fight. It was the logical next step given the times."

Jack's wartime hero is Lieutenant John Duncan "Sea Wolf" Bulkeley, winner of the Medal of Honor. Bulkeley, who from *PT-41* led Motor Torpedo Boat Squadron Three, performed a daring two-day rescue in March 1942, bringing to safety General Douglas MacArthur, commander of United States Army Forces in the Far East safely from Corregidor Island in the Philippines in advance of the nearby island of Bataan's fall to the Japanese.

Bulkeley embarks on a promotional tour touting the success of the PT boat program. More than five hundred vessels—forty-three PT squadrons each with twelve boats—would be commissioned for the war effort. A fleet of two hundred is soon to be dispatched to the Pacific theater.

In the sumptuous privacy of Kennedy's suite at the Plaza Hotel, Joe Sr. meets with the newly ranked lieutenant commander. The patriarch pitches the decorated veteran "Sea Wolf" on the navy neophyte Jack and his qualifications as skipper. Although Joe's motivations on behalf of his son—the postwar veterans' vote—are transparent to Bulkeley, he moves Jack into active duty in the Pacific.

In April 1943, Jack is in command of a PT boat.

"Without *PT-109*," presidential aide Dave Powers boldly declares, "you have no President John F. Kennedy."

CHAPTER 13

"Ship at two o'clock!" the lookout shouts to Lieutenant Junior Grade Jack Kennedy, skipper of *PT-109*. He's silenced the radios and powered down the eighty-foot craft to a single, idling engine to avoid detection by the advancing Japanese fleet.

Light, fast, and heavily armed but not heavily armored, PT boats are designed to attack in great numbers as the "Mosquito Fleet." On August 2, 1943, there are only three—*PT-109*, *PT-162*, and *PT-169*, in picket formation—on the Blackett Strait, south of Kolombangara in the Solomon Islands.

At 2:30 a.m., the ships are patrolling in total darkness. It's impossible for Jack to get his bearings on the open water, and his vessel is not equipped with radar. He doesn't have time to turn the boat, with its diminished thrust, out of the line of attack. At a speed of over thirty knots, a 1,750-ton Fubuki-class Japanese destroyer called the *Amagiri* collides with them, severing the fifty-ton *PT-109* in half.

On impact, Jack smashes into the helm. And the gas tank ruptures.

The crew sustains immediate and widespread casualties. Motor Machinist Mate Second Class (MM2) Harold William Marney and Torpedoman's Mate Second Class (TM2) Andrew Jackson Kirksey are killed instantly. The water's surface is coated with a slick of engine oil and fuel. The eleven survivors' eyes are burning as they choke on the fumes—all the while clinging to pieces of wreckage floating in the shark-infested waters.

Motor Machinist's Mate First Class (MM1) Patrick Henry "Pappy" McMahon is blasted from his post in the engine room. He's severely burned and struggling to swim. Acting on instinct, Jack supports the injured man across his own back and uses the strap of the machinist's life preserver as a towline, pulling McMahon's weight with his teeth.

McMahon's stepson, William H. Kelly, later tells the Associated Press, "Dad was burnt so bad. He thought he was holding [Kennedy] up, so he asked the [future] president, 'Just leave me. I'll be all right by myself.' But of course, he would not think of it."

Hoping for rescue, the crew clings to the hull of the boat for a dozen hours, but it begins to take on water. Creating a makeshift flotilla from the debris of *PT-109* and loading it with salvaged supplies, the strongest among the surviving crew push the injured for three or four miles toward the closest safe land they can find, Kasolo Island, nicknamed Plum Pudding Island.

Though Kick later writes home from England, "The news about Jack is the most exciting I've ever heard," only Joe Sr. knew—and he kept the message from Rose—that Jack is declared "missing in action" by the Navy Department.

Plum Pudding Island is uninhabited and without food or drinkable water, so after two days, Kennedy braves his injuries and leads the search for help, assisted by Ensign George H. R. "Barney" Ross. The two of them swim between Olasana Island and Nauro Island, where they startle "Coastwatchers"—Biuku

Gasa and Eroni Kumana—aiding the Allied forces. The native Pacific islanders don't initially trust the men, but upon discovering the stranded survivors of *PT-109*, they decide it's safe to help Kennedy.

The islander scout Gasa helps Jack use a jackknife to scratch a distress message onto a green coconut—"NAURO ISL… COMMANDER…NATIVE KNOWS POS'IT…HE CAN PILOT…11 ALIVE…NEED SMALL BOAT…KENNEDY"—that Gasa and Kumana deliver to Australian Lieutenant Arthur Reginald Evans, a fellow Coastwatcher on yet another island, who sends rescue.

The next morning, Jack awakens to four islanders looking down at him and the crew. One of them says, in a perfect British accent, "I have a letter for you, sir." Lieutenant Wincote, a New Zealander who is working with the US Army, writes, "I strongly advise that you come with these natives to me."

On August 8, after enduring six days in enemy territory, Jack and the crew reach the US base at Rendova.

Nearly two decades later, that crucial dried coconut husk is displayed on President Kennedy's desk in the Oval Office, and he remains in correspondence with Gasa and Kumana, even inviting them to his inauguration.

The machinist McMahon, whose burns covered 70 percent of his body, eventually recovers from his injuries. The onboard collision ruptured a disk in Jack's back. He will require surgery, but his psychological wounds run even deeper.

Elevated to full lieutenant and now in command of *PT-59*, Jack sees further action in the Solomon Islands until November 16, 1943, when the mentally and physically exhausted officer is ordered to the naval hospital at Tulagi Island, where he relinquishes his command. Jack returns to the United States on December 21, already having been declared a "Hero in the Pacific" by the *New York Times*.

To Rose, "he [Jack] is just the same," she declares in a family letter. "Wears his oldest clothes, still late for meals, still no money. He has even overflowed the bathtub, as was his boyhood custom."

Although many military insiders view the sinking of *PT-109* as an accident at sea, Joe Sr. works the press, convincing *Reader's Digest* to reprint for a mass readership John Hersey's rousing account originally published in *The New Yorker*. His tactics work, bringing Jack's story to a much larger readership, and fueling interest in the handsome homecoming hero.

Among the journalists now jostling for exclusive interviews is none other than Inga Arvad, Jack's Danish dream girl.

While they had ended their relationship almost two years earlier, they had continued their correspondence. "As long as you have that feeling" for survival, Jack had written Arvad during his convalescence, "you seem to get through." He confesses, "I've lost that feeling lately." He adds with heartfelt declaration, "Knowing you has been the brightest part of an extremely bright 26 years."

In January 1944, she interviews him for the *Boston Globe*. "Real heroes," he says, "are not the men who return, but those who stay out there like plenty of them do, two of my men included."

In June 1944, while in the hospital recovering from back surgery, Jack is awarded the Navy Marine Corps Medal and the Purple Heart. In March 1945, he receives a medical discharge from the navy, then signs on with the Hearst newspapers as a special correspondent.

Politics "is Joe's business," Jack would tell his cousin Joe Kane, Joe Sr.'s nephew and political adviser. "I want to go into the news business."

But with Joe Jr.'s death in August of 1944, the political mantle is passed to Jack, or as Jack put it, "[The] burden falls to me."

Joe Sr. has issued his latest orders, and Jack would not be destined for journalism. "It was like being drafted."

By the Fourth of July, 1945, the entire family has fallen into line. At the holiday gathering in Hyannis Port, Grandfather Honey Fitz makes a toast. In 1915, when Joe Jr. was born, Honey Fitz had brashly predicted, "[Joe] *is* going to be the President of the United States," the first among America's Irish Catholics. But on that night during the final days of the war in the Pacific, James A. Reed, Jack's friend from the navy, sees the former mayor look right at Joe and Rose's second born when he raises a glass to the future president of the United States.

CHAPTER 14

On May 8, 1952, at an exclusive Washington dinner on Q Street NW hosted by the journalist Charles Bartlett and his wife, Martha, a statuesque brunette catches the eye of thirty-four-year-old Congressman Jack Kennedy.

For the second time.

The Bartletts made the initial introduction at a small garden party at their home in May 1951, but it failed to spark. The then twenty-one-year-old George Washington University student Jacqueline Bouvier had had a foreboding reaction to the thirty-three-year-old, third-term Democratic representative from Massachusetts.

Jackie "had an absolutely unfailing antenna for the fake and fraud in people," the art critic John Russell later says of his long-time friend, and at first meeting, she sensed that Jack was a man who "would have a profound perhaps disturbing influence on her life."

Time magazine notes, "legend claims that Jack Kennedy 'leaned across the asparagus and asked for a date.' Jackie denies the story; asparagus, she says, was not on the menu." Either way, Jack fails to get the date.

By Christmastime 1951, Jackie has instead become engaged to John G. W. Husted Jr., whose prominent family connections in part fueled his success on Wall Street. But the life Husted offered Jackie, while financially secure, is emotionally limited. In March 1952, Jackie cancels their plans for a June wedding.

Instead, she pursues her work as the "Inquiring Camera Girl" at the *Washington Times-Herald,* where "Can you spot a married man?" is just one of the provocative questions she asks passersby on the streets of Washington, the population of which, at just over eight hundred thousand—over one hundred thousand larger than today—nevertheless has a small-town feel. As she is working at the same paper where, a decade earlier, Kick Kennedy and Inga Arvad had been on staff, it's impossible not to be drawn into the Kennedy orbit. Jackie adds Jack's book, *Why England Slept,* to her reading list.

Although Jackie would call the Bartletts "shameless in their match-making," she accepts their second invitation to dinner with a man who "looked a little lonesome and in need of a haircut and perhaps a square meal"—as Jackie's sister, Lee Bouvier, would later describe the Senate hopeful.

This latest meeting takes root, and Jackie later says she determined of their relationship, "Such heartbreak would be worth the pain." On Jack's part, Lem Billings suggests he found Jackie "a challenge," and "there was nothing Jack liked better than a challenge."

Not only is Jackie beautiful and her manners impeccable—courtesy of the esteemed Miss Porter's School—she's sharp and entertaining. In Jackie, Jack finds an equal adopter of humor as a survival tactic. "She had such a wit," her future White House social secretary, Letitia Baldridge, would observe. "She would have been terrible if she wasn't so funny." Jackie also has an enviable equestrian-set social status, inherited from her father, "Black Jack" Bouvier, to whom she bears a striking physical resemblance.

As they begin to spend time together, exchanging gifts of books on history, poetry, and art, the new couple is quick to confide parental difficulties on both sides. While many would later name her father as the only man Jackie ever truly loved, despite his philandering, "Jackie really didn't like her mother," recalls Bouvier cousin and family biographer John Davis. Jack could cut even deeper on the subject of Rose. "My mother was a nothing." And he chafes against Joe Sr.'s control. "I think my destiny is what my father wants it to be."

Jack struggles even more deeply with the numbing grief that comes from the loss of two siblings in less than five years. He bleakly describes Joe Jr.'s death in 1944 as having "a completeness...the completeness of perfection." He keeps Joe Sr.'s 1935 letter that tells of beloved younger sister Kick who "thinks you are quite the grandest fellow who ever lived and your letters furnish most of her laughs."

Impatient with his son's melancholy in the midst of a tough political contest, Joe delivers a stern mandate. A senator needs a wife. After all, Jack's younger brother Bobby has been married to Ethel Skakel since 1950 and has already had the first of what will be eleven children.

Jack is then campaigning against incumbent Republican senator Henry Cabot Lodge. "He spent half of each week in Massachusetts," Jackie recalls. "He'd call me from some oyster bar up there, with a great clinking of coins, to ask me out to the movies the following Wednesday in Washington."

The distance gives Jackie time to make her own calculations, according to opinion writer Helen Lawrenson. "Jackie knew about it all, or, if not all—[the] hundreds of other women from secretaries and hotel maids to starlets, socialites and wives of his friends—she knew the score."

On November 4, 1952, Congressman Jack Kennedy defeats Lodge by just over seventy thousand votes to become the new senator from Massachusetts.

In spring 1953, Jackie receives two big opportunities: an assignment to cover twenty-five-year-old Queen Elizabeth II's June 2 coronation, and a proposal of marriage from Jack. She first heads off to London before answering, putting an ocean's distance between them. Jackie "realized that if she married into that family, she would be expected to cater to their every whim. Kennedy women were treated like second-class citizens. Jackie wasn't prepared to tolerate that," fashion designer Estelle Parker opines. On the other hand, Jackie declares, the Kennedys "are nothing if not the most exciting family, perhaps in the world."

Despite her concerns, Jackie makes her decision and accepts Jack's proposal—and the diamond and emerald engagement ring from Van Cleef & Arpels, the two central stones totaling nearly six carats. Their engagement is announced on June 24, 1953, and she resigns from the *Times-Herald*.

"We are all crazy about Jackie," Joe declares, although at first the Kennedy women are puzzled by her disdain for athletics, her independence, her elegance, and her writerly pursuits. "'Jack-leen,' rhymes with 'queen,'" Eunice says. Dinah Bridge, a family friend, says, "Jackie was put through her paces by the whole family. And she stood up extremely well to the Kennedy barrage of questions." Rose settles on distant praise: "It would be hard to imagine a better wife for Jack."

Engagement doesn't slow Jack's philandering, however. A month before his wedding, the now thirty-six-year-old senator takes a bachelor adventure on the French Riviera. There he peels off from his Harvard roommate Torbert Macdonald to romance twenty-one-year-old Swedish socialite Gunilla Von Post, who recalls, "He spoke of his parents, his late brother, his sisters and brothers—but for the moment, there was no mention of a fiancée." In 2010 and 2011, correspondence detailing further liaisons between the socialite and the then-future president fetched six figures. Jack's last letter to Gunilla was dated 1956, three years after he wedded Jackie.

Evelyn Lincoln, Senator Kennedy's longtime executive secretary, whose upstanding Midwestern sensibility was often challenged by her employer's personal assignments, said in an interview, "Half my time was spent with women trying to find out about him."

Regardless, on September 12, 1953, eight hundred elite guests gather at St. Mary's Church in Newport, Rhode Island, to witness what Rose describes as "a splendid wedding" that introduces Jackie to "her new life as the wife of a political figure." The mother of the groom details a press account, "It took almost two hours for the guests to pass through the reception line to greet the couple."

"It was a beautiful, fairy tale of a wedding," says family friend Sancy Newman, noting how it was perfection personified. "Everyone said the most perfect things, wore the most perfect clothes, and had the most perfect manners. It was picture perfect." According to another guest, it was "just like the coronation" of Queen Elizabeth that Jackie had reported on earlier that year.

Less fittingly perfect is the incendiary rumor that their Newport wedding was not Jack's first trip to the altar. Investigative reporter Seymour Hersh claims that in 1947, Jack, on a whim, had married Palm Beach socialite Durie Malcolm.

Family friend Charles Spalding's wife, Betty, quotes Eunice as confirming the quickie marriage: "There was a drunken party and they [Jack and Durie] went off to a justice of the peace to get married" at two in the morning. Spalding admits that at Jack's request and with the help of a lawyer, he stole the marriage certificate from Palm Beach County offices, erasing any trace of a "high school prank, a little bit of daring that went too far."

But Durie, who was widowed by her fourth husband in 1996, denies the marriage to the *Sunday Times* of London: "I wouldn't have married Jack Kennedy for all the tea in China. I'll tell you why, if you want to know the truth. I didn't care for those Irish micks, and old Joe was a terrible man."

The marriage may have been quietly annulled. Certainly, there is no record of a divorce, allowing the scandalous possibility that when Jack married Jackie in 1953, he became a bigamist, clouding the family record of his children.

At the time of the wedding, the press vigorously investigates the Durie Malcolm story but doesn't print it. Meanwhile, rumors of Jack's further infidelities never quiet. Journalist and longtime family friend Arthur Krock warns of the consequences of a scandalous news story to Jack's presidential aspirations, but Joe disagrees. "The American people don't care how many times he gets laid."

"Kennedy men are like that," Jackie herself would caution Joan Bennett before she became Mrs. Ted Kennedy in 1958. "You can't let it get to you, because you shouldn't take it personally." Her words are a near echo of Josie Fitzgerald's 1929 warning to Rose over Joe's affair with Gloria Swanson.

As Jackie writes to her friend and confidant, Reverend Joseph Leonard, an Irish priest she'd met in 1950, "Jack's like my father in a way—loves the chase and is bored with the conquest—and once married needs proof he's still attractive, so flirts with other women and resents you. I saw how that nearly killed Mummy." It only takes Joan a few years of marriage to learn that her sister-in-law was right. "You just had to live with it."

The early days of the marriage are bumpy. "I was thirty-six, she was twenty-four. We didn't fully understand each other,"

Jack says, and Jackie, too remarks, "I found it rather hard to ad-just [to married life as a politician's wife]." It doesn't help that Jackie is unfamiliar with—and uninterested in—politics, and Jack is often away from home. "I was alone almost every week-end," she says. "Politics was sort of my enemy, and we had no home life whatsoever." Complicating matters was Jack's poor health, which needed to be constantly downplayed.

Had the truth about Jack's health gone to press, the American people might have felt the same way as Jackie did: *afraid.* "Jackie was usually the type to never show fear," Lem Billings recalls, "but she was scared, very much so, about all of Jack's illnesses. Not only did he have Addison's disease [caused by un-deractive adrenal glands], he had a variety of back problems. He was on different drugs and medications, so many you couldn't keep track of them all, including cortisone shots to treat the Addison's. He had muscle spasms, and was being shot up with Novocain all the time. He was always very sick."

In October 1954, thirteen months after their wedding, Jackie stands alongside the priest speaking in Latin by Jack's bedside at the Hospital for Special Surgery in New York. An attempted double fusion spinal surgery has left the senator in need of last rites. Jackie faces the very real possibility of losing her new hus-band. "I remember Jackie placing her hand on his forehead and saying, 'Help him, Mother of God,'" Lem recalls.

Miraculously, the senator survives, and in 1954 Jackie writes to Reverend Joseph Leonard, "I love being married much more than I did even in the beginning." To Jack, she writes, "You are an atypical husband," but "you mustn't be surprised to have an atypical wife—each of us would have been so lonely with the normal kind."

By August 1956, the Kennedy clan has expanded. Eunice, Pat, and Jean have all gotten married. Eunice already has two children, Ethel is pregnant with her fifth, Pat with her second—and Jackie with her first. Despite the impending birth of their first child, however, Jack has gone off to cruise the Mediterranean, smarting from having recently lost the Democratic nomination for Adlai Stevenson's Vice-Presidential running mate. So he's nowhere to be found when Jackie is rushed to the hospital on August 23, 1956, only to deliver their daughter—whom she names Arabella—stillborn.

The tragedy of that loss stays with her, but as she tells Reverend Leonard, she can see "so many good things that come out of this—how sadness shared brings married people closer together."

A little over a year later, on November 27, 1957, Jack and Jackie welcome a healthy daughter, whom they name Caroline.

Jackie is delighted to be a wife and mother, but Jack's main focus is still the possibility of a run for the presidency in 1960. While as of July 1958, Jack has still "said not a public word about wanting his party's nomination," the ambitions of "the handsome, well-endowed young author-statesman from Massachusetts" are easily understood, as outlined in a *New York Times* article entitled "How to be a Presidential Candidate."

Despite her new obligation to Caroline, Jackie isn't going to sit at home simply missing Jack again. She accompanies him on the campaign trail, to excellent effect. While Rose sniffs that her daughter-in-law is "not a natural-born campaigner," Kennedy aide Kenny O'Donnell recalls, "When Jackie was traveling with us, the size of the crowd at every stop was twice as big," and Jack finds his wife's judgment invaluable.

She cannot stay on the road with him full-time, however, but often attends functions just for the chance to see him. At one such event, she remarks, "This is the closest I've come to lunching with my husband in months!" The campaigning pays off, and in July 1960, Jack Kennedy wins the presidential nomination at the Democratic National Convention in Los Angeles. His wife, Jackie—now pregnant again—has done much to burnish his image, but many feel Jack is still a long shot against the seasoned Republican vice president Richard Nixon.

In Jack's ear is the voice of his friend Ben Bradlee, then reporting for *Newsweek,* "Do you really think—way down deep—that you can pull this thing off?"

"If I don't make a single mistake, yes," he answers.

CHAPTER 15

A man in a well-tailored suit struts into the darkened Chicago courtroom. The sound of his heavy footfalls echoes off the stone floor as he passes the jury box and witness stand. Both are empty. But Judge William Tuohy's chambers are not.

The chief judge of Cook County Civil Court rises from his desk at the sight of the man whose face is obscured by a fedora and dark glasses, taking the man's entrance as his cue for departure.

Joe Kennedy, already seated in chambers when the man arrives, won't be leaving. This is his meeting, and he's guaranteed, through the mob lawyer Robert McDonnell, that the discussion will be "very, very private."

Today's meeting is between himself and a crime boss known by many names. "Mooney," "Momo," "Sam the Cigar," and "Sam Flood," are all aliases—the FBI would identify up to nineteen—for Salvatore Giancana, whose name appears in the Nevada Gambling Commission's "Black Book" of top offenders, and who took control of the Chicago "outfit" in 1957.

There's no safer place from the ears of the FBI than a judge's chambers.

And no more dangerous person to proposition than Al Capone's onetime "trigger man." A Selective Service psychological evaluation had identified Giancana as a "constitutional psychopath with an inadequate personality."

Double-crossing the Sicilian American is a certain death sentence, even for a businessman as powerful as Joe Kennedy. Joe's got big assets in Chicago—in 1945, he bought the Merchandise Mart for just under thirteen million dollars. Under the management of Eunice's future husband, Sargent Shriver, the original Marshall Field building was transformed into the world's largest office building. Now, as the 1960 presidential election gets under way, the facility is valued at more than one hundred and fifty million dollars. But even Joe doesn't have the clout Giancana does.

"I own Chicago. I own Miami. I own Las Vegas," Giancana states to an FBI agent. Senator Jack Kennedy's efforts to break this hold have made him the chamber's second-ranked Democrat on Labor. He's joined the Select Committee on Improper Activities in the Labor Management Field, or Rackets Committee, supported by the group's chief legal counsel—Jack's younger brother Bobby.

In June 1959, Giancana and thirty-four-year-old Bobby Kennedy have a headline-making confrontation when Giancana is called to testify before the committee. Although Giancana has taken the Fifth Amendment, a legal protection against self-incrimination, Bobby reels off antagonistic questions for the record.

Since then, Giancana has been quietly building relationships with politicians and law enforcement and is well aware that an alliance with the next potential occupant of the Oval Office might protect his "outfit" from federal investigations.

Joe wants to capitalize on Giancana's power over Illinois unions, whose votes in Cook County he believes are key to Jack besting the Republican presidential front-runner, Vice President Richard Nixon, in this winner-take-all state in the Electoral College.

McDonnell, who waits with Judge Tuohy in the jury box during Joe and Giancana's meeting, later reveals to the investigative reporter Seymour Hersh how the handshake deal was executed. "There was no ballot stuffing...They just worked—totally went all out. He [Kennedy] won it squarely, but he got the vote because of what [Giancana] had done."

The mobster shifts easily between the hard-driving urban labor contingent and the glitzy denizens of the Las Vegas strip, where from the shadows he controls such top-name casinos as the Sands and the Riviera. Giancana "had the most perfectly manicured hands and nails I had ever seen," observes George Jacobs, who worked as Frank Sinatra's valet.

Giancana's close pals with Sinatra, the biggest headliner on the strip. Ol' Blue Eyes, Frank Sinatra, is the leader of the Rat Pack, a rotating cast of singers and actors that at that time included Dean Martin, Sammy Davis Jr., and Joey Bishop. The British actor Peter Lawford is a recent addition, broadly dismissed as "the least talented member of the Rat Pack," but the FBI has a theory about Lawford's inclusion. Peter Lawford is married to a Kennedy sister: Patricia. Pat and Peter's 1954 wedding had been a huge social event, attracting more than three thousand spectators outside St. Thomas More Cathedral in New York City. Rumors would also later surface of an affair between Pat and Sinatra.

But Sinatra is interested in a different Kennedy—Jack—and only Lawford can help him connect. "A well-known movie actor has been cultivated by Sinatra and they are now apparently close associates," a New Orleans special agent for the FBI reports to Director J. Edgar Hoover in March 1960, the month before the Illinois primary.

"There was a joke at the time that ended up having a lot of truth to it," cultural historian Steven Watts writes, "that in a way, Kennedy wanted to be Sinatra and Sinatra wanted to be Kennedy." Judith Campbell Exner, a dark-haired Californian whose beauty "was in the Elizabeth Taylor category," according to a Hollywood reporter, saw it happen firsthand. "They seemed to have a genuine mutual admiration society; Frank was in awe of Jack's background and his power as [future] President and Jack was mesmerized by Sinatra's swinging lifestyle."

Even more mesmerizing to Jack? Judith Exner herself.

Sinatra is holding court at his usual table at the Sands Lounge in Las Vegas, in February 1960. Among the entourage reveling in the success of yet another sold out Rat Pack show is the twenty-five-year-old Exner, who listens attentively to Sinatra—whom she'd briefly dated in 1959—until she notices two new faces around the table. She doesn't know that Jack Kennedy and his brother Ted are in politics until Sinatra introduces Jack as Senator Kennedy.

Nominally, Jack and Ted—now twenty-eight and his brother's campaign manager for the western states—are collecting advice from Hollywood influencers. Jack's poll numbers have been flagging in California, and the Democratic National Committee's nomination convention is set for July in Los Angeles. The Hollywood publicist Jim Mahoney, who represents Sinatra and Lawford, remembers strategizing, "Do a 'Youth for Kennedy' operation . . . Get the veterans behind him. He's got to do something here in California or he's in big trouble."

What the senator does do is ask Judith Cambell Exner to a

poolside lunch. They talk for hours, Jack's trademark sense of humor revealing itself in his reaction to Exner's confession that his younger brother Ted had made a failed pass at her the night before. "That little rascal. You'll have to excuse his youthful exuberance," he laughs.

"[Jack] seemed anxious to get together again. I was elated, almost giddy," Exner later tells *People* magazine.

A month of daily phone calls—"Jack was the world's greatest listener," Exner writes in her 1977 autobiography, *My Story*—culminates in a passionate meeting at the Plaza Hotel in New York, the night before the March 8, 1960, New Hampshire primary. "It was amazing to me that he could be so relaxed on the eve of the first primary of his presidential campaign but unbelievably, he didn't mention New Hampshire once during our entire night together. The next morning, he sent me a dozen roses with a card that said, 'Thinking of you...J.'"

Jack's not the only one thinking of Exner. In April, Sinatra also introduces her to his good friend "Sam Flood," an alias of Sam Giancana's. Incredibly, Exner begins carrying on two simultaneous affairs, one with a presidential hopeful, and one with the "Chicago Godfather."

She also starts carrying currency—hard cash and secret information—between her two lovers. "I feel like I was set up to be the courier," she explains to *People* magazine. "I was a perfect choice because I could come and go without notice, and if noticed, no one would have believed it anyway."

One such operation involves a plan to quash the mounting threat in West Virginia from rival Democratic candidate Senator Hubert Humphrey of Minnesota, who has been benefitting from growing voter concern over Kennedy's Catholic faith.

"I think he [Giancana] can help me with the campaign," Jack tells Exner, and puts her on a train to Chicago with a shadowy "protector" who may have been a Chicago political operative, as well as a satchel full of cash—enough to secure a meeting at the Fontainebleau Hotel in Miami Beach on April 12.

The gangster, the senator, and Exner—and likely the new mink coat she paid for with the two thousand dollars in cash Jack gave her before the train trip—are all present at the Miami Beach meeting, though she acknowledges, "The plans had all been made without me, way ahead of time."

A key part of those plans is to capitalize on a unique West Virginia campaign law that favors well-financed field operations. Paying staffers and voters money to cast their ballots is allowed, and the Kennedy dollars are flowing.

On May 10, Jack wins over 60 percent of the vote, forcing Humphrey out of the race.

Reporters laugh along with him as Jack jokes, "I just received the following wire from my generous Daddy; Dear Jack, Don't buy a single vote more than is necessary. I'll be damned if I'm going to pay for a landslide."

That many of them probably know the truth in that statement is moot.

In July, Jack accepts the Democratic Party's presidential nomination and addresses a rapt audience at the national convention in Los Angeles, stating that he sees the country's future "on the edge of the New Frontier—of the 1960s—a frontier of unknown opportunities and perils—a frontier of unfilled hopes and threats."

Unknown. Unfilled. Perils. Threats. How closely the dark elements of Jack's predictions would parallel his own last days.

Sinatra watches the nomination alongside Jack's father, Joe; Jack's brother Bobby; and Jack's brother-in-law Peter Lawford—the Rat Pack now the "Jack Pack"—and considers himself one of them, stating, "We're on our way to the White House." He's right.

On November 8, voters tip the popular vote to Jack by

the narrowest of percentages, 49.7 to 49.5 percent—a 118,550-vote margin out of 69 million votes cast. In the Electoral College, he wins 303 to 219.

That fall of 1960, Rose Kennedy writes in her diary, "I doubt [Joe Sr.] will ever get credit for the constant, unremitting labor he has devoted to making his son President."

But it's the mobster Giancana who takes credit, boasting to Exner, "Your boyfriend wouldn't be president if it wasn't for me."

CHAPTER 16

John F. Kennedy takes office in the dawn of the television age, the first occupant of the Oval Office to regularly broadcast his press conferences live.

He'd been hugely successful during the first-ever televised presidential debate against Nixon, where his image of youth and vigor dominated over the older man. It didn't matter how ill Jack truly was—the important thing was that he *looked* healthy and telegenic.

Perhaps influenced by his mother's lifelong criticisms of his sloppy appearance, Jack knows the value of presentation. "Rather vain" was Jackie's initial impression of Jack, according to Bouvier cousin John Davis's recollection. "She talked about how he had to have his hair done all the time, how he had to always look just right."

Norman Mailer saw JFK as "Superman" with a "jewel of a political machine, all discipline and savvy and go-go-go." He "had the deep orange-brown suntan of a ski instructor, and when he smiled at the crowd his teeth were amazingly white and clearly visible from a distance of 50 yards. It was a hero America needed, a hero central to his time."

Television audiences would never see that hero's utter reliance on his valet, George E. Thomas, who called the president "John F." Thomas not only plans the president's wardrobe—up to four clothing changes per day—but helps him dress. Due to lingering pain from his back injuries and osteoporosis, Jack needs help getting into his back brace and shoes, and even with navigating stairs.

During the 1960 presidential campaign, Kennedy sought out Dr. Max Jacobson—"Dr. Feelgood" to his patients—for relief from pain and exhaustion. Once in the White House, Kennedy's prescription list becomes so extensive that staff maintains the crucial "Medicine Administration Record."

True to the Kennedy ethos, one is never enough. "Doctors came and went around Kennedy," writes biographer Richard Reeves. "In a lifetime of medical torment, Kennedy was more promiscuous with physicians and drugs than he was with women."

But no amount of physical suffering deters him from implementing his ambitious social agenda. Plans to create the Peace Corps and attack poverty were in line with campaign promises, but not the idea that New Frontier would extend into outer space. On May 25, 1961, in a joint congressional session on "Urgent National Needs," the president sets an astonishing benchmark, saying, "I believe this nation should commit itself to achieving the goal, before the decade is out, of landing a man on the moon and returning him safely to Earth."

But his lofty goals are quickly, and repeatedly, interrupted by Cuban crises. The flash of the new and the blindness of inexperience soon collide in the first serious crisis of the Kennedy administration. In January 1959, two years before Jack's inauguration, General Fulgencio Batista's American-friendly government in Cuba fell to thirty-two-year-old revolutionary Fidel Castro. The new self-appointed prime minister declares himself a Communist and signs a series of pacts with Soviet premier, Nikita Khruschev.

A CIA operation funded by Kennedy's predecessor, President Dwight D. Eisenhower, identified former Cubans exiled to Miami when Castro took power, more than fourteen hundred of whom join top-secret "Brigade 2506" in 1961 and are taken to receive extensive training from US military special forces.

The three-part plan calls for the brigade to attack Castro on a Cuban beach known as the Bay of Pigs—where Castro is known to fish—followed by an airstrike and then a combined attack. The assumption is that once Castro is out of the picture, the Cuban people will turn to a more US-friendly leader.

Democrat and foreign policy expert Dean Acheson warns the president that "this was a disastrous idea."

It was.

The mission begins—and ends—on April 17, 1961. The brigade begins their attack, but at the last minute, Kennedy withholds US air support for fear of reprisal from the United Nations, leaving the exiles trapped at the landing site. Castro quickly activates his militia to kill more than a hundred, and imprisons the rest of Brigade 2506 for the next twenty months before releasing them in exchange for more than fifty million dollars in American food and medical supplies for Cuba—and the integrity of the Kennedy administration.

The Bay of Pigs fiasco shatters the president's confidence. "I have had two full days of hell—I haven't slept—this has been the most excruciating period of my life," he tells his legal adviser Clark Clifford. "I doubt my presidency could survive another catastrophe like that."

Indeed, international relations between the United States and Cuba and their powerful ally, the Soviet Union, only get worse from there, leading to the Cuban Missile Crisis, when Kruschev establishes plans to place nuclear missiles in Cuba to defend the island.

It's another test of the Kennedy administration, and at a tense cabinet meeting in 1962, when it appears that the United States and the Soviet Union are on the brink of nuclear war, Air Force Chief of Staff General Curtis LeMay tells Kennedy, "You're in a pretty bad fix, Mr. President," to which Kennedy shoots back, "You're in there with me."

Jackie chimes in with a romantic view of these dark days, though her tender feelings weren't made public for decades. "If anything happens, we're all going to stay right here with you," Jackie told her husband, according to interviews she did with Schlesinger in 1964 (unreleased until 2011).

Thankfully, the countries are able to come to a disarmament agreement, and the president comes out of the crisis with his reputation relatively intact.

Bobby Kennedy, on the other hand, has already had his own reputation stung by accusations that nepotism landed him the attorney general position at just thirty-five years old. "I can't see that it's wrong to give him [Bobby] a little legal experience before he goes out to practice law," Jack quips, but it's Bobby who takes the hits.

In the meantime, he's already concocted another plan to dislodge Castro from power. In a November 1961 meeting at the White House, Bobby writes in his notebook, "My idea is to stir things up on the island with espionage, sabotage, general disorder, run and operated by Cubans themselves with every group but Batistaites and Communists. Do not know if we will be successful in overthrowing Castro but we have nothing to lose in my estimate."

Operation Mongoose, a multiagency covert operation, is launched under Bobby's oversight. "Get rid of the Castro regime, quote-unquote," is the way the CIA officer Sam Halpern describes his orders—and when he asks for clarification on what "get rid of" means, he is told, "Sam, use your imagination." What defies imagination, given RFK's history with prosecuting the mob, is the recruitment of the Mafia. With Castro's seizure of power, the Mafia has lost their lucrative casino businesses in Cuba, and they're eager to assist.

Judith Exner is again tapped as a courier between Jack and Giancana, including helping to arrange a meeting between them in Chicago in her hotel suite, where she exiles herself to the bathroom while the president and the mob boss discuss strategy in the bedroom.

"I thought I was in love with Jack. He trusted me and I was doing something important for him," Exner later reflects. "I guess I felt I was doing something important." She claims not to have known what that something was, though, until over a decade later: "It finally dawned on me that I was probably helping Jack orchestrate the attempted assassination of Fidel Castro with the help of the Mafia."

The Mafia's plans ranged from sprinkling a CIA poison on Castro's food to an exploding cigar and poison flowing from a pen. But the assassination plans don't go anywhere, and are eventually superseded by the Cuban Missile Crisis.

President Kennedy never fulfills his father's promise of protection for the mob from the Oval Office. Instead, his brother Bobby Kennedy, the attorney general, doubles down on his pursuit, making it his important mission to obliterate the American Mafia.

Giancana fumes, "My millions were good enough for 'em, weren't they? The votes I muscled for 'em were good enough to get Jack elected. So now I'm a fuckin' greaseball, am I?" according to Chuck Giancana, author of *Double Cross*, a biography of his mobster uncle. "Well, I'm gonna send them a message they'll never forget," Giancana threatens.

Menacing words like these are what keep Judith Exner silent for the next twenty-five years. "I've gone to great lengths to keep the truth from ever coming out, which is probably the only reason I'm alive today," she tells *People* magazine in 1988. "I lied [to the Senate Select Intelligence Committee that investigated "Operation Mongoose" in 1975] when I said I was not a conduit between President Kennedy and the Mafia," she says, adding, "I would never have known mobsters if it hadn't been for Frank Sinatra."

Is Frank Sinatra the key to it all? That's what one woman in Newark, claiming to be psychic, writes to the FBI in March 1985. "Frank Sinatra is the main problem," she declares. "He is responsible for the Kennedy curse: Joe, Jack, Bobby."

The last line in Frank Sinatra's FBI file reads, "Newark [FBI] considers the captioned matter closed," but an explanation for the successive Kennedy tragedies remains very much an open matter.

CHAPTER 17

The November 22, 1963, final evening edition of the *Boston Globe* lies on the floor next to the bed of the ailing patriarch Joe Kennedy. The headline screams: "Extra! Extra! PRESIDENT SLAIN: *Assassin's Bullet Fells Kennedy on Dallas Street.*"

America's beloved president John F. Kennedy is dead, the third of Joe's nine children to die a sudden, violent death.

The seventy-five-year-old patriarch, who had long boasted of his conquests in bed and in business and even bargained with the Mafia to send union votes to his son—had suffered a paralytic stroke nearly two years earlier, on December 19, 1961. Initially, through aggressive rehabilitation, he'd successfully battled back, relearning to walk with the aid of an engraved silver and black stick, a gift from his beloved daughter-in-law Jackie. But in recent months, his condition has drastically deteriorated.

A month earlier, on Sunday, October 20, 1963, President Kennedy had visited Hyannis Port. When Joe wheeled his chair onto the porch to say good-bye, Jack kissed his father on the

THE HOUSE OF KENNEDY

forehead, turned to leave...then went back again, as if Jack believed he was seeing his father for the last time.

"He's the one who made all of this possible," Jack told his aide Dave Powers inside the helicopter, "and look at him now."

His father seemed on the cusp of death.

But the man entering his final days will not be Joe.

Ted and Eunice break the terrible news of Jack's assassination to their father, as Rose can't bear to. "We have told him but we don't think he understands it," Rose said.

Or it may be that he simply cannot stand the truth that Jack is dead.

Afternoon shadows crisscross Joe's room. The man who built the powerful House of Kennedy is left with only his memories to comfort—or taunt—him.

A few days earlier, President Kennedy and the First Lady are in Jack's White House dressing room, reviewing travel plans. The next day, they'll depart on a whirlwind two-day, five-city trip to Texas, with a final stop on November 23 at LBJ Ranch, which the vice president acquired when serving as a senator.

Richard Nixon, the Republican presidential nominee whom Kennedy defeated in 1960 and who has since been practicing law in New York City, is also in Dallas for a corporate speaking engagement. He's ready to predict a key absence from the 1964 Democratic ticket—Johnson's. "In 1960, Lyndon was a help. In 1964 he might not be," Nixon theorizes.

The president is experiencing a surge of health. "I feel great. My back feels better than it's felt in years," Jack tells White House aide Kenny O'Donnell.

Nevertheless, JFK is wearing his Nelson Kloman back brace, made at the surgical supply company in Washington, DC. As customary, his tie clip features a replica of his wartime boat, *PT-109*. Valet George Thomas coordinates the array of clothing needed for the multiple public appearances the Kennedys have planned for each day of the trip.

Jackie is also busy with preparations, from hair to wardrobe. She's written a four-page packing list to her personal assistant, Providencia Parendes, inspired by the president's advice: "Be simple—show these Texans what good taste really is."

The First Lady's signature low-heeled shoes—a narrow size 10A—are specially made, according to biographer Barbara Leaming, "to make large feet look smaller and more feminine." In her memoir *Jackie's Girl*, former personal assistant Kathy McKeon reveals another of Jackie's sartorial secrets: "[A] quarter-inch lift affixed to one heel on each pair of shoes, apparently meant to compensate for one leg being slightly shorter than the other. No one ever would have guessed."

A possible inspiration for the footwear adjustment comes from the president himself. Dr. Janet Travell, the first woman to be appointed as personal physician to the president, has been treating Jack since his third back surgery in 1955. "One of the first things I did for him," she says, "was to institute a heel lift" to correct his left leg being shorter than his right.

During her tenure as First Lady, Jackie has already become a style icon, known for her "overwhelming good taste" and her collaborations with the dress designer Oleg Cassini, informally known as "the Secretary of Style," who called her an "American Queen." "Jackie wanted to do Versailles in America," Cassini recalls. Together they create the "Jackie look."

While Jack is proud of his wife's style, he's annoyed at how much she spends—though his father, Joe, foots the bill for all of her Cassini dresses. "Just send me an account at the end of the year. I'll take care of it," he tells the designer.

For the trip to Texas, however, Jackie packs mainly Chanel.

The 1961 Lincoln Continental convertible—painted presidential blue metallic and code-named SS 100-X by the Secret Service after undergoing two hundred thousand dollars in security modifications—is ready to drive the Texas streets. It's the first presidential car outfitted with a removable transparent roof. But the top is not bulletproof, and the body of the upgraded vehicle, though heavy, lacks protective armor. Gary Mack, curator of Dallas's Sixth Floor Museum at Dealey Plaza, describes the car as an "expensive, fancy limousine." Any glare or reflection might disrupt an assassin's clear shot. And in any case, Jack, who once astounded the French president Charles de Gaulle by insisting on touring the Champs Élysées by convertible even in the rain, is against using the roof. "I don't want the bubbletop on the car," he tells Kenny O'Donnell, who is organizing his Dallas schedule. "I want all those Texas broads to see what a beautiful girl Jackie is."

Despite tensions in their marriage, and Jackie's initial discomfort at the public role of First Lady (she remarked to the *New York Times* in 1960, after Jack's election, that she felt like she had become "a piece of public property. It's really frightening to lose your anonymity at thirty-one"), she confides to a friend in 1962, "The last thing I expected to find in the White House [has been] the happiest time I have ever known—not for the position—but for the closeness of one's family." By early August 1963, that family is set to expand—Caroline is five and a half, John Jr. is two and a half, and Jackie is pregnant with another baby, due around the same time as what will be her tenth wedding anniversary, on September 12.

But on August 7, 1963, more than a month prematurely, Jackie goes into labor while vacationing on Cape Cod. The date is significant—it's the twentieth anniversary of the Japanese attack on *PT-109* that made Jack a naval hero. There is "no way in God's Earth," says Ben Bradlee, that the president wouldn't have noted the coincidence. Unlike when Jackie went into labor with Arabella, this time Jack rushes to his wife's side at Otis Air Force Base on Cape Cod, where Jackie is undergoing an emergency Cesarean.

Patrick Bouvier Kennedy is born at 12:52 p.m., suffering from hyaline membrane disease, a lung disorder common in babies born prematurely.

In 1963, the odds of the four-pound, ten-and-a-half-ounce boy surviving are only fifty-fifty, yet the *Boston Globe* optimistically predicts, "He's a Kennedy—he'll make it." An article published the day of Patrick's birth notes the White House press secretary, Pierre Salinger, saying, "The doctors are hopeful," and quotes one of those doctors describing the boy as "a lovable little monkey" whom they're treating with "tender loving care, medicine, oxygen, and everything else we can do to correct the symptoms."

Tragically, Patrick's condition worsens. He's rushed by ambulance to Children's Hospital in Boston, and Jackie is not well enough to accompany him. The president alone watches over the infant, encased in an incubator. "Nothing must happen to Patrick," Jack tells his mother-in-law, "because I just can't bear to think the effect it might have on Jackie." Yet he can only stand helpless as a team of doctors tries and fails to revive his son. Jack is able to hold him at the end, saying, "He put up quite a fight. He was a beautiful baby." But the *Washington Post* notes, "The First Lady never once held little Patrick in her arms or heard him cry."

Nor is she able to attend his funeral, in a private chapel at Cardinal Richard Cushing's Boston residence. "Overwhelmed with grief," according to Cushing, Jack throws his arms around the tiny coffin. The cardinal, who officiated at Jack and Jackie's wedding, places a hand on his shoulder. "My dear Jack, let's go, let's go, nothing more can be done."

But the president cannot be consoled. "He was genuinely cut to the bone," remembers Larry Newman, a Secret Service agent. "When that boy died, it almost killed him too."

Despite the tragedy of Patrick's death, one positive aspect is noticed by everyone near to the First Couple—this shared loss has brought the two of them closer together, and they are even publicly affectionate in ways previously unseen. "The other agents and I noticed a distinctly close relationship, openly expressed, between the president and Mrs. Kennedy," recalls the Secret Service agent Clint Hill. "Prior to this, they were much more restrained."

"It was different than I had seen them before," deputy press secretary Malcolm Kilduff says. "It was very nice." He adds, "I thought to myself how protective he was being of her." White House intern Mimi Beardsley also recalls feeling that after his son's death, the president is filled "not only with grief but with an aggrieved sense of responsibility to his wife and family," significantly curtailing, and possibly ceasing, all of his affairs.

By the time of their trip to Texas, the Kennedys are closer than they have ever been.

Jackie's mother, Janet Auchincloss, notes that "all their strains and stresses," have subsided to a point where "they were very, very, very close to each other and understood each other wonderfully."

CHAPTER 18

The president and First Lady are scheduled for a joint appearance at a breakfast at the Hotel Texas in Fort Worth on November 22, 1963, one of Jackie's first since Patrick's death in August. The people waiting outside in the hotel parking lot early that morning are chanting "Jackie! Jackie!" eager for a glimpse of the First Lady. "Mrs. Kennedy is organizing herself," Jack tells the disappointed crowd. "It takes her longer, but, of course, she looks better than we do when she does it."

The crowd inside is eager, too, thousands of them cheering when Jackie appears in an American-made "line-for-line" copy of a Chanel strawberry-pink wool suit with a matching pillbox hat ensemble that her husband found "smashing." (Although Jackie has been a longtime Chanel client, it's deemed "too foreign, too spendy" for her to buy clothes directly from Paris as First Lady—so instead Chanel sends the patterns and material to New York, to be technically created in the U.S.)

As the *Chicago Sun-Times* editorializes that morning, all hopes are riding on Jackie. "Some Texans, in taking account of the tangled Texas political situation, have begun to think that Mrs. Jacqueline Kennedy may turn the balance and win her husband this state's electoral vote."

At the hotel, Jack signs what may be a last autograph, for Texas Hotel chambermaid Jan White, on the front page of that day's *Dallas Morning News,* which features a photo of the couple in San Antonio the day before, Jackie smiling widely and wearing another chic Chanel dress, this one white and belted with a thin black bow.

Historian William Manchester says that Jackie herself later revealed to him that she and the president made love aboard Air Force One on the jaunt between San Antonio and Houston on the afternoon of the twenty-first—a detail he cloaked in his 1967 book, *The Death of a President,* as their "last hour of serenity," coyly ending with "the President emerged in a fresh shirt."

After the breakfast, the Kennedys leave the Hotel Texas and head back to Air Force One, ready for the thirteen-minute hop from Fort Worth Carswell Air Force Base to Dallas Love Field.

Dallas is the new home of former major general Edwin A. Walker, a self-proclaimed "super patriot" whom *Newsweek* labeled "the Thunder on the Right." Despite a psychiatrist deeming his actions indicative of "paranoid mental disorders"— Kennedy privately commented, "Imagine that son of a bitch having been commander of a division up till last year. And the Army promoting him?"—in September 1962, Walker's supporters were even carrying "Walker for President 64" signs.

Fellow Dallas resident and ex-marine marksman Lee Harvey Oswald is *not* one of those supporters. As a declared Communist, Oswald is exactly the kind of enemy Walker and his zealots seek to vanquish.

In 1959, twenty-year-old Oswald visits Moscow on a tourist visa with the intention to defect, but the KGB rejects him and his "outdated information," and determines that he's no double agent. "His intellectual training experience and capabilities were such that it would not show the FBI and CIA in good light if they used people like him." But a top member of the Politburo intervenes and in 1960 puts him to work at a television radio factory in Minsk, where the KGB bugs his government-issue apartment.

John F. Kennedy is inaugurated president of the United States in January 1961, and that April, Lee Harvey Oswald marries Marina Prusakova after a six-week courtship.

In June 1962, the US and Soviet governments agree to allow the "re-defector" Oswald and his family to return to the United States.

On April 10, 1963, Oswald decides to use Walker as "target practice." In the Marines, Oswald had earned a sharpshooter qualification, rated by the sergeant in charge of his training as "a slightly better than average shot for a Marine, excellent by civilian standards." Now, he trains the telescopic sight of his high-powered Mannlicher-Carcano infantry rifle—mail ordered with his family's grocery money under the alias A. Hiddell—on the former general as Walker sits at his desk inside his Dallas home.

He pulls the trigger—and misses.

"He couldn't see [properly] from his position because of the light," Walker later theorizes to the Warren Commission. "He could have been a very good shot and, just by chance, he hit the woodwork."

Although Oswald tells his wife, Marina, "I shot Walker" immediately upon returning home late that night, it's not until after the events in Dallas that the ammunition used is linked back to Oswald.

Prior to JFK's visit in November 1963, Walker, an outspoken

adversary of the president's, has his extremist associates distribute five thousand flyers. The flyers show a stylized mugshot of Kennedy alongside seven accusations of treason, from the political—"Betraying the Constitution"—to the personal—"LIES to the American people (including personal ones like his previous marriage and divorce)."

Hours before the president's plane touches down in Dallas, twenty-four-year-old Lee Harvey Oswald takes off his wedding ring and leaves it on the bedroom dresser. (Fifty years later, that ring will sell for one hundred eight thousand dollars at auction.) In recent months, he's become estranged from his wife, Marina, and she and their daughters are staying with a friend, Ruth Paine, in suburban Dallas, while Oswald has a room in a boardinghouse. But on Thursday night, November 21, he decides to stay at the Paine house, where he typically visits only on weekends.

"I was surprised to see him," Ruth Paine remarks. The couple fought often, but that evening she has "the impression that relations between the young Oswalds [are] 'cordial,' 'friendly,' 'warm'—like a couple making up after a small spat."

They sleep in the same bed, but in the middle of the night he kicks her away when her feet touch him. "My, he's in a mean mood," Marina thinks. The next morning, he sleeps late, then gets a lift to his job at the Texas School Book Depository from a coworker, Buell Wesley Frazier, one of Ruth Paine's neighbors. While they are driving to work, Frazier asks Oswald what's in the elongated brown package he's brought.

"Curtain rods," Oswald tells him.

CHAPTER 19

I t all began so beautifully. After a drizzle in the morning, the sun came out bright and beautiful. We were going into Dallas," Lady Bird Johnson observes in her diary of November 22, 1963.

The Texas native and wife of Vice President Lyndon Johnson will ride in the third car of the presidential motorcade that sets out from Love Field just before noon. The planned route is an eleven-mile drive through the city's downtown at a slow crawl of twelve to fifteen miles per hour, ending at the Dallas Trade Mart for a scheduled 1:00 p.m. luncheon.

Fifteen minutes earlier, from inside Air Force One, Jack takes in the cheering crowd of two thousand gathered around the fenced perimeter of the airfield and remarks to Kenny O'Donnell, "It looks like everything in Texas is going to be fine for us."

Earlier that morning, at the Hotel Texas in Fort Worth, Jackie had felt uneasy upon seeing a hate-filled, full-page anti-Kennedy ad from the "American Fact-Finding Committee" in the *Dallas Morning News*. The ad was bordered in mourning black, and despite a headline proclaiming "Welcome Mr. Kennedy," its tone was deeply belligerent.

On the spring day when Jackie first met Jack, she'd felt that he "would have a profound perhaps disturbing influence" on her life. Would angry Texans be the source of the disturbance she had sensed more than a decade before?

But her husband makes light of her fears, joking, "We're heading into nut country today...You know, last night would have been a hell of a night to assassinate a president," he tells her, remarking on how easy it would have been for someone among the anonymous masses lining the streets in Fort Worth with "a pistol in a briefcase...could have dropped the gun and briefcase and melted away into the crowd."

A fellow boarder at Lee Harvey Oswald's rooming house recalls his rapt attention to a televised report two days earlier, on November 20, detailing the president's upcoming visit and adding information to the maps and routes that the *Dallas Times Herald* had published on November 19.

Oswald now knows the expected timing of the presidential motorcade's passage through Dealey Plaza, then on past the Texas School Depository building where he works. He knows that the president and the First Lady will be in the lead car, along with Governor John Connally and his wife, Nellie.

As the motorcade departs Love Field, Oswald is spotted on the sixth floor by a coworker, Charles Givens, carrying a clipboard and walking toward the elevator. Givens later testifies to the Warren Commission that Oswald directs him, "When you get downstairs, close the elevator." Oswald doesn't explain himself, but Givens does as he is told.

By twelve thirty, Oswald is positioned in his sniper's perch.

Bill Greer, the president's personal driver, is at the wheel of the open-top Lincoln Continental, license plate GG-300. By order of the president, the Secret Service are not standing on the retractable foot stands but positioned in the follow-car.

In the fold-down, forward-facing jump seats are Governor Connally and his wife, Nellie. President Kennedy and Jackie are in the seats behind them. "We were indeed a happy foursome that beautiful morning," Nellie Connally writes in her book, *From Love Field: Our Final Hours with President Kennedy*. Both she and Jackie wear pink suits and carry roses, Jackie's red and Nellie's yellow. "Everything was so perfect."

As the excited crowds cheer, Nellie turns in her seat to face Jack and says, "Mr. President, you can't say Dallas doesn't love you."

The president is smiling and waving his right hand at onlookers. Jackie has in her lap the bouquet of roses Dallas mayor Earle Cabell presented to her at Love Field. The day was "hot, wild," Jackie recalls. "The sun was so strong in our faces."

"Suddenly," Lady Bird Johnson records, "there was a sharp loud report—a shot. It seemed to me to come from the right above my shoulder from a building. Then a moment and then two more shots in rapid succession."

Dallas Morning News staff writer Mary Elizabeth Woodward, along with three newsroom colleagues, watch from across Elm Street just east of the triple underpass. Woodward's article, titled "Witness from the News Describes Assassination," states, "We were almost certainly the last faces [John F. Kennedy] noticed in the crowd. After acknowledging our cheers, he faced forward again and suddenly there was a horrible, ear-shattering noise, coming from behind us and a little to the right."

What Woodward does not reveal in her eyewitness account is her lifelong hearing problem. She comes to deeply regret that omission, as the direction she gives for the source of the sound does not match the location of the Texas Book Depository where Oswald had holed up—and that discrepancy fuels decades of speculation. In her 2017 *Dallas News* obituary, she calls it "something that I have regretted the rest of my life because every conspiracy theorist in the world has quoted that. And I'm convinced that I did not hear it correctly."

Roy H. Kellerman, special agent in charge, testifies on December 18, 1963, that after hearing the first shot, he "turned around to find out what happened when two additional shots rang out, and the President slumped into Mrs. Kennedy's lap and Governor Connally fell into Mrs. Connally's lap. I heard Mrs. Kennedy shout, 'What are they doing to you?'"

Abraham Zapruder will spend the rest of his life answering that very question.

"How many times will you have a crack at [taking] color movies of the president?" Lillian Rogers, Zapruder's secretary at his apparel manufacturing company, Jennifer Juniors, tells her boss. She sends "Mr. Z"—a fifty-eight-year-old Kennedy enthusiast who'd emigrated from Russia as a teenager—home to retrieve his high-end Bell & Howell Zoomatic Director Series Camera, already loaded with eight-millimeter Kodachrome II color safety film.

The clothing factory occupies two floors of the Dal-Tex Building, located across the street from the Texas School Book Depository where the armed Oswald lurks. Zapruder walks a block toward Elm Street, steps onto a raised concrete platform, and points his viewfinder at the approaching motorcade.

The visuals Abraham Zapruder captures over the next twenty-six seconds instantly convince him that he has just witnessed an assassination. "They killed him!" he shouts at bystanders. Then, minutes later, "It was terrible. I saw his head come off."

"I think he was very sorry to be the guy who got it on film," says Zapruder's granddaughter, Alexandra, decades later. "It brought him nothing but heartbreak."

* * *

"Step on it! We're hit!" Roy H. Kellerman orders Bill Greer. As the Continental speeds toward Parkland Memorial Hospital, Jackie protectively cradles her dying husband, his bright red blood seeping into her pink suit.

"It's the image of yellow roses and red roses and blood all over the car...all over us," recalls Nellie Connally. "I'll never forget it."

Lady Bird Johnson catches a tragic glimpse as their cars speed off. "I cast one last look over my shoulder and saw a bundle of pink, just like a drift of blossoms, lying in the back seat."

CHAPTER 20

Hugh Aynesworth, a thirty-two-year-old aerospace reporter for the *Dallas Morning News*, isn't assigned to cover the president's visit, but figures he won't be missed from an empty newsroom. He works his way through the crowd and finds a place in front of the Texas School Book Depository a few minutes before twelve thirty.

Shots ring out and panic erupts around him: "My reporter instinct kicked in. I saw a man across from me pointing up to the sixth-floor window, saying, "he's up there"...He [Howard Brennan] was the only witness, and he described the shooter perfectly."

At the Dallas County Sheriff's Department, Howard Leslie Brennan, a steamfitter employed by the Wallace and Beard Construction Company, gives a sworn statement. About 12:18 p.m., he tells them, he was looking up and into the brick building across from Elm Street, where he saw a man sitting in a window. "He was just sitting up there looking down," Brennan recounts, "apparently waiting for the same thing I was, to see the President." As the presidential motorcade passes, Brennan says he heard the sound of an engine backfiring, or maybe someone throwing firecrackers from the brick building.

"I then saw this man I have described in the window and he was taking aim with a high-powered rifle. I could see all of the barrel of the gun. I do not know if it had a scope on it or not. I was looking at the man in this window at the time of the last explosion. Then the man let the gun down to his side and stepped out of sight."

Based on Brennan's description of the man with the rifle—a slender white man in his early thirties dressed in light-colored clothing—an all-points bulletin goes out. By the time Brennan leaves the sheriff's office at about 2:00 p.m., police will know just where to find the man who assassinated the president.

—————

United Press International White House correspondent Merriman Smith has a seat in President Kennedy's motorcade, in the press car, which is equipped with a radiotelephone.

Four minutes after the shooting, at 12:34 p.m., Smith breaks the first news of the assassination over UPI's A-wire: "DALLAS, NOV. 22 (UPI)—THREE SHOTS FIRED AT PRESIDENT KENNEDY'S MOTORCADE TODAY IN DOWNTOWN DALLAS."

Two minutes later, the press car arrives at Parkland Memorial Hospital following President Kennedy's car. As Smith, who would go on to win a Pulitzer Prize for his coverage of these events, writes, "I recall a babble of anxious, tense voices— 'Where in hill [sic] are the stretchers…Get a doctor out here...He's on the way...Come on, easy there.' And from somewhere, nervous sobbing."

Immediately following the shooting, Nellie Connally recalled Jackie repeating, "They have killed my husband. I have his brains in my hand."

Chief anesthesiologist Dr. Marion Thomas "Pepper" Jenkins—who within two days treats both JFK and his killer, Lee Harvey Oswald—similarly recalls his most haunting memory of November 22: the First Lady showing him that "she had been cradling his brain in her hand."

Nor will it be the last macabre mention of JFK's brain.

In 1998, the Assassinations Records Review Board releases a shocking report into the National Archives in Washington, DC. Douglas Horne, a former naval officer and the board's chief analyst for military records, states, "I am 90 to 95 percent certain that the photographs in the Archives are not of President Kennedy's brain. If they aren't, they can mean only one thing—that there has been a coverup of the medical evidence."

The case of the two "Kennedy" brains—one of them allegedly a plant showing much less damage than doctors saw during their examinations at Parkland Memorial Hospital—renewed the fevered discussion over whether Kennedy had been shot from the front, as initial medical reviews indicate, or from behind, as the Warren Commission ultimately concludes.

Rumors have long held that during the autopsy conducted at Maryland's Bethesda Naval Hospital, the president's brain had been removed and delivered in a stainless-steel container, first to the Secret Service, and then to a medical locker in the National Archives.

The author James Swanson tells the New York Post that a 1966 search for the brain proved futile, but that the probe did "uncover compelling evidence suggesting that former Attorney

General Robert Kennedy, aided by his assistant Angie Novello, had stolen the locker."

What Dr. Jenkins concludes either way, however, is that the brain injury was not survivable. While Kennedy was technically still alive when he was brought in, "He was dying." Jenkins recalls telling the priest who was there to perform last rites, "Look at this head injury. We didn't have any chance to save him."

Merriman Smith watches as two priests enter the president's hospital room to administer last rites, then rushes to the "nurses room," where acting White House press secretary Malcolm Kilduff (Pierre Salinger is on an Asian tour) calls a hasty conference to officially announce what Merriman Smith has already learned from Secret Service agent Clint Hill.

"He's dead."

At approximately 1:15 p.m., forty-five minutes after Kennedy is shot in Dealey Plaza, J. D. Tippit, a Dallas cop, is patrolling the Oak Cliff neighborhood in his cruiser. The thirty-nine-year-old married father of three is roughly three miles from Dealey Plaza when he spots a pedestrian who fits the description of the assassin. Tippit calls the man over for questioning, then exits the vehicle to investigate further.

The man, Lee Harvey Oswald, puts a .38-caliber revolver between them and, at point-blank range, shoots the officer three times. A fourth shot, to the head, proves fatal. Oswald leaves the scene and continues walking down the street as passerby T. F. Bowley comes upon the horrifying scene and uses Tippit's police radio to report the crime.

Twenty-two-year-old Johnny Calvin Brewer is listening to the radio as he works the cash register at Hardy's Shoe Store. He hears a news bulletin that Officer Tippit has been shot, and the sound of approaching sirens. Just then, a man enters Hardy's, pretending to shop for shoes while clearly trying to avoid the police activity outside. Brewer realizes this man might be Tippit's killer.

It is. Oswald exits Hardy's, moving four doors down to the Texas Theater, where the film *War Is Hell* is already screening. Ticket taker Julia Postal notices Oswald sneaking in without paying the ninety-cent admission, so when Brewer comes over to alert her to his suspicions about Oswald, Postal calls the cops.

At this point, no one other than Tippit has connected Oswald to the assassination, but they're after him for the officer shooting. About 2:00 p.m., squad cars, their sirens wailing, seal off the perimeter of the movie house. Four officers enter through the rear of the theater, checking it from front to back, discovering Oswald seated in one of the last rows.

"I was about fifteen feet away from where Oswald was seated," recalls the *Dallas Morning News* aerospace reporter Hugh Aynesworth, who has hitched a ride on a news van after tipping the crew off to the bulletin he'd heard on a police scanner. "They got him out of there in a hurry. I never understood how so many [police officers] got there so fast."

Officer Nick McDonald orders Oswald to get up and out of his seat. "Well, it's all over now," Oswald declares.

But it isn't, yet.

"He made a fist and bam, hit me right between the eyes," McDonald recalls. Then Oswald points a gun at the officer. "Bracing myself," McDonald says, "I stood rigid, waiting for the bullet to penetrate my chest." When the gun misfires, fellow officers Ray Hawkins and T. A. Hutson help subdue Oswald.

"I protest this police brutality and I am not resisting arrest!" Oswald declares.

At 2:38 p.m., U.S. district judge Sarah Tilghman Hughes administers the Oath of Office—dutifully copied by a staffer from Article 2, Section 1 of the Constitution—to Vice President Lyndon Baines Johnson.

For the first time, two presidents are aboard Air Force One.

One of them is in a coffin.

A defiantly dry-eyed Jackie refuses to change out of her bloodstained pink suit. "My whole face was spattered with blood and hair," Jackie remembers, explaining that she began to wipe it off, but immediately regretted it. "Why did I wash the blood off? I should have left it there...I should have kept the blood on."

"Somehow that was one of the most poignant sights," the suddenly new First Lady, Lady Bird Johnson, writes in her diary of that day, "that immaculate woman, exquisitely dressed, and caked in blood."

"I want them to see what they have done to Jack," Jackie says, several times.

Just after 6:00 p.m., the plane lands at Andrews Air Force Base. There are crowds of mourners waiting for Air Force One—among them, Attorney General Bobby Kennedy, who immediately boards the plane and goes to embrace his sister-in-law.

"I'm here," he tells her.

CHAPTER 21

Earlier that day, at the Lafayette Hotel in Washington, DC, Eunice Kennedy Shriver, who is six months pregnant with her fourth baby, has just sat down to a Friday lunch with her husband, Sargent Shriver, and their four-year-old son, Timmy.

The growing family hasn't had much time together since March 1961, when with Executive Order #10924, President Kennedy established the Peace Corps "to promote world peace and friendship," and named his brother-in-law Shriver as head of the new agency within the State Department.

A waiter approaches the table with word that Shriver has an urgent phone call from his secretary, Mary Ann Orlando.

An ashen Shriver soon returns to the table. "Something has happened to Jack," he tells his wife.

A second call quickly follows. The president's condition is critical.

Eunice holds fast to the belief that her big brother Jack can survive. "There have been so many crises in Jack's life—he'll pull through," she declares.

It seems only yesterday that Eunice and Jack shared a house in Georgetown. Jack was single then, in the 1940s. They'd throw raucous all-night parties, and both smoke Cuban cigars.

Eunice and Shriver rush across Lafayette Park to Peace Corps headquarters, where Eunice places a call to the attorney general's office. Her brother Bobby confirms that Jack is clinging to life. But then the unbearable news flashes on the wire service: The president is dead.

The Shrivers and Peace Corps staffers kneel on the office floor together in prayer, repeating Hail Marys.

Three days earlier, on November 19, Jack had pardoned a turkey at the White House in advance of the November 28 Thanksgiving holiday. "Let's keep him going," Kennedy had joked. Thanksgiving is less than a week away now, and in New York, Jean Kennedy Smith is doing some holiday errand-running on Friday afternoon. She notices passersby crying, listening to a news bulletin blaring from every car radio on the street.

She can't believe what she's hearing. Her husband, Stephen Smith, is at the Kennedy campaign office in the Pan Am building, strategizing for Jack's reelection. Stephen, Jean thinks, will know if the news is true.

Patricia Kennedy Lawford is at her oceanfront home in Santa Monica, California, a magnificent property previously owned by studio head Louis B. Mayer. Her husband, actor Peter Lawford—whom she will divorce in 1966, the first (but not the last) Kennedy to ever divorce—is away in Lake Tahoe performing with comedian "Ragtime Jimmy" Durante, but her best friend and neighbor, Judy Garland, makes sure Pat won't be alone. (Sociable Judy occasionally vacations with the Kennedy family in Hyannis Port, and sings to Jack over the telephone. "He'd request 'Over the Rainbow,'" Judy's third husband, Sid Luft, recalls. She "obliged the president with several renditions of his favorite melodies.")

Senator Ted Kennedy is sitting in the Speaker's chair presiding over the day's business, a job relegated to junior senators during quiet legislative stretches. Around 2:00 p.m., aide Richard Riedel rushes in with the news from Dallas. Ted is devastated, but his first thought is how his wife, Joan, will react. They've been married for five troubled years, and she's been numbing the pain of Ted's infidelities with alcohol. Ted locates Joan in Washington's Elizabeth Arden salon and has her brought to their Georgetown home. A terse call from Bobby—"He's dead"—unleashes in Joan a demonstrative grief that is too much for Ted to handle. "Just go to bed," he tells his wife. "Take a pill or something."

Rose Kennedy ventures out, bundled in "the same old but warm coat I had worn through the snows when I went to Mass the morning of Jack's inauguration." She walks on the Cape Cod beach both alone and with her nephew Joe Gargan, telling him that they "must go on living."

The matriarch takes a condolence call from now President Lyndon Johnson and his wife Lady Bird, who accompanied Jack's coffin from Dallas to Washington. "We must all realize,"

Lady Bird tells Rose, "how fortunate the country was to have your son as long as it did."

⸻

On the day of Kennedy's assassination, Special Agent Mike Howard searches Lee Harvey Oswald's Dallas apartment. He discovers a green address book—since disappeared from evidence—but records that on page seventeen, under the heading "I WILL KILL," Oswald has written the names of four men: conservative anti-Communist Edwin Walker; former vice president Richard Nixon; FBI agent James Hosty; and—at the top of the list—Texas governor John Connally. Oswald has already taken a shot at Walker, and Nixon, it turns out, is also in Dallas in November 1963 at the same time as JFK.

Yet although Governor John Connally, who denied Oswald an adjustment to his "undesirable" military discharge, is first on Oswald's kill list, it is President John F. Kennedy who is first to take a bullet from him.

⸻

By Sunday, November 24, a transfer is in process. Due to death threats against Oswald, who has now been connected to Kennedy's assassination, police are on guard. At 11:20 a.m. they lead the prisoner—handcuffed to Detective James R. Leavelle—through the basement of the Dallas city jail and into an armored truck bound for the Dallas county jail. There Oswald will await a Monday court hearing.

Dozens of print and television reporters have been waiting all morning to cover the perp walk, and millions of viewers have tuned in to the live broadcast.

"All of a sudden someone steps out, two quick steps," *Dallas*

Times Herald photographer Bob Jackson recalls. The someone is local nightclub owner Jacob Leon Rubenstein, known as Jack Ruby. "He fired, and I hit the shutter . . . My big concern was did I get it before the bullet entered [Oswald's] body."

Jackson succeeds in snapping the exact moment Ruby's bullet hits Oswald in the abdomen, his mouth agape in pain, his eyes squeezed tight, his shackled hands slightly raised, as if bracing for the next bullet.

Ruby's "right hand was contracting as though he was trying to fire another shot," Detective Leavelle later testifies at Ruby's 1964 trial. Ruby's defense? Not murder, but spasms of "psychomotor epilepsy."

Perhaps. Though Levealle testifies to hearing Ruby say, "I hope the sonof-a-bitch [*sic*] dies" as he pulls the trigger. "I saw Jack Ruby before he made his move toward Oswald," Levealle recalls. "I jerked back and tried to pull Oswald behind me. I did manage to turn his body and he was hit about three-four inches left of the navel."

Asked to explain Ruby's motivation, Levealle theorizes that the man wanted "to do something spectacular."

CHAPTER 22

In the East Room of the White House, Jackie and her brother-in-law Bobby Kennedy stand before Jack's casket.

The Marsellus Casket Company's Model 710, "The President," is closed, in accordance with Jack's wishes. "I want you to make sure they close the casket when I die," family aide Frank Morissey remembers Jack saying to him. "He seemed to have a premonition about it, and he asked that eight or nine times."

A century earlier, another fallen leader lay in state in this very room, the chandeliers identically draped for mourning with black crepe. At Jackie's request, the White House has modeled the mourning for her husband on what was done for Abraham Lincoln. "Jack really looks, acts, and sounds like young Lincoln," Rose had once said, proudly describing her son's performance in his October 1960 debate against Nixon. Now the thirty-fifth and sixteenth presidents have in common their deaths by extremist assassin's bullet.

Jackie asks Secret Service agent Clint Hill to bring her a pair of scissors so that she can snip a lock of Jack's hair.

When a pair is in her hand, Hill and Brigadier General Godfrey McHugh fold back the American flag that covers the casket—made of five-hundred-year-old solid African mahogany—and raise its heavy lid.

"When I saw President Kennedy lying there, confined in that narrow casket, with his eyes closed so peacefully just like he was sleeping, it was all I could do to keep from breaking down," Hill recalls. "Mrs. Kennedy and the president's brother walked over to view the man they had so loved. I heard the sound of the scissors, beneath the painful cries, as she clipped a few locks of her husband's hair."

The president is wearing Jackie's wedding ring. A Parkland Memorial Hospital orderly had helped her slip it on his finger moments after doctors had declared him dead.

George E. Thomas has dressed the president with extra care. The man Thomas calls Jack F. will be buried in his favorite blue suit.

When the somber, private moment is complete, Bobby carefully closes the casket lid. Hand in hand, he and Jackie exit the East Room. The honor guard resumes its vigil around the president.

⎯⎯⎯ ∞∞∞ ⎯⎯⎯

The night before, Jackie's mother, Janet Auchincloss, decides it's too much to expect Jackie to break the news of their father's death to her children. She delegates the task to British nanny Maud Shaw, instructing her to tell the children individually, starting with five-year-old Caroline.

Shaw protests, not wanting to be responsible for taking "a child's last happiness," but at Auchincloss's insistence, she manages a comforting story for Caroline, telling her that her father has gone to look after her baby brother. "Patrick was so lonely in heaven. He didn't know anybody there. Now he has the best friend anyone could have."

Caroline and John Jr. know what a fun friend their dad could be, too. Jackie later reminisces how he played with them in the Oval Office, moving along with fitness instructor Jack LaLanne on television. How he "loved those children tumbling around him in this sort of—sensual is the only way I can think of it," she says.

Before they close the casket, Jackie instructs the children, "You must write a letter to Daddy now and tell him how much you love him." Caroline dutifully does just that, and John Jr., not yet three, scribbles him a pretend note as well.

Opinion writer Jimmy Breslin famously reports from Arlington National Cemetery for the *New York Herald Tribune,* describing the exchange between gravedigger Clifton Pollard and superintendent John Metzler as they worked on Sunday, November 24, the day before the burial.

"He was a good man," Pollard said. "Yes, he was," Metzler said. "Now they're going to come and put him right here in this grave I'm making up," Pollard said. "You know, it's an honor just for me to do this."

That same day, a detail of navy enlisted pallbearers carries the president's body from the White House to the Capitol Rotunda in preparation for the lying-in-state ceremony. President Johnson lays an honorary wreath at the casket, then Jackie and Caroline kneel there together. Their departure, with Bobby, is the public's invitation to enter. People form two lines, blocks long. Even with the visitation extended overnight, each mourner is allowed only a glimpse.

In one of the first acts of Lyndon Johnson's fledgling presidency, he declares a national day of mourning in Jack's remembrance on November 25, 1963.

John Jr.'s third birthday will forever be the same day as his father's funeral. Caroline will turn six before the month is out.

Military body bearers place the president's remains on the same caisson that had carried FDR and the Unknown Soldier. It's drawn by seven gray horses and Black Jack, a riderless horse fitted with the saddle, stirrups, and backward-turned boots that symbolize a fallen leader. Twelve hundred troops cordon the route to St. Michael's Cathedral, eight blocks distant.

The temperature hovers at just over forty degrees, yet a crowd of one million people gathers in the open air. Private Arthur Carlson, Black Jack's handler, recalls, "I've never seen that many people be that quiet. It must have been eight or ten people deep, the whole way, and they were all as still as statues."

The silent crowd watches a procession of international leaders and dignitaries who, despite intense security concerns, walk nearly a mile from the White House to St. Michael's, where Cardinal Richard Cushing prepares to perform yet another Catholic rite for the Kennedy family. He married Jack and Jackie, said the funeral Mass for their son Patrick, and will now say Jack's as well.

Assembled in the pews are prime ministers and presidents — de Gaulle, Eisenhower, Truman — alongside generals and royalty. All listen as Bishop Philip Hannan recites Kennedy's 1961 inaugural address with the solemnity of scripture.

When Mass ends, Jackie stands with Caroline and John Jr. on the steps of the cathedral. The honor guard carries the coffin past them as a military band plays "Hail to the Chief." Jackie bends down and whispers in her son's ear, "John, you can salute Daddy now and say goodbye to him."

A photo of the salute the small boy gives his fallen father stands among some of the most indelible images ever taken.

The procession continues along the three-mile route from St. Matthew's Cathedral to Arlington National Cemetery. Jackie walks between Bobby and Ted, her sisters-in-law Ethel and Joan protectively shadowing them. The Kennedy sisters—Eunice, Jean, and Patricia—walk three abreast, holding a place for Rosemary in their hearts. The fatherless children, Caroline and John, ride in the motorcade.

Rose alone represents the senior Kennedys. Joe is too frail to leave Hyannis Port. His health has been so poor following his stroke nearly two years earlier, Rose has long thought her husband near death already. "Not only did she expect him to die," Kennedy chauffeur Frank Saunders says, "she even bought the dress. How awful that she had to wear it for her son's funeral."

Joe's nurse, Rita Dallas, says the rosary for him. "So it was," she recalls, "while a nation watched their President laid to rest with fitting pomp and ceremony, his father prayed alone."

As the pallbearers carry the casket from the caisson to the grave, the United States Air Force Pipe Band plays "Mist Covered Mountain."

Fifty military fighters, thirty Air Force F-105s, and twenty Navy F4Bs pass overhead in three V formations, with one missing from the last V in tribute. Air Force One makes an honorary flyover, piloted by Colonel James B. Swindal, who only days before flew the president's body home from Dallas.

Swindal speaks for many in the military when he recalls the shock surrounding the loss of the president who had so memorably served among them. "I didn't belong to the Johnson team. My President was in that box."

"Those drumbeats, I'll tell you," recalls the US Army specialist Douglas Mayfield of the funereal walk down Pennsylvania Avenue. "That presidential drumbeat was so different and haunting. For days, I could hear those drums."

Sergeant Jim Felder, one of two black pallbearers, held an

upper corner of the president's flag-draped casket. "At the time, I was so intent on doing my job that I refused to feel any emotion," he recalls in an interview with South Carolina's newspaper the *State*. "It must have been about two weeks later that I was standing at my locker and it hit me. I realized that I had lost someone I respected, admired and loved. I sat down on my bunk and cried."

In addition to the million mourners there in person, millions more watched on TV.

David Bianculli, a radio host, recalls being among the unprecedented television audience of 175 million as a ten-year-old schoolboy. "I locked the TV in my room, turned it on, and watched. Alone. And kept changing channels and watching some more, until my dad and sister came home. Then we all watched, for days, and grieved together. When Ruby shot Oswald, we were watching; when John-John saluted his father's coffin, we were watching—just like, at that point, almost everyone else in the country."

***

Down in Texas, there is another funeral occurring. President Kennedy and Officer Tippit are buried on the same day, November 25, 1963. The words of the Baptist pastor C. D. Tipps Jr., who leads Tippit's funeral service, describe the shared sacrifice of the World War II heroes. "He was doing his duty when he was taken by the lethal bullet of a poor, confused, misguided, ungodly assassin."

Marie Tippit and Jackie Kennedy are strangers brought together by tragic circumstance, two women widowed on the same day—by the same killer.

"This great tragedy prepares me to sympathize more deeply with you," Marie Tippit telegrams the White House, to which

Jackie replies by letter, "You and I share another bond—reminding our children all their lives what brave men their fathers were."

———————— ∞ ————————

Just before midnight, an exhausted Bobby and Jackie are alone in the White House residence. The family has dispersed, following a subdued birthday party for John Jr.

Bobby, whose own birthday was only five days before, on November 20, asks, "Shall we go visit our friend?"

Agent Hill escorts them by light of the eternal flame specially constructed by military engineers at the head of Jack's grave, the flame that Jackie lit for the first time only hours before, and that will never be extinguished.

On bended knee, they pray together.

———————— ∞ ————————

"During those four endless days," between Jack Kennedy's assassination and his burial, Jackie "held us together as a family and as a country," her brother-in-law Ted Kennedy later declares. "In large part because of her, we could grieve and then go on."

Part of what Jackie ensures, too, is "to make certain that Jack was not forgotten by history."

To that end, on Friday, November 29, in the midst of a nor'easter, Jackie summons a writer to Hyannis Port. He is Theodore H. White, whose political chronicle *The Making of the President 1960* won the 1962 Pulitzer Prize for General Non-Fiction.

In a congratulatory note to White, President Kennedy had written, "It pleases me that I could at least provide a little of the scenario."

Now he is the entire scenario.

White later recalls the directness of Jackie's instruction. "There was something she wanted *Life* magazine to say to the country, and that I must do it." Foremost in Jackie's mind are the "bitter people" intent on negatively defining the Kennedy presidency, as had happened at a July 1963 press conference. "The Republican National Committee recently adopted a resolution saying you were pretty much of a failure," a reporter stated, then asked, "How do you feel about that?"

At the time, Jack humorously claimed the label of failure, saying, "I presume it passed unanimously." But even—or especially—in these raw, vulnerable days, Jackie understands that failure is unacceptable. She has never been more Joe Kennedy's daughter-in-law than now.

White, who likes to call himself "a storyteller of elections," is about to expand his role on a grand scale.

Crafting a president's legacy takes time. But there isn't any time. White's editors at *Life* are holding the presses for the December 6, 1963, issue, at the cost of thirty thousand dollars an hour.

Over the next three and a half hours, White takes notes by hand as the thirty-four-year-old widow relives the events of the week that changed the world, but that only she experienced firsthand.

She has "an obsession," she confesses. Jackie is fixated on *Camelot,* a Broadway musical based on the Arthurian legend and cowritten by Frederick Lowe and Alan Jay Lerner, Jack's Choate and Harvard classmate. The show's record-breaking Broadway run, from December 3, 1960, to January 5, 1963, has roughly paralleled the Kennedy presidency, and was beloved by Jack.

"The lines he loved to hear," Jackie confides, were "Don't let it be forgot, that once there was a spot, for one brief shining moment that was known as Camelot." With Jack dead, "There'll never be another Camelot again," she tells White.

"For President Kennedy: An Epilogue," reads White's story in *Life* later that week. The byline atop the two-page spread is "Theodore H. White," but the enduring vision it puts forth is Jackie's alone.

PART FIVE

The Prophet

ROBERT FRANCIS KENNEDY

CHAPTER 23

Bobby Kennedy's just another lawyer now," Jimmy Hoffa says in January 1964 of his longtime adversary, stripped by tragedy of his powerful position of attorney general in the JFK administration.

Comparisons between Bobby and Jack are never-ending, but only their Harvard swimming coach could accurately measure Jack's "floatability" against Bobby's "heav[iness] in the water... He would sink, sink quite easily."

Since JFK's November 1963 assassination, Bobby has been deeply sunk. "It was like Daddy lost both arms," his wife, Ethel, later describes it to their daughter Rory. "It was just six months of blackness."

———

In March 1965, Bobby finally rises back into the air—up the highest unscaled peak in North America. "I was concentrating not so much on reaching the top as on getting one foot up ahead of the other," Bobby writes in his first-person account for *Life* magazine. "I don't like heights, and as we struggled over the 500-foot comb that guarded the summit with a drop of 6,000 feet, I tried to avoid looking down."

The joint expedition of the National Geographic Society and the Boston Museum of Science begins as a survey of unexplored mountains in the Saint Elias Range in Canada's Yukon Territory—and becomes a hurried secret, the original April or May climb dates accelerated to late March to prevent two known rival groups from summiting first.

"Good luck, Daddy. You'll need it," Bobby's twelve-year-old son, Joe (named for his late uncle Joe Jr.), wishes him on a telephone call to Seattle, where the press meets Bobby's incoming flight—Bobby wryly notes of one reporter, "His paper had just completed my obituary."

Any obituary would include at least two notable new changes in Bobby's life: As of January 1965, he is now a father of nine (Matthew Maxwell Taylor Kennedy was born on January 11) and he's recently been sworn in as a US senator alongside his brother Ted, for New York and Massachusetts, respectively.

Bobby's in good climbing company, led by Jim Whittaker and Barry Prather, honored by JFK for their roles on the first American team ever to summit Everest.

Though Ted was also invited on the climb, he's not among the team of eight mountaineers. Lengthy recuperation from injuries sustained in a plane crash the previous June have sidelined him, but Ted can't resist reminding reporters which brother is the superior mountaineer. "I wish to point out for the record he is not the first Kennedy to climb a mountain. I climbed Matterhorn in 1957, which is higher."

Bobby doesn't care about which one's higher. He is on a quest to become the first Kennedy to *name* a mountain.

After reaching Base Camp by Royal Canadian Air Force helicopter, Bobby acclimates to the nearly eighty-seven-hundred-foot altitude and proves a quick study in the basic mountaineering techniques he'll need to pass through High Camp at twelve thousand feet on the way to the summit, estimated at just under fourteen thousand.

"I'm getting braver now," he jokes, after surviving a blizzard at High Camp. "I've been up Everest three times in my mind."

Roped between Whittaker and Prather and carrying a forty-five-pound pack, Bobby has a headache from breathing reduced oxygen. Rose's parting words—"Don't slip, dear"—come to pass as Bobby makes a misstep and falls into a crevasse up to his shoulders, unable to see the bottom.

He extracts himself, resuming careful work with ice ax and crampons until the men reach the final approach about two hundred feet from the peak. Whittaker turns to the thirty-nine-year-old senator. "It's all yours, Bob."

In Kennedy tradition, he is the first to win the peak.

"I was so delighted because I had wanted him to get up there," Jim Whittaker later tells documentarians. He was eager for Bobby to be "the first human being to stand on the peak named for his brother," adding, "We were bawling, it was really emotional."

"I planted President Kennedy's family flag"—three gold helmets on a black background, which the Chief Herald of Ireland had presented to JFK in March of 1961—"on the summit," Bobby writes of that triumphant moment. "It was done with mixed emotion. It was a feeling of pain that the events of sixteen months and two days before had made it necessary. It was a feeling of relief and exhilaration that we had accomplished what we set out to do."

Bobby describes the peak he's newly named Mount Kennedy as a "magnificent mountain . . . lonely, stark, forbidding."

In the snow, Bobby places Jack's inaugural address and medallion, sealed in a metal container, as well as several of his brother's beloved tie-clip replicas of *PT-109*.

He is not only memorializing his brother but also burying the secrets they shared.

CHAPTER 24

On May 19, 1962, a star-studded, forty-fifth birthday salute to President Kennedy is under way at New York's Madison Square Garden. Top-tier tickets to the Democratic fundraiser cost one thousand dollars—nearly eighty-five hundred today.

Peter Lawford, married to the president's sister Patricia, is facing a demanding crowd and seems to be having an anxious moment as emcee. He's trying—and failing—to call to the stage Marilyn Monroe, the entertainment headliner. The thirty-five-year-old platinum blonde Hollywood screen siren is as notorious for pill-popping as she is for her chronic lateness to call times on set.

But Lawford is a very good actor. Tonight the joke is on the president, and the crowd of more than fifteen thousand is in on the gag. Finally, in the midst of Lawford's third introduction, Monroe emerges from the wings. "Mr. President," Lawford chuckles, "the *late* Marilyn Monroe."

The audience roars with laughter at Lawford's unwitting

double entendre, little guessing that less than three months later, she'll be dead.

But tonight, Monroe takes geishalike steps to the podium mic, literally sewn into her skintight dress, a white mink wrap slipping from her bare shoulders. The audience gasps at her "beads and skin" gold rhinestone gown designed by Academy Award–nominated, French-born Jean Louis and said to have cost twelve thousand dollars, enough to buy a dozen tickets to the show. In 2016, the dress became the "world's most expensive" when Ripley's Believe It or Not! acquired it at auction for more than five million dollars.

"It had been a noisy night, a very 'rah rah rah' kind of atmosphere," recalls *Life* magazine photographer Bill Ray. "Then *boom,* on comes this spotlight. There was no sound. No sound at all. It was like we were in outer space. There was this long, long pause and finally, she comes out with this unbelievably breathy, 'Happy biiiiirthday to youuuu,' and everybody just went into a swoon."

Despite raised eyebrows, Jackie tells her sister, Lee, "Life's too short to worry about Marilyn Monroe." Instead of attending Jack's fundraiser, Jackie and the children are at the First Family's Glen Ora estate outside Middleburg, Virginia, enjoying what she calls "a good clean life." As spectators, including her husband, ogle Monroe at Madison Square Garden, Jackie is winning a third-place ribbon at the Loudon Hunt Horse Show.

Onstage, a giant birthday cake is rolled out as the president addresses the crowd. "I can now retire from politics after having had 'Happy Birthday' sung to me in such a sweet, wholesome way," he says, with the same mischievous grin he's worn since Monroe sang her first note.

Later that evening, United Artists studio head Arthur Krim hosts a private reception for seventy-five at his town house at 33 East Sixty-Ninth Street, where official White House photographer Cecil Stoughton captures the only known photo of Marilyn, Bobby, and Jack together. Bobby is looking at Monroe's face while the president's back is to the camera.

Jean Kennedy Smith and her husband, Stephen, are in attendance at the Madison Square Garden event as well as at Arthur Krim's reception, where White House photographers also capture Stephen posing alongside Monroe.

Arthur M. Schlesinger Jr., special assistant to the president, recalls that night as the first he and Bobby met Marilyn Monroe. "I do not think I have seen anyone so beautiful," he says. "But one felt a terrible unreality about her—as if talking to someone under water. Bobby and I engaged in mock competition for her; she was most agreeable to him and pleasant to me—but then she receded into her own glittering mist."

The next day, Jackie is furious—not with the president, but with his brother. "My understanding of it is that Bobby was the one who orchestrated the whole goddamn thing," Jackie tells her sister-in-law over the telephone. "The Attorney General is the troublemaker here, Ethel. Not the President. So it's Bobby I'm angry at, not Jack."

Not long afterward—perhaps to celebrate JFK's birthday of May 29 and Monroe's, June 1—Patricia Lawford hosts a gathering at her beachfront home in California. Bobby and Marilyn Monroe meet again. The actress has been fired by Twentieth Century Fox for "spectacular absenteeism" from George Cukor's *Something's Gotta Give,* the never-completed film whose production came to a costly halt (Fox claimed two million dollars in losses) when Monroe traveled to New York to perform for the president.

In a letter dated "the early 1960s" when it went to auction in 2017, Jean Kennedy Smith writes to Monroe, "Understand that you and Bobby are the new item! We all think you should come with him when he comes back East!" (According to Kennedy biographer Laurence Leamer, Jean's unhappiness in her own marriage to Kennedy "fixer" and reputed philanderer Stephen Smith is lifted by none other than Alan Jay Lerner, lyricist of the musical *Camelot*. Though Jean vehemently denies the affair, the *Baltimore Sun* quotes Leamer as saying, "I stand by my story."

A "very often distraught" Monroe takes to phoning Bobby in Washington, and rumors swirl that the attorney general tries but fails to persuade the studio to rehire her. Yet although struggling actor Robert Slatzer (who in 1991 claims, without evidence of a marriage certificate, that he and Monroe were married for five days in 1952) quotes her as saying "Robert Kennedy promised to marry [me]," the actress herself denies a sexual relationship with Bobby. "I like him," she tells her masseur Ralph Roberts, "but not physically."

According to Florida senator George Smathers, Monroe is also making "some demands" of the president, and there are fears she'll call a press conference to reveal details of a secret relationship. Smathers tells Seymour Hersh that he sent "a mutual friend" to "go talk to Monroe about putting a bridle on herself and on her mouth and not talking too much because it was getting to be a story around the country."

Monroe has become a dangerous liability, going so far as to phone Jackie with the declaration that she was to become the second Mrs. Kennedy. Journalist Christopher Andersen reports Jackie responding, "Marilyn, you'll marry Jack, that's great. And you'll move into the White House and you'll assume the responsibilities of first lady, and I'll move out and you'll have all the problems."

Shortly after 7:00 p.m., on Saturday, August 4, 1962, Peter Lawford receives a call from a woozy Monroe at his and Patricia's Santa Monica mansion. "Say good-bye to Pat," she instructs Lawford to tell his wife. "Say good-bye to Jack and say good-bye to yourself, because you're a nice guy."

This conversation is the closest thing pointing to Monroe's state of mind or intentions that day, though there's only Lawford's word for it—for although Monroe was a lifelong diarist, no recent diaries are later found in her house. Earlier diary entries, though, give clues to her fearful state of mind. In 1956, she wrote in a green leather diary of "the feeling of violence I've had lately about being afraid of Peter [Lawford] he might harm me, poison me, etc. why—strange look in his eyes—strange behavior."

Neither are any tape recordings of her phone calls found— yet there ought to have been. After all, she'd paid for it to be done.

According to medical records released on the fiftieth anniversary of her death, two months earlier, on June 7, 1962, Monroe had made an emergency visit to Michael Gurdin, a UCLA plastic surgeon. She'd seen him previously, in 1958, under the name "Miller" (she'd been then married to playwright Arthur Miller, her third husband, though they'd divorced in 1961). Now using the alias "Joan Newman," she arrives at Dr. Gurdin's office with her longtime psychiatrist, Ralph Greenson, seeking treatment for "an accidental fall." But Dr. Gurdin is skeptical. He tells a colleague that he "thought she [Monroe] was beaten up," and discussed his suspicions that her psychiatrist had committed the abuse. Modern X-rays confirm "a minute fracture of the tip of the nasal bone."

After that, Monroe contacts Fred Otash and requests he install a bug on her phone so she can record her own phone calls—possibly as insurance against threats or blackmail.

"Marilyn wanted a mini–phone listening device," Otash reveals in records his daughter, Colleen, later shares with the *Hollywood Reporter.* "You could hide it in your bra."

The irony is that inside the walls and in the roof of Monroe's 2,624-square-foot, four-bedroom, three-bath hacienda-style home at 12305 Fifth Helena Drive—which the star had purchased only six months earlier for $90,000 (a 2010 sale fetched $3.85 million)—recording devices have already been installed by...Fred Otash.

Otash knows his way around Hollywood, first as a vice detective—he left the LAPD in the mid-1950s after wrangling with Chief William H. Parker—and then as head of the Fred Otash Detective Bureau, until he lost his state license following a 1959 conviction in a Santa Anita Race Track conspiracy. According to the *Los Angeles Times,* he drinks a quart of Scotch and smokes four packs of cigarettes a day.

As a paid "fact verifier" for gossip magazines, who also "find[s] out what the Democrats were up to on behalf of Howard Hughes and Nixon," Otash keeps copious notes on the intimate lives of celebrities, many of whom travel in Kennedy circles. James Ellroy tells *The Hollywood Reporter* that Otash "was always talking about bugging [JFK brother-in-law] Peter Lawford's beach pad and getting the goods on Kennedy. He told me Jack [sexually] was a two-minute man. But I did not trust him not to dissemble." (On that topic, columnist Earl Wilson quotes Marilyn as describing her encounters with the president this way: "Well, I think I made his back feel better.")

Otash's extensive, and only partially authorized, access to her home leads to his eventual bombshell declaration: "I listened to Marilyn Monroe die."

On that Saturday afternoon in August before Marilyn Monroe called Peter Lawford, Otash places both Lawford and Bobby at her Brentwood bungalow, deep in conflict with a highly emotional Monroe.

"She said she was passed around like a piece of meat," Otash writes. "It was a violent argument about their relationship and the commitment and promises he [Bobby] made to her. She was really screaming... Bobby gets the pillow and he muffles her on the bed to keep the neighbors from hearing. She finally quieted down and then he was looking to get out of there."

Otash should also have been able to hear Monroe's call to Lawford, though the former PI also never acknowledges another, later call, from her second husband's son, Joe DiMaggio Jr. (his mother was starlet Dorothy Arnold). Monroe and her ex-stepson, a twenty-one-year-old marine private, had remained close. "If anything was amiss, I wasn't aware of it," DiMaggio Jr. says. "She sounded like Marilyn."

Hours later, Marilyn Monroe is dead.

CHAPTER 25

In the early hours of Sunday, August 5, 1962, Marilyn Monroe's live-in housekeeper wakes with a sinking feeling. She knocks loudly at her employer's locked bedroom door, and when there is no answer, she calls Ralph Greenson.

Greenson comes over, breaking into Monroe's bedroom via the window. He finds a horrifying scene: the thirty-six-year-old movie star lying naked, lifeless, facedown on her bed, still clutching the telephone receiver.

At 4:20 a.m., Greenson alerts the LAPD.

According to a 1985 interview with the *Los Angeles Times*, Fred Otash quotes Peter Lawford as instructing him to "do anything to remove anything incriminating" at Monroe's house that could connect her to Jack and Bobby. Biographer James Spada argues that "the cover-up that was designed to prevent anyone from finding out that Marilyn was involved intimately with the Kennedy family has been misinterpreted as a cover-up of their having murdered her." But Sergeant Jack Clemmons, a homicide detective and the first LAPD officer to arrive at

Monroe's home, states, "It was the most obviously staged death scene I had ever seen. The pill bottles on her bedside table had been arranged in neat order and the body was deliberately positioned." One of the bottles—found empty—originally contained fifty Nembutal capsules, prescribed only two or three days earlier.

In a 1983 interview for the BBC, the "cover-up" concept resurfaces. Biographer Anthony Murray recalls his exchange with Marilyn's former housekeeper: "There was a moment where she put her head in her hands and said words to the effect of, 'Oh, why do I have to keep covering this up?' I said, 'Covering what up, Mrs. Murray?' She said, 'Well of course Bobby Kennedy was there [on August 4], and of course there was an affair with Bobby Kennedy.'"

Yet the housekeeper's recollections may not be entirely reliable. She changes her story, first saying she called Greenson just after midnight, and then around 3:00 a.m., leaving hours unaccounted for between Monroe's time of death and the initial call to the police. Also, she was on the verge of losing her job. "I can't flat out fire her," Monroe had told the psychiatrist. "Next thing would be a book—*Secrets of Marilyn Monroe by Her Housekeeper.* She'd make a fortune spilling what she knows and she knows too damn much."

At the autopsy, John Miner, who heads the medical-legal section in the Los Angeles DA's office, wants to know more.

It is established protocol for the chief medical examiner to conduct celebrity autopsies, but inexplicably, junior medical examiner Dr. Thomas Noguchi performs the procedure on the five-four, 118-pound actress.

Dr. Noguchi's examination is meticulous, and his subject clearly makes an impression, stirring the pathologist (who would later become known as "Coroner to the Stars" and inspire the title character on the hit television series *Quincy*) to quote the Latin poet Petrarch: "It's folly to shrink in fear if this is dying. For death looked lovely in her lovely face."

Bearing in mind that "when you are a coroner, you start from the assumption that every body you examine might be a murder victim," Dr. Noguchi examines Monroe and detects neither needle marks indicating a drug injection nor signs of physical violence beyond a fresh bruise just above her left hip. The autopsy confirms blood toxic with barbiturates, and also a stomach empty of food particles, even the yellow dye that coats Nembutal capsules. But Dr. Noguchi never performs the full range of organ tests, stopping short after analyzing the blood and the liver. "I am sure that this could have cleared up a lot of the subsequent controversy, but I didn't follow through as I should have."

The forensic pathologist Cyril Wecht interprets the autopsy results for *People* magazine as "acute combined drug toxicity, chloral hydrate and Nembutal."

But Miner holds a differing opinion. He is convinced that the actress was administered an enema (a routine Hollywood weight-loss technique, though due to months of health issues, Monroe's body was already at its lowest weight of her adult life) containing the lethal combination of Nembutal and the sedative chloral hydrate.

Though Dr. Gurdin's suspicions about the psychiatrist's involvement with Monroe's broken nose will not become known for another half century, Ralph Greenson is also an unofficial "suspect." Miner proposes that Greenson allow him to listen to recently taped sessions with the actress as a way for the psychiatrist to clear his name. Greenson (whose 1978 essay "Special Problems in Psychotherapy with the Rich and Famous" would bring him further dubious notoriety) agrees, on the condition that Miner not reveal the contents, a promise he keeps until after Greenson's death. The tapes reveal a woman willing to examine what mistakes she's made in previous relationships, and filled with conflicting references to a hopeful future and unresolved feelings for both of the Kennedy brothers.

"I tell you, doctor," Monroe said in one session. "I'm glad he [Jack] has Bobby. It's like the Navy—the president is the captain and Bobby is the executive officer. Bobby would do absolutely anything for his brother and so would I. I will never embarrass him. As long as I have memory, I have John Fitzgerald Kennedy."

According to Arthur Schlesinger Jr., "Robert Kennedy came to inhabit the fantasies of her [Monroe's] last summer," although in another session, Monroe asserts, "As you see, there is no room in my life for him [Bobby]. I guess I don't have the courage to face up to it and hurt him. I want someone else to tell him it's over," she says. "I tried to get the president to do it, but I couldn't reach him."

Life magazine gets one of Monroe's final interviews, published weeks after her August 1962 death. When asked whether many of her friends had rallied around her when she was fired by Fox, "There was silence," *Life* reports, "and sitting very straight, eyes wide and hurt, she had answered with a tiny, 'No.'"

In those final summer days, would Marilyn Monroe have counted the Kennedy brothers as "friends"?

In 1964, Frank A. Capell, an anti-Communist author, self-publishes a pamphlet titled "The Strange Death of Marilyn Monroe" (later expanding it in 1969), alleging that Bobby's affair with the actress had ended in a death sentence carried out by Communist agents hell-bent on keeping Monroe from exposing Bobby's dealings with Castro.

Numerous other conspiracy theories regarding whether Marilyn Monroe was murdered—and if so, by whom—engage public imagination to the point that twenty years later, in 1982, the LA district attorney's office agrees to review the ongoing controversy. Ultimately, however, they conclude that had the actress indeed been murdered, it "would have required a massive, in-place conspiracy covering all the principals at the death scene on August 4 and 5, 1962," and concluded, "Our inquiries and document examination uncovered no credible evidence supporting a murder theory."

Marilyn Monroe's original cause of death—a barbiturate overdose marked on her death certificate as "probable suicide"—stands.

In May 1964, the recently widowed Jackie Kennedy is playing tennis with Reverend Richard T. McSorley in McLean, Virginia, at Bobby and Ethel's six-acre Hickory Hill estate (which was briefly Jackie's—she and Jack bought the place in 1955 and lived there for a year before selling it to Bobby and Ethel). The game allows Jackie unexpected freedom and cover to talk with the priest openly about her struggles—with grief, depression, her obsessive mental replaying of Jack's violent death, and thoughts of taking her own life, an act forbidden by her Catholic faith, but one she's grown sympathetic to.

"I was glad that Marilyn Monroe got out of her misery," she says of the actress. "If God is going to make such a to-do about judging people because they take their own lives," Jackie says, to Father McSorley's alarm, "then someone ought to punish Him."

CHAPTER 26

On a sheet of ruled notebook paper, Bobby writes the word *Courage.*

It's Christmas Eve, 1963. Bobby's two younger siblings, Ted and Jean, are representing the family among eight hundred notables gathered for the rededication of New York's Idlewild International Airport as John F. Kennedy International Airport. Mayor Robert Wagner extolls the late president as "a brilliant practitioner of intercommunication."

Bobby sits alone with his notebook. He's been asked to write the foreword to the memorial edition of JFK's *Profiles in Courage.* In a few words, he must distill the bravery that marked his late brother's character. The assignment also contains a painful and private challenge for Bobby—incorporating courage into the next phase of his own life, a life without his brother.

Bobby describes the technique Jack used to successfully mask a lifetime of physical pain: "Those who knew him well would know he was suffering only because his face was a little whiter, the lines around his eyes were a little deeper, his words a little sharper. Those who did not know him well detected nothing. He didn't complain about his problem so why should I complain about mine — that is how one always felt."

By contrast, Bobby always wears his intentions on the surface. A trait, he explains, born of determination. "I was the seventh of nine children. When you come from that far down, you have to struggle to survive."

"The Kennedys moved fast," the *New York Times* columnist George Vecsey observes, humorously describing two separate occurrences when Bobby "almost knocked down" Vecsey's wife and "almost mowed down" Vecsey himself.

Bobby loves to tackle, but his real skill is tenacity. "I can't think of anyone who had less right to make varsity than Bobby," his 1947 Harvard teammate and friend Kenny O'Donnell tells biographer Chris Matthews. "If you were blocking him, you'd knock him down, but he'd be up again going after the play. He never let up. He just made himself better."

Not everyone views Bobby's forceful manner positively. When Jack begins his first Senate term in 1952, Ted Sorensen (an attorney hired as JFK's researcher, who would go on to become a speechwriter and trusted political adviser) gets a jarring introduction to Bobby's style of play.

"In a photo opportunity for a magazine article," he recalls, "JFK, RFK, and I went across the street to the Capitol lawn to simulate a touch football game in which JFK threw me a pass with RFK defending. As I reached up for the ball, I felt a powerful and unsportsmanlike shove and went down onto the muddy grass in my one good 'Senate suit.'" Sorensen developed an early impression of Bobby as "militant, aggressive, intolerant, opinionated, somewhat hollow in his convictions."

Like Sorensen, in 1952 Bobby is also a Senate staffer, working for first-term Republican senator Joseph R. McCarthy of Wisconsin. While Sorensen's position is merit-based, Bobby secures his through Kennedy connections—McCarthy's a pal of Joe Sr. and has not only vacationed with the family, but dated two of Bobby's sisters, Pat and Jean. Bobby, a 1951 graduate of University of Virginia Law School, works for just six months on the Senate Permanent Subcommittee for Investigations, but the stint tarnishes his reputation for over a decade. "In those days," Sorensen recalls, "[Bobby] was a conservative, very close to his father in both ideas and manners, sharing his father's dislike of liberals."

On January 31, 1957, Bobby becomes chief counsel for the newly formed Senate Select Committee on Improper Activities in the Labor or Management Field, popularly known as the Rackets Committee. Though Bobby has inside knowledge of his brother Jack's presidential ambitions—and according to his sister Jean, their father is "really mad" about a "politically dangerous" investigation into organized labor—Bobby sets his target on James Riddle "Jimmy" Hoffa, head of the 1.3 million-member transportation-based Teamster union.

On February 19, 1957, Eddie Cheyfitz, a lawyer for the Teamsters, invites the two men to dinner at his home. It's their first meeting, and after sizing one another up—Hoffa finds Kennedy's handshake weak; five-nine Kennedy looks down on Hoffa's five-five stature—tension builds over dinner conversation that amounts to what Bobby calls "a complete fabrication" of information about the union. He demands a physical contest: "Hoffa, I'll just bet I can beat you at Indian hand wrestling."

In both of his two memoirs, Hoffa relates the encounter. The RFK biographer Larry Tye quotes from the second: "I leaned back in my chair and looked at him as if he was crazy. I couldn't believe he was serious but he stood up, loosened his necktie, took off his jacket, and rolled up his sleeve... Like taking candy from a baby. I flipped his arm over and cracked his knuckles on to the top of the table. It was strictly no contest and he knew it. But he had to try again. Same results...I'm damn certain in my heart that Robert F. Kennedy became my mortal enemy that night."

For three years, Bobby tries and fails to prove the improper financial dealings he's alleged of Hoffa. "I used to love to bug the little bastard," Hoffa says of a series of 1957 Rackets Committee hearings televised by NBC, which reveal an entrenched rivalry between the two men.

"During the worst of the hearings," Ethel recalls, "the big semis would get off the main roads and come by Hickory Hill with the horns just blaring." In 1959, the *New York Times* reports that Bobby "received anonymous threats from a telephone caller that someone would throw acid in the eyes of his six children," who consequently, according to Bobby Jr., had "to wait after school in the principal's office" for Ethel to pick them up.

Still, staffers admire his total dedication. The assistant attorney Nicholas Katzenbach recalls working lunches at Hickory Hill. "Bobby would call up at the last minute, and say uh, 'Ethel, I'm bringing out uh, 10 of us, 12 of us, 20 of us, uh, can you fix us some lunch?' And we'd spend the afternoon discussing problems."

The feud with Hoffa escalates when Jack is elected president in 1960 and Bobby rises to the head of the Justice Department as attorney general for the Kennedy administration. Joe Scarborough writes that Bobby "ultimately succeeded in convicting Hoffa but along the way he did the unthinkable: He made him a sympathetic figure."

Although a May 1963 Gallup poll shows Bobby's favorability rating at 72 percent, he's already worrying about the effects his controversial stint as attorney general may have on Jack's chances for reelection in 1964.

Aides are surprised when on November 20, 1963, his thirty-eighth birthday, their hard-working leader (according to Joe Sr., "Jack works as hard as any mortal man can. Bobby goes a little further") gives a dispirited toast at the office party. They whisper about an impending resignation, speculating, "I guess Bob won't be here by Christmas." That night at Hickory Hill, in the midst of another bustling party for friends and family, Ethel picks up on Bobby's grave mood. In her own toast, she never mentions her husband, insisting only that guests "drink to the President of the United States."

Two days later, on November 22, 1963, it is warm enough to eat lunch on the patio at Hickory Hill. Bobby's guests are Robert Morgenthau, U.S. attorney for the Southern District of New York, and the chief of his criminal division, Silvio Mollo. The menu of clam chowder and tuna fish sandwiches honors the Catholic tradition of forgoing meat on Fridays.

At 1:45, there is a commotion by the pool. A workman with a transistor radio begins shouting, and a phone extension rings. Ethel tells Bobby that J. Edgar Hoover's on the line, which immediately alarms him, as he and Hoover are bitter rivals. (At a meeting of senior FBI agents in 1968, Hoover deputy Clyde Tolan remarks of Bobby, "I hope someone shoots and kills the son of a bitch.") Bobby later tells Arthur Schlesinger Jr., "I thought something was wrong because he wouldn't be...calling me here."

Hoover delivers his dire news: "The President's been shot." When JFK biographer William Manchester asks Bobby whether Hoover "sounded excited," Bobby replies, "No, not a bit. No, nor upset." On reflection, Bobby later says, "It wasn't the way that, under the circumstances, I would have thought an individual would talk."

Morgenthau, with whom Bobby had served in the navy, can immediately see the "shock and horror" on his face. After about a minute, Bobby repeats Hoover's message to his guests. Bobby has calls to make upstairs, but, Morgenthau says, "We didn't want to leave him."

Bobby remembers talking to Secret Service agent Clint Hill: "I asked if they'd gotten a priest, and they said they had." He waits by the phone in his home office. "Clint Hill called me back, and I think it was about thirty minutes after I talked to Hoover…and he said, 'The President's dead.'"

Bobby rejoins his guests in the television room. "Jack is dead," he tells Morgenthau. "We were just in shock," the US attorney recalls. "We just couldn't believe what we were hearing. Then he got up and walked out and left us."

Bobby's aides pour into Hickory Hill, where US marshals set up security detail. With his black Newfoundland dog, Brumus, trailing behind, Bobby walks the grounds with Edwin Guthman, the public information director for the Justice Department, confiding his fears that his relentless crusades against crime or Communism could have brought this violence on Jack. "There's so much bitterness," Bobby says to Guthman. "I thought they would get one of us, but Jack, after all he's been through, never worried about it…I thought it would be me."

"Did the CIA kill my brother?" Bobby demands of the agency's director, John McCone, not long after the assassination. He is never satisfied with McCone's answer of no.

"He had the most wonderful life," Bobby assures his children of their uncle. But his composure is cracking. Ethel hands her husband a pair of dark glasses. Soon he must prepare to meet Air Force One at Andrews Field.

Once the plane lands, newly sworn in President Lyndon Johnson will take possession of the Oval Office—and all the secrets of the Kennedy administration contained within. Bobby orders national security adviser, McGeorge Bundy to change the combinations to Jack's locked file cabinets and to remove the recording equipment installed there and in the Cabinet Room.

After he dispatches Ted and Eunice to Hyannis Port to tell Joe and Rose the news, settles Jean and Jackie in the White House residence, and consults with Sargent Shriver on the funeral arrangements, Bobby tries to rest. Chuck Spalding walks him to the Lincoln Bedroom, offering a sleeping pill, which Bobby accepts. "God, it's so awful. Everything was really beginning to run so well," Bobby tells Spalding, keeping control of his emotions until his friend closes the door.

"Then I just heard him break down...I heard him say, "Why, God?"

CHAPTER 27

Bobby grapples with his grief by means of a striking physicality.

In Hobe Sound, Florida, not long after the funeral, Kennedy aides take up a brutal game of touch football. "People were smashing into each other to try and forget that John Kennedy was dead," Pierre Salinger observes, "and Bobby was one of the toughest guys in the game."

Even so, Bobby tells Washington friends, "I don't think there is much left for me in this town." The friends are alarmed at the sight of his gaunt figure dressed in his brother's clothes—Jack's leather bomber jacket with the presidential seal, or his tweed overcoat, or his navy sea coat. Bobby, a nonsmoker, holds the silver cigarette case that commemorates Jack's defeat of Nixon. The inscription reads: "When I'm through, how about you?"

Adults attempt to comfort Bobby, but one child dares to confront him with the truth. "Your brother's dead! Your brother's dead!" journalist Peter Maas recalls a boy of around seven shouting at Bobby during a Christmas party for orphans. The event is Bobby's first public outing since the funeral, and everyone in the room is aghast. "The little boy knew he had done something wrong, but he didn't know *what;* so he started to cry," Maas reports. "Bobby stepped forward and picked him up, in kind of one motion, and held him very close for a moment, and he said, 'That's all right. I have another brother.'"

And he has eight children. The day before Jack's funeral, he writes each of them a letter and instructs his siblings to do the same with their children. "It was natural for Bobby to take charge," Ted recalls. "He's been sort of a second father to us." To Joe, Jack's godson and Bobby's oldest son, Bobby writes, "Remember all the things that Jack started—be kind to others that are less fortunate than we—and love our country."

Of his work at the Justice Department, Bobby says, "I don't have the heart for it right now," and through the end of 1963 he remains at Hickory Hill.

The naturally bright atmosphere at Hickory Hill turns somber. "At this breakfast, not long after my uncle's death," Bobby's son Michael remembers, "my father had the discipline to tell the older children to write down the significance of Jack's death to the United States." Although Michael was only five years old at the time, he says, "I remember that incident very, very well. I remember thinking, Oh, I'm glad I don't have to do that yet."

Kathleen Kennedy Townsend (the eldest of Bobby and Ethel's children) remembers the typical ambiance of Hickory Hill as a "wild, informal mixture of a children's playground, upbeat discotheque, and a humming political headquarters." Her childhood home bustled with "lots of kids. There were plenty of horses, many dogs, chickens, geese, goats. It was a menagerie . . . my brother Bobby collected reptiles. And actually the turtle was in the laundry room. The sea lion was in the swimming pool."

In late January 1964, a Pacific trip to Japan and Indonesia "restores him [Bobby] to activity," according to Arthur Schlesinger. He begins to act on the pronouncement Jack made to a reporter during his Senate service: "Just as I went into politics because Joe died, if anything happened to me tomorrow, my brother Bobby would run for my seat in the Senate. And if Bobby died, Teddy would take over for him."

Politics has changed, become more personal. One driving factor is the revelation of a long-held Kennedy secret. After her botched lobotomy in 1941, Rosemary Kennedy—now the oldest living Kennedy sibling—was shuttled around to various facilities, leaving Eunice, her closest sibling, with no idea of her sister's whereabouts "for a decade after the surgery." Since 1949, however, Rosemary has been under the care of the nuns at the St. Coletta facility in Wisconsin. Her biographer Kate Larson believes that Jack may have visited Rosemary while campaigning in 1958, though he made no mention of his sister during the national presidential contest. Only in 1960, when Jack is president-elect, is Rosemary mentioned as his "mentally retarded sister who is in an institution in Wisconsin," in a publication for the National Association for Retarded Children.

Outspoken Eunice, who, as executive vice president of the Joseph P. Kennedy Jr. Foundation since 1957, has already spent years advocating for the intellectually disabled, pushes further. "Don't bother to sit with them; they can't learn, so forget them; give them a lollypop to suck and a bench to sit on," she mocks. "That's what we've been fighting."

"You know how Eunice is if she wants you to do something for her," Jean Kennedy Smith explains to Jackie. "She won't take no for an answer. She will pester you until you will either go mad or do what she asks."

"Just give Eunice what she wants," Jack tells his aides. In 1961, the Kennedy administration forms the Panel on Mental

Retardation and in 1962, the National Institute of Child Health and Human Development (renamed in 2008 for Eunice Kennedy Shriver).

In 1962, Eunice invites photographers from the *Saturday Evening Post* to Timberlawn, her Maryland estate, where she's established a summer camp for children with disabilities—the first of its kind in the United States—staffed by volunteers recruited from local schools, diplomacy corps, and even a prison.

Images of happy children riding in pony carts and swimming in the pool accompany Eunice's September 1962 essay, "Hope for Retarded Children," the first public telling of her sister Rosemary's story (minus details of the lobotomy).

On October, 24, 1963, during what would prove to be his last weeks in the Oval Office, Jack signs into law the Maternal and Child Health and Mental Retardation Planning Bill, remarking, "We can say with some assurance that, although children may be the victims of fate, they will not be the victims of our neglect."

Though President Johnson publicly carries through on JFK's social programs and ensures the passage of the late president's sweeping Civil Rights Act on July 2, 1964, privately he resents the power and influence Bobby retains. According to Johnson, Bobby "acted like *he* was the custodian of the Kennedy dream, some kind of rightful heir to the throne."

Bobby will never forget LBJ's planned speech closing for November 22, 1963, canceled after Jack was assassinated. "And thank God, Mr. President, you came out of Dallas alive."

When the time comes in 1964 for Johnson to choose a running mate in the next election, his first at the top of the ticket, Bobby is last on his list.

"I'd waited my turn," Johnson said. "Bobby should have waited for his."

CHAPTER 28

In the summer of 1964, Ted is on the campaign trail, seeking the Democratic nomination for reelection to his Massachusetts Senate seat. On June 19, 1964, the Kennedys' pilot warns against flying into weather conditions around West Springfield, Massachusetts—site of the state Democratic convention—so Ted instead charters a small plane. Disastrously, the plane crashes near Easthampton, killing two of five on board. Ted escapes with a punctured lung and broken vertebrae in his back, though his long convalescence later causes him to miss accompanying Bobby on his historic climb up—and dedication of—Mount Kennedy.

Bobby, accompanied by federal investigator and family friend Walter Sheridan, visits Ted in the hospital. "Somebody up there doesn't like us," Bobby confides to Sheridan when they take a walk outside, continuing, "It's been a great year for the giggles, hasn't it?"

On August 24, the Democratic national convention is under way in Atlantic City. When Bobby takes the stage to deliver a tribute to JFK, he is unable to speak over the delegates' cheers and applause, which runs for sixteen minutes, confirming the enduring power of the Kennedy name. According to presidential historian Michael Beschloss, "Johnson had nightmares that he would get to the Democratic Convention in 1964, and in would come Bobby Kennedy and Jackie Kennedy—stampede the delegates to vote not for LBJ but RFK for president."

Johnson has taken precautions, not only moving Bobby's tribute to closing night (after the presidential and vice presidential nominations are secure) but assigning Bobby an FBI detail. As Atlantic City–based agent William Sullivan would later testify to the Watergate Committee, "Robert Kennedy's activities were of special interest, including his contacts with [Martin Luther] King."

These are extreme measures against Bobby, who two days before the convention had announced his intention to exit the Capital Beltway for the Empire State. He tries on the prospect of holding his first legislative office, imagining, "I'm not just a senator. I'm Senator from New York. I'm head of the Kennedy wing of the party."

To satisfy residency laws, on September 1, 1964, Bobby and Ethel (pregnant with their ninth child) move into Marymead, a home leased for them by Kennedy brother-in-law and finance manager Stephen Smith. ("Ask not what the Kennedys can do for you, but what you can do for the Kennedys," Smith riffs on his role.) The twenty-five room, three-story, Colonial-style white house in exclusive Glen Cove has a swimming pool and a view of Long Island Sound.

On September 3, 1964, Bobby resigns from the Justice Department. That day, the *New York Times* editorializes, "It is doubtful that any Attorney General before Robert Francis Kennedy entered or left office under circumstances of such strong public feeling."

Not long after the thirty-eight-year-old begins campaigning against the incumbent, sixty-four-year-old Republican Kenneth Keating, more strong public feeling arises. This time, the furor is over the identity of Bobby's new neighbor—Jackie—who has leased Creek House, a property nearby Marymead. According to Jackie's secretary, Pamela Turnure, the former First Lady personally chooses the ten-room fieldstone house for the "maximum privacy" it affords herself and her young children. But proximity inspires a round of rumors of a Bobby/Jackie romance. "Though there was no affair," says Florida senator George Smathers, "I believe Bobby's wife thought there was one."

For his part, Keating, an intense critic of the Kennedy administration's stance on Cuba, holds zero affection for Bobby. He wastes no time blasting him as a carpetbagger who hasn't lived in New York since the Kennedy family moved away from Bronxville when Bobby was twelve years old. "I think it's an unprintable outrage," a leading Democrat comments off the record to the *New York Times* about Bobby's move to New York, though the same article reports that "a new figure"—Bobby—"has caught the public fancy."

"His appearance," Bobby's daughter Kerry Kennedy writes, "is ever modern: the shaggy hair, the skinny ties, the suit jacket off, the shirt sleeves rolled." And when the crowds can get close enough to the candidate, who campaigns standing atop his car, they try to claim a piece. During a swing through Westchester and the Bronx, Bobby complains to Hubert Humphrey, Johnson's running mate, that "too many young people are pulling at him." The attention "makes me feel like a Beatle," he jokingly declares, flashing that Kennedy smile.

On October 27, 1964, in a contentious debate televised on WCBS from two different studios—each candidate seated opposite an empty chair—Senator Keating openly mocks Bobby's star appeal, saying, "The squeals of the bobby soxers could be registered in a juke box but not in an election box." Three days later, on October 30, following a face-to-face debate broadcast by radio and ending after midnight, Bobby appeals to Keating, "Let's just go home." Keating misses the chance to remind voters that Kennedy's home is a mansion.

As the race tightens, Bobby needs to secure endorsements. Jackie steps up, arranging an interview with the publisher of the *New York Post*, where instead of sidestepping Bobby's biggest perceived character flaw ("People say he is ruthless and cold"), she offers a touching explanation: "He isn't like the others. I think it was his place in the family, with four girls and being younger than two brothers and so much smaller. He hasn't got the graciousness they had. He is really very shy, but he has the kindest heart in the world."

On November 3, Election Day, the *Post* backs Bobby for senator.

He wins the Senate seat by seven hundred thousand votes. (By contrast, in the 1964 presidential election, Johnson took New York state from his Republican rival, Barry Goldwater, by a margin of nearly three million.)

Despite his win, *Village Voice* writer Nat Hentoff expresses an opinion held by many—that "Bobby the K," as Hentoff calls the senator-elect, won't be local for long. "I am bugged when Kennedy beaters of the bush try to con me by pretending New York State is anything but a way-stop for this man on the run."

CHAPTER 29

During JFK's final White House cabinet meeting, the president scrawled a single word on his notepad. *Poverty.*

Bobby now looks at that crumpled piece of paper every day. It's framed and hanging on his office wall.

Though the memory of Jack is ever-present, the Kennedy brothers' rivalry proves irrepressible. "Step back a little, you're casting a shadow on Ted," a photographer tells senator-elect Bobby during a visit with Ted in Boston's New England Baptist Hospital. "It'll be the same way in Washington," Ted answers.

Mercurial Bobby, according to the majority leader, Senator Mike Mansfield, is "*in* the Senate, but not *of* it." Ted, who in his second term is the more experienced legislator, helps Bobby launch his ambitious social agenda. It works. George Gallup documents Bobby's "meteoric rise" in popularity between February and August 1966. Though negative respondents fault the first-term senator for having a "poor personality or temper" as well as being "power hungry" and "riding on the Kennedy name" (although "being a Kennedy" is also a leading positive response), Bobby ties Johnson in a "Trial Heat" poll, roughly two years out from the 1968 presidential election.

On September 25, 1966, politics falls away when, barely two years after Ted's plane crash, yet another one leaves Bobby's family bereaved. A light plane carrying Ethel's brother George Skakel Jr., president of New York's Great Lakes Carbon Company, and four other passengers, crashes near Riggins, Idaho, during a failed landing. The fatal incident intensifies lingering grief over the 1955 deaths of Ethel's parents, George and Ann, who also'd died in a plane crash, in an Oklahoma field.

Following the loss of his brother-in-law, "Kennedy immediately went into seclusion," UPI reports. "It was not known if Mrs. Kennedy was with him." Not long afterward, Bobby tells Ted Sorensen, "You had better pretend you don't know me. Everyone connected to me seems to be jinxed."

On October 30, 1966, Bobby and Arthur Schlesinger Jr. meet at P.J. Clarke's saloon in New York City to discuss the newly released Warren Report on JFK's assassination. "RFK wondered how long he could continue to avoid comment on the report," Schlesinger recalls. "It is evident that he believes that it was a poor job and will not endorse it, but that he is unwilling to criticize it and thereby reopen the whole tragic business."

The following spring, Bobby receives a pointed reminder of the broad scope of human suffering. The source is Marian Wright, a twenty-seven-year-old Yale Law School graduate and the first black woman admitted to the Mississippi bar, who testifies before the Senate Subcommittee on Employment, Labor, and Poverty on behalf of the NAACP's Legal Defense Fund. Wright invites committee members to see for themselves the dire living conditions poor people endure. Bobby and Pennsylvania senator Joseph Clark accept, traveling with Wright to Mississippi on April 9, 1967. On April 11, John Carr, a young reporter for the *Delta-Democrat Times* in Greenville, Mississippi, gets a tip from his editor. "There's a big story checking out of the Holiday Inn."

Driving his own VW Bug, Carr follows Bobby's blue sedan nearly to the cotton fields and a cluster of fenced-off houses known in Mississippi as "quarters." Bobby "spoke in a low, breathy voice," Carr writes, "and at times we reporters and the blacks we had inflicted ourselves on had to strain to hear him." What most startles Carr is a repetitive gesture Bobby makes as he talks, first to the impoverished residents—one family's refrigerator contains only a jar of peanut butter—and then to the press. "Kennedy would...touch his neck right above the collar with his right hand. It got to be eerie; it reminded me of his brother's reaction to the first shot that had hit him."

"I've been to third-world countries and I've never seen anything like this," Bobby tells his aide, Peter Edelman. For Marian Wright (who fifteen months later marries Edelman), Bobby has an immediate and activist recommendation: "Tell Dr. [Martin Luther] King to bring the people to Washington." King agrees, and announces the Poor People's Campaign, saying that the Southern Christian Leadership Conference of which he was president, "will lead waves of the nation's poor and disinherited to Washington, DC, next spring to demand redress of their grievances by the United States government and to secure at least jobs or income for all."

Some who encounter Bobby speak of sensing a transformation in his character at this time. As Wright remembers, "I'd formed an image of him as a tough, arrogant, politically driven man from the Joseph McCarthy era. These feelings dissolved as I saw Kennedy profoundly moved by Mississippi's hungry children."

"I've been with him many times since he entered the United States Senate, and I still find him growing and changing," Kennedy speechwriter Ted Sorensen states in his memoir. This man is the opposite of the "Bad Bobby" of 1960, described by a JFK aide as "a petulant baseball player who strikes out in the clutch and kicks the bat boy."

"Somewhere in this man sits good" is Martin Luther King's assessment, while still wary of Bobby's conservative politics dating to his days as a McCarthy acolyte—and later as an attorney general who favored wiretapping many of the individuals the government was monitoring, including King himself. "Our task is to find his moral center and win him to our cause."

Bobby's cause, he himself insists, is to effect social justice, not to seek the presidency. "I would say that the chances for a Kennedy dynasty are looking very slim," he says in 1967. "Bobby had a psychic violence about him," actress Shirley MacLaine observes, adopting wartime language. "Let's be violent with our minds and get this thing changed. Let's not be violent with our triggers."

Ever mindful of his numbers—a May 10, 1967, Gallup poll shows Kennedy support declining—it's no wonder that on US Senate stationery Bobby directs Sorensen:

Teddy, old pal—Perhaps you could keep down the number of adjectives and adverbs describing me in 1955 and use a few more in 1967. OK? Bob

On March 2, 1967, Bobby gives a speech on the unpopular and ongoing war. "Three Presidents have taken action in Vietnam," Bobby said. "As one who was involved in those decisions, I can testify that if fault is to be found or responsibility assessed, there is enough to go around for all—including myself." Ironically, by taking a portion of the blame, he effectively transfers the burden from himself and his brother Jack and onto President Johnson.

That summer, antiwar activist Allard Lowenstein approaches Bobby with an ambitious plan to attack Johnson on the "immoral" conflict in Vietnam, with the ultimate goal being to "dump" Johnson from presidential contention. Bobby is intrigued, but ultimately declines to participate: "People would say I was splitting the party out of ambition and envy. No one would believe I was doing it because of how I felt about Vietnam and poor people."

Bobby sends Lowenstein a note quoting the transcendentalist philosopher Ralph Waldo Emerson. "For Al, who knew the lesson of Emerson and taught it to the rest of us. They did not yet see…that if a single man plant himself on his convictions and then abide, the huge world will come round to him. From his friend, Bob Kennedy."

During the last two days of January 1968, celebration of the Lunar New Year veers into a strike known as the Tet Offensive. The wave of surprise attacks by North Vietnamese forces on targets throughout South Vietnam results in headline-making US and South Vietnamese casualties. Addressing the Washington press on January 30, the question of a presidential run inevitably arises. Bobby declares that "under no foreseeable circumstances" will it happen.

Despite Bobby's public projection of certainty, the Kennedy inner circle is roiling with indecision on the matter.

"Is my Daddy going to run for President?" Arthur Schlesinger recalls "little David Kennedy," age twelve, asking him "gravely."

David's mother, Ethel, newly pregnant with her and Bobby's eleventh child, votes yes, even going so far as to send out an election-themed Christmas card. SANTA CLAUS IN '67 read the signs Ethel and the children are pictured holding on the front of the card; and on the back, a photo of a smiling Bobby embellished with the thought bubble "Would you believe Santa Claus in '68?"

"She [Ethel] wanted to be First Lady, that's true," says Rose Kennedy's secretary, Barbara Gibson. "But she also believed that Bobby had so much to give."

Ted's on the no side. Bobby tells *Life* magazine reporter Sylvia Wright, "My brother thinks I'm crazy. He doesn't like this. He doesn't go along. But then, we're two different people. He doesn't hear the same music. Everyone has to march to his own music."

"He usually follows his own instincts and he's done damn well," Ted admits. But while he's unsure what Jack would've advised, he's confident how Joe Sr. would lean if he wasn't incapacitated by the stroke. "I know what Dad would have said...Don't do it," he tells aide Richard Goodwin.

News from Jackie further complicates the situation. Her romantic relationship with wealthy, divorced Greek industrialist Aristotle Onassis—whom she first met through her sister, Lee, in August 1963 after the death of baby Patrick—is deepening. Their age discrepancy (she is thirty-nine; he is sixty-two) and religious differences (Onassis is Greek Orthodox, not Catholic) makes him highly controversial as a potential second husband to America's most famous widow. "For heaven's sake, don't marry him," Ethel begs. "Don't do this to Bobby. Or to me!" Jackie knows how to be a good Kennedy. Bobby's decision comes first.

On March 16, 1968, Bobby returns to the Caucus Room of the Old Senate Office Building in Washington. He's forty-two years old. Eight years earlier, he had watched proudly when Jack, then also age forty-two, had launched his 1960 presidential campaign from this very room. Now it's Bobby's turn.

Finally, Bobby is granted the respite that's been eluding him since Jack's death. Soon after his announcement, Bobby tells Nicole Salinger (wife of press secretary Pierre Salinger), "I'm sleeping well for the first time in months. I don't know what's going to happen, but at least I'm at peace with myself."

Little else about the 1968 presidential contest is peaceful. More often, it's not only heated but bitter. Bobby's announcement comes just four days after the New Hampshire Democratic primary, where antiwar senator Eugene McCarthy nearly upset Lyndon Johnson, who as sitting president is on record for having sent half a million troops into peril.

Senator McCarthy will never forgive Bobby for crashing the 1968 race. Though McCarthy remains cordial with his Senate colleague Ted, for decades McCarthy insists, "Bobby had an inferiority complex, but Jack never did."

Not twenty-four hours after the New Hampshire polls close, Bobby is quoted in the press: "I am actively reassessing the possibility of whether I will run against President Johnson." McCarthy, an Irish Catholic like the Kennedys, takes special note of Bobby's tactics and timing. "An Irishman who announces the day before St. Patrick's Day that he's going to run against another Irishman shouldn't say it's going to be a peaceful relationship."

On March 31, in a live television address, Johnson makes a surprise announcement. He's calling an end—not to the war in Vietnam, but to his bid for a second term as president. (Instead, Johnson's vice president, Hubert Humphrey, will belatedly join the race on April 27.)

"You're kidding," Bobby exclaims. "I wonder if he would have done it if I hadn't come in." Ethel breaks out a celebratory bottle of Scotch. "Well, he didn't deserve to be president anyway," she tells her husband.

A few days earlier, at a dinner party in New York, Jackie served up some provocative table talk to Arthur Schlesinger. "Do you know what I think will happen to Bobby?" Jackie told him. "The same thing that happened to Jack. There is so much hatred in this country, and more people hate Bobby than hated Jack...I've told Bobby this, but he isn't fatalistic, like me."

Just as Jackie's premonitions of violence in Dallas went unheard by Jack, so does her latest fear. Jackie is right. Bobby never does learn to respect the power of fate.

But he's not the next victim.

CHAPTER 30

On April 9, 1968, thirteen hundred mourners file into Ebenezer Baptist Church in Atlanta, Georgia. Bobby and Ted Kennedy are there, along with other men vying for the presidency—Senator Eugene McCarthy, Vice President Hubert Humphrey, and Richard Nixon. At Bobby's invitation, Jackie attends, her presence a comfort to the nation's newest famed widow, Coretta Scott King.

Five days earlier, on April 4, 1968, Martin Luther King Jr. had been shot while leaving Room 306 on the second floor of black businessman Walter Bailey's Lorraine Motel in Memphis. King had been under Memphis police protection since March 28, when his demonstration for the rights of local sanitation workers had turned violent.

Just after 6:00 p.m., on April 4, civil rights leaders Andrew Young, Jesse Jackson, and Reverend Ralph Abernathy witness King's assassination by a rifle shot that severs his spinal cord.

"I don't even think he heard the shot [a Remington-Peters, soft-point, metal-jacketed bullet] or felt any pain," recalls

Young. "You see a picture of Andy [Young] and I pointing," Jackson explains of the iconic photo of the eyewitnesses at the crime scene. "We're pointing because the police were coming to us with drawn guns and we were saying the bullet came from that way," which was a rooming house facing the hotel walkway. "And I said, 'Martin, don't leave us now, don't leave us now. We need you,'" says Jackson.

⁕

As law enforcement searches for the gunman who shot King, Bobby is campaigning in Indiana in advance of the May 7 Democratic presidential primary.

He's about to make the seventy-six-mile flight from Muncie to the state capital, Indianapolis.

On board the plane, Bobby's press team alerts him that Dr. Martin Luther King has been shot. At Muncie's Ball State University, Bobby had earlier reassured a black student who challenged, "You're placing a great deal of faith in white America. My question: It this faith justified?" In an airborne interview with *Newsweek*'s John J. Lindsay, Bobby is distressed at the response he gave the student in light of what's happened. "You know, it grieves me . . . that I just told that kid this and then walk out and find that some white man has just shot their spiritual leader."

The plane lands, along with the news that King has succumbed to his injuries and has been declared dead. According to Lindsay, Bobby seems to "shrink back, as though struck physically." Confronted with yet another reminder of Jack's assassination, he hides his face in his hands, saying, "Oh, God. When is this violence going to stop?"

Across the country, cities are erupting in riots, and more conflict is anticipated on the streets of Indianapolis, where Bobby is scheduled to speak. Mayor Richard Lugar tries to intervene, but Bobby refuses to change his plans. "I'm going to Seventeenth and Broadway," Bobby says. "I'm going there and that's it and I don't want any police going with me."

He sends a fearful Ethel on to the hotel as word of King's death continues to spread. "Dr. King is dead and a white man did it... Why does he [Kennedy] have to come here?" a black woman beseeches a white pastor in the gathering crowd, some of them armed.

Bobby's police escort leaves him on the outskirts of the ghetto (later called the Kennedy-King neighborhood). His only protection are the words of press secretary Frank Mankiewicz. "You should give a very short speech. It should be almost like a prayer."

In a parking lot, Bobby stalwartly climbs onto a makeshift podium, the back of a flatbed truck equipped with a microphone. Under the dark sky, the weather has turned. "He was up there," television correspondent Charles Quinn recalls, "hunched in his black overcoat"—one that used to belong to Jack—"his face gaunt and distressed and full of anguish."

Bobby announces King's death to a collective cry of disbelief. Though the *Washington Post* has cataloged Bobby's public-speaking flaws—"the nervous, self-deprecating jokes; the trembling hands on the lectern; the staccato alternations of speech and silence; the sudden shifts of mood"—all of these awkward mannerisms fall away as he speaks for the next six minutes.

In the midst of his remarks, Bobby makes his first public reference to Jack's assassination. "For those of you who are black and tempted to be filled with hatred and distrust at the injustice of such an act, against all white people, I can only say that I feel in my own heart the same kind of feeling. I had a member of my family killed, but he was killed by a white man."

Over one hundred cities see riots that night, but not Indianapolis. McCarthy campaign volunteer Mary Evans, sixteen, stands among high school classmates and listens to Kennedy speak. "The minute he started talking, it was like the laying on of hands. Every word out of his mouth was a balm. The whole crowd was swept up in the emotion, and I stopped being scared."

Abie Washington, a twenty-six-year-old navy veteran, says, "My level of emotion went from one extreme to another. He had empathy. He knew what it felt like. Why create more violence?" And to Black Radical Action Project member William Crawford, "The sincerity of Bobby Kennedy's words just resonated, especially when he talked about his brother."

Later that night, Bobby phones Coretta Scott King, saying, "I'll help in any way I can." When he hears of Mrs. King's plans to retrieve her slain husband's body from Memphis, Bobby makes a generous offer. "Let me fly you there. I'll get a plane down." She accepts, ignoring advisers' concerns about the possible impropriety of accepting an expensive favor from a presidential candidate.

Bobby downplays King's assassination in his campaign stops, though he does comment to journalist Pete Hamill, "It's very interesting that they can't find the killer of Martin Luther King, but they can track down some twenty-two-year-old who might have burned his draft card."

Although Memphis police arrived on the scene of King's assassination within minutes, it takes months for them to track down the gunman, easily identified as James Earl Ray from the copious fingerprints he leaves at the crime scene, including on the gun, and on a newspaper detailing Dr. King's whereabouts. Ray, a fugitive from the Missouri State Penitentiary, manages to escape Memphis for Canada and then England before finally being arrested in London two months later on June 8, 1968, and sentenced to life in jail.

Long before Ray is captured, on the eve of Dr. King's funeral, Bobby meets with the King family, as well as the leaders in the black community, who are all trying to find their way forward. Reverend Hosea Williams recalls a collective desire "that Bobby Kennedy would come up with some answers," since "after Dr. King was killed, there was just no one left but Bobby." The civil rights leader John Lewis feels the same way. "Dr. King may be gone but we still have Bobby Kennedy, so we still have hope."

But Reverend Williams warns Bobby, "You have a chance to be a prophet. But prophets get shot."

CHAPTER 31

In May 1968, pop artist Roy Lichtenstein's portrait of Bobby, his brown hair swooping over his forehead, appears on the cover of *Time* magazine. Compared to his close-cropped 1950s cut, Bobby has been growing out his hair, sixties-style.

The longer length appeals to young voters. At Hickory Hill, hours before Bobby announced his presidential candidacy, Ted had tried to intervene with Bobby's barber, saying, "Cut it as close as you can. Don't pay attention to anything he says. Cut off as much as you can."

Before the upcoming West Coast Democratic primary swing (Oregon, May 28; California, June 4), Bobby flies to Cape Cod to visit his parents. "How will you feel being the mother of two presidents?" Bobby appeals to Rose. "That makes you quite a girl, doesn't it?"

On his way to victory in the Indiana primary with 42 percent of the vote, Bobby had chipped a front tooth (when a crowd in the town of Mishawaka pushes him up against his car) and spent a fortune campaigning. (Bobby admits to six hundred thousand dollars, perhaps only half the actual amount.) Rose Kennedy, a veteran campaigner, is on hand with a page from Joe Sr.'s script on politics and money. "It's part of this campaign business. If you have money—you spend it to win. And the more you can afford, the more you spend."

Bobby has another Kennedy lesson for McCarthy. "I don't know whether people think it's so good to be second or third. That's not the way I was brought up. I was always taught it was much better to win. I learned that when I was about two."

Having run Jack's victorious senate and presidential campaigns, Bobby well knows that a candidate's fortune can turn in a day. As he admits to the press, "It's a long time until August" and the Democratic national convention that will be held in Chicago at the end of that month.

Bobby aims to keep topping the primary ballots, and sets himself a steep goal: "I *have* to be able to win in every state." But the issues of race and poverty feel less urgent to Oregon's largely white middle-class suburban constituents, who are more attuned to McCarthy's antiwar message. At Portland State College, two students wave signs at Bobby reading, "Cut your hair, then we'll vote!"

Not enough of them do vote for Kennedy on May 28. The next morning, the front page of the *Oregonian* delivers the news: "Senator Eugene McCarthy won a dramatic victory Tuesday night—becoming the first candidate to defeat a Kennedy." It's a crushing blow to the RFK campaign—and the Kennedy family. "Let's face it," Bobby admits. "I appeal best to people who have problems."

In Hyannis Port, Bobby is determined to make up the loss, confiding to his wheelchair-bound father, "Dad, I'm going to California for a few days and I'm going to fight hard. I'm going to win one for you." With the Oregon defeat rankling Bobby, there is no turning back.

Kennedy California campaign headquarters is on Wilshire Boulevard, and from there Bobby rallies his staff: "If I died in Oregon, I hope Los Angeles is Resurrection City," he tells them. There is much ground to cover before the primary, set for June 4 (the same date as the South Dakota primary). Bobby campaigns by train and in open-top cars, shaking hands until his own are painfully swollen.

The "Hollywood for Kennedy" committee, led by singer Andy Williams, offers some glamorous relief by organizing two "star-studded" nationally televised galas on May 24 in Los Angeles and June 1 in San Francisco.

On June 2, writer George Plimpton is hosting a campaign-themed live call-in radio show and has an alarming exchange with an anonymous voice on the line demanding, "Is Bobby Kennedy ready?" and then in response to Plimpton's "Ready for what?" yells, "Ready to be killed. He's doomed! He's doomed!"

Another local threat against Bobby occurs months earlier, on April 4, 1968, the same day Martin Luther King Jr. is shot. Alvin Clark, a Los Angeles trash collector, recalls a conversation with a man on his route with whom he's talked politics over the past three years. The two express mutual dismay over King's death, but when their conversation shifts to the upcoming primary, they disagree. "I told him I was going to vote for Kennedy," Clark says, recalling that the man responded, "What are you going to vote for that son of a bitch for? Because I'm planning on shooting him."

Two days before the primary, on June 3, Bobby travels more than twelve hundred California miles. In San Francisco's Chinatown, a loud popping sends Ethel crouching into the wheel wells of the convertible. Earlier in the campaign, Bobby had vowed to Charles Quinn of NBC News, "If I'm ever elected president, I'm never going to ride in one of those God-damned [bulletproof, bubble-top] cars." When the pops in San Francisco prove to be Chinese firecrackers, Bobby continues to greet the crowds there and in Los Angeles and San Diego, where he nearly collapses from fatigue.

On June 4, Bobby, Ethel, and six of their children stay in Malibu as guests of the film director John Frankenheimer. While voters take to the polls, the family enjoys the beach—until David, a week and a half shy of his thirteenth birthday, is caught in a dangerous undertow. Though Bobby rescues his son, David, a sensitive, good-looking boy ("If we ever go broke," Ethel once told journalist Dolly Connelly, "we'll make a movie star of David and live off his earnings") is traumatized by the event, and both Kennedys sustain minor bruises and scrapes.

It's a physically and emotionally exhausting experience, and later that day when adviser Richard Goodwin encounters Bobby "stretched out across two chairs in the sunlight…his head hanging limply over the chair frame; his unshaven face deeply lined and his lips slightly parted," he can't help fearing the worst. Even after realizing Bobby is only sleeping, Goodwin thinks to himself, "I suppose none of us will ever get over John Kennedy."

The polls close at 8:00 p.m. It's after six when Frankenheimer speeds along the Santa Monica Freeway toward the Ambassador Hotel, where the campaign team will watch the election returns. "Take it easy, John," Bobby Kennedy tells him. "Life is too short."

CHAPTER 32

The party in the fifth-floor campaign suite at the Ambassador is in full swing, but Bobby cautiously asks aides, "Do we know enough about it [projected returns] yet?"

He slips away to phone Kenny O'Donnell in Washington, telling him, "You know, Kenny, I feel now for the first time that I've shaken off the shadow of my brother. I feel I've made it on my own."

When, just before midnight, the numbers point to a narrow margin of victory—Kennedy, 46 percent; McCarthy, 42 percent—Bobby and Ethel descend to the ballroom. They pass through the hotel kitchen to cheers from the workers—"Viva Kennedy! Viva Kennedy!"—and emerge into a crowd singing "This Land Is Your Land." As president, Bobby has promised columnist Jack Newfield, he will make the Woody Guthrie song the new national anthem.

"I was just shocked by the fact that he didn't have any security. I think he had one person," recalls Latino activist and Kennedy campaign staffer Dolores Huerta. No police are present. Los Angeles mayor Sam Yorty is a Nixon man, and under his orders the LAPD labels Bobby as "nobody special" and not only refuses to attend his motorcades but issues the campaign twenty-three tickets on more than a hundred alleged traffic violations. Bobby's sole bodyguard, former FBI agent Bill Barry, is unarmed. Per government policy in 1968, as a mere presidential candidate, Bobby doesn't qualify for Secret Service protection.

"We are a great country, an unselfish country, a compassionate country," Bobby says after fifteen minutes of unscripted remarks. His twelve-year-old son David is the only one of Bobby's ten children (Ethel is pregnant with number eleven) awake and watching the live television broadcast. "So my thanks to all of you and now it's on to Chicago and let's win there."

As Bobby is speaking these words, his staff agrees to a press conference. The ballroom is so crowded that Bobby fears for his pregnant wife's safety. "Look after Ethel," Bobby says to Barry as they retrace their route through the hotel kitchen at 12:15.

Seventeen-year-old busboy Juan Romero shook Bobby's hand the day before, and now the candidate offers him a second handshake.

A slight, dark-haired man dressed all in blue slips in among the kitchen staff. Inside a rolled-up Kennedy poster he's hiding a .22-caliber Iver Johnson pistol loaded with eight bullets. He extends the weapon at Bobby and squeezes the trigger. A bullet pierces Bobby's head. Two more hits follow, one in his back and the other in the right shoulder. (Many will later note the similar physical positioning of the brothers' fatal injuries.) Bobby drops immediately to the floor.

News cameras continue to roll.

"Shots! Shots! Look out, look out, there's a madman in here and he's killing everybody!" someone screams.

The "madman" is the same person who trash collector Alvin

Clark remembers pledging to shoot Bobby on the day that Martin Luther King Jr. was killed. His name is Sirhan Bishara Sirhan, a twenty-four-year-old Christian Palestinian whose family fled Jerusalem for Pasadena in 1956. Sirhan—whose notebook containing repeated declarations that "RFK must die" was entered into evidence at his 1969 murder trial—rejects Bobby's pro-Israel stance.

Bill Barry wrestles the weapon away from Sirhan, but not before the gunman fires off enough rounds to wound five others. When onlookers turn on Sirhan, Barry orders Kennedy aide Jack Gallivan and football star Rosey Grier, "Take this guy. Get this guy off in a corner where people can't hit him." (LA police chief Tom Reddin later uses a camper-shell-topped pickup truck to transport Sirhan from jail to court so that he can't be killed like Lee Harvey Oswald.)

Busboy Romero is still by Bobby's side, and remembers his lips moving with words of concern. "I heard him say, 'Is everybody OK?'"

"I could feel a steady stream of blood coming through my fingers," Romero says of holding Bobby's head off the cold concrete. "I remember I had a rosary in my shirt pocket and I took it out, thinking that he would need it a lot more than me. I wrapped it around his right hand and then they wheeled him away."

At Central Receiving Hospital, 12:30 a.m., Dr. V. F. Bazilauskas tries to get a pulse. "Bob, Bob can you hear us?" the doctor pleads as a priest performs last rites.

The medical team is pumping Bobby with adrenaline and massaging his heart, bringing his vital signs back, but weakly. The doctor gives Ethel his stethoscope. "She listened," he recalls, "and like a mother hearing a baby's first heartbeat, she was overjoyed."

"They put a stethoscope to my ear, and I could hear his heart beating. It was beating…beating…beating…" Ethel later tells her personal assistant, Noelle Bombardier. "I thought, Oh my God. He's going to live. *He's going to live.*"

In preparation for surgery, Bobby is transferred to nearby Good Samaritan Hospital, a facility with superior equipment. Through the halls, Hugh McDonald, assistant press secretary, carries Bobby's size eight-and-a-half dress shoes, repeating, "I've got his shoes…I've got his shoes."

In a ninth-floor operating room, a team of neurosurgeons performs a four-hour emergency craniotomy. Twelve hours later, at 1:44 a.m., twenty-six hours after the shooting, Bobby is pronounced dead.

A second Kennedy son felled by a crazed assassin's bullets.

CHAPTER 33

The autopsy on Bobby Kennedy is conducted by Dr. Thomas Noguchi, now the Los Angeles County chief medical examiner. As a junior medical examiner, Dr. Noguchi had performed the autopsy on Marilyn Monroe in August 1962. Though he himself has called out errors he made during Monroe's autopsy, the detailed examination he performs on Bobby is lauded by independent forensic examiners as "the perfect autopsy." Bobby's cause of death is a fatal head wound. "Mr. Kennedy," Dr. Noguchi finds, "was shot from a distance of one to six inches."

John Tunney, son of the heavyweight boxing legend Gene Tunney and a close friend since law school, advises Ted against seeing his brother in the morgue. "You can't look," he tells Ted. "You've got to get out of here. Just remember him [Bobby] the way he was. Don't look at him."

"They're killing all the Kennedys," a distraught Pierre Salinger tells his wife, Nicole. Salinger, a career press man—first for Jack and then Bobby—is on the ground in Los Angeles, coordinating Coretta Scott King's arrival from Atlanta, and Jackie's from London.

The Kennedy compound at Hyannis Port is plunged into chaos. "It seemed impossible that the same kind of disaster could befall our family twice in five years," Rose later writes in her memoir. Joe Kennedy Sr.'s nurse, Rita Dallas, observes the matriarch grappling with a deeply personal pain. "With Jack, it was the death of the president," Dallas reflects. "With Bobby, it was the death of a son." There are unfounded rumors that the news of Bobby's death has killed Joe Sr.; it has not. He watches the live television coverage along with the rest of the nation.

When Air Force One arrives in Los Angeles to retrieve Bobby's body, the NBC News reporter Sander Vanocur observes, "It somehow seems ironic that on afternoons very much like this, Air Force jets bear the bodies of male Kennedys out of the west back to their resting places in the east." Though the flight manifest was not made public, on the night of June 6, David Brinkley reports on the pathos of the journey taken "in one airplane [by] three widows of three American public figures murdered by assassins"—Jackie, Coretta Scott King, and now Ethel—seen by the Secret Service agent Paul Sweeney "consoling one another."

Bobby lies in state at St. Patrick's Cathedral in New York, a site chosen by Stephen Smith to differentiate Bobby's funeral from Jack's in Washington, DC, and also as a symbolic homecoming for the New York senator. After a private family service on June 7, nearly one hundred and fifty thousand mourners line twenty-five blocks as they wait to file past Bobby's casket.

On June 8, hundreds of Washington notables headed by President Lyndon and Lady Bird Johnson, plus Hollywood stars and civil rights dignitaries, join the Kennedys for the funeral. Cardinal Richard Cushing says the televised High Requiem Mass, just as he did for Jack.

Ted steps to the flag-draped coffin and delivers a roll call of Kennedy siblings lost. "Joe and Kathleen, Jack" he intones, his voice breaking with emotion. And now Bobby. All three of his brothers are dead. All killed while serving their country.

To break the hold of unbearable grief, friends try to summon up some of Bobby's mischievous spirit. Of the solemn but lengthy service, one of them says to Richard Harwood of the *Washington Post,* "If it had gone on much longer, Bobby would have started kicking the box."

But the day of mourning has barely begun. In a nod to Abraham Lincoln's historic funeral train, the Kennedys and seven hundred guests fill twenty-one train cars and embark from New York's Pennsylvania Station. The 226-mile route runs through New Jersey, Baltimore, and into Washington's Union Station.

Over a million people of all colors line the route, waving, saluting, and holding up signs as the train passes by. "So long Bobby"; "We love you." The outpouring for Bobby prompts *Life* magazine reporter Sylvia Wright to ask herself, *What did he have that he could do this to people?*

Whatever it was Bobby possessed, Ethel is heartened to see the spark of it in her eldest son as the sixteen-year-old greets those on board the train, dressed in his father's suit and exuding that same charisma. "I'm Joe Kennedy, thank you for coming," he tells fellow passengers.

"He's got *it!* He's got *it!*" his mother crows.

When they arrive in DC, the family draws deep on their well of strength as they disembark at nine in the evening for the final procession toward Arlington National Cemetery.

As Bobby's casket travels along the National Mall near the Lincoln Memorial, it passes among the peaceful demonstrators whose presence he inspired. The march that he had suggested Marian Wright bring to Dr. Martin Luther King Jr. had coalesced into the "Poor People's Campaign," which had marched on

Washington on Mother's Day, May 12, about five weeks after King's own assassination. The demonstrators had set up a makeshift encampment called "Resurrection City" on the National Mall ever since. Jesse Jackson, who acted as mayor of the encampment, recalls, "We were still traumatized by Dr. King's assassination. Then while in Resurrection City, Robert Kennedy was killed."

At Arlington, Lady Bird Johnson looks up at "a great white moon riding high in the sky." On the ground, the cemetery is dark, lit only by mourners' candles and television cameras. The pallbearers lose their way to the gravesite, thirty yards from Jack's. In accordance with Bobby's wishes, it will be marked with a plain white cross.

"Somehow the Kennedys draw the lightning," the *New York Times* columnist James Reston writes as the world mourns. "They seem to be able to save everything but themselves."

CHAPTER 34

The Kennedys do go on to Chicago that summer, though not to the Democratic national convention. On July 20, 1968, Eunice Kennedy Shriver launches the first Special Olympics Games at Chicago's Soldier Field.

The newest Olympians are all disabled young people, coached by professional athletes in events broadcast on national television. "When she [Eunice] told me what she wanted, I thought, 'Nobody is going to watch this, a bunch of crippled kids running around,'" recalls sports host Frank Gifford, whose daughter Victoria would go on to marry Bobby's son Michael in 1981. But the former New York Giants running back quickly came around. "We captured it all on film, and it was one of the most moving things I have ever done. It took away the despair and the fear. They were just kids having fun. After we put it on television, we picked up crowds all over the country. No one could tell her it wouldn't work." Coverage expands in 1979 with a two-hour ABC special, and in 1987 on *Wide World of Sports*.

U.S. News & World Report later pronounces in a 1993 cover story, "When the full judgment of the Kennedy legacy is made—including JFK's Peace Corps and Alliance for Progress, Robert Kennedy's passion for civil rights and Ted Kennedy's efforts on health care, workplace reform and refugees—the changes wrought by Eunice [Kennedy] Shriver may well be seen as the most consequential."

The success of the Special Olympics is a bright spot in an otherwise dark time in the Kennedy family. Less than three months after Bobby's death, in the last week of August 1968, party leaders callously pit a deceased brother against a grieving one on the floor of the Democratic national convention. Johnson has long openly preferred Ted to Bobby ("I like Teddy. He's good"), but it's a low blow when Eugene McCarthy declares to Ted via his brother-in-law Stephen Smith, "I wouldn't support your brother."

Many whose lives Bobby touched are struggling in his absence.

When asked to name a favorite among her nine children, Rose always gives the same answer. "I do not have a favorite," Jean remembers her mother insisting. "Every one of you brings your own unique quality to this family and I love you all the same."

But Bobby is the only one Rose calls "my little pet," the one whose bond with children and animals draw comparisons to Saint Francis of Assisi. "It is so very difficult to speak of him," Rose tearfully tells *Look* magazine not long after his death.

Vice President Hubert Humphrey, who ultimately becomes the 1968 Democratic presidential nominee but loses the election to Richard Nixon, senses that Bobby's death brought down the entire party. "I said it and I meant it that the bullet that shot and killed Bobby Kennedy fatally wounded me...Had Bobby lived I think there'd have been a Democrat in the White House."

Ted Sorensen had watched from Bobby's hotel room as the sounds of Sirhan Sirhan's gunshots rang out over national television. "I could not believe that what I had gone through five years earlier [with Jack] was happening again," Sorensen says, never letting go of his suspicions that his deep opposition to Bobby's candidacy caused his late entry into the race, which somehow led to this tragic outcome.

"I am a much better man for knowing him [Bobby] than I ever was before," Bill Barry says. The former FBI agent and RFK bodyguard spends the rest of his life reliving those moments in the hotel kitchen, imagining how he himself might have taken the bullets that killed Bobby.

Juan Romero receives letters addressed to "the busboy" at the Ambassador Hotel. One writer accuses Romero of "being so selfish," maintaining, "If he hadn't stopped to shake your hand, the senator would have been alive."

On Bobby's funeral train, Coretta Scott King paid tribute to Ethel by saying, "I don't see how she has been able to go through this awful experience with such dignity," but Jackie sees a different side to her sister-in-law. Over lunch when talk turns to Ethel, Jackie tells Jean, speaking as someone who's endured similar tragedy, "I'm telling you here and now, she's in trouble."

The suddenly widowed mother of ten, soon to be eleven, children was four months pregnant when Bobby was killed. Although Ethel's spent around eight years of her life pregnant, she's never done so under circumstances like these before. "I don't know what will happen to Ethel if anything happens to this baby," Ted frets. As her final pregnancy progresses, she becomes increasingly reliant on Ted and his wife, Joan.

On December 12, 1968, Ethel safely delivers her and Bobby's eleventh child, whom she names Rory Elizabeth Catherine Kennedy. At a press conference at Georgetown Hospital, Ethel calls out her newfound closeness with Ted and Joan, saying, "With an aunt and uncle like these two, this new Kennedy can't miss."

The week before Christmas, on the way home to Hickory Hill, Ethel, Ted, and baby Rory share a poignant, private moment. They take the newborn to Arlington National Cemetery, where Ethel carries her to the lonely gravesite, the only place where Rory can meet her father.

PART SIX
The Senator
EDWARD MOORE KENNEDY

CHAPTER 35

Now that Bobby's gone, you're all we've got. You've got to take the leadership," Al Lowenstein says to Ted Kennedy, in the elevator down to the morgue at Good Samaritan Hospital, where Bobby lies dead.

Barely a day earlier, Bobby had asked Lowenstein to defect from the McCarthy camp to Kennedy's. He agreed. Now Lowenstein's audaciously suggesting that Ted Kennedy take his late brother's place in the 1968 presidential campaign.

"Uh, uh," says civil rights leader Charles Evers, "you're not going to do it to that family a third time."

Ted declines, anticipating a three-pronged attack from Richard Nixon—"that I was too young, that I had no record in public life strong enough to recommend me for the high office of President, that perhaps I was trying to trade on my brothers' names." He will not resume Bobby's candidacy.

Rose is forty-two when her youngest child, Edward Moore Kennedy, is born on February 22, 1932, exactly two hundred years after George Washington. Fitting, in a family where Rose states, "My babies were rocked to political lullabies," but while fourteen-year-old Jack's request to be his baby brother's godfather is granted, his other wish—that they name him George Washington Kennedy—is not.

Ted's education on world issues starts early. He's only six when his father is appointed ambassador to Great Britain in 1938, and in the fall of 1940, Joe Sr. writes to eight-year-old Ted of the nightly German bombing raids on London, "I am sure, of course, you wouldn't be scared, but if you heard all these guns firing every night and the bombs bursting you might get a little fidgety...I hope when you grow up you will dedicate your life to trying to work out plans to make people happy instead of making people miserable, as war does today."

"We were serious about serious things," Rose says of the Kennedy family, "but we liked laughing at things that weren't, including sometimes, some of our own foibles."

"I think that [Jack] really liked Teddy a lot, he really did, because he loved his sense of humor and he loved his esprit, the fact that he had such a good sense of humor about things and could laugh and joke," Ted's friend John Tunney remembers of the brothers' adult relationship.

"And the last shall be first," reads the Gospel of Matthew. Ted treasures these words Jack later inscribes on a silver cigarette case for his youngest brother. But first Ted must live the teaching, growing up with scant Kennedy allies.

Ted, whom *The New Yorker* later describes as "the youngest and reputedly stupidest of Joseph P. Kennedy's nine children," is teased incessantly about his mediocre schoolwork and his weight.

During Ted's time at the Fessenden School, a private academy in Newton, Massachusetts, Rose writes to Joe Sr., "Teddy really is such a fatty." His sister Eunice agrees, telling Joe, "He looks like two boys instead of one." And of his grades, Joe Sr. writes his eleven-year-old son, "You didn't pass in English or Geography and you only got a 60 in Spelling and History. That is terrible...You wouldn't want to have people say that Joe and Jack Kennedy's brother was such a bad student, so get on your toes."

Looking back, Ted puts a humorous spin on what must have been a terrible, even terrifying, stint: "The school had sent a notice to all the fathers of the entering boys for permission to paddle their sons, and my father was the first one to send it back, approved. In four years there I was paddled thirteen times. (This may not be good campaign material for a US Senator, but there it is, thirteen.)"

In 1946, Ted follows Bobby to Milton Academy in Massachusetts, where Bobby writes home that Ted (younger by seven years) is still struggling—by Kennedy standards—with his weight. "Teddy had his usual line of stories and seemed fat as ever," he writes.

"But Teddy was a big physical presence too. He was strong as hell," says the *Boston Globe* reporter Robert Healy. In some cases, his size worked to his advantage. His Milton coach Herbert Stokinger recalls, "Ted had really sticky fingers. He was a good all-around football player. He was able to do his blocking assignments well."

Admitted to the Harvard class of 1954 as a Kennedy family legacy, Ted pays more attention to freshman football than to his first-year coursework. In the spring semester, he is in danger of failing Spanish. Without a passing grade, Ted will lose his spot on the football roster the following fall.

He concocts a scheme to swap exam booklets with another student, but they're caught red-handed. "Ted was a bright guy.

He didn't have to cheat," says Ron Messer, who played freshman football with Ted. Joe Sr. disagrees. "Don't do this cheating thing, you're not clever enough," he rails at his errant son, then is outraged anew when Ted flubs his chosen path toward redemption: joining the military.

On June 25, 1951, one year into the Korean War, nineteen-year-old Ted enlists for a four-year term in the army, though only two are required under the draft. "Don't you even look at what you're signing?" Joe berates Ted, then smooths his way. After basic training at New Jersey's Fort Dix, Ted is assigned rarified duty in Paris, as honor guard in the North Atlantic Treaty Organization (NATO) headquarters. While he's there, Rose insists Ted learn about fine French wines, in spite of Joe's prohibition (enforced by a generous financial incentive of two thousand dollars) against any of his children drinking or smoking before age twenty-one. During an Alpine ski trip with sisters Jean and Pat, Jean writes their mother of Ted's military physique: "He may weigh 215, but it's all meat and muscles."

In 1953, Ted is readmitted to Harvard, now six-two, two hundred pounds—and two academic years behind his entering class. "He learned a lesson," his teammate Claude Hooton says of the cheating scandal that nearly derailed his chances at Harvard, especially his chances at becoming only the second Kennedy man to win a coveted varsity letter.

The first was Bobby, who played in jersey number 86, and Ted is proud to wear Harvard number 88. He's a strong player, and following the 1955 season, receives a scouting letter from Green Bay Packers head coach Lisle Blackbourn. "You have been very highly recommended to us by a number of coaches in your area and also by our talent scouts as a possible Pro Prospect." But when Joe Sr. arranges a session in a Chicago Bears practice uniform, Ted's dreams of professional football dim. "He put on the pads, took two or three hits, and said he'd never been so frightened in his life," remembers his roommate Ted Carey. "He got out of there."

Had he pursued a rookie bid and made the Green Bay Packers team, Ted would have encountered Bart Starr and Forrest Gregg as first-years on their way to the Hall of Fame. Instead, Ted famously informs Coach Blackbourn that instead of football, he's chosen "another contact sport."

Politics.

CHAPTER 36

In the fall of 1956, Ted enrolls at the University of Virginia Law School, from which Bobby had graduated in 1951. The class of 1959 has 150 members, and Ted makes a fast friend in John Tunney, whose father, former heavyweight champ Gene Tunney, owns a summer house near the Kennedy compound in Hyannis Port. The classmates partner for the prestigious multi-year elective moot-court competition (winning in their third year, where Bobby had not). They also rent an off-campus house together on Barracks Road, where their lavish parties are catered by a cook named Carmen, formerly employed by Jackie.

At one white-tie affair, which Ted's brother Bobby also attends, Mortimer Caplin compares the demeanor of the two Kennedy UVA alums. "The contrast was so dramatic. I mean Ted was the life of the party—singing, being the leader—and Bob was sitting there—thoughtful, quiet—and it stuck with me for a long time."

When Ted invites Bobby to speak on the Charlottesville, Virginia, campus, Bobby first asks (allegedly on behalf of Rose), "what side of the court my brother is going to appear on when he gets out of law school, attorney or defendant."

Bobby is referring to the speeding tickets—five of them—Ted has racked up during his time in Charlottesville. The most serious incident occurred in March 1958, when Ted was a twenty-six-year-old second-year student. That night Sheriff T. M. Whitten pursued a speeding car from the intersection of US 29 and US 250. "He cut his lights out on me and tried to outrun me," Whitten recalls, before pulling into a driveway and "[getting] down in the front seat" to hide from the officer. Whitten arrests the man, who identifies himself as Edward M. Kennedy, and Ted is ultimately convicted of reckless driving and fined thirty-five dollars.

Ted can't stay away from speed—or danger. Ted Sorensen recalls driving with then-undergraduate Ted from Cape Cod to Boston. "It was the first time in my young life that I realized when cars coming from the other direction blink their lights at you, it means there's a trooper up ahead and you ought to slow down."

During law school, Ted also earns his license to pilot single-engine airplanes. It's a two-hour drive on US 29 from Charlottesville to Bobby's Hickory Hill estate in McLean—and an even faster trip by air. John Tunney recalls Ted turning what should have been a routine flight into a wild ride. "I've never been more terrified in my life as when we came into [Washington] National Airport and they told us to follow a Colonial airplane into the airport landing strip. I point up at the plane and said, 'Ted, is that the one up there?' He said, 'I think that's it.' So that plane goes in and we start coming in after that plane. The ground controller said—I think we were in a Cessna, 'Cessna, Cessna, get out of there, get out of there! Hard left!' And so we take a hard left turn and I look behind me and there is a four-engine plane coming in. There was a United plane on our tail . . . We got out of the way, we landed, and then we flew back the next day."

Though Ted laughs off the near crash, Tunney makes a plan and sticks to it. "I wasn't going to tell him I was afraid to fly with him. I just studiously avoided it."

In 1958, Ted is appointed as "manager" of Jack's 1958 campaign for reelection to the US Senate during his third year of law school. Lester S. Hyman, a Washington lawyer and political mentor to the Kennedys, recalls, "I really got to see Ted in action. He was very helpful in the campaign, but he clearly wasn't running it."

James Sterling Young, the director of a Kennedy Oral History Project at the University of Virginia, identifies a 1960s saying: "Most people grow up and go into politics. The Kennedys go into politics and then they grow up."

"He was the show horse," John Tunney says of the decision to hand such responsibility to a young man with no political experience. "But Teddy learned fast and everybody adored him. It was clear that he had a magic with crowds; the way he spoke, the way he looked, he was very handsome . . . He [Ted] was a great politician. He just had it, and his family used to say that he was the most natural politician in the family."

In her 1998 biography of aide Kenny O'Donnell and his life with the Kennedys, his daughter Helen O'Donnell asked each of her interview subjects the same question: "Compare John Kennedy, Robert Kennedy, and Edward Kennedy." "John Kennedy was the ultimate pragmatist, [while] Bob Kennedy, when he changed, became the ultimate man of passion," Lester Hyman responds, adding, "Ted Kennedy is the perfect amalgam of the two of them, the pragmatic side and the passionate side." In his interview with the Miller Center, which specializes in presidential scholarship, the *Boston Globe*'s Robert Healy identifies a similar alchemy. "Jack was all head. Ted's all heart."

On November 4, 1958, Jack regains his seat in the Senate, and the moment sparks Ted's own political ambitions. "The day that John Kennedy was elected," John Tunney remembers, "Teddy made a decision that he was going to run for the Senate," though he would not be eligible until after his thirtieth birthday in 1962.

That night, after the victory party, the brothers make a private toast to their respective political ambitions. Ted begins, "Here's to 1960, Mr. President—if you can make it." And Jack replies, "Here's to 1962, *Senator* Kennedy, if *you* can make it."

CHAPTER 37

On October 28, 1957, the Kennedy family is dedicating a sports complex at Manhattanville College in memory of Kathleen "Kick" Kennedy, who attended the Catholic women's school. Ted's sister Jean, also an alumna, introduces her classmate Joan Bennett, a Bronxville local, to her twenty-five-year-old brother. "He was tall and he was gorgeous," Joan remembers. Joan is herself twenty-one and has modeled for Revlon and Coca-Cola. The Kennedys approve of the blond beauty, whom Jack nicknames "the Dish," and Secret Service agent Larry Newman later describes as "the kind of girl anyone would want to date, the kind who would never take a drink, never be anything but cheerful and sunny."

Only married men succeed in politics, Joe and Rose insist. So in late summer 1958, Ted fumbles his proposal to Joan, barely managing, "What do you think about our getting married?" and failing to present her with a ring. She accepts, though acknowledges to herself that Ted is a man she barely knows. Joe purchases the ring Ted finally gives to Joan when he arrives late to their engagement party.

Despite Joan's misgivings, the wedding is announced, an ivory bridal gown is chosen, and several hundred guests are invited to witness the ceremony set for November 29, 1958, at St. Joseph's Church in Bronxville, New York. Still, according to Kennedy cousin Mary Lou McCarthy, "From the beginning, she was in trouble, and she seemed to know."

Harry Bennett, a Republican and father of the bride, arranges that the wedding be filmed. But when newlywed Joan watches the footage, she receives not the wedding gift her father intended but the shock of her life. Jack, forgetting that he was miked, can be heard reassuring Joan's new husband, "Being married doesn't really mean you have to be faithful to your wife."

He isn't.

Although Kennedy biographer Barbara Leaming calls Joan "the perfect polished wife" and notes that she and Ted "were a couple of such attractiveness that they seemed to belie all the laws of time and nature," early in the marriage, Joan finds in her bed a gold necklace that doesn't belong to her. When, over lunch in Washington, she asks Jackie's advice, her sister-in-law is blunt. "No woman is ever enough for a guy in that family," she says, then insists, "Make sure Ted knows you found that necklace."

Ted does share one secret with his new wife: his longing to leave the Kennedy East Coast strongholds. He tells John Tunney that "he was thinking of going west, going out to maybe California and putting his roots down. He even talked about having part ownership of a football team, an NFL team."

Ted does go west, but only on sanctioned Kennedy business. He's the manager of thirteen western states in Jack's 1960 presidential campaign. Tirelessly canvassing for signatures, organizing field staff, and subsisting on a diet of fast food, Ted steadily gains weight. ("He was terrible with candy and ice cream," Lester Hyman explains, but "when he runs for election he drops twenty pounds.")

Ted excels in finding daring, newsworthy ways to bring in pledged votes for Jack—riding a bucking bronco in Miles City, Montana, and landing a 180-foot ski jump outside of Madison, Wisconsin. In the weeks leading up to the New Hampshire primary—during which his and Joan's first child, Kara Anne Kennedy, is born on February 27, 1960—he even climbs into strangers' cars to affix campaign stickers to interior windows until an unseen dog attacks him. "Yes, he went west and he delivered Wyoming," Robert Healy recalls.

Jack makes Ted a dare that he should, by FAA regulations, have refused. Though Ted is licensed to fly only single-engine planes, during a swing through Nevada, Jack convinces his youngest brother to pilot the Kennedys' twin-engine campaign plane, the *Caroline*. Ted does, and brings the aircraft in for a rough landing.

There is more turbulence on election night, when the votes promised to Ted in the field don't appear in the election returns. Ten of the thirteen states under Ted's watch land in Nixon's column. Jack's victory, though narrow, should be a triumph for all Kennedys. To lessen the sting of his father and brothers' disappointment in him, Ted sends a humorous telegram from Africa, where Jack had exiled him on a press junket: "Can I come back if I promise to carry the Western States in 1964?"

On February 7, 1961, less than a month after Jack is inaugurated president, Ted also takes a new job, for the standard Kennedy public-service salary of a dollar per year, assisting Suffolk County district attorney Garrett Byrne. The Boston location is decidedly not in any of the western states where Ted and Joan have privately discussed moving. Regarding the change of heart, "All I remember," Joan says, "is that Ted told me his father wanted him to run for United States Senate."

It is to be the patriarch's last major political power play. The week before Christmas, 1961, Joe Sr. loses consciousness on a golf course near the Kennedy mansion in Palm Beach. He is rushed by ambulance to St. Mary's Hospital, where the Kennedys have been generous donors, previously dedicating a room in memory of Joe Jr. In the room next door, doctors determine that Joe has suffered a stroke, and a priest performs last rites. When he stabilizes, he's found to have lost his speech and mobility on the right side of his body.

"The stroke was devastating," Robert Healy explains. Previously, Joe "would call all of them [including Teddy] every day . . . and then when he had the stroke, you know, he couldn't talk but he still called them."

Out of the whole family, Ted is the one who can best understand and communicate with his father. But Ted's devotion—he alone stays by his father's hospital bed for three days—is mixed with devilish merriment.

Rita Dallas, newly hired as a live-in caregiver for Joe, is caught completely off guard when Rose asks her to carry a stack of towels to the sauna in Hyannis Port and comes "face to face with Teddy and his friends, milling around, stark naked." Ted addresses Rita by name, though they have never met before, as he "was dancing around jovially full of fun and laughter. Draping his arm around my shoulder, which was stiff with shock, he made a flamboyant point of introducing me to his friends. Never before, or ever since, have I been introduced to a naked man."

With Joe incapacitated, the responsibility of convincing voters of Ted's worthiness for a Senate seat now falls to President Kennedy.

Though Ted's 1951 withdrawal from Harvard for cheating on his Spanish exam did not make headlines at the time, the

Kennedys are well aware that the eleven-year-old tidbit will feel fresh once Ted—finally eligible to run for Senate now that his thirtieth birthday has passed in February 1962—will be up against Eddie McCormack, state attorney general and favorite nephew of John W. McCormack, Speaker of the House of Representatives, in the Democratic state primary contest.

JFK chooses Robert Healy to break the story for the *Boston Globe,* after a protracted negotiation over where to bury the lede. "He [the president] wants it in a biographical sketch of Teddy," Healy recalls. "I'd write that story, put it in the tenth paragraph and the AP [Associated Press] would lead with it all over the country that Teddy got caught cheating at Harvard. No way am I going to do that."

They agree on an interview-style headline—"Ted Kennedy Tells About Harvard Examination Incident"—and that the contents of the article will not identify the student who took the Spanish exam in Ted's place.

"Jack could swear like a pirate," Healy says, recalling the president's next words. "I'm having more fucking trouble with this [Harvard cheating story] than I did with the Bay of Pigs."

McGeorge Bundy, a former Harvard dean of arts and sciences who is also on the call with Healy, agrees. "And with about the same results."

The scandal successfully contained, the campaign confronts the next challenge, the "Teddy-Eddie" debate to be televised on August 27, 1962, from South Boston High School. McCormack is circulating a campaign brochure listing his numerous achievements against Ted's sole qualification ("Brother of the President"), and on debate night builds that theme into a personal attack. "If his name was Edward Moore, with his qualifications, with your qualifications, Teddy, your candidacy would be a joke," McCormack sneers. "But nobody's laughing because his name is not Edward Moore. It's Edward Moore Kennedy."

"Ted almost fell apart at that point," Lester Hyman says, and remembers bracing for McCormack to surge at the polls. "But it was just the opposite, particularly the women. You know, you don't do that to a Kennedy. Kennedys can do no wrong, and it just turned the other way around. And that's how Teddy won the nomination."

In the statewide general election on November 6, 1962, Ted faces yet another political heir—Republican George Cabot Lodge, son of Henry Cabot Lodge, whom Jack had defeated to win his first Senate seat in 1952. History repeats itself as another Kennedy bests another Cabot Lodge.

Ted's victory, with 54 percent of the votes, at once cements the Kennedy dynasty and launches what will become the third-longest career in the Senate.

CHAPTER 38

Mississippi senator James O. Eastland, head of the power-ful Senate Judiciary Committee, initiates the freshman senator Ted Kennedy into rarified, competitive congres-sional culture.

As Ted tells the story, he arrives in Eastland's office for an early-morning meeting where the only choice of refreshment is bourbon or Scotch. After three stiff drinks, Ted finds himself named to the Immigration, Constitution, and Civil Rights sub-committees.

"So of course I go back to my office, and the sitting room is filled with people—the 9:00 meeting, the 9:30 meeting, the 10 o'clock meeting—and I walk in there smelling like a brewery. Here's our little Senator, thirty years old; he's been down here two weeks, and he's stiff as a billy goat at ten in the morning."

In an April 1963 interview with *Newsweek*'s James M. Can-non, President Kennedy dissects his family dynamic. "The pres-sure of all the others on Teddy came to bear so that he had to do his best," the president says. "It was a chain reaction started by Joe, that touched me, and all my brothers and sisters."

"What an extraordinary family man he [Ted] was," says John Tunney. "I can tell you from the inside, it was that way. They were just bound to each other."

Lester Hyman recalls flying as Ted's passenger in a two-seater plane to Hyannis Port so that Ted could visit his father. "I always remember Ted being so patient and just talking at him, telling him everything that had happened and telling him stories. I was told later that of all the children in the family, he was the one who most came to see the father, over and over again."

That November, it falls to Ted to break the news of Jack's death to Joe. He shares the family's fear that the patriarch, who has never fully recovered from his 1961 stroke, will not survive news of the loss. The next day, Ted takes Joe for a car ride. They set out, along with nurse Rita Dallas, for a seemingly aimless trip along the roads of Cape Cod. Determined to keep his father away from news of preparations for the national day of mourning in Jack's honor, Ted stretches the drive for hours, pretending to be lost so that Joe can point out the turns back home.

Back in Washington, Ted doesn't have to pretend. He channels his feelings of grief and loss into the words of his first major speech on the Senate floor, in support of the Civil Rights Act of 1964 that Jack had originally championed. "My brother was the first President of the United States to state publicly that segregation was morally wrong," he says on April 9, 1964, with Joan looking on from the gallery. "His heart and his soul are in this bill. If his life and death had a meaning, it was that we should not hate but love one another; we should use our powers not to create conditions of oppression that lead to violence, but conditions of freedom that lead to peace."

Ted's words ring controversial to the powerful contingent of southern senators, who argue and filibuster the measure for longer than two months. On June 19, a final debate lingers into the evening.

Ted banters with his travel coordinator Ed Moss about making a grand entrance at their next stop, the Massachusetts State Democratic Convention in West Springfield, where the delegates are expected to endorse Ted for his first full term in the Senate. In their one-two patter, Senator Kennedy asks, "What do you want me to do, crack up an airplane?" and his aide answers, "Nope, just parachute out of it into the convention."

At 7:40 p.m., the Civil Rights Act of 1964 passes the Senate by a vote of 73–27. Ted and Moss, plus Indiana senator Birch Bayh (at Ted's invitation, keynote speaker at the West Springfield convention) and Bayh's wife, Marvella, rush to National Airport.

At thirty-four years old, Bayh is the next youngest in the Senate. He wins his Indiana seat in the same 1962 midterm special election as Ted, and quickly becomes a close friend. Ted is not only the youngest senator, but the only one whose brothers are the sitting president and attorney general, respectively.

"It's bad weather," Kennedy pilot Howard Baird warns from Hyannis Port. "The fog is really rolling in." But Moss engages pilot Ed Zimny to fly a chartered Aero Commander 680 twin-engine aircraft to Barnes Airport in Westfield. The flight takes off after 8:00 p.m.

Minutes before 11:00 p.m., Zimny radios Barnes control tower that he'll attempt an instrument landing through the zero-visibility conditions. With his trained pilot's eye, Ted could tell what was going on: "I was watching the altimeter and I saw it drop from eleven hundred to six hundred feet," Ted recalls. "It was just like a toboggan ride, right along the tops of the trees for a few seconds. Then there was a terrific impact into a tree."

Bayh is brought back to consciousness by his wife's screams. The plane—which "opened as though a kitchen knife sliced

Twenty-six-year-old Joseph P. Kennedy and Twenty-four-year-old Rose Fitzgerald on their wedding day in Boston, October 7, 1914. (*Photo by Morgan Collection/Getty Images*)

Rose and Joe Sr. at their beloved family vacation home, "La Guerida," in Palm Beach, bought at a bargain price during the Depression. It's later nicknamed the "Kennedy Winter White House" once Jack begins using it as a presidential retreat. (*Photo above by Morgan Collection/Getty Images. Photo left by Donald Uhrbrock/The LIFE Images Collection via Getty Images/Getty Images*)

Joe Sr. makes a splash as a Hollywood studio head during the 1920s, and Gloria Swanson (right) stars in his notorious film *Queen Kelly*. His calls to her are cited as "the largest private telephone bill in the nation during the year 1929." (*Photo above by Morgan Collection/Getty Images. Photo right by United Artists/Kobal/Shutterstock*)

Jack (left) and Lem Billings (right), his childhood best friend, traveling in Europe in 1937. (*Photo by © CORBIS/Corbis via Getty Images*)

Joe Sr. (center) demands great things of his two eldest sons, Joe Jr. (left) and Jack (right). (*AFP via Getty Images*)

The Kennedys at Hyannis Port. From left: Jack, Jean, Rose, Joe Sr., Patricia, Bobby, Eunice, and Ted (holding football). (*Photo by © CORBIS/Corbis via Getty Images*)

Eunice (left) and Rosemary (right), smiling and waving. "Rosemary, you have the best teeth and smile in the family," Eunice tells her older sister. (*Photo by Bettmann Archive/Getty Images*)

Rosemary and Joe Sr. in England, where he serves as ambassador. Rosemary adores her father; he says of her, "I don't know what it is that makes eight children shine like a dollar [coin] and another one dull." (*Photo by Bettmann Archive/Getty Images*)

The Kennedys en route to England in 1938. From left: Kathleen, Patricia, Rose, Ted (in front), Bobby, and Jean. (*Photo by Express/Express/Getty Images*)

Kathleen, nicknamed Kick, with William Cavendish, Marquess of Hartington. Kick declares her days in England made her "a person in her own right, not just a Kennedy girl." (*Photo by Bettmann Archive/Getty Images*)

Kick marries Cavendish in wartime London. Despite his noble title, Kick's Catholic family oppose her marrying a Protestant—except Joe Jr. (behind Kick), who gives the bride away. (*Photo by Everett/Shutterstock*)

Joe Jr. (left) joins the war as a Navy pilot, and Jack (above) as a lieutenant in the Navy. Lifelong sibling rivals, Joe downplays the medal Jack receives for heroism when his PT Boat is sunk, but concedes, "To get anything out of the Navy is deserving of a campaign medal in itself." (*Photo left by Bettmann Archive/Getty Images. Photo above by Denver Post via Getty Images*)

Posted to DC before shipping off to the South Pacific, young Jack falls in love with Inga Arvad, a twice-married Danish journalist suspected of being a Nazi spy, whom Hitler once called "the most perfect example of Nordic beauty." (*Photo left by Bettmann Archive/Getty Images. Photo right by Bettmann Archive/Getty Images*)

A decade later, Jack has to work hard to woo Jacqueline Bouvier; but as friend Lem Billings says, "there was nothing Jack liked better than a challenge." (*Photo by Bettmann Archive/Getty Images*)

Jack, seated under an early campaign sign and photos of his parents, first enters congress at the age of 29 in 1947, but is often mistaken for a staffer, given his youth and often disheveled appearance. (*Photo by Yale Joel/The LIFE Images Collection via Getty Images/Getty Images*)

Jack is known to call up Judy Garland (seen here campaigning for Kennedy in 1960) to request she sing him "Somewhere Over the Rainbow" by telephone. (*Photo by ullstein bild/ullstein bild via Getty Images*)

Judith Exner, who briefly dated Frank Sinatra, acts as a liaison between mobster Sam Giancana and Jack Kennedy. (*Photo by Earl Leaf/Michael Ochs Archives/Getty Images*)

Founding member of the "Rat Pack" Frank Sinatra is a big Kennedy booster, and considers himself part of the "Jack Pack" inner circle. (*AFP/AFP via Getty Images*)

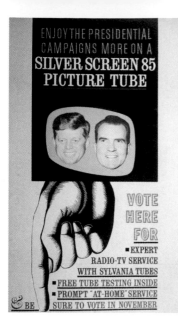

Advertisement for the 1960 Presidential TV debates between Kennedy and Nixon, and a "Youth for Kennedy" campaign button. (*Photo left by David J. & Janice L. Frent/Corbis via Getty Images. Photo above by David J. & Janice L. Frent/Corbis via Getty Images*)

Jack and Jackie in a ticker-tape parade. (*Photo by Frank Hurley/NY Daily News Archive via Getty Images*)

Marilyn Monroe is one of many stars at JFK's forty-fifth birthday gala, where she performs her iconic "Happy Birthday, Mr. President" in a "beads and skin" gold rhinestone gown. (Monroe seen here at the after-party with Stephen Smith, Jean Kennedy's husband.) (*Photo above by David J. & Janice L. Frent/Corbis via Getty Images. Photo left by Cecil Stoughton/AP/Shutterstock*)

The Kennedy women. From left: Joan Bennett Kennedy, Jean Kennedy Smith, Eunice Kennedy Shriver, Jacqueline Bouvier Kennedy, and Ethel Skakel Kennedy. (*Photo by The Estate of Jacques Lowe/Getty Images*)

Joe Sr. and Jack playing golf with Stephen Smith (left) and Peter Lawford (right). (*Photo by Bettmann Archive/Getty Images*)

Jack and Jackie in Hyannis Port with their children, Caroline and John Jr. (*Photo by Brooks Kraft LLC/Sygma via Getty Images*)

Jack frequently visits Hyannis Port after Joe Sr. suffers a debilitating stroke in 1961, from which he never fully recovers. (*Photo by AP/Shutterstock*)

President Kennedy and the First Lady in Dallas on November 22, 1963, only hours before JFK is assassinated. (*Photo by Art Rickerby/The LIFE Picture Collection via Getty Images*)

One of Bobby Kennedy's toughest fights on the Senate Labor Racket Committee is against Teamster President, Jimmy Hoffa (right)."I used to love to bug the little bastard," Hoffa recalled. (*Photo by Bettmann Archive/Getty Images*)

In March 1965, Bobby commemorates his brother's death by ascending the highest unclimbed peak in North America and christening it Mount Kennedy. (*Photo by Anonymous/AP/Shutterstock*)

Ethel and Bobby with their son David at a senate campaign rally. (*Photo by Bettmann Archive/Getty Images*)

After his brother's death, Bobby claims the "chances for a Kennedy dynasty are looking very slim," but eventually decides to join the presidential race, focusing on social issues like poverty and education. (*Photo left by Bill Eppridge/The LIFE Picture Collection via Getty Images. Photo above by Boris Yaro/Los Angeles Times via Getty Images*)

In addition to his own brood of (ultimately) eleven, Bobby is close with Jack's children. Clockwise from top: Bobby's daughter Kerry, son Michael, son David, nephew John Jr., niece Caroline, and daughter Courtney. (*Photo by George Silk/The LIFE Picture Collection via Getty Images*)

"Bobby is Good" is a sentiment shared by many, including those who knew him back in his harsh "Bad Bobby" days. Supporters and detractors alike agree that he seems to have truly grown and changed. (*Photo by Steve Schapiro/Corbis via Getty Images*)

Ethel and Bobby on June 5, 1968, celebrating his win in California towards securing the Democratic presidential nomination, moments before his assassination. (*Photo by Julian Wasser/The LIFE Images Collection via Getty Images/ Getty Images*)

Dr. Thomas Noguchi, the LA coroner known as the "Coroner to the Stars," performed autopsies on both Marilyn Monroe and Bobby Kennedy. (*Photo by Paul Harris/ Getty Images*)

Joan and Ted Kennedy, during an early senate campaign. Ted's win in 1962 launches what will become the third-longest career in the Senate. (*Photo by Carl Mydans/The LIFE Picture Collection via Getty Images*)

In 1964, Ted nearly dies in a plane crash that kills two of the five people on board. He escapes with a punctured lung and broken vertebrae in his back. (*Photo by Bettmann Archive/Getty Images*)

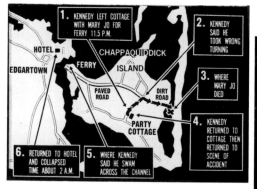

On July 18, 1969, Ted drives a car off a bridge in Chappaquiddick Island, resulting in the death of former RFK staffer Mary Jo Kopechne. Ted, seen here attending Mary Jo's funeral in a neck brace, is charged with leaving the scene of an accident. (*Photo above by Express Newspapers/Getty Images. Photo right by Bettmann Archive/Getty Images*)

The Kennedys' compound in Hyannis Port, Massachusetts, is the scene of many family get-togethers, often involving athletic competitions or spirited games of football. (*Photo above by Stew Milne/AFP via Getty Images. Photo right by Ron Galella/Ron Galella Collection via Getty Images*)

Senator Kennedy with his mother, Rose. Of all the Kennedy children, youngest son Ted is the one most devoted to their parents. (*Photo by Jam/AP/Shutterstock*)

Ted with Bobby's daughter Courtney, his close friend and fellow senator John Tunney, and Bobby's widow, Ethel. (*Photo by Ron Galella/Ron Galella Collection via Getty Images*)

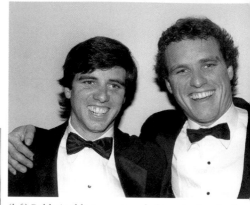

(*left*) Bobby's oldest son, Joe, shaking the hands of passengers aboard his father's funeral train from California to DC in 1968, leading to speculation on the 16-year-old's own political possibilities. Joe goes on to win his first term in congress in 1987, taking over from Tip O'Neill the same seat his uncle Jack once held. (*above*) Joe and his brother Michael (*left*). (*Photo left by Bettmann Archive/Getty Images. Photo above by Mario Suriani/AP/Shutterstock.*)

Ethel's nephew Michael Skakel has been accused of killing neighbor Martha Moxley in 1975, when both were teenagers, but Bobby Jr. staunchly defends his cousin's innocence. (*George Etheredge/ The New York Times/Redux*)

JFK Jr. (left), a Manhattan Assistant DA, leaves a Palm Beach courthouse with his cousin William Kennedy Smith (right) in 1991. Willie's rape trial is the first case ever broadcast on Court TV. (*Photo by Kathy Willens/AP/Shutterstock*)

Bobby with his young son David (above) in 1958. The two have a special connection, and Bobby is extra-protective of his most sensitive child. David (right) struggles throughout his adolescence and twenties, never regaining equilibrium after witnessing his father's assassination live on television. (*Photo above by The Estate of Jacques Lowe/Getty Images. Photo right by Ron Galella/ Ron Galella Collection via Getty Images.*)

When Saoirse's Eyes Are Smiling

When Saoirse's eyes are smiling
Sure, 'tis like the morn in
Spring
In the lilt of Irish laughter
You can hear the angels sing
When Saoirse's heart is happy
All the world seems bright
and gay
And when Saoirse's eyes are
smiling
Sure, they steal your heart
away

Bobby and Ethel's granddaughter, Saoirse Roisin Kennedy Hill. Saoirse, Courtney's daughter, is open about her struggles with depression, and about not stigmatizing it. (*Photo by David L Ryan/The Boston Globe/Pool/ EPA-EFE/Shutterstock*)

Young John Jr. adores planes and helicopters. President Kennedy jokes that people will falsely assume his son is racing to embrace him when he disembarks, but "Little do they know—that son would have raced right by his father to get to that helicopter." (*Photo left by Estate of Stanley Tretick LLC/Corbis via Getty Images. Photo above by Estate of Stanley Tretick LLC/Corbis via Getty Images*)

John attempts to board any plane or helicopter he comes near, "weeping bitterly" when he is left behind, though his father often consoles him with toy planes. (*Photo by Harvey Georges/AP/Shutterstock*)

Jackie walking with John Jr. (right), Caroline (left), and her nephew Anthony Radziwill (center). John Jr. and Anthony grow up together and remain close their whole lives, speaking nearly every day. (*Photo by PA Images via Getty Images*)

Jackie is a devoted mother, who wants Caroline and John Jr. to have "normal and fun" childhoods. "I don't want my young children brought up by nurses and Secret Service men," she tells the *New York Times*. (*Photo left by Ron Galella/WireImage. Photo below by Ron Galella/ Ron Galella Collection via Getty Images*)

Jackie shocks the world when she marries Greek shipping magnate Aristotle Onassis on October 20, 1968, though she credits him with bringing her "into a world where one could find happiness and love." (*Photo by Everett/Shutterstock*)

Teenage Caroline and John. (*Photo by Ron Galella/Ron Galella Collection via Getty Images*)

John Jr, seen wearing a "Shriver" life-jacket in Hyannis Port, is used to life-long paparazzi attention. *People* magazine even names him 1988's "Sexiest Man Alive." (*Photo by Ron Galella/Ron Galella Collection via Getty Images*)

Instead of politics or law, John Jr. ultimately chooses to go into journalism, founding the celebrity-tinged political magazine *George* in 1995. (*Photo by Larry Busacca/Contour by Getty Images*)

In 1996, John Jr. and Carolyn Bessette manage to elude the paparazzi completely when they slip away to be married on a tiny island, though their daily lives are relentlessly documented. (*Photo by Lawrence Levine/AP/Shutterstock*)

John Jr. and Carolyn taking off in John's first plane, Cessna Sky-lane N529JK, in 1998. John later upgraded to a Piper Saratoga shortly before his ill-fated voyage in 1999. (*Photo by* Boston Herald/*Shutterstock*)

through it," he recalls—has crashed in an apple orchard. He surveys the scene to discover that Zimny and Moss are dead, and that Ted is trapped in the wreckage.

"We've all heard adrenaline stories about how a mother can lift a car off a trapped infant," Bayh explains. "Well, Kennedy was no small guy, and I was able to lug him out of there like a sack of corn under my arm."

On the convention floor, the press surround Kennedy staffer Edward Martin. "There's a plane down. You don't think it's Kennedy?" When he learns it is, Martin has the White House locate a Kennedy, any Kennedy—finally relaying to Sargent Shriver, "Ted is injured in an accident. He's going to live, but will you notify all the Kennedy family members?"

"He's going to be fine," Joan tells reporters on the way to the emergency room in Northampton's Cooley Dickinson Hospital, where Ted is undergoing a blood transfusion.

Despite suffering three crushed vertebrae, a punctured lung, and broken ribs, on the morning of June 21, Ted is able to call his family himself. "Let me talk to Dad," he instructs cousin Ann Gargan, telling Joe: "You'd better get out here as soon as you can because they're talking about my back. Nobody knows more about backs than you do."

Recalling the grave complications of Jack's back surgeries, Joe is against the doctors at Boston's New England Baptist Hospital operating on Ted. "Dad doesn't think that's a very good idea," Ted explains, as he braces himself for a five-month recovery within the rigid confines of a Stryker frame bed.

"They would turn him upside down and turn him around," John Tunney recalls. "[But] he was educating himself as he was lying there...He used to get people to come out from Harvard to give him lectures and talk to him about economics and things like that."

Ted receives a constant stream of visitors from celebrities and politicians, including President Lyndon Johnson, who likes Ted more than his brothers and bestows on the youngest Kennedy a departing kiss on the cheek. Senator Birch Bayh, who walked away from the crash with only minor injuries, remembers bringing Ted his favorite treats, such as "the biggest, nicest strawberries" he could find.

Despite the seriousness of his injuries, Ted continues his campaign. Joan steps up for him. Though she has two young children—Ted Jr. joined Kara in September 1961—and has recently suffered her second miscarriage, Joan shakes off her fragility and resumes the campaigning on her husband's behalf. "Joan became the candidate herself," Joe Gargan recalls, "and was willing to go to every village and town in Massachusetts to appear for Ted." Her work leads to the senator's overwhelming victory on November 3, 1964, over Republican Howard Whitmore.

Bobby, now New York senator-elect, and Ted, from a wheelchair, give a joint news conference on their respective Senate wins, Ted's being significantly more substantial at 75 percent of the vote. "He's getting awful fresh since he's been in bed and his wife won the campaign for him," Bobby says.

On December 16, 1964, Ted leaves the hospital under his own power. "Is it ever going to end for you people?" Jimmy Breslin questions Bobby, who gives the reporter a serious answer. "If my mother hadn't had any more children after her first four she would have nothing now...I guess the only reason we've survived is that...there are more of us than there is trouble."

But there's more than enough trouble.

"It's a curse," Joan tells Jackie. "Look at the things that have happened. Can we just chalk it up to coincidence?"

CHAPTER 39

T eddy and Bobby"—who call each other "Robbie" and "Eddy"—"were unbelievably close," John Tunney says. "I think that Bobby was Teddy's best friend."

In March 1967, Bobby flies to Boston to meet Ted for the St. Patrick's Day parade, the day after Bobby's announced presidential candidacy.

"We don't have any signs," Ted says.

"The stores are all closed," Lester Hyman remembers. "It's St. Patrick's Day, and literally, Ted took the paper lining out of drawers in the house, and we sat with crayons, writing up signs, *Welcome Bobby!*, so there would be some signs available for the parade."

Ted and Lester Hyman get in the car with the driver Jack Crimmins to pick Bobby up at the airport. "It wouldn't start. I remember Teddy putting his head down and then up again as he said, 'The fucking Kennedy machine rides again.'"

When Ted and Joan's son Patrick Joseph Kennedy II is born on July 14, 1967, Ted and Joan decide they want to live closer to Bobby and Ethel. In 1967, they leave Georgetown for a property in McLean, Virginia, not far from Hickory Hill. Ted hires architect Carl Warnecke, who designed Jack's grave.

On the night of the 1968 California Democratic presidential primary, Ted is in San Francisco, where he has been working on Bobby's campaign. While Joan is in France visiting Ted's sister Eunice and brother-in-law Sargent Shriver, now ambassador to France (though many believe President Lyndon Johnson appointed him to keep the ambitious politician Shriver out of American politics), Ted has been keeping company with Helga Wagner, the blond, Austrian-born wife of the American shipping heir Robert Wagner. An unnamed source tells the *Washington Post* of "several days of partying, scheduled around campaign events and a society wedding" as well as a number of dinners out.

At San Francisco's Fairmont Hotel, Ted's aide, Dave Burke, watches Bobby deliver his victory speech at the Ambassador Hotel. Ted is returning from a victory party when Bobby is shot, and it falls to Burke to procure an air force plane to get Ted from San Francisco to Los Angeles. San Francisco congressman Phil Burton adds weight. "I am standing here with Senator Edward Kennedy," Burton says to an air force major, "whose brother has just been shot and who may be the next President of the United States. You are at a point I call a career decision, Major. Either you get that plane, or your career is over."

Burton's bravado is enough to get Ted to Bobby's bedside, but no one can save the stricken candidate. Ted is devastated. As Ted tells his close friend Tunney, he fears that he, too, might disappear. "Teddy, you know, he was not able to function effectively for a while. Part of his brain was not working, and it was because of this extraordinary grief that he felt, and almost to the degree that was fatalistic, that he was going to be gone, he was dead, he was going to kill himself, he wouldn't be around much longer," Tunney says. "In the early days, after Jack was killed and after Bobby was assassinated, I think he was getting all kinds of death threats all the time. I think that he thought his days were numbered, too, that he probably was going to be assassinated, that somebody was going to go for the third one and knock them all off."

One (unsubstantiated) threat logged in Ted's FBI file comes from none other than Bobby's convicted killer, Sirhan Sirhan. A fellow prison inmate claims Sirhan "offered him one million dollars and a car in exchange for killing Senator Kennedy," the file records.

Ted was not alone in his suffering. On June 22, 1969, Judy Garland, a longtime Kennedy family friend, dies in London of barbiturate poisoning. She'd been close with many of the Kennedys, especially Pat Kennedy Lawford, a California neighbor, and had vacationed with them all in Hyannis Port (Judy's daughter Lorna Luft recalls "so many Kennedys, they just seemed to multiply as you watched," so eventually she and her brother "just sort of blended in with the crowd of kids and enjoyed ourselves"). Judy had often visited Bobby and Ethel in Hickory Hill, and after Ted's 1964 plane crash, had sent him a telegram wishing him a speedy recovery that said "We need you so much."

Her relationship with Jack had been especially warm, and multiple sources recall how he'd never let her off the phone without singing at least a few bars of "Over the Rainbow," one of his favorite songs. As she later wrote in a letter to Harold Arlen, composer of The Wizard of Oz, that song transcended the film. "It's become part of my life. It is so symbolic of all my dreams and wishes that I'm sure that's why people sometimes get tears in their eyes when they hear it."

Ted's façade of strength is as insubstantial as the late Judy Garland's rainbow. True to Kennedy form, he deals with his own grief by pushing himself physically. Richard Goodwin, speechwriter and adviser to both Jack and Bobby, recalls, "He was really terribly shaken up by Bobby's death. He used to sail all night long by himself in the days and weeks after that happened, just sailing."

In August 1968, at College of the Holy Cross, Ted makes his first public speech since Bobby's funeral at St. Patrick's Cathedral. "There is no safety in hiding," he states to the crowd assembled in Worcester, Massachusetts. "Like my brothers before me, I pick up a fallen standard. Sustained by memory of our priceless years together, I shall try to carry forward that special commitment to justice, excellence, and courage that distinguished their lives."

Teddy had always leaned on the influence and support of his older brothers, but now he had to stand alone. "You've got to learn to fight your own battles," sixteen-year-old Bobby had once told nine-year-old Ted, as a new boarding student at Portsmouth Priory in Rhode Island.

On his way to being a contender for the 1972 Democratic presidential nomination, Ted's passion for Bobby's social causes also burns brightly. Now Bobby's prophetic words stand in stark relief.

Ted makes a renewed commitment to his legislative role, embarking on a vigorous—and ultimately victorious—contest against the Senate veteran Russell B. Long of Louisiana to become the youngest man, at age thirty-six, ever elected majority whip, also known as the assistant leader of the Senate.

And Ted, now the de facto Kennedy family spokesman, is also thrust into the role of father figure, not only to his own three children but also to Jack's two and Bobby's eleven. Ethel in particular needs all the help she can summon. But Ted's family devotion too often skips over his immediate family with Joan, including Kara, Ted Jr., and Patrick. By spring 1969, Joan is pregnant again, though for years she has battled her own perceived inadequacies, reinforced by Ted's infidelities. "It was difficult to hear all the rumors," she once explained. "And I began thinking, well, maybe I'm just not attractive enough."

Joan was "so fragile," Lester Hyman recalls, though Joan bristles at the characterization. "They would all write how vulnerable I was, and everybody felt sorry for me," she retorts. "If only they knew that I was so strong, I was stronger than anyone else just to be able to survive. It was very hard." Not even their shared family traumas warmed the strained relationship between Joan and Ted. "Rather than get mad or ask about rumors of Ted and his girlfriends, it was easier for me to just go and have a few drinks and calm myself down. As if I weren't hurt or angry," Joan explains many years later. This was a dangerous tactic given her family history of alcoholism.

Hyman remembers a distressing encounter during a party at Ted and Joan's home in McLean. "Joan came over to me, and she had a water glass, and she said, 'Could you do me a favor?' I said, 'What's that?' And she said, 'Take this water glass and just fill it with vodka, please.' I said, 'Joan, do you think you should?' She said, 'Please, just do this for me, and don't tell Ted.'"

Ted is struggling with his own drinking. In April 1969, the senator embarks on a visit to Alaska and the native people of that state in his brother Bobby's honor. But on the return flight to Washington, his travel companions catch a rough glimpse of the usually jovial senator. "Teddy used to be so much fun," a close friend tells the *Vanity Fair* reporter Dominick Dunne. "He kept the whole family laughing. After the deaths of Jack and Bobby, his dark side appeared, which can only be described as melancholy. That was when the indiscretions started."

Aides and reporters watch in shock as a drunken Ted stalks the aisles of the commercial jet, pelting them with airline pillows and repeating "Es-ki-mo power" amid ramblings about his potentially enduring a fate similar to his brother's: "They're going to shoot my ass off the way they shot Bobby..."

After witnessing the spectacle, at once poignant and alarming, John J. Lindsay of *Newsweek* attempts to sound the alarm about what he assesses as Ted's deteriorating mental state.

Lester Hyman recalls receiving a call from Lindsay directly following the Alaska trip. "I want to tell you that your friend Ted Kennedy is in deep psychological trouble," Lindsay tells Hyman. "Everybody else is just saying, 'Ah, he just had a few drinks.' This is a guy who is suffering, and if you guys don't do something soon, something terrible will happen. And by God, it did."

CHAPTER 40

Friday, July 18, 1969, marks a hard stop in Ted's packed Washington calendar. He catches a flight north to Boston, telling his seatmate, Speaker of the House Tip O'Neill, a fellow Massachusetts native, "I've never been so tired in my life."

As Ted is sharing that confidence, *Apollo 11* is orbiting the moon. NASA astronauts Neil Armstrong and Buzz Aldrin are two days from realizing Jack's space-race vision of Americans making the first lunar landing.

Thirty-seven-year-old Ted has a mission of his own—a return to the Edgartown Yacht Club regatta on the eastern shore of Martha's Vineyard. He was too deep in grief for Bobby to attend in the summer of 1968, but this year Ted, along with cousin Joe Gargan and a crew, will race *Victura,* a twenty-five-foot wooden sailboat the Kennedys acquired in 1932, the year Ted was born. Their boat places ninth.

On the small island of Chappaquiddick, reachable from Edgartown only by car ferry across a narrow channel, Joe Gargan has rented a cottage. After the regatta, a party of twelve—

six men Ted's age or older, five of them married; six single women all under thirty—gathers to enjoy steaks and drinks, and to reminisce about the women's days as "Boiler Room Girls," who'd done tireless liaison work for Bobby's presidential campaign from a top-secret central room in his headquarters in Washington. The women have asked Ted and Joe Gargan to "take us sailing again" as they did in Hyannis Port the previous summer.

Twenty-eight-year-old Mary Jo Kopechne currently works in DC at the political consulting firm Matt Reese Associates. She holds a two-year business-secretarial degree from New Jersey's Catholic Caldwell College for Women and had volunteered on JFK's 1960 presidential campaign. In March 1968 she distinguishes herself by assisting with Bobby's presidential announcement.

Her Caldwell College classmate and Washington friend Elly Gardner calls Mary Jo the kind of party guest who's "always the first to leave and never had more than one drink." Owen Lopez, a lawyer who dated Mary Jo in Washington, agrees, noting that she "wasn't the life of the party by any means. She tended to be subdued and measured in her speech. In fact, that's why I think she was so trusted by the Kennedy staff. They looked for unconditional loyalty and discretion in the people they hired."

Loyal and discreet would also describe Ted's driver, sixty-three-year-old Jack Crimmins, a South Boston native who, according to Senate staffer Edward Martin, is not only "a real character" but "an invaluable asset to the senator, not only his driving but humor." He's been with the senator since Ted's 1961 days as a Boston assistant district attorney and looks after the senator's 1967 black four-door Oldsmobile Delmont 88 ("Don't ride around in new cars," Joe Sr. insists). Tonight, Crimmins is one of Ted's five male guests, and brings to the party gallons of alcohol, including vodka, Scotch, and beer.

But Crimmins won't be driving that evening.

Instead, the senator leaves with the keys—and Mary Jo Kopechne.

Testimony as to what happens next runs to 763 pages in the inquest document released nearly eighteen months later, on April 29, 1970.

In short: Ted was driving the Olds, with Mary Jo as his passenger, when they went off Dike Bridge into eight feet of water in Poucha Pond.

He lives. She drowns.

His next actions shadow him forever after. The consequences of the accident are compounded by questionable choices. When Ted gets out of the water, his first instinct is not to seek help from police, but to return on foot to his friends at the party, a little over a mile away. "So then he [Ted] went back up to the house and he was very badly advised by others who had probably had too many drinks as well," Ted's best friend John Tunney, who is not at the party, later relates. "So everything fell apart over the next several hours."

"That was the tragedy of it. All of the people there [at the party] were dependent upon him in one form or another," Tunney declares. "It's so sad. It was so sad that he didn't have somebody at that party to say we've got to get hold of the police immediately."

Instead, Joe Gargan recalls fellow party guest Ray LaRosa, who works for the Massachusetts Department of Civil Defense, calling him and attorney Paul Markham out to the rented white Plymouth Valiant parked in the driveway, where Ted has collapsed. "The senator said to me, 'The car has gone off the bridge down by the beach and Mary Jo is in it,'" Gargan says. "With that I backed up the car and went just as fast as I could toward the bridge."

When a second attempt to rescue Mary Jo fails, Kennedy later testifies that he instructs Gargan and Markham, "You take care of the girls; I'll take care of the accident." Gargan and Markham return to the "Boiler Room Girls" and the cottage, while Ted, who's missed the last ferry of the night, swims across the five-hundred-foot channel to Edgartown and the Shiretown Inn.

Once there, Ted makes a number of phone calls—but not to the police. Nor does he call his wife, Joan, but Gargan has also suggested his cousin call Kennedy family lawyer Burke Marshall and personal assistant David Burke. Ted pauses his phone calls at 2:25 a.m. to interact with the innkeeper, Russell Peachey—an encounter, some later surmise, meant to start establishing a timeline of his actions over the past several hours. He doesn't mention the accident to Peachey.

He does reach Helga Wagner, his companion during Bobby's California campaign, a "tall, slim, blond, athletic" woman whom one admirer calls "a veritable female 007." Helga later insists to *People* magazine that she's a friend to "all the Kennedys," and Ted's call that night is only to get the phone number where he can reach his brother-in-law (and known family fixer) Stephen Smith, vacationing in Spain.

Christopher Lawford remembers how his mother, Pat Kennedy Lawford, exhibits telltale Kennedy secretive behavior. "Nobody said a word about what happened. There were all these hushed phone conversations and then my mother packed her bags and said she had to go to the Cape. That was the way we were always informed of crises—someone arriving in a hurry, or someone leaving in a hurry."

John Tunney receives one of those urgent calls. "I was in California campaigning for the Senate," he recalls. "I got a call from Pat Lawford. She said, 'Your best friend is in terrible trouble. He's had a terrible accident and you'd better come back right now. You've got to get back here with him.'"

"It was a terrible thing," Ted tells Tunney. "I shouldn't have been there. I shouldn't have been in a car when I've had a few drinks. I tried to save her but I couldn't. I tried to dive down and I couldn't. I almost drowned myself. I had water in my lungs. I didn't see her and I thought she had gotten out." Despite the beach being a well-known "lovers' lane" spot, Ted insists to his friend that "he'd never had any kind of sexual relationship with that girl."

As to "the morality of her death," however, "I don't feel guilty," Ted says. "Obviously, I can be faulted terribly from a judgment point of view, but from the point of view of was it a killing, absolutely not. It was an accident."

CHAPTER 41

Police Chief Dominick "Jim" Arena responds to an 8:30 a.m. call from two young fishermen who spot the Oldsmobile submerged in Poucha Pond.

Arena has been on the job in Edgartown for two years, and he swims out to make a routine survey of the wreck. He's unable to enter the car, but is struck by a chilling thought. "Something told me it was more than just a car in the water. Sitting there [on the undercarriage], I had the feeling that there was someone in that car."

Deputy Sheriff Christopher S. "Huck" Look Jr. witnesses the vehicle being pulled from the water and has a startling revelation—it's the same big black car he'd noticed while patrolling the night before about 12:45 a.m. (contradicting the police statement Ted gives on Saturday morning, July 19, where he notes the time he was driving the car as "approximately 11:15 p.m." When Walter Steele, special prosecutor for the Vineyard learns of the incident, he says, "That's impossible. They [the Kennedys] don't drive anywhere").

Look had specifically noticed two sevens in the license plate number, just like his high school jersey. Police confirm that the wrecked car with license plate L78207 is registered to Senator Edward M. Kennedy.

After a diver retrieves Mary Jo's body, the associate county medical examiner, Dr. Donald Mills, examines it at around 9:30 a.m. Though he does not perform an autopsy, Dr. Mills puts Mary Jo's time of death at no earlier than 12:30 in the early hours of that morning, and her cause of death as drowning. The doctor's time line doesn't square with Ted's—that the accident happened shortly after 11:15 p.m., and that there was a second rescue attempt made at 12:20 a.m. in the rented white Valiant (license Y98-746).

"I believe," Look, who in 1971 will be appointed sheriff, says, "that I know the difference between a big black car and a little white car."

Look is speaking as an investigator seeking to prepare a criminal case. Though local law enforcement is first on the scene, the FBI is the first to break the news to the White House.

On Saturday, July 19, J. Edgar Hoover, still FBI director, receives a teletype "flashing the first news of the drowning, initially misidentifying Ms. Kopechne as 'Mary Palporki.'" The communication is entered into Ted's FBI file with a notation that the "fact Senator Kennedy was driver is not being revealed to anyone."

Diaries kept by White House chief of staff, H. R. Haldeman, reveal that Nixon becomes obsessed with the Chappaquiddick incident, ordering aide John Ehrlichman to get investigators "working on what really happened."

According to the *Boston Globe*'s Robert Healy, "He had a fixation, Nixon did, on the Kennedys. Of course, what the hell? He was looking down the barrel of a gun at Bobby and Jack, and the guy was paranoid anyway and the Kennedys just wiped him out . . . [A]ll he wanted to talk about was Ted Kennedy."

The Boston-area papers, led by the *Globe,* are in the incredible situation of having to decide whether to "lead with the moonwalk or Chappaquiddick." Robert Healy describes the front-page layout: "We did a dual job that [Saturday] night"—in advance of the Sunday, July 20, paper. "Split right in half."

"It was the greatest moment in John F. Kennedy's presidential [legacy] happening at the worst possible moment for Ted Kennedy—the senator's personal legacy," Taylor Allen, screenwriter of the 2017 film *Chappaquiddick,* opines.

But attempts at in-depth reporting on the story prove frustrating. In terms of first-person fact-finding, Adam Clymer of the *New York Times,* who later becomes Ted's biographer, is completely shut out. "I tried to interview people about it. Not only Kennedy, but I knew a couple of the women who were there. They wouldn't discuss it with me."

"You knew you weren't going to get anything from the Kennedys," Robert Healy says of the *Globe's* strategy on reporting the case. They tried to get info out of Police Chief Arena, but even though "he wasn't a pal [of the Kennedys] . . . I think he was being careful about dealing with the United States Senator from Massachusetts."

"I was the driver," Ted admits to Chief Arena, though he doesn't say as much when he calls Mary Jo's mother, Gwen Kopechne, on Saturday morning. By noon, he has boarded a short flight to Hyannis Port, where he must face his father.

In the presence of Rita Dallas, Ted begins his awful story. "Dad," he says, "I'm in some trouble. There's been an accident, and you're going to hear all sorts of things about me from now on. Terrible things. But, Dad, I want you to know they're not true. It was an accident. I'm telling you the truth, Dad; it was an accident."

Jackie has her own opinion, and it implicates Joe and the

ethos he created in the House of Kennedy. "I believe Ted has an unconscious drive to self-destruct," Jackie tells Kennedy biographer J. Randy Taraborrelli. "I think it comes from the fact that he knows he'll never live up to what people expect of him. He's not Jack. He's not Bobby. And he believes that what he is, is just not enough."

Rita Dallas recalls Ted undergoing a medical examination by a doctor in Hyannis Port, who "recommended that Teddy's spine be tapped. This was done at Teddy's house on Squaw Island. The diagnosis was 'wear your neck brace,' but Teddy shook his head saying, 'No, I can't do it. I can't let people think I'd be trying to get their sympathy. I can't.'" The doctor also detects a mild concussion, similar to the one Ted sustained in the 1964 plane crash he also survived.

In the aftermath of Chappaquiddick, Joan (then thirty-two years old and four months pregnant) hears of the scandal directly from her husband's mouth—though he's not talking to her. According to Joan's secretary, Marcia Chellis, Joan picks up a phone extension only to overhear a conversation between Ted and Helga Wagner.

"Ted called his girlfriend, Helga, before he or anyone else told me what was going on," Joan tells Chellis. "I couldn't talk to anyone about it, I had to stay upstairs."

Three days after the incident, on July 22, Ted and Joan, along with Ethel, travel from Hyannis Port to attend Mary Jo's funeral at St. Vincent's Roman Catholic Church in Plymouth, Pennsylvania. The congregation of five hundred buzzes when the Kennedy party enters, observing, "The senator, wearing a heavy neck brace, seemed to have trouble kneeling after they entered the front pew." The three highly visible mourners then travel to the cemetery in Larksville by chauffeured limousine.

That same day, the *Boston Globe* reports on the findings of Edgartown's associate medical examiner, Dr. Mills. Mary Jo's blood tests showed "a degree of alcohol, but it was very well down. She was not drunk at the time this happened. She was not drinking immoderately," he said. (In 1969, the Massachusetts blood alcohol concentration [BAC] limit was .15 percent; in 2000, the national limit dropped to .08 percent; Mary Jo's blood tested for .09.)

Chief Arena didn't test Ted's blood alcohol levels, explaining, "If a man comes into my station clear-eyed and walking steadily on his feet with no semblance of alcohol on his breath," he explains, "I have no business in giving a Breathalyzer."

On Friday, July 25, Ted, Joan, and Stephen Smith cross Nantucket Sound by Kennedy yacht for a hearing at the Edgartown courthouse presided over by Judge James Boyle. Ted pleads a barely audible "Guilty" to a misdemeanor charge (lacking evidence of criminal negligence, the most serious possible charge) of leaving the scene of an accident.

After handing down a suspended two-month sentence, Judge Boyle says, "It is my understanding that he [Ted] has already been and will continue to be punished far beyond anything this court can impose."

The bewildered public has endured seven days of silence from the Kennedys, but on that same Friday night, Ted makes a thirteen-minute nationally televised speech from the library of the family's Hyannis Port home. While Ted is the one to deliver the speech, however, the message is crafted by Jack and Bobby's finest wordsmiths and political operatives.

According to Lester Hyman, however, key influencers—speechwriters Ted Sorensen and Richard Goodwin, aides Milton Gwirtzman and David Burke, lawyer Burke Marshall, and brother-in-law Stephen Smith—"were John Kennedy's people. I believe that they were there to preserve John Kennedy's reputation, not Teddy's, and I think they disserved him [Ted]."

Viewers now know that Ted's wife, Joan, was absent from

the party at the cottage on the night of July 18 "for reasons of health" (a euphemism for her pregnancy with their expected fourth child), and that Ted feels grief and remorse over Mary Jo's death. Part of this is a prelude to a political appeal, as Ted directly addresses the voters of Massachusetts, asking "whether my standing among the people of my state has been so impaired that I should resign my seat in the United States Senate."

A quickly commissioned Gallup poll shows that "extremely favorable" ratings of the senator have dropped fifteen points (from 49 to 34 percent) following his televised speech, but Ted's Boston office is besieged with favorable calls. The polished senatorial rhetoric has convinced one crucial person: Mary Jo's grieving mother, Gwen Kopechne, who passes a handwritten note to the reporters surrounding her house during Ted's broadcast. "I am satisfied with the senator's statement, and do hope he decides to stay in the Senate."

The Kopechnes decide not to sue. "We figured that people would think we were looking for blood money," Mary Jo's father, Joseph Kopechne, explains, though the family does accept $90,904 from Ted, as well as $50,000 from his insurance company. The money "was damn little, considering," Joseph Kopechne angrily tells *Ladies Home Journal* in 1989.

Ted and his family spend the August Senate recess at the family compound in Hyannis Port. On August 28, Ted goes on the annual Kennedy family camping trip, but Joan feels too ill to join him. That night, her sisters-in-law Jean and Ethel take her to Cape Cod Hospital, where she suffers a miscarriage, her third. "Asked by a newsman whether the miscarriage was the result of a fall or accident," the *Desert Sun* reports, Ted, who visits Joan on August 29, says, "No, she just didn't carry."

The couple's personal tragedy counts among yet another life lost—among the Kennedys, and those who dare to get close to them.

⌑⌑⌑

On Ted's first day back in the Senate, he invites Lester Hyman to lunch at his desk. Hyman recalls Ted "raised his hand just like a little kid" in an oath as he begins to tell his story.

"Lester, I swear to God," Ted says, "I had nothing to do with Mary Jo Kopechne, and I was not drunk," Hyman relates. "I said, Ted, I believe you, I really do. But the problem is not so much that but your conduct afterwards. And he said, Well, let me explain that to you. I said, Good. At that point, the buzzers rang in the Senatorial office for a vote call and he had to leave. By the time he came back, he wasn't ready to talk any more, and I always wondered what he would have said."

Ever mindful of the looming 1972 campaign, President Nixon is already actively working every advantageous angle. In a 2010 interview with the *New York Times,* John W. Dean III, who rose from an assistant in the Justice Department to White House counsel, explains that if Nixon were to face the senator he wanted to make certain "that he could hang Chappaquiddick around Kennedy's neck." On October 17, 1969, Dean requests that the FBI research the activities of Mary Jo Kopechne, specifically stating in his memo, "both the deputy attorney general and the attorney general are anxious to discretely find out if Mary Jo Kopechne (deceased) had visited Greece in August, 1968," when Ted is known to have traveled with Jackie on his way to meet with Aristotle Onassis.

At clubby Sans Souci Restaurant in Washington, Lester Hyman and Senator Eugene McCarthy are seated at separate tables, but McCarthy is "talking about Chappaquiddick, and dripping with sarcasm" at a volume loud enough for Hyman to overhear McCarthy say, "Isn't it ironic that the entire Kennedy dynasty has been brought down by a mere Polish secretary?"

The judicial inquest into the death of Mary Jo Kopechne is set to begin on January 5, 1970, six months after the fatal accident. In advance, Stephen Smith has secured witness testimony from an insider source, the Massachusetts state detective Bernard J. Flynn. At Boston's Logan International Airport, Flynn advises Smith and a Kennedy attorney, "Have Ted Kennedy tell the truth. We don't have any other witnesses. He has nothing to fear."

More than twenty witnesses are called, including Senator Kennedy. He testifies for more than two hours, although, per standard inquest procedure, he is not cross-examined. Questioning closes January 8.

Just two weeks later, Ted Kennedy experiences another blow. On January 21, the *New York Times* front page headline screams "KENNEDY OUSTED AS WHIP" in bold, capital letters. Ted loses to Senator Robert Byrd of West Virginia in what the press describes as a political coup capitalizing on Ted's vulnerabilities in the wake of Chappaquiddick. Byrd takes a stance against the stiff-drink negotiations that Ted has favored both on and off the Hill. "I despise cocktail parties," he says. "You just stand around and waste time."

Yet if cocktails will keep Ted's inhibitions loosened, the next round is on President Nixon. While Ted's reputation has been severely damaged, he's still a Kennedy, and the Kennedys are still widely beloved. On June 23, 1971, White House chief of staff, H. R. Haldeman, strategizes about capitalizing on reports of Ted's continued philandering. "We need to take advantage of this opportunity and get him [Ted] in a compromising situation if we can."

A grand jury declines to take further legal action against

Ted in the Chappaquiddick case, yet his peers stand in extended public judgment. In a 1979 essay titled "Prelude to the Bridge," *New York Times* columnist William Safire compiles a list of Ted's damning actions—from his expulsion from Harvard to his excessive speeding in Virginia to leaving the scene of a deadly accident—for which Ted has seemingly suffered no consequences. "When in big trouble," Safire writes, "Ted Kennedy's repeated history has been to run, to hide, to get caught, and to get away with it."

A former LBJ staffer offers the dire prediction, "This is the fall of the House of Kennedy."

But Ted's confidante Helga Wagner, whose connection to Ted and Chappaquiddick is exposed as part of a Scientology investigation, advises, "People have to forgive and forget."

CHAPTER 42

My uncle stuck to whatever it is that he does," Patricia Kennedy Lawford's son, Christopher, writes. "It usually works, especially in Massachusetts."

But if Ted's going to create a lasting legacy—as a sitting senator, or future president—he must expand his vision to a national scale. The issue he chooses in 1970, universal health care, is personal. In his 1972 book, *In Critical Condition: The Crisis in America's Health Care,* Ted mentions his sister Rosemary's "struggles," his brother Jack's "many ailments, diseases, and near-death experiences," not to mention his own experience in 1964, when he spent five months in a Boston hospital recovering from his extensive injuries sustained in the plane crash that killed two others. "I knew the care was expensive, but I didn't have to worry about that," Kennedy writes in *Newsweek,* arguing, "Every American should be able to get the same treatment that U.S. senators are entitled to."

For more than four decades, Ted pursues the passage of universal health care, calling it "the cause of my life."

The issue turns suddenly and urgently personal again in November 1973, when his son, twelve-year-old Ted Jr., is diagnosed with bone cancer. (Thirty years later, in 2002, his daughter, Kara, will also receive a cancer diagnosis, this time for lung cancer.) Joan "breaks down" when she hears the news while traveling in Europe, and rushes home to help prepare her son for a November 16 surgery at Georgetown University Hospital. To save his life, Ted Jr. must lose his leg, which is amputated above the knee.

Ted's twenty-two-year-old niece Kathleen Kennedy, Bobby's eldest daughter, is to be married that same day, and Ted is supposed to stand in for his brother and escort her down the aisle. On the day of Ted Jr.'s surgery, he rushes from the hospital to Washington's Holy Trinity Church, walks Kathleen to the altar to where her groom, David Townsend, is waiting, then before he returns to the hospital, closes down the wedding reception to a tearful chorus of his favorite song, "When Irish Eyes Are Smiling."

Ted Jr.'s surgery is successful, and he later fondly recalls an incident during a snowstorm the winter he was first learning to use his prosthesis. Father and son decide to sled down the driveway on the family's Flexible Flyer. The conditions are so icy that Ted Jr. slips and falls as he tries to climb back up the hill. "And I started to cry and I said, 'I can't do this. I said, I'll never be able to climb that hill.'

"And he lifted me up in his strong, gentle arms and said something I will never forget, he said, 'I know you can do it. There is nothing you can't do. We're going to climb that hill together, even if it takes all day.'"

Ted Jr.'s November 1973 illness coincides with the tenth anniversary of JFK's assassination. Throughout these ten tumultuous years, all of the Kennedys have been searching for a way to preserve Jack's—and the family's—legacy.

By October 20, 1979, architect I.M. Pei has turned aspiration into a physical repository. Seven thousand invited guests gather to behold the John F. Kennedy Library, a concrete and glass tower standing on Dorchester Bay across from the Boston skyline. Ted dedicates it to the memory of his late brother. "It was all so brief," he says of the JFK presidency. "Those thousand days are like an evening gone. But they are not forgotten."

Ted's pointed references to time are not lost on President Jimmy Carter, with whom he shares the stage. Though their relations that October day are cordial, the two men are as yet undeclared rivals for the 1980 Democratic presidential nomination. After the terrible events on Chappaquiddick and the death of Mary Jo Kopechne, there was no chance of Ted running in 1972, and even 1976 seemed too soon.

Even so, Carter has had to withstand years of speculation that he only won the Democratic Party's nomination back in 1976 because Ted chose not to run, and that even now as the incumbent president, he might still be pushed out by Ted in the 1980 election. Carter has already made clear that a Kennedy challenge was call for a fight. "I'll whip his ass," Carter predicted with assurance.

As the 1980 campaign gears up, despite spirited assistance from veteran Kennedy operative Al Lowenstein, assurance is something uncharacteristically lacking in Ted. Roger Mudd of CBS News flies to Cape Cod for a two-part interview with Ted, the first on September 28, 1979, at his home on Squaw Island, not far from the Kennedy compound in Hyannis Port; the second, on October 12, in his Senate office. Ted, in his memoir *True Compass,* calls his participation in the interviews a "personal favor" to Mudd. Mudd calls Ted's on-camera answer to one now infamous question "a politically embarrassing incident."

Mudd asks Ted what should be an easy question for him

to answer: "Why do you want to be President of the United States?"

Ted is stumped. For the first time in his life, he is unable to come up with a response. He hesitates, stumbles, and stammers, finally managing to cobble together a rambling, unpersuasive answer.

The *Boston Globe*'s Robert Healy has a theory as to why. "I think he didn't think about it because it was so obvious to him. 'I want to promote my brother's—legacy'...He wanted the legacy."

Journalist Chris Whipple, then a reporter for *Life* magazine and a witness to Mudd's interview, has a different take. "Kennedy had no clue," he says. "His heart just wasn't in it," Whipple speculates, wondering, "Was it consciously or otherwise an act of political destruction?" Author Garry Wills puts it in even more macabre terms, saying of Ted that he "has to keep living three lives at once...[He] has no one but ghosts at his side, and they count more against than for him, eclipse him with bright images from the past," adding, "Once brother drew on brother for fresh strength; now brother drains brother, all the dead inhabiting the one that has lived on."

The Mudd interview airs in November, a few days before Ted makes his official announcement. But his bid for nomination may as well be over before it begins. The voting public sees not preservation but panic. Ted's nonanswer to Mudd's defining question becomes the symbol of a struggling campaign.

Another blow comes just before 4:00 p.m. on March 14, 1980, when seven shots ring out in New York's Rockefeller Center. A mentally ill man walks into former New York congressman Al Lowenstein's law office and shoots him several times, point blank. Lowenstein, whom the *Washington Post* calls "a Pied Piper to three generations of student activists," had been a friend to Bobby and an adviser to Ted's campaign.

His tragic murder sounds a symbolic death knell to the latest Kennedy presidential campaign, though it limps along until the Democratic convention in August 1980, where Senator Kennedy concedes the party's nomination to President Carter. According to *The New Yorker,* Ted's appearance is "solemn and enigmatic." On the floor of Madison Square Garden, where eighteen years earlier Marilyn Monroe had serenaded Jack, are signs that read, "We Love Ted—But Jimmy's All Right, Too."

Asked by the *New York Times* if she is perhaps relieved that her brother Ted has not won the Democratic presidential nomination, Jean Kennedy Smith replies, "I don't dwell on the past and I don't think Ted does. My father always said to worry about the things that you can change, not the things you can't. Ted lost. And now we move on to the next thing."

Many expect him to try again in 1984, but by the end of 1982, Ted officially declares that it's too "soon to ask them [his family] to go through it all again." Plus, Ted says it'll be too hard on the kids—twenty-two-year-old Kara, twenty-one-year-old Ted Jr., and fifteen-year-old Patrick—given that he and Joan are finally divorcing after several years of separation. (August 1978 cover stories of *McCall's* and *People* had both touted Joan's newfound sobriety and independence.)

The question of Ted's running for president rears up with nearly every election, but he never makes another serious attempt at it. Instead, he focuses his political attention on his Senate career—and the voters in Massachusetts reward him with nine terms, making him the third-longest serving member of the Senate in history, and earning him the moniker "The Liberal Lion of the Senate."

And while he "picked up the torch of his fallen brothers" and continued to valiantly fight "to advance the civil rights, health, and economic well-being of the American people," so too was he dogged by stories of his own debauchery, poor personal choices—and ironically, the Kennedy name itself. As political journalist Teddy White puts it, "Ted Kennedy had inherited a legend along with his name and he was almost as much trapped by the legend as he was propelled by it."

PART SEVEN

The Next Generations

THE KENNEDY COUSINS

CHAPTER 43

S enator Ted Kennedy wants a nightcap. It's close to midnight, but not even the soothing sound of ocean waves lapping the shoreline next to the family's Palm Beach mansion can compel the senator to stay at home tonight, on Good Friday, 1991.

Ted and his youngest child, Patrick—now twenty-three, and already following family tradition into politics as a member of the Rhode Island House of Representatives—are down in Palm Beach for Easter weekend, at the invitation of Ted's recently widowed sister, Jean Kennedy Smith. Also among the group of family and friends is Jean's younger son, William "Willie" Kennedy Smith, thirty, a medical student weeks shy of graduating from Georgetown University.

The senator rustles up his son Patrick and his nephew Willie and persuades them to join him for a bachelor boys' night out.

It's been twenty-two years since Chappaquiddick. Ted and Joan divorced in 1983, and their oldest son, Ted Jr., now a lawyer, has long since recovered from his childhood diagnosis of bone cancer which resulted in the amputation of his right leg. Their daughter, Kara, is a TV producer working with her aunt Jean, Willie's mother, at Very Special Arts, the international organization on arts, education, and disability that Jean founded in 1974.

In a matter of twenty-four hours, between now and Easter Sunday, another Kennedy scandal will unfold, one that will dominate national print headlines and television news crawls.

This time, a Kennedy will go on trial for rape.

But for now, the trio hits the town for a late supper, then a few drinks at Au Bar, a trendy Palm Beach watering hole known as a magnet for the nouveau riche and B-list celebrities like Donald Trump's recent ex-wife, Ivana, or Roxanne Pulitzer, whose scandalous 1980s divorce made the front pages of every tabloid with claims she'd been kinky with a trumpet.

The fifty-nine-year-old senator orders his usual double Chivas Regal on the rocks, while Patrick chats with twenty-seven-year-old Michele Cassone, and Willie meets a twenty-nine-year-old single mother named Patricia Bowman. Willie tells her he's about to become a doctor, and Bowman tells him about her two-year-old daughter's health problems.

"I really felt like I could trust him. He seemed to be an intelligent man, a likable man," Bowman says of Willie. "During our dancing he'd never laid one hand on me. He had never done anything suggestive at all."

The Kennedys join Bowman's friend Anne Mercer and Mercer's boyfriend, Chuck Desiderio, at their table. The conversation is barely audible above the pulsing music, but at some point, Mercer starts arguing politics with the senator. Ted decides to leave with Patrick, who invites Michele Cassone back to the Kennedy mansion for a drink and a million-dollar view of the Atlantic. She accepts, following Patrick and his father's white convertible in her own car.

The Kennedy mansion at 1095 North Ocean Boulevard is a Mediterranean-style home designed by architect Addison Mizner in 1923, and has been in the Kennedy family since 1933, when Joe Sr. bought it during the Depression for a steal at a hundred and twenty thousand dollars. JFK wrote *Profiles in Courage* while vacationing there, as well as his inaugural address. The mansion is known as "La Guerida" but has been nicknamed the "Kennedy Winter White House" ever since Jack began using it as a presidential retreat. Despite the home's fashionable pedigree, however, most first-time visitors in the 1990s are surprised at its shabby-chic décor. "It was dark, dingy, and smelly," recalls Michele Cassone, cracking, "If it was my house, I'd have it exterminated."

Ted, Patrick, and Cassone chat in the living room, where Cassone switches from flutes of nightclub bubbly to glasses of white wine. Everyone else in the house is apparently asleep.

"Ted was very drunk, and Patrick and I had a nice buzz on," she recalls.

The senator disappears from the room. Patrick and Cassone head into a bedroom the cousins are sharing for the weekend and start making out.

Then Ted comes into his son's room to say good night. But he's not wearing any pants, only underwear and his long-tailed shirt.

"I got totally weirded out," Cassone recalls. "I said, 'I'm outta here.'"

Patrick escorts Michele Cassone to her car and politely says good night.

Farther down the beach, things are unfolding differently.

Left without a ride when his uncle and cousin took off earlier, Willie asks Patricia Bowman for a lift home when Au Bar closes at 3:00 a.m. She's happy to oblige, and when they arrive, the two of them go for a walk on the sand, despite a brisk breeze.

According to Bowman's version of what happens next, Willie then asks her if she'd like to go skinny dipping. She declines. But he goes ahead, stripping off his clothes and wading into the cold surf.

Bowman turns to go up to the house and to her car. "I've had a nice night with a nice guy," she later recalls thinking as she left. "It would be nice if he called again, but hey, let's be realistic, he's a Kennedy."

But as she reaches the concrete steps, she claims, she feels a hand grab her bare ankle from behind. She trips and falls. It's Willie, who she says has suddenly undergone a "surreal" aggressive transformation. She breaks free and starts "running, to get away," but Willie, who is six-two and around two hundred pounds, tackles her on the lawn by the pool.

"I tried to arch my back to get him off me," five-six, 130-pound Bowman will later testify, "and he slammed me back into the ground. I was yelling, 'No!' and then 'Stop!'"

But Willie won't stop. "I was struggling, and he told me to 'Stop it, Bitch,'" she alleges. "Then he pushed my dress up and he raped me. I thought he was going to kill me."

Per her police report, Bowman "remembers hearing herself screaming and wondering why no one in the house would come out and help her, especially since she knew that Senator Kennedy was in the house."

Yet Ted and Patrick will swear in court they never heard any screams—nor did the other dozen or so people staying in the house. Willie's mother, Jean Kennedy Smith, was sleeping at the Palm Beach estate that night, but says she didn't hear anyone crying for help, or any other noises. Other houseguests, including William Barry (the former FBI agent who wrested the gun from Sirhan Sirhan after he shot Bobby Kennedy) and two prosecutors from the Manhattan district attorney's office (friends of John Kennedy Jr.'s) also assert it was a peaceful night.

Nevertheless, Patricia Bowman says she finally manages to escape from Willie and runs into the house, where she hides in the kitchen. When she spots a phone on the counter, she uses it to call her friend Anne Mercer.

"I wanted somebody to come and help me feel safe. And I didn't know that the police would care or would come," Bowman says, explaining why she calls Mercer instead of 911. "I had just been raped by a Kennedy. And I didn't know what power they held," she says. "These are political people and... maybe they owned the police."

As soon as she hangs up, Bowman says, she hears Willie calling for her. He finds her hiding in the kitchen and pulls her into another room. But this time Bowman confronts him.

"I told him that he raped me, and he looked at me, the calmest, smuggest, most arrogant man, and he said, 'No one will believe you.'"

CHAPTER 44

Anne Mercer and her boyfriend, Chuck Desiderio, arrive at the Kennedy estate about fifteen minutes after getting the call from Patricia Bowman. "She was literally shaking and she looked messed up, her hair and makeup was running," Mercer recalls. Willie, on the other hand, looks "disheveled" but calm.

Mercer and Desiderio take Bowman back to Mercer's house, but before leaving the house on North Ocean Boulevard, they swipe a few small items—a framed photo, a notepad, a decorative urn—as proof they have indeed all been there.

Mercer gives Bowman a change of clothes.

Nine hours later, Patricia Bowman is at the Palm Beach County Sheriff's office to file a report of rape—and to name her attacker. The Kennedy name drops with a thud.

Later that afternoon, Bowman is at Humana Hospital, where she undergoes forensic tests and is treated for minor back injuries. "I felt all this fear and this dirtiness," she says. "I was just so afraid and confused by everything that had happened to me. I was a mess."

The attending physician, Dr. Rebecca Prostko, is convinced "there was a traumatic event of some sort." She later testifies, "Regressive behavior is a little hard to fake."

While Bowman is being examined at the hospital that Saturday afternoon, Ted hosts a luncheon at the mansion. At the quiet gathering, there is no mention of the previous night's "incident," though there is talk between the cousins. As per the police investigation, Patrick recalls Willie telling him Bowman was "really whacked out," and that they'd had sex without protection, later adding, "This is really a setup, isn't it?" Another witness statement notes an overheard conversation at Chuck & Harold's, a Palm Beach celebrity hangout, where a nearby patron hears the senator say to Willie, "And she will say it is rape."

Regardless of what else is going on, the Kennedys hold fast to holiday tradition. On Easter Sunday, the clan attends Mass at St. Edward's Catholic Church. But rumors that something shocking has happened at the Kennedy estate are already spreading, although some locals take a rather blasé attitude.

"Over the years I've been to many parties at the Kennedy house," socialite Susan Polan tells *People* magazine. "One plays tennis there, one goes to parties there, but there are times when you don't go up to the Kennedy house unless you expect to be raucous. They're a lot of fun, but they're just boys, and boys will be boys."

Nevertheless, by late afternoon on Monday, April 1, 1991, Palm Beach detectives are knocking at the door of the mansion, though most of the family has already left town.

Sadly, it's not the first time Palm Beach detectives have needed to talk to the Kennedy family at Easter.

Seven years earlier, over Easter week 1984, Ethel and Bobby Kennedy's twenty-eight-year-old son David Anthony Kennedy was found dead of a fatal overdose in Room 107 of the Brazilian Court Hotel in Palm Beach.

The family is devastated, but not shocked—for years they've all been asking each other what to do about David and his escalating addictions.

David—the fourth of Bobby and Ethel's eleven children, after Kathleen, Joe, and Bobby Jr.—has always been a sensitive, small boy. Family friend Chuck McDermott remembers, "There was some level on which David tapped his father's sensitivity. You would find him walking with David or with his arm around David. David just seemed to need it."

In April 1968, Bobby consults the child psychologist Robert Coles when twelve-year-old David has a run-in with police, who catch the boy throwing rocks at motorists passing near Hickory Hill. Coles recalls Bobby's eyes widening when he makes the connection that David "was a little like him, throwing rocks at strangers—or LBJ," as Bobby had been metaphorically doing since Jack's death in 1963.

A few months later, on June 4, David nearly drowns while swimming in the Pacific, but his father is able to jump in to save him. Later that same night, while up watching Bobby's victory in the California primary, David is horrified to witness his father's assassination live on TV.

His near-death experience "made Bob even larger than life to David," remarks Kennedy family friend John Seigenthaler. "And then 12 hours later, he lost this father in a most horrible way." Ethel similarly notes to her personal assistant, Noelle Bombardier, that Bobby "saved David's life the very same day he lost his own, and David really never could understand any of it," theorizing, "It was as if he thought God had traded his life in for his dad's."

The boy's trauma is largely swept under the rug, however. "No one ever talked to me about what I was feeling," David states. When he tries to bring it up to his mother, Ethel snaps that "It's not a subject I want to discuss." What they do instead, apparently, is medicate his emotional pain away. "We took him to the doctor and the doctor put him on some medication. One thing led to another," Ethel tells Bombardier. David moves on to recreational drugs, and by the time he's fifteen, he and his cousin Christopher Lawford are hitchhiking to New York City and buying heroin in Central Park. "David and I sort of decided together that there really wasn't any reason to be good any more, so we might as well be bad," Chris recalls.

In August 1973, when David is eighteen, he's injured in a jeep accident on Nantucket caused by his older brother Joe. Joe, David, and five teenage girls, including David's eighteen-year-old girlfriend, Pamela Kelley, are all in the car at the time. Joe "was doing his SuperKennedy act," as David puts it. "There was all this crazy energy. I suppose Teddy was that way before Chappaquiddick."

"It was typical Kennedy horseplay," Kelley agrees. "We were all laughing as Joe spun the Jeep 'round and 'round and 'round." Of the passengers, she is the most seriously injured—permanently paralyzed in both legs. David's injuries are less severe, but after receiving morphine at the hospital, he becomes ever more reliant on drugs.

By 1976, David has dropped out of Harvard and Boston College, and in 1978 suffers an overdose (though publicly his uncle Stephen Smith, the Kennedy family spin doctor, labels it "pneumonia").

For the next several years, David's in and out of various rehab clinics, making optimistic attempts to get better but always backsliding. So it comes as no surprise to the clan when Ethel's son is arrested in 1983 after overdosing on heroin.

Except it's not David.

It's Bobby Jr.

"David was the Kennedy screw-up, not Bobby," his cousin Christopher Lawford points out. "This was a real wake-up call."

Fortunately for Bobby Jr., his stint in rehab is far more successful than David's many attempts, which in some ways leaves David feeling worse than ever. "Kennedys don't fail," his uncle Ted tells him. Yet David has failed sobriety over and over.

He feels like he's been letting his family down, failing to meet their high expectations. Once, when the question of what it means to be a Kennedy is posed to him, David replies, "It means that we're exactly the same as everybody else, except better." Yet the Kennedy he most relates to in his darker moments is Rosemary: "She was an embarrassment; I am an embarrassment. She was a hindrance; I am a hindrance."

On March 19, 1984, he again attempts a stint in rehab, and a month later, heads to spend Easter with his extended family and ailing Grandma Rose in Palm Beach, Florida. Instead of staying at the "Kennedy Winter White House," David checks in to the Brazilian Court Hotel, along with several other family members, as the house on North Ocean Boulevard couldn't hold them all. Over the course of the next week, he rotates between dutiful visits to Rose and heavy drinking; various friends, family members, and hotel staff all later remark on David's ability to consume staggering amounts of alcohol. ("I've heard it said that God invented alcohol to keep the Irish from ruling the world," Chris Lawford later writes in the opening line of his 2005 memoir. "My family almost proved Him wrong.")

Ethel isn't down in Palm Beach for Easter that year, but she becomes increasingly concerned when she cannot reach her son after multiple calls to the hotel. She sends David's cousins Caroline Kennedy and Sydney Lawford to check on him, but although the young women make two visits to the hotel, they are unable to locate him. On April 25, 1984, Ethel calls the hotel to request they open the door to David's room. Ten minutes later, they call her back—but before they can inform her of what they've found, Ethel knows.

"He's dead, isn't he?" she says, gasping and hanging up on learning she is right. She's later overheard lamenting to a friend, "When David died, my chance to be a better mother died with him."

Press coverage of David Kennedy's death in Palm Beach is extensive yet respectful. Seven years later, however, when his cousin Willie's Easter scandal breaks, again in Palm Beach, the entire Kennedy family finds themselves drawn not only into the court of public opinion—but into an actual courtroom, where they witness one of their own stand trial.

And this time, the treatment the Kennedys face will be very different.

CHAPTER 45

The bombshell allegations of rape on the beach outside the Kennedy mansion are splashed across the world from Au Bar, which doubles as the reporters' impromptu Palm Beach newsroom.

Reporter Steve Dunleavy gets a sit-down scoop with Anne Mercer, who is paid forty thousand dollars for two ill-advised interviews broadcast on the tabloid TV show *A Current Affair*. And despite knowing nothing about what happened between Willie and Patricia Bowman, Michele Cassone charges multiple TV talk shows a thousand dollars each for dishing on Ted's pantsless antics on that night.

On May 11, 1991, Willie turns himself in to the Palm Beach police on a sexual battery charge, and immediately posts bail. He calls the charges against him "an outrageous lie" and says he's looking forward to being vindicated at trial.

By the time Case No. 91-5482—*The State of Florida v. William Kennedy Smith*—comes to trial, *Newsweek* predicts it "will be the most-watched legal proceeding in American history." The brand-new Courtroom Television Network secures live broad-cast rights, agreeing to obscure Bowman's identity. "This trial was perfect for TV of course," Alan Dershowitz points out, "it had sex [and] the Kennedys."

The trial is watched by millions on television, but the Palm Beach County courtroom itself is small and cramped, allowing only three seats apiece for Patricia Bowman's family and Willie's. The extended Kennedy family comes out to support Willie—most notably his mother, Jean, and his aunts Ethel, Eunice, and Patricia, who rotate their supportive presence under close watch of the cameras.

Though his aunt Jackie doesn't appear, John F. Kennedy Jr. makes two celebrity cameos at his cousin's trial, and the public vie for glimpses of the famous family members. The *Sun-Sentinel* prints a "Spectators' Guide" to "Smith and his entourage," while local businesses cash in on the hundreds of reporters in need of photocopies, A/V hookups, and parking—not to mention entrepreneurs selling novelty Ted Kennedy-in-his-underwear T-shirts, or Sprinkles, the scoop shop with "trial flavors" like "Willi Vanilli," "Teddy's Best" (a boozy option), or "Lupo Lemon" (a reference to the judge's sourpuss expression). As one TV reporter notes of the media coverage, "It looks more like a football game than a news event."

———— ⌘ ————

The trial begins on December 2, 1991. William Kennedy Smith's attorney is Roy Black, a celebrity Miami criminal de-fense trial lawyer known as "The Professor." Unlike prosecutor Moira Lasch, who's been given the nickname "The Ice Queen" and disdains the press, Black always seems to find time to give interviews.

Despite Lasch's excellent reputation and conviction record,

she fails to convince Judge Mary Lupo to allow testimony from three other women who all claim to have been similarly assaulted by Willie over the previous decade.

In 1983, "Lisa" was a nineteen-year-old law student dating Willie's cousin Max (Matthew Maxwell Taylor Kennedy, the ninth of Bobby and Ethel's children). She meets then-twenty-three-year-old Willie at a party in Manhattan, and finds him "quite charming." Since he "in no way" seems to be coming on to her, she accepts Willie's invitation to stay in a guest room at a nearby Kennedy home. Once there, however, Lisa says "he attacked me." Then, when she managed to get free, "he tried to convince me that that wasn't what had happened."

Lisa tells her boyfriend, Max, of the disturbing encounter, which he downplays—although after his cousin's arrest in Palm Beach, she states in court papers, Max apologizes for not taking her seriously back then, telling her, "Sounds like Willie has a really big problem. He needs some help."

A second woman, "Lynn," now a doctor, says that when she was a Georgetown student in the spring of 1988, Willie invited her to a family get-together. When Lynn arrives, Willie claims the others are all in the pool, although it's clear there is no one else at the house. To Lynn's dismay, Willie then "take[s] off his clothes" before diving nude into the water. Back inside, Lynn is even more surprised and frightened when Willie comes at her: "He threw me over the couch and I landed on my back, pinned to the floor by his wrist with him on top of me." When he eventually lets her up, she quickly leaves.

The third woman is "Michele," who states that when she was a grad student in 1988, she got drunk at a college picnic and Willie—"somebody that I knew…somebody that I trusted"—offers her a ride home. Instead, however, he takes her to his Georgetown carriage house, where he "started just getting more and more aggressive," she recalls, "almost animal-like" and "ferocious." He attempts to force her to give him oral sex, but "That's when I kind of lost it, and I just passed out." When she woke up the next morning, Michele says Willie was condescending and dismissive.

Judge Lupo rules the women's depositions inadmissible.

In her opening statement, Moira Lasch portrays Patricia Bowman as a normal, hard-working single mother and Willie as a man who can't accept rejection, while Roy Black says that following a "consensual act of sexual intercourse," Bowman was the one who then felt slighted and resentful.

Lasch calls Anne Mercer as her first major witness. The night before the trial, the second of Mercer's two paid interviews airs and during cross-examination, Black portrays Mercer as a liar and opportunist. He accuses her of changing her story to embarrass Senator Kennedy and of using the TV payout to finance a vacation in Mexico. Mercer is "a disastrous witness," and Black later jokes, "I have to thank Steve Dunleavy for what he did," regarding his interview with Mercer on *A Current Affair*.

Black is slowly managing to turn Willie into the victim.

CHAPTER 46

I t's the fourth day of the trial. Over the previous two days, Patricia Bowman has testified about her experiences in the early morning hours of March 30, 1991. While occasionally tearful, she's direct and poised.

Roy Black, Willie's defense attorney, highlights the gaps and contradictions in Bowman's memory of events—discrepancies intensified by Judge Lupo's exclusion of the prosecution's expert on rape-trauma syndrome—but she's resolute in her story. What Bowman says she struggles to understand, however, is "how this nice guy had turned into that one, the one who had raped me."

Despite the allegations, a "nice guy" is how a number of people describe Willie, the second of Jean and Stephen Smith's four children (his older brother by two years is Stephen Jr.; sisters Amanda and Kym are six and twelve years younger, respectively). A Georgetown friend calls Willie "a regular guy who happens to come from this amazing family," while a supervisor notes Willie "doesn't have any violence in him." An ex-girlfriend says the rape allegations are "inconceivable," stating that Willie is "a gentle person." According to an article in the *Washington Post,* Willie has dated a "harem of women," including Meg Ryan when they were both in their late twenties and she was filming *When Harry Met Sally.*

But other sources say Willie's otherwise "unassuming" personality undergoes drastic changes when he drinks, and according to a sworn statement by James Ridgeway de Szigethy, John Jr.—now a Manhattan assistant district attorney—told de Szigethy that his cousin Willie is guilty, and that the family "'should have done something about Willie years ago when he first started doing this,' meaning get help for him when he first started raping women."

Publicly, the Kennedy family provides a united front, repeatedly declaring themselves "a very close family" who all express their complete support. Privately, one family friend says, "They'll stick by Willie through thick and thin, but when this is over, and they're all alone, they'll beat the shit out of him."

Throughout the trial, Willie's extended family take their turns in the limited seats available in courtroom 411, and the press runs warm and fuzzy photos of Willie with his new dog, or out with his family, or kneeling at prayer. James Ridgeway de Szigethy recalls confronting John Jr. over the family staging such photos, thereby indicating "a public expression of confidence and trust in his cousin," to which he says John Jr. replies, "You just don't understand the pressure I'm under." John Jr. reveals to de Szigethy that he doesn't *want* to attend Willie's trial, but is being forced to do so. The older Kennedys aren't taking any chances; *Newsweek* reports that Willie's mother, Jean, "has reportedly imposed a dating and drinking ban on young Kennedys" and *Vanity Fair* quotes a local hostess as having been told that the Kennedys "have a strategy session every night at dinner at the compound."

"I'm the one who's on trial," Willie tells reporters and spectators at the courthouse, "but it's difficult not to feel sometimes that my family is on trial for me."

That certainly does seem true of his uncle Ted.

As Dominick Dunne writes in the October 1991 issue of *Vanity Fair,* "Senator Kennedy [is] already at the lowest point in his career," but while "he has been forgiven his trespasses over and over again," Ted now "has the earmarks of a man who has given up hope, of whom too much has been asked, who wants to abdicate all responsibility. And he drinks."

Expectations are not high as the Massachusetts senator enters the courthouse, although cheers go up from scores of court watchers who have lined up for hours. But Ted acquits himself well—his voice cracking as he recounts his motivation for taking the boys out that night. How the recent death from cancer of Willie's father, Stephen Smith, has left him severely depressed over the loss of a close friend. He talks about how close the family is, how he, Ethel, Eunice, Patricia, and Jackie have all rallied around their sister Jean. Willie tears up, too. One of his attorneys offers him a handkerchief.

"I wish I'd gone for a long walk on the beach instead," Ted says of that Good Friday. "But I went to Au Bar."

As for Willie, "I was very moved by a lot of things my uncle said," he tells the press later that day. "I think this process has been unfair to him. I don't say that in a bitter way. I just mean it in my heart."

Next on the stand is Ted's son Patrick, visibly nervous and less polished than his senator father. That same week the *National Enquirer* has exposed Patrick's cocaine habit, revealing that he had a stint in rehab at age sixteen. Despite testimony that occasionally contradicts his father's, after two hours on the stand and no questions from the defense, Patrick walks away unscathed.

Now it's Willie's turn. He confidently strides to the witness stand, comfortable enough to make friendly eye contact with the six jurors, four women and two men. Patricia Bowman watches Willie's testimony from a TV in the prosecutor's office.

Willie carefully unfolds his version of events. He turns the tables and accuses Bowman of having picked *him* up at Au Bar, of being the aggressor in consensual sex, claiming she was the one who unzipped his pants, and who "massaged" him to climax before he went into the water for a swim, after which they again had sex.

Then, he says, he accidentally calls her by the wrong name, at which "she got very, very upset, told me to get the hell off her."

Willie says he walks her to her car and she drives away, yet when Willie meets up with his cousin Patrick back in the house, Bowman is inexplicably there.

By this time, he says, Anne Mercer has also arrived, and Bowman then leaves with her pal.

Moira Lasch attacks Willie's testimony, but the three-hour cross barely fazes him. At one point, in response to the prosecution's sarcastic questioning, Willie says, "Miss Lasch, I've searched myself every night since March 29 to try to find out why [she] would make an allegation against me that's not true, that's going to destroy my family, destroy my career, possibly send me to jail for fifteen years. I don't know why she would do that. I don't understand why anyone would do that." When questioned why Bowman would have made up her accusations, Willie offers several possibilities, then quickly adds, "But that's not the issue here. The issue here is I'm innocent. And how do you defend yourself from somebody who says the word 'rape' over and over again... I'd like you to tell me how to deal with it?"

After ten days of testimony, with forty-five witnesses called, the attorneys give their closing arguments. The six jurors head out to deliberate—but are back with a verdict after only seventy-seven minutes, barely an hour.

When the court clerk announces the verdict, Patricia Bowman, watching via television from the prosecutor's office, faints. "I remember just leaning up against this door frame. And I remember the words, 'Not guilty.' And the next thing I remember is... they were helping me off the floor," she tells Diane Sawyer in an interview on ABC's *Primetime Live*.

Willie, meanwhile, is all smiles. Outside the courthouse, hundreds of onlookers have gathered, chanting "Willie! Willie! Willie!" Willie looks visibly relieved, and even his mother, Jean, declares, "I feel great, just great!"

From Boston, Ted Kennedy again highlights the family bond. "If there's anything good that has come out of this whole long experience, it's the renewed closeness of our family and friends," he tells reporters.

"I have an enormous debt to the system and to God, and I have a terrific faith in both of them," Willie says. "I'm just really, really happy." Of the jurors, Willie says, "My life was in their hands and I'm so grateful for the job they did."

Several of the six-member jury later appear on talk shows. One of the most outspoken is Lisa Lea Haller, founder of an eponymous cosmetics company, and the youngest juror at thirty-seven. She tells the *New York Times* that the lack of physical evidence was most persuasive. "There was nothing on the dress," she says, asking, "What about all the screaming? Nobody heard it."

Shortly after his news conference, Willie is whisked back to La Guerida in the family's 1989 wood-paneled Mercedes station wagon, where his friends and family have already gotten the victory party started. Roy Black claims on several TV shows that at the party, they held a prayer circle and "said a prayer for Patty."

Despite the verdict, Patricia Bowman releases a statement declaring, "I do not for one moment regret the action I have pursued," and as her lawyers' own statement says, "A not-guilty verdict does not equate to innocence."

She also points out that the media circus of the televised trial—which arguably begins the era of real-life court cases as popular spectacle—was hard for her to take. "To some people, this has been entertainment," she says. "It was a tragedy. It was a trauma for me."

Among those who especially profit from the trial is Roy Black, who not only gains a television career and more celebrity clients, but even romance—about nine months after the trial ends, Roy Black runs into juror Lea Haller at a Coral Gables bar. The two begin dating, and marry in 1994. From 2011 to 2013, Haller appears as a main cast member on three seasons of Bravo TV's reality show *The Real Housewives of Miami,* where Black occasionally appears with her on camera.

Willie earns his medical degree from Georgetown, but finds himself again in the news in 1993, when he's arrested on October 23 for assaulting a bouncer in Virginia. He pleads no contest to the charges, and sidesteps the court date that had been scheduled for December 3, in part to avoid what would've been "a circus" as well as "to be with his mother in Ireland for the holidays," as Jean Kennedy Smith had just been named the US ambassador to Ireland a few months earlier.

He founds a Chicago-based humanitarian group but resigns as the head in 2004, after a lawsuit (later dismissed) alleges that three separate employees had come forward with claims of sexual harassment. Willie denies the charges, claiming, "Family and personal history have made me vulnerable to these kinds of untruths."

CHAPTER 47

When you look at the third generation of Kennedy men, much of what remains of a once powerful dynasty is good teeth, good hair and the best public relations a trust fund can buy," *Time* magazine announces in May 1997.

While the family as a whole remains devoted to public service, whether through government (Kathleen Kennedy Townsend is lieutenant governor of Maryland, while her brother Joseph Kennedy II and their cousin Patrick Kennedy are both congressmen in the U.S. House of Representatives, for Massachusetts and Rhode Island, respectively) or philanthropy (founding programs such as the Special Olympics, Citizens Energy, or Physicians Against Land Mines), it's certainly true that the once-mythologized Kennedy image has taken a few hits over the last decades.

"For those of us who were born after the assassination, I don't think we have the same perspective or the same investment," remarks one twenty-something in 1997. "I'm more in touch with the scandals that have been coming out lately than the whole higher mythology."

A caustic *Newsweek* cover story entitled "Dynasty in Decline" reminds readers how in the 1960s, JFK and RFK embodied prosperity and social justice; now in the 1990s, "the drama is not so grand... [the younger Kennedys] are emblems of a tabloid time, a fin-de-siècle moment when public life seems less important and stories about sex more titillating."

The combination of Kennedys and sex is nothing new, of course, but what's prompting these latest critiques of Joe and Rose's grandchildren are two salacious stories that land within days of each other. The first involves Bobby and Ethel's oldest son, Joe Kennedy II, who's taken a hit in the polls with the publication of his ex-wife Sheila Rauch Kennedy's book *Shattered Faith,* about her resistance to Joe's petition to have their twelve-year marriage annulled so that he can marry his fiancée and staff member, Beth Kelly, in the Catholic Church. It's the details that truly hurt the forty-four-year-old, six-term congressman—accusations that he was a bully who decried his ex as a "nobody," his lack of concern over Sheila's objections, that he was insensitive enough to serve her the annulment papers while on vacation in the Caribbean with his girlfriend, even his characterization of the annulment itself as just "Catholic gobbledygook."

Joe's been openly planning a run for Massachusetts governor, and allegations of his callous behavior causes backlash among his mostly Irish Catholic constituents, though at first it seems there's every chance the ground he's losing can be recovered over the year and a half between the book's publication and the election.

But less than two days after Sheila appears on *Primetime Live* to launch her book tour, an even bigger Kennedy scandal overwhelms the annulment pushback. On April 25, 1997, the

Boston Globe breaks the shocking story about an alleged affair between Joe's younger brother Michael Kennedy, a thirty-nine-year-old married father of three, and Marisa Verrochi, his family's nineteen-year-old former live-in babysitter. Even more disturbing—and potentially constituting statutory rape—are accusations that the affair began as far back as five years earlier, putting the babysitter at a mere fourteen years old.

"I'm told Ethel is devastated over this," biographer Jerry Oppenheimer, author of *The Other Mrs. Kennedy,* says, adding that in his estimation, this was the "seamiest" Kennedy scandal yet. "Michael was the apple of her eye. He was among the Kennedys who were seen as the future of the clan."

Indeed, Michael LeMoyne Kennedy, the middle child in Bobby and Ethel's brood of eleven, is the one Bobby Jr. calls "Mummy's favorite." Not that the other siblings resent that title, he says. "No one was jealous of her love for him because he was everyone else's favorite, too." Both Teddy and Ethel notice a certain similarity to his father in Michael. "Ethel always felt that he was a lot like Bobby. Very bright, quick," a family friend notes, while Teddy recalls once glancing at Michael in profile and feeling overcome: "The resemblance was so striking, I had to just sit there and stare at him for a moment," he says.

In 1981, Michael marries Victoria Gifford, daughter of football great Frank Gifford, and they have three children: a son, Michael Jr. in January 1983, and two daughters, Kyle Francis in July 1984 and Rory Gifford in November 1987. Like many Kennedys, Michael goes to Harvard, and, like his father and uncle Ted, the University of Virginia Law School. After graduating in 1984, he goes to work with his brother Joe at Citizens Energy, a company Joe started to help low-income families with heating oil. When Joe wins his first term in Congress—taking over from Tip O'Neill the seat his uncle Jack had held from 1947 to 1953—Michael becomes president and CEO at Citizens Energy.

Among the notoriously competitive siblings, Michael and Joe are said to be the most competitive with each other. "They resent each other because neither one gets what the other does," says one family friend. "Michael didn't get to run for Congress; Joe did. Joe, on the other hand, resents Michael because Michael made money, while Joe never did."

But a race to see who can tarnish the Kennedy name faster is not a competition either brother wishes to win.

CHAPTER 48

On January 22, 1995, Michael's wife, Vicki, woke up to find her husband missing from their bed. Perplexed, she begins looking for him throughout their million-dollar home in Cohasset, a seaside suburb of Boston. She can't find him anywhere.

Surely he's not in Marisa's room?

The soon-to-be-seventeen-year-old is the daughter of Michael's close friend, neighbor, and Democratic donor, billionaire entrepreneur Paul Verrochi. It's well known that even before Marisa moved in, "Michael Kennedy would call her parents and say they were going to be out late and that [Marisa] should sleep over," neighbor Dan Collins tells *Time* magazine.

She's been living with the Kennedys since last spring, at Michael's suggestion, and has been babysitting for them since she was in middle school. She's even traveled with Michael and the kids on a few family vacations—whitewater rafting, skiing, etc.—trips that his wife hadn't joined in on. With Vicki absent, people have been starting to notice an uncomfortable intimacy between Michael and the teenager.

Vicki opens the door.

Michael is there, in Marisa's bed.

Vicki screams, waking the children, causing Marisa to cry, and Michael to deny knowing how he got there. He begs Vicki to forgive him, and blames it all on booze.

Michael's drinking *has* increasingly been a problem over the past year. Until recently, he was known as a "straight arrow," the calm and even-keeled one within the family. But then "something snapped," as a family associate recalls. "Michael started drinking heavily and got depressed. He wasn't a mean drunk, just reckless."

Concern over Michael's drinking culminates in a family intervention earlier that same month, at which Michael agrees to check himself into rehab by February 1. Michael swears to Vicki that he will clean up his act. But there will be no waiting the extra week now. He checks in to Father Martin's Ashley rehab center in Havre de Grace, Maryland, that same day, January 22, 1995. "I have come to recognize I had a dependence on alcohol," Michael is quoted as saying in *People*.

"No one has hidden behind alcoholism as an excuse for inappropriate behavior," Michael's younger brother, thirty-three-year-old Christopher Kennedy, says. "But all of us clearly understand the link."

News of Michael's entry into rehab is surprising to outsiders but overshadowed by the death of his grandmother later that same day. The 104-year-old matriarch of the Kennedy family, the "indomitable" Rose Fitzgerald Kennedy, dies of pneumonia at home in Hyannis Port, and is buried on January 24, 1995. Six of the other grandchildren, including Michael's oldest sister, Kathleen, the new lieutenant governor of Maryland, serve as pallbearers for her funeral in the same church in Boston's North End where Rose was baptized in 1890.

Privately, the family is furious with Michael, but publicly, they close ranks to keep the sordid news from leaking out.

"I wanted to kick his [ass]," Christopher Kennedy says of when he first heard the news about his brother Michael's affair with the babysitter, but the natural impulse among the family, as always, is to circle the wagons. Word spreads quickly among the cousins. "We talk to each other a lot, partially because we don't really know who we can trust," explains Ted Jr.

John F. Kennedy Jr. and his friend Stephen Styles-Cooper go to visit Michael in rehab about three weeks into his stay. The abstinence from alcohol may be working, but John Jr. is taken aback that his cousin seems as devoted to his teenage paramour as ever, even producing for them a photo of Marisa, which Michael tells them he's kept hidden in his sock.

"*This* is the girl you're going to hell for?" Stephen Styles-Cooper recalls John Jr. exclaiming, pronouncing her "just a kid" and taking the photo away with them when they leave. On their four-hour-long trip back to New York City, Stephen says John seems "shut down," remarking, "I couldn't tell if he was angry, hurt, sad, confused...or what."

Whatever's going through his friend's mind, Stephen is surprised by what happens as they finally part: "[He] looked at me and said three words I never thought I'd hear coming from him: '*Fucking Kennedy Curse.*'"

CHAPTER 49

By April 1995, Michael is home from rehab and Marisa has moved out of the house—but he and the seventeen year old are still seeing each other. Associated Press photos even show her (but not Michael's wife and kids) at the Kennedy compound on Labor Day 1995, causing John Jr. to reportedly observe, "Aunt Ethel must really be on the warpath." Still, Vicki and Michael more or less manage to keep their marital problems out of the public eye—but they can't keep a lid on local gossip.

Especially not when it seems the affair has been an open secret among Marisa's prep school classmates at Thayer Academy all along. The girl, whom *People* reports had been named "Most Beautiful" by her fellow students, has apparently been boasting about it throughout high school. "She used to brag all the time about sleeping with the Kennedy guy. But nobody believed her until the stories came out," scoffs one former classmate. Marisa even "told people she had been caught in bed with him," another one confirms.

Over the next year, as Michael and the teen continue their relationship, the only people who somehow *don't* seem to get wind of the affair are Marisa's parents, June and Paul Verrochi. By the fall of 1996, however, enough people are talking that friends of the Verrochis finally broach their suspicions directly to June and Paul. When confronted by her parents, Marisa at first denies it . . . but then admits everything.

According to J. Randy Taraborrelli in his book *The Kennedy Heirs*, Marisa's father, Paul, marches directly over to Michael's office and unloads on him in front of witnesses. "Paul asked me how I could do it," Michael later tells a family member. "And he kept asking me and asking me *and asking me*. And the only thing I could think of was that I was sure someone with a heart could've answered the question. But that wasn't me," he says. Michael's own estimation of himself is "I'm not normal. I don't feel things."

Vicki has had enough, and she and the children move out of the family home.

Marisa starts her freshman year at Boston University and breaks things off with Michael.

Though he tries to change Marisa's mind, Michael also initially hopes to repair his marriage to Vicki, but by April 1997, the couple announces a separation after sixteen years of marriage.

Yet what seems like a conclusion is only the beginning, since it's soon after Vicki and Michael's separation is announced that reporters from the *Boston Globe* break the salacious affair story. And while it's no surprise that news of an alleged relationship between a Kennedy and a teenage babysitter is almost immediately picked up across the country, what *is* surprising is that no one in the Kennedy camp makes much attempt to deny it. There's a tacit agreement that yes, the affair took place; the only real fight is over when it may have begun (in Massachusetts, the legal age of consent is sixteen).

The press has a field day with this scandal, and Cohasset police launch inquiries into the statutory rape allegations, but true to form, the Kennedys clam up.

As one family friend tells *Vanity Fair*, "I have a sense that all of the Kennedys are in a castle with a moat around it and a gangplank that lifts up, and they're all in there with boiling oil for journalists. They're in a siege mentality all the time, and I think it colors their whole relationship with other people."

That familial devotion is both admirable and a source of frustration to outsiders, many of whom view loyalty taken to this extent as disrespectful to the victims, even Mafia-esque. "The only time the family intervenes is when there's an embarrassment in the press," a close friend of the Kennedys points out. "The infraction is not considered important, only the public embarrassment."

Even when Joe speaks out on the dual family dramas, it is only to say vaguely, "I view these as private and personal matters," while acknowledging, "Sometimes in my family it doesn't always work out that way." Nevertheless, he states firmly of Michael, "I love my brother very much, I will always love my brother, and I will stand by my brother"—an attitude *Vanity Fair* deems "*Omertà,* Irish-American-style."

So the question remains: Who leaked to the press?

Among the Kennedy inner circle, the finger of betrayal is pointed at their cousin Michael Skakel.

CHAPTER 50

Michael Christopher Skakel was born on September 19, 1960, the fifth of seven children. His father, Rushton Skakel Sr. (himself one of seven children in a family that includes younger sister Ethel Kennedy), is left to raise the six boys and one girl as a single parent when their mother, Anne, passes away from cancer at age forty-one in March 1973.

The Skakel family was already "Greenwich royalty" in Belle Haven, an exclusive neighborhood in the tony Connecticut town, even without the added luster and celebrity that Ethel's marriage to Robert Kennedy gave them by association. Besides, the Skakels are reportedly even wealthier than the Kennedys, and traditionally Republican, which didn't change when Ethel married into a Democratic family, not even when her brother-in-law ran for president.

According to Kennedy biographer J. Randy Taraborrelli, Ethel's brother Jim Skakel says the family "supported Nixon, not Jack, in the 1960 election," and claims their brother George

Jr. thumbed his nose at the Kennedys by handing out the in-auguration tickets Ethel gave him to the homeless. In a 1966 piece on George Jr. in the *Stanford Daily*, William F. Buckley Jr. tells a similar story, but claims that George Jr. felt the Kennedy staff was acting "a little pompously" at the 1961 inauguration, "whereupon he took the seating pass of an august Cabinet member and conferred it ceremoniously on a Negro porter, throwing protocol into utter panic."

Ethel and Rushton's father, George Skakel Sr., "was even more a self-made man than Joe Kennedy," going from a railroad clerk to owner of the Great Lakes Carbon Corporation, one of the largest privately held businesses in the world. Following George Sr.'s 1955 death in a plane crash—and eleven years later, oldest son George Jr.'s—Rushton Sr. takes over as chairman of Great Lakes Carbon, and grows even wealthier.

Rushton Skakel's children are known to be ill behaved—a frustrated former nanny who worked for the family in the mid-sixties remarks, "They didn't like discipline—the kids or the parents"—though this, too, seems in keeping with Skakel family tradition, as Ethel's brothers were also considered terrors in their Greenwich neighborhood while growing up. However, after their mother, Anne, passes away, "an even more intense level of chaos came to rule our household," Michael Skakel recalls. He was twelve years old at the time of her death, left with little supervision and an often-absent father who handed his children off to "friends, relatives, servants, a coterie of priests and nuns and a series of live-in tutors."

In the fall of 1975, Rushton Jr. is nineteen, Julie is eighteen, Thomas is seventeen, John is sixteen, David is eleven, and the youngest in the family, Stephen, is nine. Michael turns fifteen that September. Their friends and neighbors diagonally across the street are the Moxleys, who moved to the exclusive Belle Haven neighborhood in 1974 with their two teenagers, John and Martha. Martha, who makes friends quickly and is deemed "Best Personality" at her new school, is also fifteen, just a month older than Michael Skakel.

"You've heard it said there was no adult supervision in the [Skakel] house," remarks former detective Mark Fuhrman. "They had no intelligent supervision whatsoever. It was 'The Addams Family,' and the Moxleys were 'Leave It To Beaver.'"

On Halloween of that year, Martha is found viciously murdered on her front lawn. "Her killer bludgeoned young Martha with a golf club and then dragged her body nearly 100 yards to hide it," the New York Times reports in December 1975. It's a brutal beating, violent and bloody, and the fifteen-year-old was left exposed, her underwear and jeans pulled down, though there's no sign of sexual assault.

The murder weapon is discovered to be a rare Toney Penna six-iron, a distinctive golf club, which broke into at least three pieces from the force of the blows. Martha is stabbed through the throat with one of the pieces; another section is never found. The six-iron is revealed to have come from a set that once belonged to the late Anne Skakel, and Martha's time of death is determined to have been the evening prior. Among the group of teenagers she was last seen with the previous evening—Mischief Night—are both Thomas and Michael Skakel.

Early investigations glide over the possibility of the teens having any significant involvement, focusing more strongly on troubled twenty-something men like the Skakels' latest live-in tutor, Kenneth Littleton, though seventeen-year-old Thomas Skakel is also intensely questioned. But despite police efforts, the investigation quickly hits a wall, and decades go by without any arrests in the case.

With a family predilection toward drinking and no one to stop him, by age thirteen, Michael Skakel was already a self-described "full-blown, daily-drinking" alcoholic. At seventeen, in 1978, he's convicted of drunk driving, and sent by his father to a notoriously harsh teen rehabilitation center in Maine called the Élan School (shut down in 2011), specializing in "tough love and discipline" that attendees liken to abuse. He tries to run away several times, and is ultimately allowed to leave in 1980.

After that, Michael focuses on sobriety and sports, becoming a strong enough speed skier that he nearly makes it to the 1992 Winter Olympics. He also develops a warmer relationship with his aunt Ethel's kids, especially David and Bobby Jr., who also struggles with sobriety. "He helped me to get sober, in 1983," Bobby credits his cousin. Despite the family connection, the Skakels and the Kennedys had not previously been close. "I rarely saw the Skakel boys growing up, and would not have been able to identify Michael or his brothers" until they were all well into their twenties, Bobby Jr. says of his Skakel cousins.

By 1996 Michael Skakel is twelve years sober and has a reputation for being friendly and nonjudgmental. "His primary passion in life is helping other alcoholics in recovery," Bobby Jr. states. Ethel's youngest son, Douglas Kennedy, also vouches for his cousin, saying, "Michael is one of the most honest and open people I know. He cares about people more than anybody I've ever met."

He also becomes something of a Kennedy dogsbody, working as a driver on Ted Kennedy's campaign and then with Michael Kennedy at Citizens Energy. Though his official title is 'Director of International Programs,' in reality, he is mainly a driver there, too, as well as a travel companion and confidant to Michael Kennedy. As the two spend more time together, Michael Skakel becomes known simply as "Skakel" to avoid confusion with his cousin Michael Kennedy.

Skakel, whom another Kennedy relative calls "the sweetest human being that you have ever met," is the sort of person people feel comfortable turning to if they have something awkward to discuss. People tend to confide in him.

Skakel is who Michael's wife, Vicki Gifford Kennedy, calls when she finds Michael in bed with the family babysitter. He's who she entrusts to drive her husband straight to rehab, and the one who takes the heat from Aunt Ethel about the unexpected change in plans. He's even the one who helps Marisa's distraught mother, June Verrochi, when she's found bewildered on the roof of their town house due to "some very disturbing news."

"In hindsight, the strangest detail in press reports of that incident was that Michael Skakel had been on the scene and accompanied Mrs. Verrochi to the hospital," *Vanity Fair* notes.

Although maybe not so strange, given that—odd as it may seem—Skakel is also a close confidant of Marisa's. He's apparently the one who futilely attempts to discourage the teenager from having a romantic relationship with the much older and married Michael (in fairness, he also tried unsuccessfully to convince his cousins to intervene, but "neither Michael nor his siblings seemed to feel a Skakel had any business telling a Kennedy what to do"), and the one who sets Marisa up with a therapist, further incensing his cousin and his aunt. "That is not your place," Ethel reportedly chastises her nephew.

"He's been trying to save everyone, left and right," Bobby Jr. says of his cousin. "But you know what they do to saviors," he notes. "They crucify them."

Skakel's attempts at diplomacy are partially why suspicions fall on him as the leak on Michael's inappropriate relationship with the teen. Plus, Skakel's known to speak openly at his AA meetings—and quite possibly has been oversharing the details of his cousin's drama, and someone in one of those meetings likely contacted the media. According to a source in *Vanity Fair*, "he [the fellow AA member] admitted to me he did [contact the press]." And when authorities come looking for corroboration on the statutory rape accusations, Michael Skakel is the only one willing to talk.

The family feels betrayed.

"Nobody can stab you in the back quite like the guy who says he loves you," Joe Kennedy sneers.

The cold shoulder that the Kennedys turn on Michael Skakel in 1997 in the wake of the babysitter scandal couldn't have come at a worse time for him.

While down in Palm Beach, Florida, reporting on the William Kennedy Smith rape trial for *Vanity Fair* in 1991, author Dominick Dunne heard and repeated a rumor that Willie might've been at the Skakels' home sixteen years earlier, on the night of Martha Moxley's murder. "I checked it out, and it was a bum rap," Dunne says—unsurprising, since aside from his aunt Ethel, Willie had never met any Skakels—"but it got me interested in the story again."

So interested, in fact, that Dunne goes on to write a best-selling roman à clef inspired by the case, *A Season in Purgatory,* a novel in which the scion of a Kennedy-esque family covers up the murder of a young woman. In 1996, the book is made into a TV miniseries, sparking further interest in the original Martha Moxley case. At first, Dunne tells the press that he's convinced Thomas Skakel was the killer, but over time switches his suspicions to Michael. "I firmly believe that Michael Skakel is guilty of this murder," he tells news outlets.

More nonfiction books on the case follow shortly, keeping public interest stoked, and even Michael Skakel considers writing a tell-all about his family, going so far as to shop around a book proposal in 1999 under the title "Dead Man Talking: A Kennedy Cousin Comes Clean."

It backfires spectacularly.

In January 2000, Michael Skakel is arrested and charged with Martha Moxley's 1975 murder. Excerpts from taped conversations between Skakel and the ghostwriter he planned to use for his memoir feature heavily in his prosecution. While there are no actual admissions of guilt, prosecutors deem it "a web in which he has ultimately trapped himself."

With no physical evidence or eyewitnesses, "the state's case is entirely circumstantial," the *New York Times* points out when the case goes to trial in 2002, yet they convincingly cite opportunity and means, alleging motive as "unrequited feelings" between Skakel and Martha. They also bring in fellow former students from the Élan School, who state that they recall Skakel making oblique confessions to the murder.

During the monthlong trial, Marisa Verrochi is called as a witness for the defense to rebut testimony from a former roommate of hers who claims that Skakel had attended a party at her condo in 1997 where he joked about committing the murder. Marisa denies that any of that had taken place and confirms to prosecutors that she and Skakel had been "close friends" at the time, and that he'd provided her with support, protection, and comfort during her own scandal.

Surprising some and thrilling others, Michael Skakel is found guilty of the 1975 murder and given a twenty-year prison term. But in 2013, his conviction is vacated, citing poor representation by his legal counsel. Then in 2016, his conviction is reinstated . . . and again overturned in 2018.

"The state of Connecticut had a very, very, very good case, and we absolutely know who killed Martha," Dorthy Moxley, Martha's mother, declares in January 2019. "If Michael Skakel came from a poor family, this would have been over. But because he comes from a family of means they've stretched this out all these years."

"The evidence shows that Michael [Skakel] spent eleven years in prison for a crime he did not commit," Skakel's attorney, Roman Martinez, rebuts. "The Supreme Court's decision rejecting review should end this case once and for all."

Throughout his cousin's trials, Bobby Jr. stands by Skakel's side, convinced of his innocence. In 2016, he writes a book called *Framed: Why Michael Skakel Spent Over a Decade in Prison for a Murder He Didn't Commit.*

"Michael dished some pretty nasty dirt on [the family]," says Timothy Dumas, a Greenwich local and former classmate of Martha's, and author of the book *A Wealth of Evil: The True Story of the Murder of Martha Moxley in America's Richest Community.* "But the Kennedys are known for their loyalty and for drawing together in times of crisis."

CHAPTER 51

Despite Norfolk district attorney Jeffrey Locke's willingness to pursue the allegations of statutory rape, if it can be shown that Marisa Verrochi was under sixteen when her sexual affair with Michael Kennedy began, by July 1997 the investigation is dropped due to lack of cooperation.

The Verrochis release a statement citing fears of the same media hysteria that dogged the William Kennedy Smith rape trial a few years earlier, pointing out how "a protracted investigation and trial, accompanied by unrelenting media coverage, would cause potentially irreparable harm to the victim of this outrageous conduct." So while "Michael Kennedy has caused us great pain and suffering by his outrageous conduct and his breach of the trust we placed in him as a neighbor and friend," their priority is their daughter's "health and well-being [which] . . . cannot be further jeopardized."

Michael's wife, Vicki, steps in as well, denying any knowledge that her estranged husband committed a criminal act.

"Without the willing involvement of the victim, there is no

basis to proceed further," Locke concedes, and Michael quickly issues a statement, saying, "I deeply apologize for the pain I have caused. I intend to do all I can to make up for the serious mistakes I have made and to continue to obtain the help I need."

Nevertheless, fallout from the revelations about Michael's illicit relationship with the babysitter continues, sparking more stories in the press about the less-than-admirable behavior of the younger Kennedys in decades past, dredging up David's death from overdosing, Bobby Jr.'s drug arrest, the jeep accident Joe caused which paralyzed Pamela Kelley. And there's no denying that a high percentage of the family are admitted alcoholics: "It's easier to get an AA meeting together than a touch-football team now," Christopher Kennedy quips.

But the articles largely ignore how "none of the RFK sisters appears to have suffered a turbulent youth or later moral failings." In fact, the oldest Kennedy grandchild, Kathleen, has "none of the rakehell appetites of the Kennedy men," and founder of the *Washington Monthly*, Charlie Peters, calls her "the embodiment of the best the family represents. She's stayed loyal to the true faith." The sisters Michael is sandwiched between, Kerry and Courtney, are both active in humanitarian issues, and Rory, the baby of the family, is a serious documentary filmmaker who focuses on social justice issues. Even reformed addict Bobby Jr. is now described as "messianic" in his impulse to continue his father's work. "After my father died, I had a feeling I should pick up the torch...er, pick up the flag," he tells reporters.

The attitude toward the family is still rather askance after these latest scandals, however, and after examining his poll numbers, in August 1997 Joe Kennedy decides to bow out of the governor's race. Earlier that year, the president of the Massachusetts Women's Political Caucus, Samantha Overton, had noted, "Everyone I know was saying Joe Kennedy could just walk right into the governor's office," but after the "one-two punch" of the annulment and babysitter scandals, women voters are no longer looking favorably on Joe. "I don't know if he can get beyond it," she'd cautioned at the time, and it seems Joe agrees.

The most unexpected media blow comes from one of their own.

In the September 1997 issue of his pop-political glossy magazine, *George,* John F. Kennedy Jr. appears to take a potshot at his troubled cousins. In an issue that evokes the Garden of Eden, with a photo of Kate Moss and a snake on the cover and JFK Jr. himself with an apple in the interior (both seemingly nude), the editor's letter John Jr. writes references "temptation" and "desire" and "the distraction of gawking at the travails of those who simply couldn't resist."

He goes on to specify how "two members of my family chased an idealized alternative to their life" and in so doing, "became poster boys for bad behavior." Paraphrasing Grandma Rose's favorite Bible verse, John Jr. writes, "To whom much is given, much is expected, right? The interesting thing was the ferocious condemnation of their excursions beyond the bounds of acceptable behavior. Since when does someone need to apologize on television for getting divorced?"

Multiple media outlets pick up on the phrase "poster boys for bad behavior" as proof of John Jr. chastising and attempting to distance himself from his cousins. Despite Joe himself having previously appeared on *Good Morning America* a few months earlier to also decry his brother's "bad behavior," he's clearly miffed at being lumped in with Michael in John Jr.'s magazine, and lashes out: "I guess my first reaction was 'Ask not what you can do for your cousin, but what you can do for his magazine.'" Kathleen takes a more tempered view, saying of their cousin

John, "I think he probably wishes he hadn't written it. I'm sure he wishes that."

Lingering resentments are expected to blow over, however, and be largely forgotten. "A year from now, Michael and the Baby Sitter and Joe and the Annulment will have joined Amy and Joey and Donald and Marla in the landfill of tabloid dreck," predicts *Time* magazine.

But unfortunately, it would only be a few months before Michael Kennedy is back in the headlines.

CHAPTER 52

The past year, 1997, has been a challenging one for the Kennedy clan, and for Bobby and Ethel's sons in particular. Even so, former JFK speechwriter and family intimate Ted Sorensen tells the *LA Times,* "It's a family that is accustomed to both controversy and criticism. Sometimes withstanding it is all you can do—just accept it and go on."

Holding their heads high and soldiering on is something the family has long been taught to do. As Lem Billings—for whom Michael LeMoyne Kennedy is named—used to remind the younger generation after the deaths of Jack and Bobby, "Remember what Grandma Rose used to say: 'Never forget that you are a Kennedy. A lot of work went into building that name. Don't disparage it.'"

"The Kennedys all take care of each other," Beth Dozoretz, a Washington Democratic activist, remarks. "They have an overwhelming sense of a continuing commitment to public service, through all the trials and tribulations of their lives," says Thaelia Tsongas Schlesinger, a Massachusetts Democrat.

Despite his setbacks, Michael's family encourage him, "You're a *Kennedy*. You have to pull it together." Pulling oneself together and moving on is "just Kennedy 101," his cousin Patrick insists.

As 1997 comes to a close, Michael Kennedy is among extended family and friends congregating for the holidays in Aspen, Colorado, as they do nearly every Christmas season. Even though their divorce is imminent, Michael's estranged wife, Vicki, is also staying in nearby Vail with her father and stepmother, Frank and Kathie Lee Gifford. "Probably the central thing in Michael's life was his wife and his children," Michael's friend Larry Spagnola remarks. "It was his intention to reconcile."

On New Year's Eve, Michael and about twenty friends and relatives—a group that includes his younger brother Max and sister Rory, plus his three children—gather near the 11,212-foot-high summit, awaiting their last run down Aspen Mountain. They're about to play a favorite Kennedy game, known as "ski football." "They hang at the top of the mountain till everybody is off the hill, so they don't endanger anybody else," a family friend says of the game, which involves skiing downhill while tossing a small foam football back and forth. "It is Kennedyesque. There is a lot of laughing, vigor, excitement and a big rush."

There are conflicting reports as to whether the family has been warned earlier that week against playing the made-up sport, but the daredevil game is certainly rife with potential danger.

The possibility of disaster doesn't bother Michael, whom longtime friend James Hillard notes "really had a tremendous drive for living on the edge. Whether it was kayaking or skiing, he just did it." It's not a new attitude, or even exclusive to Michael. The Kennedy cousins are known to goad each other to jump from extreme heights, and Bobby Jr. notes of their child-hood, "If we went more than two weeks without a visit to the emergency room, it was unusual."

And in a family known for daring athleticism, Michael is touted as the best of them all. His brother Max calls him "an un-believably good athlete," and Joe agrees, remarking on Michael's "amazing physical gifts" and deeming him "fearless—on the slopes, on water skis, wherever he could test himself at the edge."

Bobby Jr. claims Michael's "the greatest athlete of our gener-ation," and notes, "In all my life I've never seen anyone ski as beautifully as Michael." Even Bob Beattie, a former US Olympic ski coach, has praised Michael's talent for skiing. "Michael is the best skier, a tremendously gifted athlete who could ski downhill backwards and blindfolded," another friend notes. He's confi-dent enough to not only forgo his ski poles but often to video-tape the action as the group tosses and receives the brightly colored foam ball, though on this occasion the *New York Times* notes that it's his ten-year-old daughter who is "videotaping their antics."

They've played this game many times before, including ear-lier that week. The columnist R. Couri Hay, who was present on New Year's Eve, says, "Michael is the ringleader, without question," and recalls that the previous game had ended in a tie. "Then they said, 'We'll play tomorrow—death to the loser.'"

It's mild weather, a little after four o'clock in the evening, and the group is about halfway down the run when Michael calls out to his buddy Blake "Harvey" Fleetwood, "Pass me the ball, Harve!" Michael catches it. He's looking uphill and considering where to throw the ball again, not realizing he's about to collide with a three-foot-wide spruce tree.

"Stop! Stop!" Rory tries to warn her brother.

But it's too late.

Michael crashes headfirst into the tree and is knocked unconscious.

"There was blood all over the snow," says R. Couri Hay.

Michael's sister Rory is the first to reach him. She races over and begins administering CPR. "Michael," she tells him, while others move to shield the two from the children's view, "now is the time to fight. Don't leave us!"

Paramedics from the ski patrol arrive within minutes and take over CPR as the children yell, "It's my father! Please help my daddy!" R. Couri Hay recalls, "Several of the Kennedys were on their knees saying the Lord's Prayer."

The paramedics work feverishly to stabilize Michael's neck with a cervical collar, loading him onto a toboggan for emergency transport to Aspen Valley Hospital. "On-mountain treatment included intensive cardiac care, spinal immobilization, and respiratory support," a prepared statement from the resort reads.

Despite best efforts, Michael Kennedy is pronounced dead at Aspen Valley Hospital at 5:50 p.m. The Pitkin County coroner's office notes cause of death is multiple injuries from blunt-force trauma to the head and neck, and is deemed accidental. No trace of drugs or alcohol are found in his body.

Aspen Club Lodge bellman and driver Matthew Malone recalls picking up a female passenger at 6:00 p.m. that evening, with instructions to bring her to the hospital. "Should I drop you off at Admissions or Emergency?" he inquires, to which she responds in a "tone sharp with anger and sorrow.

'He's dead. Wherever you go for that.'"

CNN reports that Michael's body is flown home to Hyannis Port on actor Kevin Costner's jet, and shortly after he is buried next to his brother David, near their grandparents, Joe and Rose.

It's a sadly familiar scene, stoic Kennedys in mourning.

"We don't know what to make of another Kennedy death," Kevin Sowyrda, a Massachusetts Republican political analyst, tells the *Washington Post*. "We almost expect it now."

"The Kennedys play too hard and live too hard," one former White House correspondent observes. "They push the envelope, and sometimes it blows up."

Others are more compassionate.

Boston's Mayor Thomas Menino says, "I don't know anyone who can match the sort of continuum of sadness this family has had," adding, "Maybe that's the price you pay for great glories."

To a packed church of mourners and hundreds of spectators, Michael's brothers Bobby Jr. and Joe eulogize him, focusing on his achievements in business and human rights. "He was not made for comfort or ease," Joe remarks. "He was the athlete dying young of A. E. Housman's verse: 'Like the wind through the woods, through him the gale of life blew high.'"

"He died, three years sober, on a forty-degree day under a blue sky in the company of his children, his family, and friends he loved," Bobby Jr. says. "He caught the ball, turned to a friend, and said his final words: 'This is really great!' The last thing he saw was his children. The next thing he saw was God."

Even in a year as difficult as 1997, the Kennedys still celebrate "a nugget of happy news," as the *New York Times* proclaims when announcing the birth of Ethel and Bobby's twenty-first grandchild on May 22.

Both Courtney Kennedy (the fifth of Ethel and Bobby's brood, between brothers David and Michael) and her husband of four years, Paul Hill, are in their forties when their first and only child, Saoirse (pronounced "Searsha") Roisin Hill, is born.

"I couldn't understand a word he said," Courtney recalls of first hearing Paul's thick Belfast accent, "but I thought: 'He's gorgeous.'" They meet in 1990, when Courtney is recovering from a broken neck sustained in a skiing accident, and Paul—an Irishman known as one of "the Guildford Four"—is recently released from fifteen years in prison for an IRA bombing he didn't commit, as dramatized in the Oscar-nominated 1993 movie *In the Name of the Father*. (Ironically, Courtney's cousin Caroline Kennedy had once nearly been the victim of an IRA bombing herself. In October 1975, when she was seventeen and living in London, a bomb under the car Caroline was scheduled to take exploded prematurely, tragically killing a neighbor, a renowned cancer researcher.)

Courtney has a particular affinity for the Kennedys' ancestral land, recalling the feeling of her first visit to Ireland as a teenager, "I felt like I was at home." Her aunt Jean Kennedy Smith begins a five-year ambassadorship to Ireland in 1993, the year of Paul and Courtney's marriage.

Reclusive Courtney, according to *Vanity Fair*, is "the most sensitive and emotionally vulnerable of the [RFK] bunch." She also grapples with lifelong depression, though she doesn't blame it on the circumstances of her upbringing. "My difficulty was being able to say 'I'm a Kennedy and I'm suffering from depression.'"

That she and Paul name their daughter Saoirse—which means "Freedom" in Gaelic—is profound, but Courtney wavers on passing along the Kennedy. "I just thought it would be one name too many," she explains. Though at first the sole Kennedy grandchild not to use the name, in later years Courtney's daughter seems happy to claim it, signing her name "Saoirse Kennedy-Hill."

In 2002, Courtney and Paul decide to move their family to Ireland, where they can bring their daughter up in a "less manic" environment. "Being here," Courtney notes, "is the best medication I can think of," for her lingering depression. And Saoirse, both her parents say, is "very Irish." The marriage doesn't last, however, and when the couple separates in 2006, Courtney and Saoirse, then eight years old, move back to the United States.

Courtney's cousin Timothy Shriver calls his niece "an only child with a hundred brothers and sisters," and her uncle Bobby Jr. agrees, saying, "She became a sister or daughter to a hundred Kennedys, Shrivers, and Lawfords. We all considered her our own."

Bobby Jr. affectionately calls her "an outgoing imp with a rebellious nature, an irreverence towards authority and deep commitment to mischief," attributes he says are likely inherited from her parents—Courtney and Paul.

Nevertheless, like her mother, Saoirse suffers from depression. At age eighteen, she bravely writes a personal essay in Deerfield Academy's paper, the *Deerfield Scroll*. "Although I was mostly a happy child, I suffered bouts of deep sadness that felt like a heavy boulder on my chest," Saoirse explains, urging her high school classmates and community to be more compassionate. "We are all either struggling or know someone who is battling an illness; let's come together to make our community more inclusive and comfortable."

Saoirse also helps found Deerfield Students Against Sexual Assault, motivated by her own experience. "I did the worst thing a victim can do," she reveals, "and I pretended it hadn't happened. This all became too much, and I attempted to take my own life."

She graduates in 2016, moving on to Boston College as a communications major and vice president of the College Democrats. Bill Stone, a fellow BC student, describes Saoirse as "very kind, funny, bright, smart," but adds, "I knew she had her demons."

She also possesses great empathy. In 2014, on the thirtieth anniversary of her uncle David's death more than a decade before she was born, she addresses David online: "You were a kind, gentle spirit that went through unimaginable struggles in your life," she writes. "It saddens me to know that we will never meet in this world, but I know I will see you up in heaven with my grandfather, Uncle Michael, and other family members."

Her words come true far sooner than anyone could have expected.

Twenty-two-year-old Saoirse spends the night of July 31, 2019, in Hyannis Port—finishing up some schoolwork and watching the Democratic presidential debates with her ninety-one-year-old Grandma Ethel. Later, although "she wasn't a partier or anything," a family source notes, she heads out with a friend for a night of karaoke and dancing, ending with a sunrise swim.

And then, as her uncle Bobby put it, "Saoirse woke up with God."

Emergency workers respond to a call at the Kennedy compound for a suspected overdose at 2:30 p.m. on August 1, 2019, but it's already too late. Though unresponsive, Saoirse is rushed to the hospital, where she is declared dead. Three months later, on November 1, 2019, toxicology results reveal "methadone and ethanol toxicity as well as other prescription medications were found in Hill's system," though her death is ruled accidental.

"If anyone ever wondered whether God loves the Kennedys," Bobby Jr. says during his eulogy for Saoirse in Our Lady of Victory Church on August 5, 2019, "the proof is that he gave us Saoirse, this brilliant beam of light and laughter."

While there have been a few other sad losses (Ted's daughter, Kara Kennedy, age fifty-one, and Patricia's son Christopher Lawford, age sixty-three, both die unexpectedly from heart failure in 2011 and 2018, respectively), Saoirse's tragic death reignites public curiosity about the family, whose younger generation is more often known for who they're dating than for what political roles they may be taking.

The juiciest gossip stories involve Bobby Jr.'s son Conor, who dates singer Taylor Swift in 2012 while he's still a high school student at Deerfield Academy; his cousin Patrick Schwarzenegger (son of Eunice's daughter Maria Shriver and Arnold Schwarzenegger, the movie-star-turned-politician), who has a relationship with pop star Miley Cyrus in 2015—while his sister Christina Schwarzenegger simultaneously dates Miley's brother Braison Cyrus; and their older sister, Katherine Schwarzenegger, is best known for marrying actor Chris Pratt in the summer of 2019.

John F. Kennedy biographer Robert Dallek remarks that the Kennedys are "a case of triumph and tragedy, great success and terrible suffering, and in many ways it's the American story" especially poignant in today's more jaded era. People are "reverting back to the Kennedys," he opines, "to hold on to something that they admire."

Although there is a brief blip in 2012 when Ted's son Patrick chose not to seek reelection to the Rhode Island House of Representatives, W Magazine points out that, "Every year between 1947 and 2011, and then from 2013 onwards, at least one Kennedy family member has held federal elective office." It's Bobby Jr.'s son Joe Kennedy III who steps in to continue the legacy; in 2013, at age thirty-two, he takes over retiring Barney Frank's seat in Congress, and is reelected in 2014 and 2016. "All eyes have been on Joe to continue to carry the torch for the family," biographer J. Randy Taraborrelli points out.

But a 2010 opinion piece in Brookings notes, "One-quarter

of the Kennedy cousins have been treated for drug or alcohol abuse, which is well above the national average. For all the glamour associated with the family, it seems that it is not easy, psychologically or emotionally, being a Kennedy."

As Ethel Kennedy herself says, "Being a Kennedy isn't for the faint of heart."

PART EIGHT

The Prince

JOHN FITZGERALD KENNEDY JR.

CHAPTER 53

John Fitzgerald Kennedy Jr. has been famous since before he was born—on Thanksgiving Day, November 25, 1960, just weeks after his father is elected the thirty-fifth United States president.

The president-elect is riding in the Kennedys' private plane (the *Caroline*, named for John Jr.'s older sister, who will turn three two days later), when he is briefed that "Jackie has been rushed to the hospital" and is undergoing an emergency cesarean section. "I'm never there when she needs me," Jack is overheard to worry. Jackie's pregnancies have been difficult before—although Caroline was born healthy, Jackie previously suffered a miscarriage along with the devastating stillbirth of their first child, Arabella (and will later endure the heartbreaking loss of yet another child, Patrick, in 1963). Though this baby is not due for another month, given her history of complications, a cesarean had already been planned for December 12. As soon as they land at Palm Beach International Airport, Jack immediately charters an American Airlines D-6 for a return flight to Washington. Shortly after 1:00 a.m., while still en route, the announcement of the baby boy's birth is made over loudspeaker to applause from those on board. Captain Dick Cramer passes his headset to JFK so he can hear for himself that mother and child are "doing well."

"It was really something, wasn't it?" Jack says of his son's unexpected arrival. Reporters standing outside the Kennedys' home at 4:35 a.m. that morning note, "He was particularly pleased when asked the name of his son. 'Why, it's John F. Kennedy Jr.,' he said, almost reverentially: 'I think she decided—it has been decided—yes—John F. Kennedy Jr.'" Though it delights him, in years to come, Jackie tells several people that she regrets giving their son Jack's name. "We would never have named him John after his father if we had known what was going to happen," she says. According to biographer Steven M. Gillon, "The irony is that in the effort to honor her husband, she inadvertently made her son's life more challenging."

At thirteen days old, John Jr. is baptized at Georgetown University Hospital's chapel. Jackie chooses her sister Lee's husband, Prince Stanislas Radziwill, as godfather and Martha Bartlett—who first introduced Jackie to Jack—as his godmother. While posing for press photos, Jackie holds her son, saying, "Isn't he sweet, Jack? Look at those pretty eyes." John's "pretty eyes" are brown like Jackie's, not blue like Jack's.

The first baby to live in the White House since 1893, John Jr. makes headlines with every move. "Gift for Kennedy Baby," the *New York Times* reports on the stuffed donkey, rabbits, and dogs that Madame Charles de Gaulle presents the new parents at the French Foreign Ministry on May 31, 1961.

In advance of his first birthday, White House press secretary Pierre Salinger reports, "John Fitzgerald Kennedy Jr. still has a cold and will not be brought [to Hyannis Port] for a joint birthday observance with his sister Caroline," who turns four on November 27.

Citizens even vote on John Jr.'s "Little Lord Fauntleroy" hairstyle, which Jackie allows to curl over his collar. Dollar bills arrive at the White House along with instructions for Jackie to cut John Jr.'s hair (she refuses, though Jack reportedly asks Maud Shaw, the children's nanny, to at least trim his son's bangs, and to blame it on the president if Jackie objects).

Jackie revels in her role as mother, setting up play groups and a small kindergarten for Caroline at the White House, along with a tree house and a swing set for both children on the South Lawn. Caroline is even allowed to ride her pet pony, Macaroni, on the White House grounds; the sight of the happy little girl on her horse delights tourists and visitors (including singer/songwriter Neil Diamond, who credits the image as providing the inspiration for his beloved hit song "Sweet Caroline").

Jack is also an involved father, one who, Jackie says, "loved those children tumbling around him," and is often seen teasing and playing with John Jr. and Caroline. "It was John's treat to walk to the [Oval] Office with him every day," Jackie recalls. He'd often let them romp around the Oval Office, resulting in a famous series of photographs of John Jr. playing under the president's desk. He also enjoyed telling them stories. "He didn't like to read books to them much. He'd rather tell them stories. He'd make up these fantastic ones . . . you know, little things that had to do with their world," Jackie recalls.

Arthur Schlesinger Jr. also remembers JFK telling the children stories that featured themselves on grand adventures—Caroline winning the Grand National or John Jr. sinking destroyers—and had one ongoing story about a white shark that ate socks. "One day, when the President and Caroline were sailing with Franklin Roosevelt Jr.," Schlesinger says, Jack "pretended to see the white shark and said, 'Franklin, give him your socks; he's hungry.' Franklin promptly threw his socks in the water." Not only does this greatly entertain Caroline, but as biographers Collier and Horowitz point out, it's "an oblique pun on that day twenty-five years earlier when his father [FDR] had asked Joseph Kennedy to drop his pants." Crucially, Lem Billings notes, everyone learns that when Jack starts in on those tales, "it was time to move to another part of the yacht" or risk having to feed the sharks, too.

The children are doted on by the public, but Jackie does her best to impress upon them that their time in the White House is temporary. "I'd tell them little stories about other Presidents and [how] there would be a President after Daddy," she recalls, "so they never got to think that all this was going to be forever."

Jackie often takes John Jr. and Caroline out of Washington to Glen Ora, the four-hundred-acre horse farm they rent in Middleburg, Virginia, where they can be a little less in the spotlight, and she can participate in rituals like nightly baths and reading stories. "Jackie wanted her kids to have what she grew up with, and to make their lives normal and fun," a friend recalls. "She applied effort and ingenuity to that."

"I don't want my young children brought up by nurses and Secret Service men," Jackie tells the *New York Times*.

She also does her best to pass along her love of horseback riding to the children, but nothing compares to John Jr.'s true love: flying. John Jr. takes his first airplane ride—from Washington to Palm Beach—at fifteen days old, and his obsession with it never wavers. Even his Secret Service code name, "Lark," is prescient.

Jack indulges his son's fascination with flying machines, taking him on helicopter rides and letting him "fly" his toy version on the floor of the president's secretary's office. Nanny Maud Shaw says that even as a toddler, John Jr. "liked to put on the pilot's helmet and push the control stick around and press the buttons, flicking the switches and making all the right noises for starting up and taking off," and recalls "one wonderful memory of the time I went looking for John on a Saturday afternoon. This time I had a good idea where he would be—down in the hangar. Sure enough, he was. And so was the President. Both of them were sitting at the controls of the helicopter with flying helmets on. The President was playing the game seriously with his son, taking orders from Flight Captain John, thoroughly absorbed in the whole thing. I retreated quietly and left father and son very happy together."

Joe Sr.'s nurse, Rita Dallas, also fondly remembers John Jr.'s childhood obsession with planes. "He adored airplanes and did everything he could to 'bum a ride' on anything that flew," she says, adding that JFK often tries to accommodate him, but when he couldn't, he instead leaves John Jr. a little toy plane. "He must have bought them by the gross," Dallas notes, "for they were everywhere." In a White House photo of John Jr. dated January 21, 1963, the smiling two-year-old is seen with a glossy press photo of Marine One airborne over the South Lawn, and a double-rotor replica model within reach.

The toy planes "usually pacified young John," Dallas says, "but if it failed, the President would bend down and whisper in his ear, 'You fly this one, son, and as soon as you grow up, Daddy's going to buy you a real one.'" John Jr. would make him solemnly promise, at which point, "Little John would run off telling everyone the news. He'd tug at us, wave his toy plane, and say, 'My daddy's going to get me a real one when I grow up.'"

John Jr.'s passion for airplanes and helicopters is so fierce, JFK reveals some concerns over what they'll do "when he's old enough and wants to learn to fly," as he tells his aide Kenneth O'Donnell, who also recalls how John Jr. "would race over and get on a helicopter, and when it came time for us to leave, he refused to get out of it," to the point that "the poor Secret Service would take John kicking and squabbling off the helicopter or the plane."

One such incident is recorded in an AP photo dated October 3, 1963, which shows the toddler "weeping bitterly" over being left behind when Jack boards Air Force One on a flight to Arkansas. Not even a return flight to the White House by helicopter consoles him. Similarly, Ted Kennedy recalls another photo that "showed John racing across the lawn as his father landed in the White House helicopter and swept up John in his arms. When my brother saw that photo, he exclaimed, 'Every mother in the United States is saying, "Isn't it wonderful to see that love between a son and his father, the way John races to be with his father?" Little do they know—that son would have raced right by his father to get to that helicopter.'"

Soon John and Caroline will see their father off on his last flight out of Washington. On November 21, 1963, Jack and Jackie board Marine One for a chopper ride to Andrews Air Force Base, where Air Force One will take off for Carswell Air Force Base in Fort Worth. The next time John wants to see his father, he will have to look at a photograph.

Or a painting.

In December 1963, shortly after vacating the White House for President Lyndon and Lady Bird Johnson, Jackie, Caroline, and John are living in a house belonging to JFK's undersecretary of state, W. Averell Harriman, on Washington's exclusive N Street.

Secretary of Defense Bob McNamara and his wife, Marg, who are close to Jackie, send over two portraits of Jack. But Jackie's grief is so fresh, she can only bear to look at a single photograph of her husband, one that shows his back, not his face. She props the paintings in the hallway, intending to return the thoughtful yet distressing gift.

Before she can, three-year-old John Jr. spots the portrait of his father at eye level, and he kisses it, saying, "Good night, Daddy." Despite John Jr.'s sweet reaction, Jackie sees it as proof that the emotional danger of having Jack's image close by is too high.

The paintings are returned.

CHAPTER 54

Suddenly, in 1968, John and Caroline gain a new member of the family: stepfather Aristotle Onassis.

When JFK made his spring 1961 state visit to France, President Charles de Gaulle was fascinated by the "unique" Jackie, predicting to his Minister of Culture, Andre Malraux, "I can see her in about ten years from now on the yacht of a Greek oil millionaire."

He's only off by a few years.

After Bobby's assassination in June 1968, Jackie has an ever-present fear: "If they're killing Kennedys, my kids are number one targets." More than anything else, it fuels in her a desire to leave the United States. It also opens her up to the possibility of remarrying.

Although she has several other suitors, Jackie is most drawn to millionaire Greek shipping magnate Aristotle Onassis, despite the twenty-three-year age gap between them. She fondly credits Onassis for the comfort he offered her in August 1963, when she traveled to Greece while in mourning over the death of her son Patrick. Onassis had been crucial in buoying her spirits back then.

Perhaps he could do so again now.

More than anything, Jackie's former assistant says, "I think she was very lonely. She needed somebody to talk to."

Jackie herself agrees, telling one former suitor, "I know [my marriage] comes as a surprise to so many people," but that Onassis understands her situation, and "wants to protect me from being lonely. And he is wise and kind."

"Not a single friend thought Jackie should marry Onassis," journalist Peter Evans remarks. "But now that Bobby was gone, there was no one who could stop her."

On October 20, 1968, Jackie and Onassis marry on Skorpios. "We are very happy," Jackie tells reporters. Patricia Kennedy, who attends the wedding, tells her mother, Rose, that the bride did seem happy—leading Jackie's former sister-in-law and mother-in-law to conclude, "Who wouldn't be with 400 or 500 million dollars and a ruby [a wedding gift from Onassis], which is worth $1,000,000?"

But another guest had a harsher take, observing that "It was like a business transaction," and that "Jackie's glance kept turning anxiously toward Caroline." Jackie's ten-year-old daughter and seven-year-old son are candle-bearers at the ceremony. Afterward, just as Charles de Gaulle had foreseen, the couple holds their wedding reception aboard Onassis's luxury yacht, *Christina*, named for Onassis's then-seventeen-year-old daughter. ("The fabled vessel," proclaims *People* magazine, "remains in a class of its own," and has been site to several other celebrity wedding celebrations, including that of movie star Grace Kelly and Prince Rainier III of Monaco in 1956, and supermodel Heidi Klum and musician husband Tom Kaulitz in 2019.)

But the devotees of the Camelot legend Jackie created are shocked that she is rewriting the ending. "Jackie, How Could

You?" pleads a Swedish newspaper headline. On what would have been her fiftieth wedding anniversary to Onassis, the *Washington Post* reflects:

"Fifty years ago, the world mourned the end of Jacqueline Bouvier Kennedy.

'The reaction here is anger, shock and dismay,' declared the *New York Times.*

'The gods are weeping,' read a quote in the *Washington Post.*

A German newspaper announced: 'America has lost a saint.'

But Mrs. Kennedy hadn't died. She had only become Mrs. Onassis."

The marriage is not destined to last as long as that, however. Although the former First Lady—thereafter nicknamed "Jackie O"—says "Aristotle Onassis rescued me at a time when my life was engulfed in shadows. He meant a lot to me. He brought me into a world where one could find happiness and love." From the start they tend to live two separate lives. Jackie's assistant recalls, though, that in addition to being famous for his extravagant gift-giving—according to *Newsweek,* he buys John a speedboat, a jukebox, and a Jeep—Onassis "was a good father to John and Caroline," who "would sit with them at the dining room table and ask how was school. He might have been an older man, but he paid attention to them, and they loved him."

Still, Jackie never cuts the ties she's been building with the Kennedy family for fifteen years, as a daughter-in-law, and as a protector of heirs to an American dynasty. "Her [Caroline's] father was gone, but her mother never flinched or withdrew from her obligations. She handled the loss, as a widow and mother, quietly and taught her only daughter the grace of dignity," Rita Dallas observes of Jackie. "After her marriage, she still maintained her home on the compound and saw to it that both of her children remained Kennedys."

But Jackie's new union is clouded by a second premonition—one far more troubling than de Gaulle's. Just as Jackie had sensed when she met Jack that he "would have a profound perhaps disturbing influence on her life," Onassis's daughter, Christina (who is not a fan of her new stepmother), similarly believes that she will bring tragedy upon her father, cruelly blaming Jackie for the deaths of her husband and brother-in-law. When a number of Onassis's business ventures start to downturn—and, most tragically, after his son Alexander is killed in a plane crash in January 1973—Onassis's health takes a sudden decline. He bitterly reflects on his daughter's warning (though Christina's prediction may have been self-fulfilling: in 1988, she dies of a heart attack determined to be caused by years of drug abuse), and he and Jackie separate, though they do not officially divorce.

"I was a happy man before I married her," Onassis takes to saying. "Then I married Jackie and my life was ruined."

By February 1975, Onassis is dead. Now forty-five, Jackie is again a widow

And it's back to being just Jackie, Caroline, and John Jr.

CHAPTER 55

Shortly after JFK's death, Jackie had feared her own wish to die would prevent her from being an effective parent, especially a solo one. "I'm no good to them. I'm so bleeding inside," she tells her confidant, Father Richard T. McSorley. For a time, she contemplates accepting Ethel's offer to raise Caroline and John Jr. among their cousins at Hickory Hill, but Father McSorley cautions against that arrangement, citing the public and family pressures on Ethel. "Nobody can do for them except you," he says.

Not to mention that Ethel and Jackie have nearly diametrically opposite approaches to parenting. Kennedy biographer Jerry Oppenheimer notes, "John, after his father's death, was brought up by a controlling and domineering mother, but one who obsessively looked out for his care and well-being." Conversely, life at Hickey Hill among Bobby and Ethel's children is much more rough-and-tumble, and later, after Bobby's death, Ethel's "moods could swing drastically," Oppenheimer writes. Grief makes Ethel alternately neglectful or abusive, and the troubled kids lash out. (Bobby Jr. even starts a gang he calls "The Hyannis Port Terrors.")

Jackie listens to Father McSorley's counsel and instead moves her family of three from Washington to New York City's Upper East Side, where she grew up. They move into a five-bedroom, five-and-a-half-bath apartment spanning the entire fifteenth floor of a limestone prewar building at 1040 Fifth Avenue, with views of Central Park and the reservoir (eventually named for Jackie in 1994). Between interest from Kennedy family trusts and an annual government widow's pension of ten thousand dollars, Jackie has an income of approximately two hundred thousand dollars a year. Impressive, even by today's standards, but for Jackie it requires careful spending. The Kennedy family friend Chuck Spalding voices the impossible challenge: "Jackie on a budget?"

All that changes, of course, after her brief marriage to Aristotle Onassis—money is not something she need worry about again—but even beforehand, one thing Jackie can afford to give her children is personal independence. Although she threatens the Secret Service, "If anything happens to John, I won't be as nice to you as I was after Dallas," she insists her son "must be allowed to experience life," citing the dire consequence that "unless he is allowed freedom, he'll be a vegetable."

But only so much freedom. In the spring of 1973, Caroline (now fifteen) begins to exhibit the same obsession with flying machines her now twelve-year-old brother has shown since before the age of three. Lem Billings, without telling Jackie, brings the siblings to Hanscom Field in Middlesex County, Massachusetts, where a flight instructor takes Caroline up in a Cessna. *"Me too,"* John begs, but he is too young.

When Jackie learns what Lem has done, she puts a stop to it. "We cannot tempt fate in this family," Jackie tells Benedict F. Fitzgerald Jr., Rose and Joe Sr.'s attorney as well as a licensed pilot. "We've had enough tragedy. I will never let my children fly. Never."

Jackie understands better than anyone what disasters have come from the longstanding Kennedy tradition of pressing the odds. On hand for Ted's protracted recovery following his 1964 plane crash, Jackie is privy to the dramatic yet accurate opinion of family physician Dr. Watt, who says, "These people [the Kennedys] are jumping all over the place. Joe Jr. was warned that his plane had a problem. Kathleen was on a small plane. Ted tried to find a pilot who would fly in bad weather when his crash occurred." Not only that, but Ethel has also lost both her parents and her older brother to plane crashes, and just months earlier, Jackie's twenty-four-year-old stepson, Alexander Onassis, suffered the same fate.

Jackie is far more tolerant of earthbound adventures. When thieves set upon thirteen-year-old John Jr. in Central Park and steal his pricey Italian bicycle, Jackie says "the experience was good for her son, that it would help him to grow up like other boys."

Jackie did send teenage John to boarding school at prestigious Phillips Academy in Andover, Massachusetts. The English instructor and dorm master Meredith Price remembers, "When he was in tenth grade, he was full of life and somewhat happy-go-lucky. There was absolutely nothing pretentious about him."

"He had to deal with some incredible pressure," John Jr.'s school friend Jim Bailinson remarks, but notes, "He turned out remarkably normal for someone who led such an abnormal existence. He did totally normal teen stuff, but his mother kept a pretty tight rein on him."

The new student lives with a roommate, and, since he's never taken public transportation, has to ask how the bus system works (though as an adult, he prides himself on navigating New York City's public transit). Jackie "was a great boarding school mother," sending cookies and care packages and coming for visits with Caroline. "Not all parents are attentive as she was," Price says.

John Jr. uses his natural charm to "push the disciplinary envelope at Andover," fellow alumnus and author William D. Cohan notes. "He didn't intentionally flaunt the rules as much as sort of pretend they never really existed in the first place, since it was pretty clear from his own experiences in life that the rules of the road would never apply to him anyway."

Admissions officers at Brown University see evidence of this when in 1979 Jackie completes John Jr.'s undergraduate application for him, since John is out of the country on an educational trip to Africa. She is careful to avoid trading on the famous Kennedy name. On the application, Jackie merely lists his late father's occupation as being "in government" and that "mother, sister grew up in New York City."

John Jr. may have opted out of traditional Kennedy alma mater Harvard, but not the academic struggles that his father and uncles variously encountered. When John fails to complete his freshman-year coursework, Jackie writes to a Brown official in July 1980. "I have never asked for special consideration for my children because I feel that is harmful to them," she explains, "but there was an extra burden John carried this year that other students did not—and I would like to mention it. He was asked to campaign almost every weekend for his uncle." She is referring to Ted Kennedy, then in the thick of his ultimately failed quest for the 1980 Democratic presidential nomination.

At school, John Jr. is naturally popular, even though he had the "bad habits of borrowing money and of losing his wallet, which occasionally had some borrowed money in it," says Cohan. *Newsweek*'s Martha Brant writes of John's need "to borrow a quarter every night for coffee," contextualizing, "Like many rich people—including his own father—Kennedy often has to borrow cash, and he is sometimes forgetful about paying it back."

John Jr. graduates in 1983 with a bachelor's degree in American studies, and returns to New York. While at Brown, he had pursued a passion that sparked at Phillips Andover—acting—and on August 4, 1985, John makes his off-off-Broadway debut at the Irish Arts Center on Manhattan's West Side, starring in Brian Friel's *Winners,* set in Northern Ireland. On stage, he can be his character (a Catholic teenager with a pregnant fiancée), not a Kennedy. In the climactic scene, John plays a drowning victim (which many viewers consider loaded with symbolic reference to Chappaquiddick), though his mother and sister are out of town throughout the play's six-show run and never see him perform.

"He's one of the best young actors I've seen in years," director Nye Heron recalls of John Jr., but feels he lacks the focus and determination needed to hone his natural talent to a professional-level skill. "John's problem as an actor was that he didn't take it seriously," says Don Wilmeth, who directed John in Brown Theater Department productions. "He did it for fun and lacked discipline. He would work hard for short stints and then go off and lose it."

"It's only a hobby," John tells reporters, mainly for Jackie's benefit. When he talks of applying to Yale School of Drama, his mother steers him away from the stage and toward the courtroom. He lands at New York University Law School, earning his degree in 1989. In May 1990, the *New York Post* trumpets the humiliating news—"THE HUNK FLUNKS . . . AGAIN"—of John's second failed attempt to pass the New York State Bar Exam. "I am very disappointed," he tells the press. "God willing, I will be back [to take the test] in July. I am clearly not a legal genius."

Even though John's been working under the watchful eye of

Manhattan district attorney Robert M. Morgenthau (who was with Bobby at Hickory Hill when J. Edgar Hoover called to break the news of JFK's death), should he fail the test a third time, he'll be forced to leave his position. In July 1990, he passes, is appointed assistant district attorney, and in August 1991, wins his first victory at trial. "This case would have posed serious difficulties for any defense," says veteran lawyer William Kunstler of the robbery defendant known as the "Sleeping Burglar" (apprehended while napping in his victim's apartment, pockets filled with her stolen jewelry), but John Jr. takes the high road, declaring, "Winning is better than losing."

CHAPTER 56

Despite Jackie's repeated warnings of the dangers of paparazzi ("Don't let them steal your soul," she tells him), John Jr. continues to live his life fully in the public eye. Photographers swarm to document his string of celebrity girlfriends—including Cindy Crawford, Daryl Hannah, and Sarah Jessica Parker—and his frequent, bare-chested outings in Central Park, where he Rollerblades and plays Frisbee with his dog, Friday. Photographer Victor Malafronte recalls "trying to get this gorgeous image of the man skating down West Broadway," when John stepped in for a handshake. "Hi, I'm John" (his preferred form of address—no middle initial or suffix; the "John-John" nickname was used purely in the press). "I was blown away," Malafronte says, and so are the editors at the *New York Post* and *People,* who deem his close-up pictures cover-worthy.

In the summer of 1988, twenty-seven-year-old John Jr. starts dating thirty-year-old pop star Madonna (still technically married to, but estranged from, actor Sean Penn). John and

Madonna quarrel over how to handle fame—she seeks it; he shuns it. According to J. Randy Taraborrelli, they're running through the park, arguing. "I'm just a guy," John says. An eyewitness takes in Madonna's response. "You're not 'just a guy,' you're a *Kennedy*."

That September, *People* magazine names John F. Kennedy Jr. 1988's "Sexiest Man Alive." But according to his personal assistant RoseMarie Terenzio, John has a major hang-up about one aspect of his appearance. "He hated his hair," Terenzio says. "He was constantly putting stuff in it to hold it down. That's why he always wore a hat, 'cause he hated his hair."

"Whenever he would get on one of those best-dressed lists," recalls Richard Wiese, a college friend, "we would just howl." Just as Rose always criticized Jack for sloppiness, John Jr. "would always be walking around with some stain on his shirt. He was a mess."

Of the magic of Camelot, Richard Goodwin, a former aide to JFK and RFK, observes that Jackie's creation is in little peril—if only its caretakers remember that "magicians are only as good as their last illusions."

In 1993, John Jr. finally chooses to seek out light from the Kennedy flame. While still employed by the city of New York, he and his friend Michael Berman approach potential investors with a concept for a political magazine. John is less than receptive to concerns over limited interest in the topic. "It was the worst presentation I have ever seen in my life," says one publisher who took the pitch. "He was like, 'I'm JFK, so there you go.'"

In an interview with JFK Jr. biographer Steven M. Dillon, Berman reveals a unique duality in his business partner. "It must be interesting to be you," he says to John in a crowded restaurant dining room, watching heads whirl in recognition of the son of the late president. "You don't know a soul here, but they all know who you are."

"That's not the weird part," John answers. "The weird part is they all remember [JFK], and I don't."

John was only two years old when his father was killed, after all—he spent his third birthday famously saluting his father's casket. But he's reluctant to delve deeper into the meaning his name carries, or the accompanying responsibility. "It's hard for me to talk about a legacy or a mystique," Kennedy states in 1993. "It's my family. The fact that there have been difficulties and hardships, or obstacles, makes us closer."

Of his sister Caroline, John Jr. tells Oprah, "We're obviously very close. As a younger brother, you look up to your sister. I was the 'man' of the family, as it were. I feel so lucky to have such a close relationship with her."

He's especially close with his cousins on his mother's side, his aunt Lee Bouvier Radziwill's children, particularly his cousin Anthony. "Anthony was more of a brother than a friend to John. He was the closest family member to John and they really did grow up together. They remained close throughout their lives and they spoke nearly every single day," RoseMarie Terenzio recalls.

Anthony's wife, Carole Radziwill, agrees, saying, "Given the life that John led so publicly, I think he really felt completely himself around Anthony. He knew Anthony had his back, and Anthony felt the same way about him. That was a nice thing to see, and it was nice to be around—that feeling of complete trust."

John's relationships with his Kennedy cousins are mainly warm if somewhat distant, and occasionally competitive. Chris Lawford describes the relationship between John Jr. and Joe, Bobby's oldest son, as the most fraught. "I think he [Joe] loved

John, hated John, and wanted to *be* John all at the same time," Chris says, pointing out that rivalry among the cousins is to be expected, after all: "We were all, every one of us, raised to be President."

As authors Collier and Horowitz remark of the Kennedy cousins in their 1981 book, *The Kennedys,* "Together in one place, they looked like a remarkable experiment in eugenics—several strains of one particularly attractive species." Eunice's children are "darkly handsome...with their father's sensitive eyes and their mother's aggressive jaw"; Teddy's kids are "blond and surprisingly frail"; Jean's children have a "round-face impassivity"; while Pat's have her ex-husband's "good looks—and a hint of his troubled vulnerability"; and Bobby's kids have the "big bones and imposing size of Ethel's family." Unsurprisingly, Caroline and John Jr., "posing for nonstop photography since infancy...had acquired a poise all the others lacked."

But the authors also note that Bobby and Ethel's children (who tend to see themselves as "the most Kennedy") "would sometimes tell their cousins, 'You're not Kennedys, you're only Shrivers [or Smiths or Lawfords].'" They taunted John Jr. as a "'Mama's boy' and said he wasn't a 'real Kennedy.'"

To the rest of the world, though, no one embodies the Kennedys more than John Jr. "I understand the pressure you'll forever have to endure as a Kennedy, even though we brought you into this world as an innocent," his mother writes him. "You, especially, have a place in history. No matter what course in life you choose, all I can ask is that you and Caroline continue to make me, the Kennedy family, and yourself proud."

John Jr. is thirty-three when Jackie dies at age sixty-four on May 19, 1994, not long after receiving a diagnosis of non-Hodgkins lymphoma. In her eulogy, Ted names Caroline and John as "her two miracles." At Arlington National Cemetery, under a headstone reading "Jacqueline Kennedy Onassis," she is buried alongside JFK, only the second First Lady, after Mrs. William Howard Taft, to be so honored.

So it falls to Ethel, the new Kennedy matriarch, to assess the latest woman to appear in John's life: twenty-eight-year-old Carolyn Bessette, who was voted "Ultimate Beautiful Person" at Catholic St. Mary's High School in her hometown of Greenwich, Connecticut, and is now head of public relations at the fashion label Calvin Klein. "She's an ordinary person," John tells his friend John Perry Barlow, but "he couldn't get his mind off her."

Barlow, best known as a former lyricist for the Grateful Dead, finds Carolyn charismatic, quirky, and a little reminiscent of Jackie herself, but after a Labor Day weekend introduction to the Kennedy clan at the Hyannis Port compound, where Carolyn fails miserably at Kennedy political and athletic gamesmanship, Ethel is less impressed. "I'm afraid Carolyn isn't everything she portrays herself as being," she tells her son Joe. Citing the knowledge that comes with raising four Kennedy daughters, Ethel adds, "If there's one thing I know, it's girls. Trust me, that one is all smoke and mirrors."

"Oh, he definitely chased her," says Brian Steel, who works alongside John as a Manhattan assistant district attorney, in an interview for the ABC documentary *The Last Days of JFK Jr.* "Early on he would be frustrated. He would say, 'I called her and she hasn't called me back.'"

Carole Radziwill recalls John, her husband's cousin, being "really besotted" with Carolyn. "He was so enthralled with her, and she with him, but she was kind of fierce. She was very confident. He liked that. She was very much her own person. She was this great combination of kind of seriousness and wild child," she says.

Carolyn's elusive behavior is reminiscent of Jackie's resistance to Charles and Martha Bartlett's "shameless" matchmaking between her and Jack. And like then, it works—by the spring of 1995, Carolyn and John Jr. are living together, and over the Fourth of July 1995, during a fishing trip on Martha's Vineyard, John proposes. Carolyn "held the proposal off for about three weeks"—just as Jackie had done when she traveled to London to cover Queen Elizabeth II's coronation—"which I think just made him all the more intent on marrying her," a friend of the couple tells *People*.

The engagement story, broken by the *New York Post* just before Labor Day, nearly overshadows John's other surprise announcement, scheduled for September 7, 1995: that he's launching a new magazine. "For almost two and a half years," he tells *USA Today*, "it was like I didn't have a job. I was sort of [developing this magazine] in secret and everyone was like, 'What's John been doing with his time?'"

The answer is *George*, a celebrity-tinged political magazine backed by publisher Hachette Filipacchi which debuts with a double issue in October/November 1995. The inaugural issue features a cover portrait by celebrity photographer Herb Ritts of supermodel (and former JFK Jr. flame) Cindy Crawford, dressed as a midriff-baring George Washington.

"He called my hotel," Cindy Crawford recalls of John's request she be his first cover model. "He reached out directly. And who's going to say no?"

The first two issues sell out and break magazine-industry financial records, and the unusual office atmosphere quickly becomes the stuff of publishing legend. Two associate editors recall going "rollerblading with John in Central Park at midnight. And it was just the fucking coolest."

But not even the novelty of JFK Jr. as publisher can easily overcome the substantial challenges of publishing expensive-to-produce glossy magazines profitably. Even in the early glow of success, investors are on watch.

John and Carolyn live together in John's TriBeCa loft at 20 North Moore Street, and at times publicly reveal that each of them possesses a tempestuous temper. On February 25, 1996, during a heated argument in Central Park, Carolyn removes her engagement ring and throws it at John. The entire exchange is photographed, and worth a quarter of a million dollars to the *National Enquirer*.

"That video was terrible for her, because it framed her as this sort of mean harpy," says George Rush, one half (with his wife, Joanna) of the *New York Daily News* gossip column Rush & Malloy. "She never recovered from that branding, really."

Six months later, however, on September 21, 1996, when the *George* magazine staff believes John and Carolyn are traveling in Ireland, the couple is actually exchanging wedding vows. The ultraprivate ceremony takes place on remote Cumberland Island off the coast of Georgia, once a retreat for Carnegies and Rockefellers, in a hand-built, wood-frame First African Baptist Church. The church, lit only by natural light and candlelight, has personal and historic significance. On November 22, 1963, islanders gathered there to mourn John's father, President John F. Kennedy.

But today, thirty-three years later, it's a celebration—and hardly anyone knows it's happening. "If Mr. Kennedy wanted privacy, this was a good place to find it," says a Cumberland Island official from the National Park Service. "We were so excited to have fooled everybody," says one of only a few dozen guests, who include Oprah Winfrey, multiple Kennedys, and John's cousin and best man, Anthony Radziwill. His sister, Caroline, is the matron of honor, and her three children are the flower girls and ring bearer.

Staffers at the local Greyfield Inn sign confidentiality agreements about the wedding and reception details, and a fifty-person security team is brought in to cover the island—"In other words," one outlet later notes, "there was more security than wedding guests."

Carolyn wears a bespoke Narciso Rodriguez white silk crepe bias-cut gown that to this day inspires the flattery of imitation. "There is something mysterious and female in the world, and she has a good connection to it," says John's friend John Perry Barlow of the bride. "It's deep and primordial and lovely."

But the feeling of privacy is fleeting. The couple is recognized three days into their Turkish honeymoon. Two weeks later, at home in New York, John begs the relentless paparazzi for "any privacy or room you could give" his new bride. The *New York Daily News* translates John's polite plea into tabloid language: "JUST LEAVE HER ALONE."

For John, the paparazzi are a part of life. The demands of fame he feuded over with Madonna back in the late 1980s have only intensified. "We're used to a certain degree of being watched," he tells Oprah in a September 1996 interview not long before the wedding. He's only half joking when he says that if he weren't a Kennedy, "you wouldn't have invited me on your show." As RoseMarie Terenzio observes, "John was never not famous. He was born famous. So for John, it was a part of his life."

For Carolyn, however, it's a much bigger adjustment. "There were times when I went to their apartment on Moore Street, and you would see the paparazzi just waiting outside, behind cars, in cars, just on the sidewalk for her to leave her apartment," Carole Radziwill recalls. "A lot of times we wouldn't leave. We would order food from Bubby's on the corner. Who wanted to leave and have to go walk through that? That was, like, every day of her life for the first year or more."

CHAPTER 57

On Friday, July 16, 1999, a Justice Department special arbitration panel meets in Washington, DC. In a split yet binding decision, the members order the US government to pay the Zapruder family sixteen million dollars for rights to the twenty-six-second film made by Abraham Zapruder, the one-of-a-kind documentation of the assassination of President John F. Kennedy.

The dollar amount tops any price previously paid for an American artifact. But before news of the record-breaking award ever hits the wire, it's held for an even bigger story—a triple fatality.

The name dominating the headlines is once again Kennedy.

⊙≋⊙

In December 1997, a student calling himself "John Cole" registers for pilot training at the Flight Safety Academy in Vero Beach, Florida. On April 22, 1998, he earns his private pilot certificate, licensing him to fly under visual flight rules (VFR) and returns for further study of instrument flight rules (IFR).

"To Flight Safety Academy, The Bravest people in aviation," the student—a no-longer-incognito John F. Kennedy Jr.— inscribes a personal photo to his flight instructors, "because people will only care where I got my training if I crash."

On one of John's trips to Vero Beach, he visits the local Piper Aircraft factory and makes a three-hundred-thousand-dollar purchase—a 1995 Piper Saratoga II. The single-engine aircraft, though used, is an upgrade from his starter plane, a Cessna Skylane.

John is finally realizing his childhood dream of flying. He likes to study at the CJ Cannon's restaurant at the local airport, where he can watch the planes take off and land. On several occasions, waitress Lois Cappelen and her famous customer talk about Jackie ("She was very strict with me," John shares with her. "Caroline could get away with anything, but I always had to be good"), the Kennedys, and finally, flying. "He said he had wanted to fly all his life," Cappelen recalls. "But he told me his wife didn't want him to do it." (Or his mother, who'd taken Lem Billings to task for allowing Caroline to try it. Unbeknownst to Jackie, John had actually begun flight training fifteen years earlier, while he was a student at Brown in 1982, but never completed it.)

However, John tells *USA Today*, "The only person I've been able to get to go up with me, who looks forward to it as much as I do, is my wife. The second it was legal she came up with me." At the Martha's Vineyard airport restaurant, Carolyn tells another waitress, Joann Ford, a markedly different story. "I don't trust him," Ford recalls Carolyn saying of her husband's flying.

Still, on May 1, 1999, Carolyn does agree to a flight with John, from New York to Washington, for the White House Correspondents Dinner. The DC appearance is part of John's exploratory process; he's considering running for the seat a four-term Democratic senator from New York has decided to vacate in the year 2000. He also needs to invigorate support for *George*, the ad sales of which are declining just as Jack Kliger is taking over as new CEO of Hachette. Some staff changes in January 1999 have also raised eyebrows with business insiders, though John is still touted as having "brilliant editor instincts." And everyone understands the cachet he brings. "Would this magazine exist without John?" the *Observer* notes. "Would anyone delude themselves that it would?"

The couple makes an indelible impression on White House reporter Helen Thomas. "They never looked more content and in love than they did that evening," she recalls. "My God, this is Jack and Jackie all over again, isn't it? They were so compelling, you actually couldn't take your eyes off them. The way photographers swarmed them. It really reminded me of the old days, the so-called Camelot days."

The feeling of romantic nostalgia is persuasive, but it might be a performance. According to friends of the couple who speak off the record to the press, John, thirty-eight, and Carolyn, thirty-three, are in marital counseling, working through issues salaciously reported as including infidelities on both sides, John's insensitivity toward his wife, and Carolyn's increasingly erratic behavior, often attributed to prescription and recreational drug use—though Carole Radziwill counters those claims, saying, "That's not the truth of what was going on." What they were all actually dealing with, she says, is her husband Anthony's impending death from cancer. "I'm not going to sugarcoat it. It was a very difficult, stressful summer for all of us," she says. "My husband was dying, and it was difficult for John to really accept that."

John's friend and personal assistant RoseMarie Terenzio agrees. "Anthony's [cancer] was emotionally devastating to

John," she tells a reporter at Fox News. "I think John knew that Anthony's passing would change his life profoundly. I don't think we were ready for it. I don't think he could have ever been ready for it."

On July 14, 1999, *George* staffers overhear John Jr. shouting into his office phone, presumably to Carolyn, "That's it. You've gone too far. Get your stuff, get out of my apartment and get out of my life."

John checks into an uptown hotel.

Terenzio quickly gets Carolyn's side of the story. "I'm not a priority," Carolyn tells her. "It's always something else. *George*. Somebody getting fired. An event. A trip to Italy to meet advertisers."

John's cousin Rory Kennedy (Ethel's youngest daughter, the one born six months after her father's assassination) is getting married in Hyannis Port three days later, on July 17, 1999. John Jr. tells Terenzio that he'll be attending solo, as Carolyn is adamant that she doesn't want to go. But somehow Terenzio and Carolyn's older sister, Lauren (a thirty-four-year-old investment principal at Morgan Stanley Dean Witter), convince her. Lauren is hopeful that the trip might help her sister and brother-in-law reconcile.

"Come on," Lauren says. "It will be fun."

On Friday, July 16, John and Lauren drive together from Manhattan to meet Carolyn on the tarmac at Essex County Airport in suburban Fairfield, New Jersey. The two-leg flight will first stop in Martha's Vineyard, where Lauren will attend a cocktail party with her new love interest, John's cousin Bobby Shriver, a forty-five-year-old film and television producer.

John Jr. arrives at the airport on crutches, still recovering from a broken ankle he'd sustained in a Memorial Day weekend paragliding accident. He needs the full strength of both legs to work the controls on his new plane.

"You know just enough to be dangerous," comments friend John Perry Barlow. "You have confidence in the air, which could harm you...You're going to find yourself flying in instrument conditions because you think you can."

By FAA standards, he can't. Not yet.

A little over two weeks earlier, on July 1, John Jr. flew the Saratoga to Martha's Vineyard alongside a certified flight instructor who must assist in taxi and landing because John's ankle was still in a cast. The instructor states, "The pilot was not ready for an instrument evaluation and needed additional training."

Nevertheless, there will be no assistance on tonight's flight, even though John is on crutches as he makes the flight preparations, including a check of the National Weather Service's aviation forecast. Since he will be flying under visual flight rules, he is not required to file a flight plan.

According to the *New York Post*, "Not only was Kennedy suffering emotional ups and downs that day, he was still taking Vicodin to relieve the pain of a recently broken ankle, plus Ritalin for attention-deficit disorder and medication for a thyroid problem." The thyroid problem is known as Graves' disease (similar to the Addison's disease his father suffered).

Carolyn is the last to arrive, having done some last-minute shopping for the perfect dress to wear to the wedding. She calls her friend Carole Radziwill from the plane, a little after 8:00 p.m. "I remember at the end she said, 'I love you.'...For some reason, I didn't say I love you back, and that always stuck with me. And she said, 'I'll call you when I land.' And that was the last I ever heard from her."

As dusk falls and the weather reports take a turn, an experienced pilot named Kyle Bailey cancels his own planned flight to Martha's Vineyard. Another pilot, Roy Stoppard, who has just flown down from the Cape, tells John Jr. that he "ran into a thick haze on the way down" and that John "might want to wait a while."

"No chance," John answers. "I'm already late," exhibiting an attitude that experienced aviators like Bailey and Stoppard call "get there-itus."

A flight instructor offers to join the flight as copilot, but John says "he want[s] to do it alone" even though a spokesman for the Aircraft Owners and Pilots Association later explains, "Flying at night over featureless terrain or water, and particularly in haze or overcast, is a prime set-up for spatial disorientation, because you've lost the horizon."

The flight takes off at 8:38 p.m., and at 8:40, John Jr. makes his sole radio transmission of the flight. "North of Teterboro. Heading eastward."

By 8:49 p.m., there is already a problem. In his ascent, John has erroneously strayed into the airspace of an American Airlines Flight 1484, descending toward Westchester Airport with 128 passengers and 6 crew on board.

Air traffic controllers are able to redirect the American Airlines flight in time to avoid a midair collision, but radio communications make it clear that John is at fault.

FLIGHT 1484: "I understand he's not in contact with you or anybody else."

CONTROLLER: "Uh nope doesn't [sic] not talking to anybody."

At a cruising altitude of 5,500 feet, John Jr. guides the Piper Saratoga through thirty minutes of smooth airtime. Then the haze that the pilots on the ground in New Jersey had warned of envelops the plane.

At just after 9:34 p.m., John is seven and a half miles from the Martha's Vineyard airport. Private pilot Michael Bard, who had returned to Connecticut from Martha's Vineyard about twenty minutes earlier, describes the conditions as "very hazy, and it was very dark, and it was very hard to see the horizon." Under those conditions, Bard tells the *New York Times,* "if you're not instrument rated, it could be difficult maintaining the airplane in an upright condition."

Radar records the plane's erratic descent from 2,200 feet at 9:40, dropping several hundred feet every few seconds, the altimeter spinning toward zero as the Piper goes into a "graveyard spiral" that may have lasted as long as thirty seconds.

At 9:41 p.m., the plane disappears from radar.

At midnight, Carole Radziwill is startled awake by her ringing telephone. "Are they there with you?" a friend of John's is asking. "I'm at the [Martha's Vineyard] airport and they're not here."

Radziwill, a former reporter for ABC News, spends hours making calls. Around 2:00 or 3:00 a.m., she calls the Coast Guard. "I said, 'My cousin's missing.' He took the name, and there was a little bit of a gasp on the other end of the phone."

Rory Kennedy's wedding is postponed as the family gathers at the Kennedy compound to await news of John, Carolyn, and Lauren.

"If Jackie was alive," Ethel says, "I don't know how she would handle this. In fact I don't think she could bear it." She adds, "I always thought of Johnny as one of my own."

President Bill Clinton orders the deployment of USS *Grasp,* a navy recovery ship. Addressing complaints over preferential treatment for the Kennedys over citizen accident victims, Pentagon spokesman Kenneth H. Bacon says, "It's a family that has distinguished itself through public service for more than thirty years." By the next afternoon, crash debris begins washing up along the shore: Lauren's suitcase, a headrest and wheel from the plane, a bottle of prescription medication bearing Carolyn Bessette's name.

After a three-day search, on July 20, 1999, an underwater sonar camera locates the main cabin at a depth of approximately 120 feet off Aquinnah (known until 1997 as Gay Head). Its wings have been sheared.

On July 21, Senator Ted Kennedy and his sons, Patrick and Ted Jr., are aboard the *Grasp* to witness the recovery of John, Carolyn, and Lauren's crash-ravaged bodies. "It was very grim, very quiet and we left [Senator Kennedy] completely alone," one of the eight crew members recalls.

"At this moment, the weight of the successive tragedies crashes down on Ted. All these years," Kennedy adviser Lester Hyman explains, "Ted refused to see a psychiatrist or anything like that because there was just so much. He didn't think he wanted to open the can of worms. I can think of twelve tragedies in that family, at least, just one after another after another, and the one that almost broke him was John Kennedy Jr."

On July 22, John's long-held wishes for a burial at sea are honored, alongside his wife, Carolyn, and her sister Lauren. All three are cremated, and their ashes spread from a naval destroyer in the Atlantic, within a mile of the crash site. "Catholic priests conducted the thirty-minute civilian ceremony on the 'fantail' of the USS *Briscoe,* a guided missile destroyer," CNN reports, noting, "There is a provision allowing for such burials for people providing 'notable service or outstanding contribu-tions to the United States,'" and that "protocol allows sea burials for the children of decorated Navy veterans. President Kennedy was a naval officer wounded and cited for heroism in World War II."

Kennedy and Bessette family mourners are not far from where, in July 1995, John proposed marriage to Carolyn. "He asked me to marry him out on the water, on the boat," she told friends. "It was so sweet. He told me, 'Fishing is so much better with a partner.'"

They were together to the last. And now, forever.

"The water had more jellyfish in it than anyone had ever seen," Bobby Kennedy Jr. writes in his diary. "When they let go of the ashes, the plume erupted and settled in the water and passed by in the green current like a ghost. We tossed flowers onto the ghosts."

A private memorial service follows in New York, at Jackie Kennedy Onassis's parish, the Church of St. Thomas More on East 89th Street. As he had for his brother Bobby, and for John's mother, Senator Ted Kennedy delivers the eulogy for John Jr., who, he says, "seemed to belong not only to our family, but to the American family. The whole world knew his name before he did."

John's beloved cousin Anthony Stanislas Radziwill comes for-ward to read the Twenty-Third Psalm. Radziwill's wife, Carole, can't shake the feeling that "John's last hours were spent think-ing about Anthony's eulogy, and then it's Anthony who must read at John's funeral. And the whole time, he's thinking, 'It was supposed to be me.'"

Three weeks later, Anthony, too, is dead.

Lisa DePaulo, an original staffer at *George,* says, "I don't believe John ever fathomed that he would die at thirty-eight. He didn't buy into things like the Kennedy Curse. Stuff like that made him hurl."

In language befitting a Kennedy, Eunice Kennedy Shriver offers her own interpretation of the clan's repeated brushes with fate. "I've come to believe that it's not what has happened to our family that has been cursed as much as it's the fact that we've never been able to deal with it privately... If there's a curse, surely it's that."

On August 4, 1999, comes the announcement of the sixteen-million-dollar Zapruder settlement, held since July 16 due to the deaths of John, Carolyn, and Lauren. The *New York Times* reports, "The film's worth had been enhanced by the soaring prices commanded for Kennedy historical memorabilia in recent years."

Yet the latest pieces of the Kennedy story are emerging in fragments.

In a hangar at the U.S. Coast Guard Air Station on Cape Cod, investigators for the National Transportation Safety Board (NTSB) recover pieces of John's Piper Saratoga II, assembling them in an approximation of the aircraft's pre-crash configuration. The propeller shows "rotational damage" indicative of hitting the water while turning.

On July 6, 2000, the NTSB issues its Aviation Accident Final Report, citing pilot failure as the cause of the accident, and further explaining that "spatial disorientation as a result of continued VFR flight into adverse weather conditions is regularly near the top of the cause/factor list in annual statistics on fatal aircraft accidents."

John "made a stupid mistake," says Andrew Ferguson, president of Air Bound Aviation that operates out of Essex County Airport. "Like going through a stop sign. But when a Kennedy goes through a stop sign, there always seems to be an 18-wheeler truck coming from the other side."

CODA

By November 1969, lingering complications from Joe Kennedy Sr.'s 1961 stroke have turned end-stage. He's lost his appetite, his eyesight, his ability to breathe without the assistance of an oxygen tank.

"My poor Joe. How cruel, how cruel," Rose murmurs as she sits by her eighty-one-year-old husband's bedside. They have been married for fifty-five years.

On November 15, Jackie arrives with kind words for her beloved "Grandpa."

"I know he could sense the tears in her eyes," Joe's nurse, Rita Dallas, says.

Pat and Jean are next to arrive, then Eunice and Sargent Shriver. "Now," Dallas says, "Mr. Kennedy seemed to exist for only one thing—the sound of Teddy's footsteps."

Not four months have passed since Ted delivered his televised speech on Chappaquiddick from his father's house. "Dad, I've done the best I can," he said to Joe that night. "I'm sorry."

On November 16, Joe fails to recognize the sound of Ted's voice.

"Please answer me," Ted says, but Joe cannot. His father is dying, and Ted is convinced that his actions have pushed Joe toward his grave. "The pain of the burden was almost unbearable," he says.

On November 18, Rose brings a rosary to her husband's lips, then wraps it around his clasped hands resting on his chest.

The children are gathered in a semicircle around his bed. Eunice begins to recite the Lord's Prayer: "Our Father, who art in Heaven / Hallowed be thy name."

In turn, each sibling speaks a line. "Thy Kingdom come / Thy will be done / On earth, as it is in Heaven."

"Amen," Rose says, in blessing on the creator of the House of Kennedy.

He is dead.

Joe is buried in the Kennedy family plot at the Hollyhood Cemetery in Brookline, Massachusetts.

"As the twenty funeral cars moved away," the *Boston Herald* reports, "a woman in black, appearing to be in her sixties, knelt alone in front of the grave. She remained there for several minutes. The woman, who was well-dressed, walked alone and declined to give her name."

"I wonder if the true story of Joe Kennedy will ever be known," Rose Kennedy once said, according to an essay by Gore Vidal for the *New York Review of Books*. The same question is asked of any and all Kennedys, as the family story continues to be written—and lived.

In 2010, Juan Romero, the busboy who comforted Bobby Kennedy on the night he was shot, has more to say to Kennedy, and in person. Dressed in the first suit he ever owned, he travels to Arlington National Cemetery and stands at Kennedy's grave, marked with a plain white cross.

"I felt like I needed to ask Kennedy to forgive me for not being able to stop those bullets from harming him. When I wore the suit and I stood in front of his grave, I felt a little bit like that first day I met him. I felt important. I felt American. And I felt good."

As JFK himself predicted on October 26, 1963, days before his death, "A nation reveals itself not only by the men it produces but also by the men it honors, the men it remembers."

THE KENNEDYS TODAY

THE END OF AN ERA

Though many Kennedy lives have been cut short, Jean Kennedy Smith endures into her nineties.

By 2020, Jean—the eighth of Joseph P. Kennedy and Rose Fitzgerald's nine children—has seen all of her siblings laid to rest: from the early deaths of oldest brother, Joseph, and sister, Kathleen, in the 1940s, to the assassinations of brothers John and Robert in the 1960s, to the twenty-first-century deaths of sisters Rosemary, Patricia, and Eunice, and even the death of her youngest sibling, Ted Kennedy, two weeks after Eunice in 2009.

In contrast to her high-profile relatives, Jean is known as the "quiet" and "shy" member of the family who eschews the glare of the spotlight, despite her frequent proximity to it as sister (and sister-in-law—the *New York Times* notes that Jean befriended Ethel, Jackie, and Joan before they went on to marry her brothers Bobby, Jack, and Ted, respectively) to her more famous siblings; wife to Stephen Smith, who spearheads all three of her brothers' presidential campaigns; or mother to William Kennedy Smith, notorious for his 1991 rape trial in Florida.

But in 1993, Jean has a surprising third act all her own when President Bill Clinton appoints the then-sixty-five-year-old widow to serve as U.S. ambassador to Ireland—more than half a century after President Franklin D. Roosevelt named her father, Joe, ambassador to the United Kingdom.

Despite her lack of diplomatic experience, Jean is warmly embraced. "The Irish people were willing to take me at face value," she reflects, per the *New York Times,* "to give me the benefit of the doubt because I was a Kennedy."

And Jean uses that goodwill to leverage aggressive measures to achieve peace in Northern Ireland. Her work paves the way for a ceasefire in August 1994, and the historic 1998 Belfast Agreement between the British and Irish governments, later credited with helping to end much of the violence. "Jean may well be the best politician of all the Kennedys," historian and longtime Kennedy insider Arthur Schlesinger Jr. marvels to the *Irish Times* of her successes. In 1998, the same year Jean steps down as ambassador, Irish president Mary McAleese makes her an honorary Irish citizen.

In February 2011, President Barack Obama presents Jean with the Presidential Medal of Freedom. Among other efforts on behalf of people with disabilities—in keeping with the same spirit that led her sister Eunice to help establish the Special Olympics—Jean assists in founding the nonprofit organization Very Special Arts in 1974, dedicated to providing artistic programs to the mentally and physically handicapped.

After more than a decade as the last surviving sibling of President John F. Kennedy, Jean passes away in her Manhattan home on June 17, 2020, at the age of ninety-two.

Her death reminds scholars of "the triumphs of the family

and their great accomplishments that still shape our lives today," retired Boston University history professor Patrick Maney tells the AP. "The Kennedys still have a hold on us in a way that nobody since that time has held a generation spellbound."

"There's still something about the Kennedy mystique that remains," Maney says, even as the passing of the Kennedy torch from one generation to the next is complete.

"She lived a great life," one of Jean's four children, Kym Smith, tells CNN of her mother. "It is the end of an era."

AN UNEXPECTED TRAGEDY

Months earlier, in the spring of 2020, Bobby and Ethel's granddaughter Maeve Kennedy McKean—Kathleen Kennedy Townsend's daughter—relocates her family to her mother's vacant house on Chesapeake Bay in Maryland.

Maeve, a forty-year-old lawyer and mother of three, is known for her humanitarian efforts. Kathleen, the former lieutenant governor of Maryland, describes her daughter as "a Peace Corps Volunteer who pursued a career in law to give voice to the voiceless." Eunice Kennedy's son Tim Shriver calls his cousin's daughter "smart as a whip, tough as nails, and kind as a human being can be." Maeve serves in the Obama administration as a human rights senior adviser, and as an executive director of Georgetown University's Global Health Initiative.

But on the afternoon of Thursday, April 2, 2020, Maeve McKean's primary focus is a kickball match with her oldest child, her eight-year-old son, Gideon.

During their game, the ball gets kicked into the water, a relatively shallow cove behind the house. Maeve and Gideon hop into a nearby canoe to retrieve it.

But the winds are stronger than expected—the Coast Guard reports twenty-nine-mile-per-hour winds and waves of up to three feet—and the little canoe is pushed out into the open bay. Neither mother nor son is wearing a life jacket.

About a half hour later, around 4:30 pm, a concerned citizen spots the two people in the canoe "trying to paddle to a ball," and immediately calls 911. Captain Russ Davies of the Anne Arundel County Fire Department says, "It looked like they were being pushed out into the water and were having a hard time returning to shore."

The *New York Times* reports that the Coast Guard searches more than 3,600 square miles via air, sea, and land for Maeve and Gideon, producing only their capsized canoe and paddle, miles away from where they entered the water.

"It is now dark again," David McKean, Gideon's father and Maeve's husband of eleven years, writes that Friday evening on Facebook. "It has been more than 24 hours, and the chances they have survived are impossibly small. It is clear that Maeve and Gideon have passed away."

When the Coast Guard suspends rescue efforts, Kathleen Kennedy Townsend issues a statement. "With profound sadness, I share the news that the search for my beloved daughter Maeve and grandson Gideon has turned from rescue to recovery."

The grieving mother and grandmother concludes: "My heart is crushed, yet we shall try to summon the grace of God and what strength we have to honor the hope, energy and passion that Maeve and Gideon set forth into the world."

Grandmother Ethel adds her condolences. "God bless Maeve and Gideon, who are up there in Heaven with Grandpa, David, Michael, Mary [Bobby Kennedy Jr's second wife, who passed away unexpectedly in 2012] and Saoirse. You have all my love—and you are in my heart and my arms are around you."

Tim Shriver tells *People* magazine that while their family is "lucky that we've been given—through our parents' generation and our grandparents' generation—a kind of strength in the face of adversity that sustains us," even so, "it's not enough to end the pain."

On Monday, April 6, 2020, Maeve's body is discovered about two and a half miles away from where the canoe had entered the water. Two days later, Gideon's body is located about two thousand feet away from his mother's. The medical examiner determines the cause of death to be accidental drowning.

The search and its grim resolution are national news, the latest tragedy suffered by a family that has already suffered so much.

"While the idea of a curse is something that should have been buried with the end of the middle ages, certainly this family is no stranger to very sad news," Peggy Drexler, a psychologist and author, writes on CNN's website, adding that the Kennedys "are proof that privilege doesn't shield anyone from catastrophe. And yet, they've largely soldiered on—bereft, diminished, surely, but undeterred. What could be more American than that?"

THE BOUNTY OF WAR

In June 2020, La Guerida, the "Kennedy Winter White House" in Palm Beach, Florida, makes headlines when *Forbes* reports that the legendary 1095 North Ocean Drive estate has just been sold, off-market, for a record $70 million—more than five hundred and eighty-three times the amount of the $120,000 purchase price (under $2.4 million in 2020) Joe Sr. paid in 1933. Of course, the Kennedy mystique is a unique value-add.

Though Joe Sr. officially designated La Guerida (loosely translated as "the bounty of war"—some sources claiming it was La Querida, meaning "the dear one," that somehow became portentously corrupted) his legal residence in 1941, for more than half a century, from 1933 until 1995, the Kennedys mainly use the home for family vacations and winter escapes.

According to the November 4, 1962, edition of the *Palm*

Beach Post-Times, after JFK's election "some 50,000" tourists troop past La Guerida to peer "at the high garden walls and the old weather-beaten Spanish-style doorway that gives entrance to the premises where the President and his family reside" in "but 16 rooms."

The *Post-Times* comparatively deems nearby Mar-a-Lago, with "more than 100 rooms" and "courtyards, patios, formal gardens and covered walks," the "largest and most ostentatious of the many mansions that have helped to make Palm Beach famous." Indeed, the original owner of Mar-a-Lago—Marjorie Merriweather Post, heiress to the General Foods Corporation fortune—envisions the property as a future Winter White House. Upon Post's death in 1973, she donates Mar-a-Lago to the United States, only to have the government reject her gift due to exorbitant maintenance costs. The estate is instead purchased by Donald Trump in 1985 for a mere $8 million—and in January 2017, Post's wishes are fulfilled when the new president-elect tweets, "Writing my inaugural address at the Winter White House, Mar-a-Lago."

For decades after President Kennedy's assassination, La Guerida continues to serve as a relaxing retreat for the ever-expanding Kennedy family, even as the home slips into genteel disrepair. ("The Kennedys have kept up the plumbing and electric and stuff, but it hasn't really been renovated in any manner since 1928," the *New York Times* quotes an architect.) After matriarch Rose's death in January 1995, the Kennedys decide to sell the furnished beach house for $4.9 million.

Future owners undertake massive renovations, though with care. "We do feel, to some degree, we're protecting a legacy," the home's owner tells the *Palm Beach Post* in 2001, convinced that JFK's "vision for our country may well have come from the fact that he was able to sit there on the lawn and reflect on where the country should go."

Twenty years on, in 2015, the property again changes hands, for $31 million. Its reconfiguration into an eleven-bedroom manse with over a dozen bathrooms and extensive outbuildings, gardens, and pool and tennis areas is closely watched; the *Palm Beach Daily News* calling the largely interior renovations a "rehabilitation-and-restoration project" while *Architectural Digest* describes it as "a careful top-down overhaul." The new owner observes that La Guerida "is part of the rich history of Palm Beach—it is fun to think of all the people who have spent time here and have walked these halls."

The latest $70 million purchase price more than doubles La Guerida's market value only five years earlier.

That's the kind of "bounty of war" certain to earn Joe Sr.'s approval.

HICKORY HILL HEIRLOOM

A fight over a personal and nostalgic item from a Kennedy residence brings one family member to legal blows in 2020.

Hickory Hill, a large nineteenth-century home located in McLean, Virginia, outside of Washington, DC, is purchased in 1955 by then-Massachusetts senator Jack Kennedy and his wife, Jackie, from the family of former Supreme Court justice Robert Jackson, only for Jack to resell it about a year later to his younger brother Bobby. Historian Carole Herrick notes, "The youthful energy of the charismatic, athletic Kennedy clan put an imprint on the estate simply by the way they lived."

Even after Bobby is assassinated in 1968, Ethel raises their family at Hickory Hill and remains there for another forty years.

In 2009, the family decides to sell—a move one former Kennedy aide calls "a shock; putting Hickory Hill on the market is like selling Mount Vernon." Ethel instructs each of the eleven adult children, all with families of their own, to choose a keepsake.

Kerry Kennedy, seventh of the eleven, picks a tall decorative urn. "It was something her parents treasured," the *Washington Post* reports, "because it was one of the few things they had that had also belonged to President Kennedy."

But Hickory Hill's new owners are loath to part with it, and instead agree to return the urn to Kerry in ten years' time. This agreement is both verbal and explicitly corresponded over email, but despite writing that they relinquish "any right to it" and stating that as of June 16, 2020, Kerry would be "free to take the urn," when Bobby's daughter attempts to reclaim the four-foot-tall heirloom in the summer of 2020, she is refused.

Herrick says that the new homeowners "relish the history of the property." But upon discovery that the urn actually predates the Kennedys by having first belonged to Justice Jackson, they now claim Kerry has no real right to it.

"Hire a lawyer," Kerry says the current owners tell her.

She does, and makes headlines when she sues for breach of contract.

Kerry's not about to let a piece of her history go without a fight.

"It belonged to the people who are so important to me," she says in the *Boston Globe*. "I'm going to put it in Hyannis Port, where my children live, my mother lives, all of my family comes every summer, so they can have this connection to our family's history."

HOME TOGETHER

The Kennedy family continues to march—or crawl—into the newest generation.

On August 10, 2020, Katherine Schwarzenegger—granddaughter of Eunice Kennedy and Sargent Shriver, and daughter of TV journalist Maria Shriver and actor and former California governor Arnold Schwarzenegger—reveals on Instagram that she and her husband of one year, actor Chris Pratt, have welcomed a baby girl, Lyla Maria Schwarzenegger Pratt.

Like any new parents, they are thrilled. Katherine's mother, Maria Shriver, at sixty-four a first-time grandmother, tells *Today* show co-host Hoda Kotb that awaiting the baby brings "a little light" during the 2020 coronavirus quarantine, when "we don't really have much to look forward to."

Maria also finds another co-host in her twenty-six-year-old son, Patrick, with whom she creates an interview series on Instagram Live called "Home Together."

"Staying at home is a form of service," Maria tells *ET*, "because our leaders are asking us to stay at home to help out healthcare workers." The show, she explains, is "our form of being of service, trying to highlight all these nonprofits and people that are doing remarkable things."

"It's everyone coming together to do their part," Patrick says.

Caroline Kennedy—the only surviving child of JFK and Jacqueline Bouvier Kennedy—also tells Savannah Guthrie on *Today* of "seeing courage all around us." Caroline and her son, Jack Schlossberg, announce in May 2020 that they intend to award the John F. Kennedy Profile in Courage Award to frontline heroes battling the COVID-19 pandemic, with the ceremony to take place "when it is safe to gather in person."

Joining in the Kennedy tradition of public service and advocacy are Maria's brothers, Tim and Mark Shriver.

Tim, who is also chairman of the Special Olympics, organizes "The Call To Unite," a twenty-four-hour live-stream event. On May 1 and 2, 2020, hundreds of boldface names—including Oprah Winfrey, Julia Roberts, Yo-Yo Ma, and presidents George W. Bush and Bill Clinton—gather to inspire goodwill.

"People are very divided," Tim tells *Forbes*. "So we wanted to take this moment to say, 'We need each other now more than ever.'"

Mark, the next youngest Shriver sibling and CEO of the Save the Children Action Network, also chooses May 1, 2020, to launch a monthlong Virtual Advocacy Summit alongside the not-for-profit World Central Kitchen. Acclaimed chef and founder José Andrés concludes an online chat with Mark by saying that "small gestures by all of us" allow for the formation of "a very powerful army of good."

And like with baby Lyla, the family still takes time to celebrate milestones and uphold traditions—as when Eunice Julia Shriver, Anthony Shriver's daughter, dons her namesake grandmother's vintage Dior wedding dress from 1953 for her own intimate wedding in October 2020.

"The dress has aged into a French vanilla ivory, and there are a few holes in it, but I didn't care," Eunice tells *Vogue*. Extra precautions are taken in restoring the delicate dress, which fit perfectly at the waist but requires a bodice to be refashioned. "I was afraid to even sit!"

And her "something borrowed, something blue"? Grandmother Eunice provides that as well—Eunice's father, Anthony, lovingly restores his mother's baby blue 1965 Lincoln Continental, just in time to use it for his daughter's wedding.

"I just felt like all these parts of my grandmother were with me," Eunice relates to *Today*. "I felt like it was her making everything click."

TAKING REFUGE

In September 2020 on Martha's Vineyard, a huge public conservation project commences courtesy of the Kennedy family.

On January 16, 1978, Jackie Kennedy Onassis purchased Red Gate Farm for $1.1 million. The twice-widowed former first lady values privacy after her high-profile marriages and decades spent in the public eye, and she finds it at the former sheep farm, which spans several hundred acres near Aquinnah on the western tip of Martha's Vineyard. To design the grounds, the *Wall Street Journal* reports, Jackie hires her friend Bunny Mellon, who also worked on the White House Rose Garden when Jackie was First Lady.

While reminiscent of the Kennedy compound in Hyannis Port, Red Gate Farm is Jackie's solo project—possibly her first. "Forty years ago, my mother fell in love with Martha's Vineyard. When she found Red Gate Farm, it was the perfect expression of her romantic and adventurous spirit," Caroline Kennedy says when the family first begins exploring a sale of the property twenty-five years after Jackie's death in 1994.

(In 1999, there is a poignant familial connection when the private plane that Jackie's son John Kennedy Jr. is piloting goes down nearby, wreckage and debris from the fatal crash washing ashore near the property's private beach.)

In September 2020, Caroline reaches an agreement to sell three hundred and four acres (another approximately hundred acres, where family homes are located, are to be retained by the Kennedy-Schlossberg family) for a purchase price of $27 million. At less than half the listing price of $65 million, the below-market sale reflects special circumstances—the family has chosen to sell to local Martha's Vineyard land conservators.

"Our family has endeavored to be worthy stewards of this magnificent and fragile natural habitat, and its sites of cultural significance. We are excited to partner with two outstanding island organizations, and for the entire island community and the general public to experience its beauty," Caroline declares in a family statement.

The deal, set to close in December 2020, will rename the property "Squibnocket Pond Reservation," and there are plans for hiking trails plus beach and kayaking areas. Conservators state to the AP, "Upon completion of a standard biological species inventory and final management plan, the majestic dunes, windswept beach, kettlehole pond, wooded trails and open meadows will be open to the public."

There's a great deal of gratitude for Kennedy-Schlossberg's choice. "You've got to give credit where credit is truly due," the executive director of the Martha's Vineyard Land Bank tells the *Vineyard Gazette*. "They had many, many, many options and they chose conservation."

A MORAL COMPASS

In June 2020, Victoria "Vicki" Reggie Kennedy, Ted Kennedy's widow and the board president of the Edward M. Kennedy Institute for the United States Senate, released a statement saying, "Violence against black people and racism must end now. We stand in solidarity with millions of Americans across this country who have stood in peaceful protest against police brutality and the systemic discrimination that has, since the birth of this nation, denied equal justice to black Americans."

Vicki goes on to highlight Ted's Senate speech in support of the Civil Rights Act of 1964. "'We should use our powers not to create conditions of oppression that lead to violence,' he said, 'but conditions of freedom that lead to peace.' Those words are truer today than ever before."

And even more so upon the death of Congressman John Lewis in July 2020. Ted's niece, Kerry Kennedy, president of the Robert F. Kennedy Human Rights organization, honors the one-time Freedom Rider, calling him "the conscience of Congress, a civil rights icon" and "a moral compass for the nation." Lewis was not only a member of RFK Human Rights's board, but also a friend and ally to her father, Bobby.

"I truly believe something died in all of us," Lewis told Kerry of Bobby's assassination. "I know something died in me... That's why you have to keep going, moving on, and trying to inspire more young people to stand up, to get up."

It is in this spirit that Kerry further takes up the cause of bail reform and systemic racism. She writes op-eds in the *New Orleans Advocate,* calling bail "a racial justice issue" and stating in Memphis's *Commercial Appeal* that there "can be no justice if the laws and the administration of those laws protect those with means while punishing the poor." In the *Chicago Sun-Times,* she decries that the city's unnecessarily incarcerated are at heightened—potentially fatal—risk of the COVID-19 virus "spreading within the jail's walls." The Robert F. Kennedy Human Rights organization directs $60,000 to a $120,000 bailout fund. "The aim: to save lives and demonstrate the absurdity and inhumanity of detaining people pretrial because they cannot afford to buy their way out."

It's unlikely Kerry Kennedy anticipated the breadth of the coronavirus crisis or the racial justice groundswell behind Black Lives Matter protests (despite both being very much at the forefront for her ex-husband, New York governor Andrew Cuomo, with whom she shares three daughters). But even less likely—that she'd expected to spar with Harry Potter author J. K. Rowling.

Just a few months earlier, in December 2019, Kerry had presented Rowling with the Robert F. Kennedy Human Rights organization's Ripple of Hope Award, which "celebrates outstanding leaders who have demonstrated a commitment to social change." Previous recipients include Barack Obama, Archbishop Desmond Tutu, and Bono.

In her acceptance speech, Rowling notes her appreciation for receiving the award from Bobby Kennedy's daughter. "Robert Kennedy embodied everything I most admire in a human being," she says. "I count this one of the highest honors I've ever been given."

Eight months later, Rowling returns the award.

The issues begin in June 2020, with a series of tweets by

Rowling which draw fire for her apparently restrictive view of transgender people. Rowling pursues her position in subsequent Twitter posts and a lengthy entry on her website, continuing to escalate her argument to the point that on August 3, 2020, Kerry Kennedy feels compelled to address the matter.

In a statement on the Robert F. Kennedy Human Rights website, Kerry writes, "Trans rights are human rights. J.K. Rowling's attacks upon the transgender community are inconsistent with the fundamental beliefs and values of RFK Human Rights and represent a repudiation of my father's vision."

Rowling's response is to deny any transphobia. She laments that given "the very serious conflict of views between myself and RFKHR, I feel I have no option but to return the Ripple of Hope Award bestowed upon me last year." She adds, "No award or honour, no matter my admiration for the person for whom it was named, means so much to me that I would forfeit the right to follow the dictates of my own conscience."

A GOVERNMENT OF CHAOS

In late September 2020, Bobby and Ethel's grandson Max Kennedy Jr. (son of their ninth child, Matthew Maxwell Kennedy) reveals himself to *The New Yorker* as the anonymous whistleblower who'd contacted the House Oversight Committee back in April with serious concerns over how the administration was mishandling and purposefully downplaying the coronavirus crisis.

In March 2020, twenty-six-year-old Max Jr. volunteers for the White House COVID-19 Supply-Chain Task Force. "It didn't seem political—it seemed larger than the Administration," he says of his decision to work at a Republican White House, despite being a lifelong Democrat and the grandnephew of John F. Kennedy. But Max is jolted by the reality that he and about a dozen other young and untrained volunteers are meant to be "the entire frontline team for the federal government."

What he sees from inside the administration is "like a family office meets organized crime, melded with *Lord of the Flies*. It was a government of chaos."

Horrified at the lack of mobilization and by pressure to manipulate data and prioritize requests by supporters rather than by need, Max reaches out anonymously to Congress. "If you see something that might be illegal, and cause thousands of civilian lives to be lost, a person has to speak out," he says of breaking his nondisclosure agreement.

Unable to effect any change from within, Max quits the task force soon thereafter.

KENNEDYS IN OFFICE

It wouldn't be an American election cycle without some Kennedys in the mix.

Amy Kennedy is a New Jersey native married to Ted Kennedy's youngest child, Patrick J. Kennedy, who represented Rhode Island in the US House of Representatives from 1995 to 2011. In January 2020, Amy, a political neophyte, announces she's running for the Democratic nomination for the Second Congressional District in south New Jersey, challenging Republican incumbent Jeff Van Drew, a former Democrat who switched parties in December 2019. "I'm running for Congress because the future of our children, our country, and our world is being decided now, and everything is on the line," she says in a campaign video.

She stresses her experiences as a public school teacher, mother of five (four with Patrick, one from a previous marriage), and education director for the Kennedy Forum, which Patrick founded in 2013 to advocate for nationwide mental health and addiction treatment as evidence that she knows "the importance of instilling good values in our kids. But too many of our leaders have lost their moral compass."

Amy runs an anti-establishment campaign yet also draws on Kennedy connections. Martin Luther King III voices her radio ads, and her campaign literature features photos of John F. Kennedy's presidential inauguration and Ted Kennedy, her late father-in-law, with Barack Obama.

"The Kennedys as outsiders—that is how they're marketing this," her opponent in the Democratic primary, Brigid Callahan Harrison, incredulously tells the *Washington Post*. The strategy works, and by mid-October the *Philadelphia Inquirer* puts Amy up 5 points in the poll against Republican Jeff Van Drew, though by election day the race is considered a dead heat and too close to call. But three days later, it's evident that the party-switching incumbent has pulled ahead, and Amy Kennedy concedes.

In Massachusetts, the upset is more seismic.

Joe Kennedy III, son of Bobby and Ethel's oldest son, Joseph Kennedy II, has the air of a rising star powered by a decades-long, multigenerational family winning streak. He wages a primary battle against incumbent Massachusetts senator Ed Markey.

Up until that point, a Kennedy has never lost an election in Massachusetts (though Kathleen Kennedy Townsend and Mark Kennedy Shriver have each dropped US House races in Maryland). The widespread assumption is that Joe Kennedy III, the grandson of Robert F. Kennedy and grandnephew of John F. Kennedy and Ted Kennedy, will carry on this tradition; the polls give him a significant advantage from the moment he announces his candidacy in September 2019.

But by September 1, 2020, Joe is the one trailing in the polls, the family dynasty on the line.

Thirty-nine-year-old Joe has served Massachusetts's Fourth District in the House of Representatives since 2013. His announcement that he will forgo a fifth congressional term in order to challenge the seventy-four-year-old Markey comes as a surprise to many. Former Massachusetts governor and 1988 Democratic presidential nominee Michael Dukakis speaks for many when he tells *New York Magazine* that he's a fan of both Ed Markey and Joe Kennedy but not a fan of this contest: "I can't for the life of me understand why he [Joe] is putting us all through this to defeat a fine U.S. Senator."

As retired Massachusetts representative Barney Frank explains to the *Los Angeles Times,* running for office in 2020 may be more complicated than trading on one's political pedigree. "Kennedy got the benefit of being a Kennedy, but he also got the problem that it's hard to look like the challenging underdog."

An unusual comparison crops up between the two candidates—sneakers. Markey's old Nike Air Revolution high-top sneakers feature prominently in his advertising, a signal that he's a man of the people rather than a "legacy in a fancy suit with a compound," as the *Wall Street Journal* quotes Peter Loge, a George Washington University political communication professor. Massachusetts radio host Chris McCarthy publishes an op-ed saying Markey is "signaling he is 'woke' to Black Lives Matter with his sneakers," but notes that Nikes are made in China—while the response ad for Joe features New Balance sneakers, which happens to be a Massachusetts-based company. "The working people in places like New Bedford, Fall River, Attleboro, and Brockton understand the difference between Nike and New Balance and they are looking for a senator who does, too," McCarthy opines.

But Joe can't quite get out from under his famous last name. "President Kennedy's not on the ballot, my grandfather's not on the ballot, my dad's not," he says. "This is about me." But Markey flips the script, invoking JFK in a campaign ad. "We asked what we could do for our country. We went out, we did it," Markey says, adding, "With all due respect, it's time to start asking what your country can do for you." (Vicki Kennedy, Joe's aunt and Ted Kennedy's widow, takes umbrage at this, telling the *Boston Herald,* "It's not been about what somebody can do for us—ever. If you can figure out what it means to ask what your country can do for you, let me know.")

House Speaker Nancy Pelosi offers a late endorsement of Joe Kennedy, but it isn't enough. The tally on September 1, 2020, confirms what the polls have been saying: Markey collects 55 percent of the vote, an impressive ten-point victory.

"The senator is a good man. You have never heard me say otherwise," Joe tells his followers after conceding, subsequently teaming with Markey at a Massachusetts "unity event" supporting the Joe Biden/Kamala Harris presidential ticket. But Joe's political future—and his family's continued legacy—remains up in the air.

"The Kennedy name has lost some of its magic in the Bay State," Jim Manley, a longtime advisor to Ted Kennedy, tells the *Los Angeles Times.* "Things are changing, and a political dynasty doesn't mean what it used to."

Says Boston University presidential historian Thomas Whalen to the *Boston Herald*: "Joe Kennedy, unlike previous Kennedys, seems out of step with the times. For the Kennedys to move forward and remain relevant, they are going to have to rebrand themselves."

Then again, bouncing back is nothing new in the House of Kennedy.

NOTES

PROLOGUE

vi "Daddy. Oh, Daddy": Dallas, *The Kennedy Case*, 19.

vii "curse actually did hang": Joe McGinniss, "The End of Camelot," *Vanity Fair,* September 1993.

PART ONE
THE PATRIARCH: JOSEPH PATRICK KENNEDY

CHAPTER 1

4 "When my great-grandfather": Thomas Maier, *The Kennedys: America's Emerald Kings* (New York: Basic Books, 2003), 7.

7 "power came from money": Richard J. Whalen, "Joseph P. Kennedy: A Portrait of the Founder," *Fortune,* 1963 (Fortune Classics, April 10, 2011).

7 Hostile takeover attempts: Whalen, "Joseph P. Kennedy."

7 "learned from Daddy": Robert McCrum, "Eunice Kennedy and the Death of the Great American Dream," *Guardian* (UK), August 15, 2009.

8 "They were very conscious": Jean Kennedy Smith, *The Nine of Us: Growing Up Kennedy* (New York: Harper, 2016), 10.

8 83 Beals Street: Bruce Gellerman, "John F. Kennedy, a Son of Massachusetts," WBUR News, November 1, 2011.

8 "no place to bring up children": Maier, *The Kennedys,* 91.

8 1963 *Fortune* profile of Kennedy: Whalen, "Joseph P. Kennedy."

8 "why he hadn't told her": Ronald Kessler, *The Sins of the Father: Joseph P. Kennedy and the Dynasty He Founded* (New York: Warner Books, 1996), 38.

9 "Very, very happy times": "The Kennedy Family—Their Ties to Bronxville," *My Hometown Bronxville,* September 2, 2009.

9 "Home holds no fear for me": Edward M. Kennedy, *True Compass* (New York: Twelve, 2009), 30–31.

9 "Dinner at Uncle Joe's": Kessler, *The Sins of the Father,* 42.

9 "fly into a rage": Thomas Reeves, *A Question of Character: A Life of John F. Kennedy* (New York: Free Press, 1991), 34–35.

9 "taught us to listen": Adam Clymer, "Rose Kennedy Is Lauded for Her Faith," *New York Times,* January 25, 1995.

10 "burdens of business": Maier, *The Kennedys,* 74.

10 "Took care of children": Barbara A. Perry, *Rose Kennedy: The Life and Times of a Political Matriarch* (New York: W. W. Norton, 2013), 69.

10 "memory of mine": Rose Fitzgerald Kennedy, *Times to Remember* (Garden City, NY: Doubleday, 1974), 75.

10 "symbol of 'American efficiency'": Fitzgerald Kennedy, *Times to Remember*, 73.

10 "I see him on TV": Seymour M. Hersh, *The Dark Side of Camelot* (New York: Little, Brown, 1997), 15–16.

CHAPTER 2

11 "couldn't for the life of him understand": Gloria Swanson, *Swanson on Swanson* (New York: Random House, 1980), 331.

12 "just like Joe Stalin": Cari Beauchamp, "The Mogul in Mr. Kennedy," *Vanity Fair,* April 2002.

12 "wild meat": Robert Dallek, *An Unfinished Life: John F. Kennedy, 1917–1963* (New York: Little, Brown, 2003), 24.

13 Swanson's extravagant expenditures: Peter Sheridan, "Gloria Swanson: A Star Ahead of Her Time," *Express* (UK), August 17, 2013.

13 Average American income: Treasury Department Bureau of Internal Revenue, *Statistics of Income for 1927* (Washington, DC: Government Printing Office, 1929).

13 Gloria Productions, Inc.: Swanson, *Swanson on Swanson,* 349.

13 "a letter to the files": Beauchamp, "The Mogul in Mr. Kennedy."

13 "taken the business load off": Swanson, *Swanson on Swanson,* 366.

13 "the largest private telephone bill": Dallek, *An Unfinished Life,* 24.

13 "No longer, no longer": Swanson, *Swanson on Swanson,* 356–57.

14 "no Kennedy baby": Swanson, 366.

14 "If he was in Europe": Kessler, *The Sins of the Father*, 274.

14 "your beloved husband is no different": Doris Kearns Goodwin, *The Fitzgeralds and the Kennedys: An American Saga* (New York: Simon & Schuster, 1987), 396.

14 "poor little Gloria": Ronald Kessler, *The Sins of the Father: Joseph P. Kennedy and the Dynasty He Founded* (New York: Warner Books, 1996), 79.

14 "Was she a fool": Barbara A. Perry, *Rose Kennedy: The Life and Times of a Political Matriarch* (New York: W. W. Norton, 2013), 76.

15 "only outsider to fleece Hollywood": Beauchamp, "The Mogul in Mr. Kennedy."

15 "I've never had a failure": Swanson, *Swanson on Swanson*, 373.

15 *Queen Kelly*: Stephen Harvey, "*Queen Kelly* Opens—More Than Fifty Years Late," *New York Times,* September 22, 1985.

16 Alexander Pantages: Kessler, *The Sins of the Father,* 57–59.

17 "He's a charmer": Beauchamp, "The Mogul in Mr. Kennedy."

17 Frances Marion's salary: Erin Blakemore, "This Forgotten Female Screenwriter Helped Give Hollywood Its Voice," *Time,* January 21, 2016.

17 "Frances rarely said": Beauchamp, "The Mogul in Mr. Kennedy."

CHAPTER 3

18 "shoeshine boy": Ronald Kessler, *The Sins of the Father: Joseph P. Kennedy and the Dynasty He Founded* (New York: Warner Books, 1996), 82.

18 "It takes a thief": Seymour M. Hersh, *The Dark Side of Camelot* (New York: Little, Brown, 1997), 45.

19 "simple and honest": Address of Honorable Joseph P. Kennedy, chairman, Securities and Exchange Commission, National Press Club, July 25, 1934.

19 "sweep them into the sea": Richard J. Whalen, "Joseph P. Kennedy: A Portrait of the Founder," *Fortune,* 1963 (Fortune Classics, April 10, 2011).

19 Marwood: Daniela Deane, "Where the Kennedys and Gores Played," *Washington Post,* February 14, 2004.

20 "not expecting too much": Thomas Maier, *The Kennedys: America's Emerald Kings* (New York: Basic Books, 2003), 83.

20 Arthur Krock: Hersh, *The Dark Side of Camelot,* 62.

20 "foster-father": Hersh, *The Dark Side of Camelot,* 62.

20 "Secretaryship of Commerce": Arthur Krock, recorded interview by Charles Bartlett, May 10, 1964, John F. Kennedy Library Oral History Program, 4.

21 "the power of the presidency": James Roosevelt, *My Parents: A Differing View* (Chicago: Playboy Press, 1976), 208–10.

CHAPTER 4

22 "Nine Children and Nine Million Dollars": Barbara A. Perry, *Rose Kennedy: The Life and Times of a Political Matriarch* (New York: W. W. Norton, 2013), 95.

22 "Jolly Joe": Richard J. Whalen, "Joseph P. Kennedy: A Portrait of the Founder," *Fortune*, 1963 (Fortune Classics, April 10, 2011).

22 "royal family that England wanted": Peter S. Canellos, ed., *Last Lion: The Fall and Rise of Ted Kennedy* (New York: Simon & Schuster Paperbacks, 2010), 19.

23 "I would not be surprised": Barbara Leaming, *Kick Kennedy: The Charmed Life and Tragic Death of the Favorite Kennedy Daughter* (New York: Thomas Dunne Books, 2016), 31.

23 "an absolute liberation": Paula Byrne, "'Kick' Kennedy: JFK's Forgotten Sister," *Telegraph* (UK), May 20, 2016.

23 "not just a Kennedy girl": Leaming, *Kick Kennedy,* 63.

23 "worth shedding blood for": Edward J. Renehan Jr., *The Kennedys at War, 1937–1945* (New York: Doubleday, 2002), 63.

23 "brought it on themselves": Phillip Whitehead, "The Bootleg Politician: He Could Have Anything He Wanted, Except the Thing He Wanted Most," *Independent* (UK), October 11, 1992.

24 Joe's call to FDR: E. Fuller Torrey, MD, *American Psychosis: How the Federal Government Destroyed the Mental Illness Treatment System* (Oxford: Oxford University Press, 2014), 1.

24 Rosemary stays in UK: Torrey, *American Psychosis,* 2.

24 "bring about a better understanding": Seymour M. Hersh, *The Dark Side of Camelot* (New York: Little, Brown, 1997), 63.

24 "what young Joe is going to do": Cari Beauchamp, "Two Sons, One Destiny," *Vanity Fair,* December 2004.

25 "a little family dinner": Klein, *The Kennedy Curse,* 121.

25 *"Nine hostages to fortune":* Klein, 123.

PART TWO
THE TWO ROSES: ROSE FITZGERALD KENNEDY AND
ROSE MARIE "ROSEMARY" KENNEDY

CHAPTER 5

29 "crazy about traveling": Barbara A. Perry, *Rose Kennedy: The Life and Times of a Political Matriarch* (New York: W. W. Norton, 2013), 23.

29 "Gee, you're a great mother": Barbara A. Perry, "Like Mother, Like Son? Ten Traits JFK Inherited from Rose Kennedy," *UVAToday*, May 25, 2019.

30 "on her knees": Donald Spoto, *Jacqueline Kennedy Bouvier Onassis: A Life* (New York: St. Martin's Press, 2000), 97.

30 "I wish I was sixteen": Godfrey Hodgson, "Obituary: Rose Kennedy," *Independent* (UK), January 24, 1995.

30 "My father didn't think": *Rose Kennedy Remembers*: Transcript of interview with Rose Kennedy for the British Broadcasting Corporation Television Service (New York: Time-Life Multimedia, 1975).

31 "screaming and yelling": Kate Clifford Larson, *Rosemary: The Hidden Kennedy Daughter* (Boston: Houghton Mifflin Harcourt, 2015), 14–15.

32 "no romance outside of procreation": Doris Kearns Goodwin, *The Fitzgeralds and the Kennedys: An American Saga* (New York: Simon & Schuster, 1987), 392.

32 Spanish influenza: "1918 Pandemic (H1N1 Virus)," Centers for Disease Control and Prevention.

32 Dr. Frederick Good: Larson, *Rosemary*, 3–4.

32 "a beautiful child": Eunice Kennedy Shriver, "Hope for Retarded Children," *Saturday Evening Post*, September 22, 1962.

33 "good idea to be around quite often": Perry, *Rose Kennedy*, 57.

33 "I had never heard of a retarded child": Larson, *Rosemary*, 43.

33 "What can they do for her": Shriver, "Hope for Retarded Children."

33 "mother of a great son or daughter": Rose Fitzgerald Kennedy, *Times to Remember* Garden City, NY: Doubleday, 1974), 415.

CHAPTER 6

34 "I had heard that chorus girls were gay, but evil": Kate Clifford Larson, *Rosemary: The Hidden Kennedy Daughter* (Boston, Houghton Mifflin Harcourt, 2015), 32.

35 "During the darkest days": Cari Beauchamp, "Two Sons, One Destiny," *Vanity Fair,* December 2004.

35 "bigger and better": Rose Fitzgerald Kennedy, *Times to Remember* (Garden City, NY: Doubleday, 1974), 65.

35 "Goethe or Voltaire": Kevin Cullen, "Finding Her Way in the Clan: Diaries Reveal a More Complex Kennedy Matriarch," *Boston Globe,* May 13, 2007.

35 Spankings: Fitzgerald Kennedy, *Times to Remember,* 116.

35 Children roughhousing: Larson, *Rosemary: The Hidden Kennedy Daughter*, 39.

36 "Joe banging Jack's head": Evan Thomas, *Robert Kennedy: His Life* (New York: Simon & Schuster, 2000), 39.

36 Rosemary's love of music: Eunice Kennedy Shriver, "Hope for Retarded Children," *Saturday Evening Post*, September 22, 1962.

36 "child rearing as a profession": Cullen, "Finding Her Way in the Clan."

36 "something quite special": Fitzgerald Kennedy, *Times to Remember,* 78.

36 "saddle shoes": Kennedy, 103.

36 "Mother is a perfectionist": Barbara A. Perry, *Rose Kennedy: The Life and Times of a Political Matriarch* (New York: W. W. Norton, 2013), 1.

36 "charm a bird off a tree": Perry, *Rose Kennedy,* 75.

37 "the young Kennedys": Laurence Leamer, *The Kennedy Women* (New York: Villard Books, 1994), 209–10.

37 "I get lonesome everyday": Perry, *Rose Kennedy,* 85.

37 "I would do anything": Perry, *Rose Kennedy,* 85

37 "She loved compliments": Shriver, "Hope for Retarded Children."

38 "terribly serious": Perry, *Rose Kennedy,* 161.

38 "the summer of 1941": Fitzgerald Kennedy, *Times to Remember,* 242.

38 "I was always worried": Doris Kearns Goodwin, *The Fitzgeralds and the Kennedys: An American Saga* (New York: Simon & Schuster, 1987), 640.

38 "My great ambition": Perry, *Rose Kennedy,* 50.

39 American Medical Association on lobotomies: "Frontal Lobotomy," *JAMA*, August 16, 1941.

39 "restore the person": Perry, *Rose Kennedy*, 164.

39 Kick investigates: Leamer, *The Kennedy Women*, 319.

39 "Oh, Mother, no": Larson, *Rosemary*, 161

39 "through the top of the head": Ronald Kessler, *The Sins of the Father: Joseph P. Kennedy and the Dynasty He Founded* (New York: Warner Books, 1996), 243–44.

39 "They knew right away": Kearns Goodwin, *The Kennedys and the Fitzgeralds*, 642.

40 "eight children shine like a dollar": John Seigenthaler, recorded interview by William A. Geoghegan, July 22, 1964, John F. Kennedy Library Oral History Program, 87.

40 "my daughter Rosemary": Fitzgerald Kennedy, *Times to Remember*, dedication page.

PART THREE
THE FAVORITES: JOSEPH PATRICK KENNEDY JR.
AND KATHLEEN "KICK" AGNES KENNEDY

CHAPTER 7

44 "So long and good luck": James W. Graham, *Victura: The Kennedys, a Sailboat, and the Sea* (Lebanon, NH: University Press of New England, 2015), 83.

44 *Unternehmen Loge*: Ron Mitchell, "The London Blitz," part 3 of WW2 People's War: An Archive of World War II Memories—Written by the Public, Gathered by the BBC. BBC website, 2003–6.

44 "star of our family": "Joseph Kennedy Jr.'s Death Recalled," *New York Times*, March 20, 1970.

45 Harold Laski: John Seigenthaler, recorded interview by William A. Geoghegan, July 22, 1964, John F. Kennedy Library Oral History Program, 88–89.

45 "when you are president?": Cari Beauchamp, "Two Sons, One Destiny," *Vanity Fair*, December 2004.

45 "building a spirit": Beauchamp, "Two Sons, One Destiny."

45 Hitler's "excellent psychology": Beauchamp, "Two Sons, One Destiny."

46 "Roosevelt's several million": Alan Axelrod, *Lost Destiny: Joe Kennedy Jr.*

and the Doomed Mission to Save London (New York: Palgrave Macmillan, 2015), 68.

46 "Kennedy was such a good pilot": Mary Gail Hare, "Essex World War II Veteran Served with JFK's Elder Brother in Navy," *Baltimore Sun,* November 10, 2011.

47 "most dangerous type of flying": "Joseph P. Kennedy Jr.," John F. Kennedy Presidential Library and Museum website.

47 "do something different": Edward Klein, *The Kennedy Curse: Why America's First Family Has Been Haunted by Tragedy for 150 Years* (New York: St. Martin's Press, 2003), 147–48.

CHAPTER 8

48 "twice as much as I need": Daniel F. Harrington, "The Last Flight of Joseph P. Kennedy Jr., Heir Apparent," *Providence Journal,* September 2, 2014.

48 "never an occasion": Doris Kearns Goodwin, *The Fitzgeralds and the Kennedys: An American Saga* (New York: Simon & Schuster, 1987), 687.

48 Joe Jr.'s combat missions: "Joseph P. Kennedy, Jr.," John F. Kennedy Presidential Library and Museum website.

49 "served in the United States Navy": "John F. Kennedy: World War II Naval Hero to President," John Fitzgerald Kennedy National Historic Site, National Parks Service website, December 2, 2015.

49 "My congrats": Robert Dallek, *An Unfinished Life: John F. Kennedy, 1917–1963* (New York: Little, Brown, 2003), 106.

49 "They sank my boat": "John F. Kennedy and PT 109," John F. Kennedy Presidential Library and Museum website.

49 "European campaign medal": Dallek, *An Unfinished Life,* 106.

49 Code phrase "Spade Flush": Alan Axelrod, *Lost Destiny: Joe Kennedy Jr. and the Doomed Mission to Save London* (New York: Palgrave Macmillan, 2015), 248.

50 "Nothing larger than a basketball": Axelrod, *Lost Destiny,* 249.

50 "exploded in mid-air": Martin Cherrett, ed., "Joseph P. Kennedy Jr. Dies in Secret Drone Mission," *World War II Today* (website).

50 "trails of smoke": "Brother of JFK Died in Air Crash over Suffolk During WW2," *ITV Report,* December 9, 2014.

50 Subsequent investigations: Steven Russell, "The Kennedy Curse: Tragedy

in the Skies over Suffolk," *East Anglian Daily Times,* November 22, 2013.

50 "Erector set and Lincoln Logs": Axelrod, *Lost Destiny,* 235.

51 Interrogation of Joe Kennedy Jr.: "Joe Kennedy Death Story Is Refuted," *Chicago Tribune,* November 11, 1986.

51 "program killed more American airmen": Rick Long/Cape Cod Curmudgeon, "August 12, 1944, Operation Aphrodite," *Today in History* (blog), August 12, 2017.

51 General Carl "Tooey" Spaatz: Edward J. Renehan Jr., *The Kennedys at War, 1937–1945* (New York: Doubleday, 2002), 304.

51 Hitler's missile men: "Joseph Kennedy Jr.'s Death Recalled," *New York Times,* March 20, 1970.

CHAPTER 9

52 "missing in action": Rose Fitzgerald Kennedy, *Times to Remember* (Garden City, NY: Doubleday, 1974), 257.

52 "let's go sailing": James W. Graham, *Victura: The Kennedys, a Sailboat, and the Sea* (Lebanon, NH: University Press of New England, 2015), 84.

53 Final letter from Joe Jr.: Daniel F. Harrington, "The Last Flight of Joseph P. Kennedy Jr., Heir Apparent," *Providence Journal,* September 2, 2014.

53 "Joe's courage and devotion": "Joseph Kennedy Jr.'s Death Recalled," *New York Times,* March 20, 1970.

53 "Luckily, I am a Kennedy": Doris Kearns Goodwin, *The Fitzgeralds and the Kennedys: An American Saga* (New York: Simon & Schuster, 1987), 697.

53 "the Big One": Barbara Leaming, *Kick Kennedy: The Charmed Life and Tragic Death of the Favorite Kennedy Daughter* (New York: Thomas Dunne Books, 2016), 30.

54 "they can not have what they want most": Thomas Maier, *The Kennedys: America's Emerald Kings* (New York: Basic Books, 2003), 149.

54 "two Joes": Leaming, 18.

54 "Kick's soul": Edward Klein, *The Kennedy Curse: Why America's First Family Has Been Haunted by Tragedy for 150 Years* (New York: St. Martin's Press, 2003), 145.

54 "Thursday—Engaged": Paula Byrne, "'Kick' Kennedy: JFK's Forgotten Sister," *Telegraph* (UK), May 20, 2016.

55 "MARRIED LIFE AGREES WITH ME": Leaming, *Kick Kennedy,* 157.

55 "nothing but goodbyes": Leaming, 158.

55 Patricia Wilson: Kearns Goodwin, *The Fitzgeralds and the Kennedys,* 670.

55 "I had better get a gal": Kearns Goodwin, 685.

56 Personal Effects Distribution: Rick Long/ Cape Cod Curmudgeon, "August 12, 1944, Operation Aphrodite," *Today in History* (website), August 12, 2017.

56 Peter Fitzwilliam resembling Rhett Butler: Leaming, *Kick Kennedy*, 235-6.

56 Rose opposes marriage to divorced man: Leaming, *Kick Kennedy*, 241.

56 "Darling Daddy": Leaming, *Kick Kennedy*, 241.

56 "I'd like to get Dad's consent": Peter Collier and David Horowitz, *The Kennedys: An American Drama* (New York: Summit Books, 1984), 169.

57 boozy lunch: Edward Klein, *The Kennedy Curse: Why America's First Family Has Been Haunted by Tragedy for 150 Years* (New York: St. Martin's Press, 2003), 159.

57 Discovery of bodies: Collier and Horowitz, *The Kennedys*, 169-70.

58 "he will be forgotten": Jennifer Newton, "Calls Grow for Memorial to JFK's Older Brother Joe to Be Built in English Village Where WW2 Bomber Exploded—Paving the Way for Younger Sibling to Go on and Become President," *Daily Mail* (UK), December 6, 2014.

58 "dinner during an air raid": Edward J. Renehan Jr., *The Kennedys at War, 1937–1945* (New York: Doubleday, 2002), 314.

PART FOUR
THE PRESIDENT: JOHN FITZGERALD KENNEDY

CHAPTER 10

61 "your blue underwear": Thomas Bilodeau, recorded interview by James Murray, May 12, 1964, John F. Kennedy Library Oral History Program, 3.

62 "godawful suits": Robert Dallek, *An Unfinished Life: John F. Kennedy, 1917–1963* (New York: Little, Brown, 2003), 2.

62 "best sense of humor": Doris Kearns Goodwin, *The Fitzgeralds and the Kennedys: An American Saga* (New York: Simon & Schuster, 1987), 464.

62 "never thought Jack would do anything": Ronald Kessler, *The Sins of the Father: Joseph P. Kennedy and the Dynasty He Founded* (New York: Warner Books, 1996), 286.

62 "shadowboxing": Edward J. Renehan Jr., *The Kennedys at War, 1937–1945* (New York: Doubleday, 2002), 314.

63 Rose's belief that Jack had a lower IQ: Barbara A. Perry, *Rose Kennedy: The Life and Times of a Political Matriarch* (New York: W. W. Norton, 2013), 51.

63 "never wanted us to talk about this": Seymour M. Hersh, *The Dark Side of Camelot* (New York: Little, Brown, 1997), 15.

63 "sick so much": Donald Spoto, *Jacqueline Kennedy Bouvier Onassis: A Life* (New York: St. Martin's Press, 2000), 87.

63 "a very definite flair": Kearns Goodwin, *The Fitzgeralds and the Kennedys,* 481.

63 "good motion": Ian Young, "The Man Who Loved JFK," review of *Jack and Lem: The Untold Story of an Extraordinary Friendship,* by David Pitts, *Gay & Lesbian Review,* September 1, 2007.

64 "Jack's winning smile": Alexis Coe, "Portrait of a Troublemaker: A Rare Glimpse of John F. Kennedy's Life at Boarding School," *Town and Country,* May 2017.

64 Jackie's gifts as a mimic: Spoto, *Jacqueline Bouvier Kennedy Onassis,* 47.

64 "two boys from the same family": Kearns Goodwin, *The Fitzgeralds and the Kennedys,* 487.

64 "a nearly impossible task to restore it": Kearns Goodwin, 489.

64 "Most Likely to Succeed": Kearns Goodwin, 489.

CHAPTER 11

65 Ralph Horton: Cari Beauchamp, "Two Sons, One Destiny," *Vanity Fair,* December 2004.

65 "frightened to death they'd get VD": Thomas Maier, *The Kennedys: America's Emerald Kings* (New York: Basic Books, 2003), 85.

65 "mother him or marry him": Robert Dallek, *An Unfinished Life: John F. Kennedy, 1917–1963* (New York: Little, Brown, 2003), 5.

66 "what did not interest him": Nik DeCosta-Klipa, "Four Things You Might Not Know About John F. Kennedy's Years at Harvard," Boston.com, May 25, 2017.

66 Mildred Finley: Lorna Hughes, "Teachers' Account of How She Was Shipwrecked and Met JFK in Glasgow Within a Few Fateful Days in September 1939," *Daily Record* (UK), September 8, 2013.

67 "wisdom and sympathy": DeCosta-Klipa, "Four Things."

67 "Appeasement at Munich": Joseph M. Siracusa, *Encyclopedia of the Kennedys: The People and Events That Shaped America* (Santa Barbara, CA: ABC-CLIO, 2012), 25.

CHAPTER 12

69 "Nordic beauty": Scott Farris, *Inga: Kennedy's Great Love, Hitler's Perfect Beauty, and J. Edgar Hoover's Prime Suspect* (Holland, OH: Dreamscape Media, LLC, 2016), 137.

69 "a boy with a future": Barbara Leaming, *Kick Kennedy: The Charmed Life and Tragic Death of the Favorite Kennedy Daughter* (New York: Thomas Dunne Books, 2016), 101.

70 Arvad's pieces on Goering and Hitler: Farris, *Inga,* 13.

70 Autographed photo from Hitler: Farris, 148.

70 "gooey eyes": Leaming, *Kick Kennedy,* 100.

70 "He had the charm": Leaming, 100.

70 "could be a spy?": Farris, *Inga,* 106.

70 "in big trouble": Seymour M. Hersh, *The Dark Side of Camelot* (New York: Little, Brown, 1997), 83.

70 "drag up the big guns": Leaming, *Kick Kennedy,* 104.

71 "It took the FBI": Frederick M. Winship, "New Book: Kennedy's 'Greatest Love'—but Was She a Spy?" United Press International, October 14, 1992.

71 "one thing I don't want": Dallek, *An Unfinished Life,* 85.

71 "The breakup with Inga": Edward J. Renehan Jr., *The Kennedys at War, 1937–1945* (New York: Doubleday, 2002), 220.

71 "Over the side, boy": Thomas Bilodeau, recorded interview by James Murray, May 12, 1964, John F. Kennedy Library Oral History Program, 8.

72 "always had something to prove": Renehan, *The Kennedys at War,* 220.

72 The postwar veterans' vote: Joseph McBride, *Searching for John Ford* (Jackson: University Press of Mississippi, 2011), 403 (footnote).

72 "Without *PT-109*": William Doyle, *PT-109: An American Epic of War, Survival, and the Destiny of John F. Kennedy* (New York: William Morrow, 2015), xi.

CHAPTER 13

74 "burnt so bad": Dennis Georgatos, "*PT-109* Survivor Saved in War by JFK Dead at 84," AP, February 21, 1990.

74 "most exciting I've ever heard": Rose Fitzgerald Kennedy, *Times to Remember* (Garden City, NY: Doubleday, 1974), 112.

75 Carving into coconut: "John F. Kennedy and *PT 109*," John F. Kennedy Presidential Library and Museum website.

75 "letter for you": Doris Kearns Goodwin, *The Fitzgeralds and the Kennedys: An American Saga* (New York: Simon & Schuster, 1987), 657.

75 Inviting Pacific Islanders to inauguration: Kat Eschner, "Why JFK Kept a Coconut Shell in the Oval Office," Smithsonian.com, August 2, 2017.

76 "still late for meals, still no money": Robert Dallek, *An Unfinished Life: John F. Kennedy, 1917–1963*, (New York: Little, Brown, 2003), 101.

76 "you have that feeling": Kearns Goodwin, *The Fitzgeralds and the Kennedys*, 559–60.

76 "real heroes": Dallek, *An Unfinished Life*, 98.

76 "Joe's business": Ronald Kessler, *The Sins of the Father: Joseph P. Kennedy and the Dynasty He Founded* (New York: Warner Books, 1996), 288.

76 "burden falls to me". Carl Beauchamp, "Two Sons, One Destiny," *Vanity Fair*, December 2004.

77 "like being drafted": Kessler, *The Sins of the Father*, 288.

77 "going to be the President": Kearns Goodwin, *The Fitzgeralds and the Kennedys*, 262.

77 James A. Reed: Kessler, *The Sins of the Father*, 288.

CHAPTER 14

78 A small garden party: Sarah Polus, "A History Buff with an Affinity for the Kennedys Just Bought the Home Where JFK Met Jackie," *Washington Post*, March 15, 2018.

78 "unfailing antenna": Robert D. McFadden, "Death of a First Lady; Jacqueline Kennedy Onassis Dies of Cancer at 64," *New York Times*, May 20, 1994.

78 "disturbing influence": Donald Spoto, *Jacqueline Kennedy Bouvier Onassis: A Life* (New York: St. Martin's Press, 2000), 75.

78 "leaned across the asparagus": *Time*, "Women: Jackie," January 20, 1961.

79 "shameless in their match-making": Spoto, *Jacqueline Kennedy Bouvier Onassis,* 83.

79 "a little lonesome": Spoto, 85.

79 "Such heartbreak would be worth the pain": Spoto, 86.

79 "a challenge": Spoto, 91.

79 "such a wit": McFadden, "Death of a First Lady."

80 "didn't like her mother": Spoto, *Jacqueline Kennedy Bouvier Onassis,* 43.

80 "My mother was a nothing": Ronald Kessler, *The Sins of the Father: Joseph P. Kennedy and the Dynasty He Founded* (New York: Warner Books, 1996), 44.

80 "my father wants": Spoto, *Jacqueline Kennedy Bouvier Onassis,* 85.

80 "completeness of perfection": Thomas Maier, *The Kennedys: America's Emerald Kings* (New York: Basic Books, 2003), 445.

80 "grandest fellow": Doris Kearns Goodwin, *The Fitzgeralds and the Kennedys: An American Saga* (New York: Simon & Schuster, 1987), 486.

80 "spent half of each week": Spoto, *Jacqueline Kennedy Bouvier Onassis,* 85.

80 "she knew the score": Helen Lawrenson, "Jackie at 50," *Washington Post Weekend Magazine,* July 28, 1979.

81 "if she married into that family": J. Randy Taraborrelli, *Jackie, Ethel, Joan: Women of Camelot* (New York: Warner Books, 2000), 64–65.

81 "nothing if not the most exciting": Taraborrelli, *Jackie, Ethel, Joan,* 64.

81 "crazy about Jackie": Spoto, *Jacqueline Kennedy Bouvier Onassis,* 99.

81 "Jack-leen": Taraborrelli, *Jackie, Ethel, Joan,* 60.

81 "put through her paces": Taraborrelli, 63.

81 "a better wife": Rose Fitzgerald Kennedy, *Times to Remember* (Garden City, NY: Doubleday, 1974), 301.

81 "no mention of a fiancée": Spoto, *Jacqueline Kennedy Bouvier Onassis,* 101.

82 Jack's last letter: Emily Saul, "Letters Reveal Steamy Affair JFK Began Weeks Before Marrying Jackie," *New York Post,* November 23, 2015.

82 "Half my time": Godfrey Hodgen, "Obituary: Evelyn Lincoln," *Independent* (UK), May 20, 1995.

82 "a splendid wedding": Fitzgerald Kennedy, *Times to Remember,* 301.

82 "picture perfect": Taraborrelli, *Jackie, Ethel, Joan,* 66.

82 "like the coronation": Spoto, *Jacqueline Kennedy Bouvier Onassis,* 104.

82 Hersh reports on Durie Malcolm: Seymour M. Hersh, *The Dark Side of Camelot* (New York: Little, Brown, 1997), 326–40.

83 "I wouldn't have married Jack": Hersh, *The Dark Side of Camelot*, 329.

83 Possibility that Jack was a bigamist: Hersh, 328.

83 "American people don't care": Barbara Leaming, excerpt of *Mrs. Kennedy* (CITY: Publisher, 2001), *New York Times*, November 24, 2001.

83 "Kennedy men are like that": Taraborrelli, *Jackie, Ethel, Joan*, 48.

83 "You can't let it get to you": Sally Bedell Smith, "Private Camelot," *Vanity Fair*, May 2004.

83 "how that nearly killed Mummy": "Jackie Kennedy Letters Shine Light on Her Marriage and Mourning," NBC News, May 13, 2014.

83 "You just had to live with it": Taraborrelli, *Jackie, Ethel, Joan*, 48.

83 "didn't fully understand each other": Spoto, *Jacqueline Kennedy Bouvier Onassis*, 106.

84 "I was alone": Spoto, 108.

84 Jack's health: Taraborrelli, *Jackie, Ethel, Joan*, 67.

84 "Jackie placing her hand": Taraborrelli, 67.

84 "I love being married": "Jackie Kennedy Letters Shine Light."

84 "atypical husband": Caroline Hallemann, "Jackie Kennedy's Love Letter to JFK Offers a Rare Glimpse into Their Marriage," *Town & Country*, October 29, 2018.

85 "sadness shared brings married people closer": "Jackie Kennedy Letters Shine Light."

85 "handsome, well-endowed": Cabell Phillips, "How to Be a Presidential Candidate," *New York Times*, July 13, 1958.

85 "not a natural-born campaigner": Spoto, *Jacqueline Kennedy Bouvier Onassis*, 133.

85 "When Jackie was traveling with us": Spoto, 131.

85 "lunching with my husband": Spoto, *Jacqueline Kennedy Bouvier Onassis*, 134.

86 "Do you really think": Ben Bradlee, "Jack Kennedy, My Friend, My President," *Newsweek*, January 17, 2011.

CHAPTER 15

87 "very, very private": Seymour M. Hersh, *The Dark Side of Camelot* (New York: Little, Brown, 1997), 136.

87 Giancana's name in the "Black Book": John M. Glianna, "Sam Giancana's

Daughter Aims to Cash in on Gangster's Memorabilia," *Los Angeles Times,* November 21, 2014.

88 "constitutional psychopath": Glianna, "Sam Giancana's Daughter."

88 "I own Chicago": Glianna, "Sam Giancana's Daughter."

88 RFK interrogation: Hersh, *The Dark Side of Camelot,* 134.

89 "no ballot stuffing": Hersh, *The Dark Side of Camelot,* 136.

89 "most perfectly manicured": Steve Chawkins, "George Jacobs Dies at 86; Frank Sinatra's Longtime Valet," *Los Angeles Times,* December 31, 2013.

89 "least talented member": Bruce Fessier, "Brother-in-Lawford Was Sinatra's Key to White House," *Desert Sun,* October 20, 2015.

89 Affair between Pat Kennedy and Sinatra: Lee Server, "The Real Reason Frank Sinatra Was Banned from the Kennedy White House," *Town & Country,* November 7, 2018.

89 "well-known movie actor": Fessier, "Brother-in-Lawford was Sinatra's Key to White House."

90 "Kennedy wanted to be Sinatra": Diana Pearl, "New Book Details John F. Kennedy's Short-lived, Intense Friendship with Frank Sinatra," *People,* November 28, 2016.

90 "Elizabeth Taylor category": Hersh, *The Dark Side of Camelot,* 296.

90 "a genuine mutual admiration society": Kitty Kelley, "The Dark Side of Camelot," *People,* February 29, 1988.

90 Sinatra introduction of Judith Exner to Kennedys: Hersh, *The Dark Side of Camelot,* 294.

90 "Do a 'Youth for Kennedy'": Fessier, "Brother-in-Lawford Was Sinatra's Key to White House."

91 "That little rascal": Kelley, "The Dark Side of Camelot."

91 "anxious to get together": Lindsay Kimble, "The Truth Behind JFK's Mobbed Up Mistress—and What She Might Have Known About the Assassination," *People,* September 19, 2017.

91 "world's greatest listener": Sara Stewart, "All The President's Women," *New York Post,* November 10, 2013.

91 "Thinking of you": Kelley, "The Dark Side of Camelot."

91 "set up to be the courier": Kimble, "The Truth Behind JFK's Mobbed Up Mistress."

91 "help me with the campaign": Hersh, *The Dark Side of Camelot,* 303.

92 Mink coat: Hersh, 303–4.

92 "plans had all been made without me": Hersh, 304.

92 West Virginia campaign law: Marc J. Selverstone, "John F. Kennedy: Campaigns and Elections," Miller Center for Public Affairs at the University of Virginia.

92 "Don't buy a single vote more": Elaine Kamarck, "The 1960 West Virginia Primary: Can It Happen Again?" *Brookings*, May 10, 2016.

92 "hopes and threats": Selverstone, "John F. Kennedy: Campaigns and Elections."

92 "way to the White House": Pearl, "New Book Details John F. Kennedy's Short-Lived, Intense Friendship with Frank Sinatra."

93 "constant, unremitting labor": Rose Fitzgerald Kennedy, *Times to Remember* (Garden City, NY: Doubleday, 1974), 320.

93 "Your boyfriend wouldn't be president": R. C. Longworth, "Woman Says She Was JFK's Mob Liaison," *Chicago Tribune*, October 7, 1991.

CHAPTER 16

94 "Rather vain": J. Randy Taraborrelli, *Jackie, Ethel, Joan: Women of Camelot* (New York: Warner Books, 2000), 56.

94 JFK as "Superman": Robert McCrum, "Eunice Kennedy and the Death of the Great American Dream," *Guardian* (UK), August 15, 2009.

95 George E. Thomas: Barbara A. Perry and Alfred Reaves IV, "Inside the Unsung Life of the Man Who Was John F. Kennedy's Most Personal Assistant," *Time*, November 20, 2018.

95 "Dr. Feelgood": Robert Dallek, *An Unfinished Life: John F. Kennedy, 1917–1963* (New York: Little, Brown, 2003), 398.

95 "more promiscuous with physicians": Dallek, *An Unfinished Life*, 399.

95 "Urgent National Needs": Douglas Brinkley, "How JFK Sent the U.S. to the Moon," *Wall Street Journal*, April 4, 2019.

96 "this was a disastrous idea": Mark White, "Bay of Pigs Invasion: Kennedy's Cuban catastrophe," *BBC History Magazine*, May 2011.

96 "Two full days of hell": White, "Bay of Pigs Invasion," *BBC History Magazine*.

97 "a pretty bad fix": Rick Klein, "JFK Tapes: New Insight Into White House Tensions During Cuban Missile Crisis," ABC News, September 24, 2012.

97 "stay right here with you": Associated Press, "Jackie O's Antiquated Views 'Horrified' Grandkids," NBC News, September 14, 2011.

97 "I can't see that it's wrong": "New Administration: All He Asked..." *Time Magazine*, February 3, 1961.

97 "stir things up": "Operation Mongoose," *American Experience*, PBS.org.

97 "Get rid of the Castro regime": "Operation Mongoose."

98 "I thought I was in love with Jack": Kitty Kelley, "The Dark Side of Camelot," *People*, February 29, 1988.

98 "message they'll never forget": Sam Giancana and Chuck Giancana, *Double Cross: The Explosive Inside Story of the Mobster Who Controlled America* (New York: Warner Books, 1992), 430.

99 "I've gone to great lengths": Kelley, "The Dark Side of Camelot."

99 "Frank Sinatra is the main problem": Jeff Leen, "AKA Frank Sinatra," *Washington Post Magazine*, March 7, 1999.

CHAPTER 17

100 "Extra! Extra!": *Boston Globe*, November 22, 1963, final evening edition.

101 "He's the one who made all of this possible": Thomas Maier, *The Kennedys: America's Emerald Kings* (New York: Basic Books, 2003), 445.

101 "We have told him but we don't think he understands it": Robert Dallek, *An Unfinished Life: John F. Kennedy, 1917–1963* (New York: Little, Brown, 2003), 697.

101 "In 1960, Lyndon was a help": Timothy Noah, "The Day Before JFK Was Assassinated," MSNBC.com, November 21, 2013.

101 "My back feels better than it's felt in years": Noah, "The Day Before JFK Was Assassinated."

102 Providencia Parendes: Jennifer Schuessler, "Jacqueline Kennedy's Notes for Dallas Are Found, Starting a Quiet Tug of War," *New York Times*, July 2, 2018.

102 "show these Texans": Cathy Horyn, "Jacqueline Kennedy's Smart Pink Suit, Preserved in Memory and Kept Out of View," *New York Times*, November 14, 2013.

102 Narrow size 10A: Steven Stolman, "The Under-the-Radar Shoe Designer Jackie Kennedy Adored," *Town & Country*, October 4, 2017.

102 "Make large feet look smaller": Barbara Leaming, excerpt of *Mrs. Kennedy* (New York: Free Press, 2001), *New York Times*, November 24, 2001.

102 "quarter-inch lift affixed to one heel": "The Weird Thing Jackie Kennedy Did with Her Shoes," *Harper's Bazaar,* April 28, 2017.

102 "One of the first things I did": Janet G. Travell, recorded interview by Theodore C. Sorensen, January 20, 1966, John F. Kennedy Library Oral History Program, 3.

102 "overwhelming good taste": J. Randy Taraborrelli, *Jackie, Ethel, Joan: Women of Camelot* (New York: Warner Books, 2000), 24.

102 "American Queen": Linnea Crowther, "Oleg Cassini and the Jackie Look," Legacy.com, 2017.

102 "Jackie wanted to do Versailles in America": Sally Bedell Smith, "Private Camelot," *Vanity Fair,* May 2004.

102 "Just send me an account": Bedell Smith, "Private Camelot."

103 Presidential blue metallic: Christopher Wynn, "Would a Bubble-Top Have Saved Kennedy? More Answers from the Strange Story of JFK's Lincoln Limo," *Dallas News,* November 19, 2018 (originally May 5, 2013).

103 "expensive, fancy limousine": Wynn, "Would a Bubble-Top Have Saved Kennedy?"

103 Convertible in the rain: Freya Drohan, "How JFK's Love for Open-Top Convertible Cars Led to His Assassination," *Irish Central* (UK), February 12, 2018.

103 "don't want the bubbletop": Edward Klein, *The Kennedy Curse: Why America's First Family Has Been Haunted by Tragedy for 150 Years* (New York: St. Martin's Press, 2003), 161.

103 "lose your anonymity at thirty-one": Donald Spoto, *Jacqueline Kennedy Bouvier Onassis: A Life* (New York: St. Martin's Press, 2000), 146.

103 "last thing I expected": Bedell Smith, "Private Camelot."

104 "no way in God's Earth": Thurston Clarke, "A Death in the First Family," *Vanity Fair,* July 1, 2013.

104 Patrick Bouvier Kennedy vital statistics: Steven Levingston, "For John and Jackie Kennedy, the Death of a Son May Have Brought Them Closer," *Washington Post,* October 24, 2013.

104 "He's a Kennedy—he'll make it": Levingston, "For John and Jackie Kennedy."

104 "lovable little monkey": Alvin Spivak, "Doctors Hopeful for New JFK Son," United Press International, August 7, 1963.

104 "Nothing must happen to Patrick": Clarke, "A Death in the First Family."

104 "The First Lady never once": Bedell Smith, "Private Camelot."

104 "Overwhelmed with grief": Bedell Smith.

105 "genuinely cut to the bone": Taraborrelli, *Jackie, Ethel, Joan,* 194.

105 "distinctly close relationship": Levingston, "For John and Jackie Kennedy."

105 "different than I had seen them before": Seymour M. Hersh, *The Dark Side of Camelot* (New York: Little, Brown, 1997), 439.

105 "aggrieved sense of responsibility": Clarke, "A Death in the First Family."

105 "very, very, very close to each other": Taraborrelli, *Jackie, Ethel, Joan,* 178.

CHAPTER 18

106 "Mrs. Kennedy is organizing": Monica Hesse, "Four Shattering Days," *Washington Post,* November 13, 2015.

106 American-made: Cathy Horyn, "Jacqueline Kennedy's Smart Pink Suit Preserved in Memory and Kept out of View," *New York Times,* November 15, 2013.

106 "smashing": Randi Kaye, "Fifty Years Later, Jackie Kennedy's Pink Suit Locked Away from View," CNN, November 21, 2013.

106 "too foreign, too spendy": Leah Chernikoff, "Karl Lagerfeld Says Oleg Cassini Knocked Off That Pink 'Chanel' Suit Jackie Kennedy Wore The Day JFK Was Assassinated," Fashionista.com, April 10, 2014.

106 "Some Texans": "A Last Thing Signed: John F. Kennedy Autographs a Dallas Newspaper on the Morning of His Murder There," Shapell Manuscript Foundation, Shapell.org.

107 Black-and-white Chanel: Bonnie Wertheim, "Jackie Kennedy's Packing List for Texas, Chic and Poignant," *New York Times,* July 3, 2018.

107 "last hour of serenity": Philip Nobile, "JFK, Jackie, Joined Mile-High Club Day Before His Death," *New York Post,* November 17, 2013.

107 "super patriot": Alan Peppard, "Before Gunning for JFK, Oswald Targeted ex-Gen. Edwin A. Walker—and Missed," *Dallas News,* November 19, 2018.

107 "paranoid mental disorders": Peppard, "Before Gunning for JFK."

107 "Imagine that son": Peppard.

107 "Walker for President 64": Peppard.

108 "intellectual training experience": Bill Rockwood, "Twenty-Four Years: Who Was Lee Harvey Oswald?" *Frontline,* November 19, 2013.

108 "target practice": Rockwood, "Twenty-Four Years."

108 "shot for a Marine": Rockwood.

108 "he couldn't see": Peppard.

108 "I shot Walker": Rockwood.

109 "Betraying the Constitution": "Photos: Kennedy Hatred in 1960s Dallas Looks a Lot Like Obama Hatred Today," *The New Republic,* November 18, 2013.

109 Oswald takes off his wedding ring: Robert Wilonsky, "Jack Ruby's Handwritten Version of What Happened on November 22, 1963, Goes to Auction," *Dallas News,* November 2017.

109 "surprised to see": Michael S. Rosenwald, "Oswald's Chilling Final Hours Before Killing Kennedy: Speaking Russian, Playing with His Daughter, Sleeping In," *Washington Post,* October 26, 2017.

109 "My, he's in a mean mood": Rosenwald, "Oswald's Chilling Final Hours."

109 "Curtain rods": "The Assassin," chapter 4 of the JFK Assassination Records, Warren Commission Report, National Archives.

CHAPTER 19

110 "began so beautifully": Lady Bird Johnson, transcript of audio diary, National Archives, November 22, 1963, p. 1.

110 "everything in Texas". "Howdy, Mr. President!": A Fort Worth Perspective of JFK, University of Texas Arlington Libraries, Special Collections.

110 "American Fact-Finding Committee": Dan Evon, "Did John F. Kennedy Predict His Own Assassination?" Snopes.com, November 25, 2016.

111 "profound perhaps disturbing": Donald Spoto, *Jacqueline Bouvier Kennedy Onassis* (New York: St. Martin's Press, 2000), 75.

111 "nut country": Edward Klein, *The Kennedy Curse: Why Tragedy Has Haunted America's First Family for 150 Years* (New York: St. Martin's Press, 2003), 175.

111 Maps and routes: "The Assassin," chapter 4 of the JFK Assassination Records, Warren Commission Report, National Archives.

111 "close the elevator": "The Assassin."

112 "happy foursome": Mimi Swartz, "The Witness," *Texas Monthly,* November 2003.

112 "so perfect": Swartz, "The Witness."

112 "can't say Dallas": James Wolcott, "Well, Mr. President, You Can't Say Dallas Doesn't Love You!" *Vanity Fair,* March 11, 2011.

112 "hot, wild": Thomas Maier, *The Kennedys: America's Emerald Kings*. (New York: Basic Books, 2003), 452.

112 "sharp loud report": Johnson, transcript of audio diary, p. 1.

112 "the last faces": Mary E. Woodward, "Witness from the News Describes Assassination," *Dallas Morning News*, November 23, 1963.

113 "every conspiracy theorist": Joe Simnacher, "Mary Pillsworth, ex-DMN Editor Who Witnessed Kennedy Assassination, Dies at 77," *Dallas News*, April 17, 2017.

113 "What are they doing to you?": John F. Kennedy Assassination Collection, Key Persons Files, Statements of Agents and Law Enforcement Officers in Presidential Motorcade on November 22, 1963, in Dallas: Roy H. Kellerman, National Archives.

113 "color movies": Michael E. Ruane, "As He Filmed, Abraham Zapruder Knew Instantly That President Kennedy Was Dead," *Washington Post*, November 21, 2013.

114 "killed him!": Ruane, "As He Filmed."

114 "nothing but heartbreak": Steve Hendricks, "Zapruder Captured JFK's Assassination in Riveting Detail, Fueling Decades of Conspiracy Theories," *Washington Post*, October 26, 2017.

114 "Step on it!": John F. Kennedy Assassination Collection, Key Persons Files, Statements of Agents and Law Enforcement Officers in Presidential Motorcade on November 22, 1963, in Dallas: Roy H. Kellerman, National Archives.

114 "yellow roses": "Nellie Connally Dies; Rode with JFK on Fateful Day," National Public Radio, September 2, 2006.

114 "drift of blossoms": Johnson, transcript of audio diary, page 1.

CHAPTER 20

115 "My reporter instinct kicked in": Hugh Aynesworth, "The Assassination of JFK: An Eyewitness Account," *BBC History Extra*, HistoryExtra.com.

116 "sitting up there": Howard Leslie Brennan, Records of the John F. Kennedy Assassination Collection: Key Persons Files, National Archives.

116 "saw this man": Brennan, Records of the John F. Kennedy Assassination Collection.

116 "THREE SHOTS FIRED": Bill Sanderson, "Merriman Smith's Account of JFK's Assassination," Pulitzer Prizes Archives, Pulitzer.org.

116 "a babble of anxious, tense voices": Merriman Smith, "Merriman Smith's Account of JFK's Assassination," November 23, 1963, United Press International Archives.

117 "killed my husband": Monica Hesse, "Four Shattering Days," *Washington Post,* November 13, 2015.

117 "she had been cradling": Beverly DeVoy, "Dallas Doctor Recalls Day He Tried to Save Dying JFK," *Deseret News,* October 28, 1993.

117 "90 to 95 percent certain": George Lardner Jr., "Archive Photos Not of JFK's Brain, Concludes Aide to Review Board," *Washington Post,* November 10, 1998.

118 "stolen the locker": Gary Busio, "RFK May Have Swiped JFK's Missing Brain," *New York Post,* October 20, 2013.

118 "He was dying": DeVoy, "Dallas Doctor Recalls."

119 "fifteen feet away": Aynesworth, "The Assassination of JFK."

119 "all over now": Associated Press, "Officer Who Arrested Oswald Dies at 76," NBC News, January 27, 2005.

119 "made a fist": Associated Press, "Officer Who Arrested."

119 "bracing myself": Associated Press.

119 "protest this police brutality": Gary Mack, "An End to Conspiracy? Rare Photo of Lee Harvey Oswald's Arrest Suggests Why He's Guilty," *Time,* November 21, 2013.

120 "My whole face": James Swanson, "Inventing Camelot: How Jackie Kennedy Shaped Her Husband's Legacy," *New York Post,* November 10, 2013.

120 "poignant sights": Lady Bird Johnson, "Selections from Lady Bird Johnson's Diary of the Assassination," November 22, 1963, PBS.org.

120 "I want them to see": Johnson, "Selections from Lady Bird Johnson's Diary."

120 "I'm here": Chris Jones, "The Flight from Dallas," *Esquire,* September 16, 2013.

CHAPTER 21

121 Lafayette Hotel: Stanley Meisler, *When the World Calls: The Inside Story of the Peace Corps and Its First Fifty Years* (Boston: Beacon Press, 2011), 62–64.

121 "world peace and friendship": "Peace Corps Established, (March 1, 1961)," *This Day in History,* History.com, July 21, 2010.

121 "so many crises": Robert McCrum, "Eunice Kennedy and the Death of the Great American Dream," *Guardian* (UK), August 15, 2009.

122 Eunice and Jack shared a house: Evan Thomas, "The Fierce Rebellion and Compassion of Eunice Shriver." *Washington Post,* April 13, 2018.

122 "keep him going": White House Historical Association, "Thanksgiving: President Kennedy Pardons a Turkey," November 19, 1963.

123 "request 'Over the Rainbow'": Liz McNeil, "Guess Which Song JFK Asked Judy Garland to Sing to Him over the Telephone," *People,* January 31, 2017.

123 "go to bed": J. Randy Taraborrelli, *Jackie, Ethel, Joan* (New York: Grand Central Publishing, 2012), 227.

123 "old but warm coat": Rose Fitzgerald Kennedy, *Times to Remember* (New York: Doubleday, 1974), 379.

123 "go on living": Thomas Maier, *The Kennedys: America's Emerald Kings* (New York: Basic Books, 2003), 455.

124 "how fortunate": Fitzgerald Kennedy, *Times to Remember,* 380.

124 "I WILL KILL": James Reston Jr., "Lee Harvey Oswald's Little Green Book Shows JFK Wasn't the Real Target," *Los Angeles Times,* November 22, 2016.

124 "steps out": Jeremy P. Meyer, "Bob Jackson's Iconic Photo of Ruby Shooting Oswald Still Resonates," *Denver Post,* November 22, 2013.

125 "right hand was contracting": "WITNESS ASCRIBES MALICE TO RUBY; Quotes Him as Saying He Hopes Oswald Would Die," *New York Times,* March 5, 1964.

125 "do something spectacular": Jim Boyle, "JFK Series: Dallas Detective Still Answering Questions About JFK Assassination," *Elk River Star News,* November 10, 2013.

CHAPTER 22

126 "I want you to make sure": Thomas Maier, *The Kennedys: America's Emerald Kings* (New York: Basic Books, 2003), 446.

126 "Jack really looks, acts": Barbara Perry, *Rose Kennedy: The Life and Times of a Political Matriarch* (New York: Norton, 2013), 243.

127 "clipped a few locks": Clint Hill, "Jackie Kennedy's Secret Service Agent Remembers President Kennedy's Funeral," *Town & Country,* November 22, 2016.

127 JFK's valet, George E. Thomas: Barbara A. Perry and Alfred Reaves IV, "Inside the Unsung Life of the Man Who Was John F. Kennedy's Most Personal Assistant," *Time,* November 20, 2018.

127 "a child's last happiness": Monica Hesse, "Four Shattering Days," *Washington Post,* November 13, 2015.

128 "children tumbling": Associated Press, "Jackie O's Antiquated Views Horrified Grandkids," September 14, 2011.

128 "letter to Daddy": J. Randy Taraborrelli, *Jackie, Ethel, Joan,* (New York: Grand Central Publishing, 2012), 232.

128 "a good man": Jimmy Breslin, "Digging JFK Grave Was His Honor," *New York Herald Tribune,* November 1963 (republished in *Newsday,* November 22, 2013).

129 "still as statues": Hesse, "Four Shattering Days."

129 "salute Daddy now": James Swanson, "Inventing Camelot: How Jackie Kennedy Shaped Her Husband's Legacy," *New York Post,* November 10, 2013.

130 "son's funeral": Taraborrelli, *Jackie, Ethel, Joan,* 239.

130 "prayed alone": Rita Dallas, *The Kennedy Case* (New York: G. P. Putnam's Sons, 1973), 249.

130 Fifty military fighters: B. C. Mossman and M. W. Stark, *The Last Salute: Civil and Military Funerals, 1921–1969* (Washington: Department of the Army, 1972), 188–214.

130 "My President": Richard Goldstein, "James Swindal, 88, Pilot of Kennedy's Presidential Plane, Dies," *New York Times,* May 1, 2006.

130 "Those drumbeats": Peter Rowe, "Carrying the Weight of JFK's Casket," *San Diego Union Tribune,* November 16, 2013.

131 "feel any emotion": Dwaun Sellers, "How SC man became pallbearer at JFK Funeral," *State* (South Carolina), October 27, 2017.

131 "locked the TV": David Bianculli, "How Live TV Helped America Mourn the Loss of JFK," *Fresh Air,* National Public Radio, November 22, 2013.

131 "ungodly assassin": Michael Whittaker, "Police Officer J. D. Tippit Buried," United Press International, November 26, 1963.

131 "This great tragedy": Dave Lieber, "JFK's Assassin Shot Her Husband; All She Wants Is to Be Buried Next to Him," *Dallas News,* November 19, 2018.

132 "visit our friend": Larry McShane, "The Day America Watched a Son's

Final Salute to Slain Father, JFK, as Nation Buried a Beloved Leader," *New York Daily News*, November 17, 2013.

132 "four endless days": "Death of a First Lady; Eulogies; Because of Her, We Could Grieve and Then Go On," *New York Times*, May 24, 1994.

132 "Jack was not forgotten": Swanson, "Inventing Camelot"

132 "It pleases me": Eric Pace, "Theodore White, Chronicler of U.S. Politics, Is Dead at 71," *New York Times*, May 16, 1986.

133 "*Life* magazine to say": Swanson, "Inventing Camelot."

133 "passed unanimously": Tom Hintgen, "JFK's Humor Broke the Ice," *Daily Journal* (Fergus Falls, MN), November 29, 2010.

133 "a storyteller of elections": Pace, "Theodore White."

133 "lines he loved": Swanson, "Inventing Camelot."

PART FIVE
THE PROPHET: ROBERT FRANCIS KENNEDY

CHAPTER 23

137 "just another lawyer now": Peter Collier and David Horowitz, *The Kennedys: An American Drama* (New York: Summit Books, 1984), 321.

137 "sink quite easily": Collier and Horowitz, *The Kennedys*, 179.

137 "like Daddy lost both arms": Lou Lumenick, "Ethel Kennedy Spills Family Secrets," *New York Post*, January 20, 2012.

137 "I was concentrating": Robert Kennedy, "Our Climb Up Mount Kennedy," *Life*, April 9, 1965.

138 "Good luck, Daddy": Kennedy, "Our Climb Up Mount Kennedy."

138 "His paper had just completed my obituary": Kennedy.

138 "I climbed Matterhorn in 1957": "Nine Things You Probably Didn't Know About Bobby Kennedy," New England Historical Society website, 2019.

139 "up Everest three times in my mind": Michael Jourdan, "Mountain Tribute to JFK Evoked by Kennedy Trip to Yukon," *National Geographic*, August 5, 2013.

139 "Don't slip, dear": Kennedy, "Our Climb Up Mount Kennedy."

139 "I was so delighted": Alexia Fernandez, "Robert Kennedy's Friend Recalls the 'Emotional' Moment He Climbed Peak Named after Late JFK," *People*, November 6, 2019.

139 "President Kennedy's family flag": Jourdan, "Mountain Tribute to JFK Evoked."

139 Kennedy family flag: "Kennedy Family Crest," Green Studio, Jacqueline Bouvier Kennedy Onassis Personal Papers, John F. Kennedy Presidential Library and Museum.

139 Chief Herald of Ireland: Correspondence from Gerard Slevin, the Chief Herald of Ireland, Jacqueline Bouvier Kennedy Onassis Personal Papers, 17 May 1963–68, June 1968.

139 "lonely, stark, forbidding": Arthur M. Schlesinger Jr., *Robert Kennedy and His Times*, fortieth anniversary edition (New York: Houghton Mifflin Harcourt, 2018), 811.

CHAPTER 24

141 Thousand-dollar tickets: Henry Machirella and Paul Healy, "E. Side, W. Side Chorus 'Happy Birthday' to JFK, *New York Daily News*, May 20, 1962 (republished as "John F. Kennedy Celebrates Birthday in Madison Square Garden in 1962," *New York Daily News* website, May 18, 2015).

141 "The *late* Marilyn Monroe": Jesse Greenspan, "'Happy Birthday, Mr. President' Turns 50," History.com—A&E Television Networks, May 18, 2012.

142 "beads and skin": Enid Nemy, "Jean Louis, 89; Dressed Stars and Socialites," *New York Times*, April 24, 1997.

142 "world's most expensive": "See the World's Most Expensive Dress!" Ripley's Believe it or Not—Ripley Entertainment Inc., Ripleys.com.

142 "a very 'rah rah rah' kind of atmosphere": Ben Cosgrove, "Behind the Picture: Photos from the Night Marilyn Sang to JFK, 1962," *Time*, April 30, 2014.

142 "Life's too short to worry about Marilyn Monroe": J. Randy Taraborrelli, *Jackie, Ethel, Joan: Women of Camelot* (New York: Warner Books, 2000), 129.

142 "such a sweet, wholesome way": Taraborrelli, *Jackie, Ethel, Joan*, 130.

143 Photo of Marilyn, Bobby, and Jack: Olivia B. Waxman, "The Story Behind the Only Known Photo of Marilyn Monroe and John F. Kennedy Together," *Time*, August 3, 2018.

143 Photo of Stephen Smith and Marilyn: "Dress Marilyn Monroe Wore

for John F. Kennedy Birthday Song Sells for $4.8 Million," NBC-Chicago.com, November 18, 2016.

143 "I do not think I have seen anyone so beautiful": Arthur M. Schlesinger Jr., *Robert Kennedy and His Times,* fortieth anniversary edition (New York: Houghton Mifflin Harcourt, 2018), 590–91.

143 "orchestrated the whole goddamn thing": Taraborrelli, *Jackie, Ethel, Joan,* 131.

143 "spectacular absenteeism": Alexandra Pollard, "Something's Got to Give: The Story of the Marilyn Monroe Film That Never Got Made," *Independent* (UK), March 29, 2019.

144 "you and Bobby are the new item!": Louise Watt, "Marilyn Monroe's Dresses, Notes, Checkbook Seen Before Sale," Associated Press, September 27, 2016.

144 Jean Kennedy Smith affair: Laura Lippman, "Two Books Unveil Details, from Sex to Silverware," *Baltimore Sun*, August 12, 1994.

144 "Very often distraught": Schlesinger Jr., *Robert Kennedy and His Times*, 591.

144 Robert Slatzer claims of marriage: "'Marilyn and Me' dramatizes possible fourth marriage," *Baltimore Sun*, September 22, 1991.

144 "Robert Kennedy promised to marry": Schlesinger Jr., *Robert Kennedy and His Times,* 591.

144 "I like him": Schlesinger, 591.

144 "talk to Monroe about putting a bridle on": Seymour M. Hersh, *The Dark Side of Camelot,* (New York: Little, Brown, 1997), 104–5.

144 "you'll marry Jack, that's great": Julie Miller, "Jackie Kennedy Gave Marilyn Monroe Her Snarky Blessing to Marry J.F.K., New Book Claims," *Vanity Fair,* August 5, 2013.

145 "say good-bye to yourself": Ellis S. Conklin, "Marilyn Monroe's Last Words Were a Farewell to President..." United Press International, September 24, 1985.

145 "the feeling of violence": Sam Kashner, "Marilyn and Her Monsters," *Vanity Fair,* October 5, 2010.

145 "a minute fracture": Joan Kron, "The Mystery of Marilyn Monroe's Plastic Surgery," *Allure,* October 9, 2013.

146 "a mini–phone listening device": Stephen Galloway, "Rock Hudson's Wife Secretly Recorded His Gay Confession," *Hollywood Reporter,* June 6, 2013.

146 Monroe's house: Lindsey Campbell, "Inside Marilyn Monroe's Brentwood Home," *House Beautiful,* October 28, 2014.000 Fred Otash: Myrna Oliver, "Fred Otash; Colorful Hollywood Private Eye and Author," *Los Angeles Times,* October 8, 1992.

146 "on behalf of Howard Hughes and Nixon": Galloway, "Rock Hudson's Wife Secretly Recorded."

146 "I did not trust him not to dissemble": Galloway.

146 "Well, I think I made his back feel better": Peter Collier and David Horowitz, *The Kennedys: An American Drama* (New York: Summit Books, 1984), 413.

146 "I listened to Marilyn Monroe die": Galloway, "Rock Hudson's Wife Secretly Recorded."

147 "passed around like a piece of meat": Galloway.

147 "sounded like Marilyn": Tracy Connor, "Spotlight Gave a Jolt to Joe's First Family," *New York Post,* March 9, 1999.

CHAPTER 25

148 Monroe's housekeeper calls Greenson: J. I. Baker, K. C. Baker and Liz McNeil, "Why Marilyn Monroe's Death Is Still a Mystery," *People,* June 29, 2017.

148 "remove anything incriminating": Myrna Oliver, "Fred Otash; Colorful Hollywood Private Eye and Author," *Los Angeles Times,* October 8, 1992.

148 "misinterpreted as a cover-up": Baker, Baker, and McNeil, "Why Marilyn Monroe's Death Is Still a Mystery."

149 "most obviously staged death scene": Richard Belzer and David Wayne, *Dead Wrong: Straight Facts on the Country's Most Controversial Cover-Ups* (New York: Simon & Schuster, 2012), Chapter 4.

149 Nembutal capsules: Howard Hertel and Don Neff, "Marilyn Monroe Dies; Pills Blamed," *Los Angeles Times,* August 6, 1962.

149 "affair with Bobby Kennedy": Baker, Baker and McNeil, "Why Marilyn Monroe's Death Is Still a Mystery."

149 "I can't flat out fire her": "John Miner" (Obituary), *Telegraph* (UK), March 4, 2011.

150 Dr. Noguchi's impression of Monroe: John Preston, "Dr Thomas Noguchi: LA Coroner Confidential," *Telegraph* (UK), September 10, 2009.

150 "might be a murder victim": Preston, "Dr Thomas Noguchi."

150 "acute combined drug toxicity": Baker, Baker, and McNeil, "Why Marilyn Monroe's Death Is Still a Mystery."

151 "I tell you, doctor": Seymour M. Hersh, *The Dark Side of Camelot* (New York: Little, Brown, 1997), 104.

151 "Robert Kennedy came to inhabit": Arthur M. Schlesinger Jr., *Robert Kennedy and His Times,* fortieth anniversary edition (New York: Houghton Mifflin Harcourt, 2018), 591.

151 "no room in my life for him": "John Miner" (Obituary).

151 "eyes wide and hurt": Alexandra Pollard, "Something's Got to Give: The Story of the Marilyn Monroe Film That Never Got Made," *Independent* (UK), March 29, 2019.

151 "The Strange Death of Marilyn Monroe": Peter Collier and David Horowitz, *The Kennedys: An American Drama* (New York: Summit Books, 1984), 323.

152 she and Jack bought the place: Matt Blitz, "Hickory Hill and the Kennedy Mystique," *Arlington Magazine,* June 4, 2018.

152 "no credible evidence": Larry Tye, *Bobby Kennedy: The Making of a Liberal Icon* (New York: Random House, 2016), 192.

152 "got out of her misery": Barbara Leaming, "The Winter of Her Despair," *Vanity Fair,* September 18, 2014.

CHAPTER 26

153 Rededication of Idlewild: Ted Reed, "Fifty Years Ago, Idlewild Airport Became JFK," TheStreet.com, December 20, 2013.

153 "Those who knew him well": "An Excerpt from 'The Revolution of Robert Kennedy,'" MSNBC.com, June 6, 2017.

154 "seventh of nine children": Larry Tye, *Bobby Kennedy: The Making of a Liberal Icon* (New York: Random House, 2016), 13.

154 "Kennedys moved fast": George Vecsey, "The Game Stopped," *New York Times,* November 21, 1983.

154 "He never let up": Chris Matthews, *Bobby Kennedy: A Raging Spirit* (New York: Simon & Schuster, 2017), 66.

154 "powerful and unsportsmanlike shove": Ted Sorensen, "RFK Assassination: Aide Recalls Tragedy Repeated" and "Excerpt: 'Counselor,'" *Morning Edition,* National Public Radio, June 5, 2008.

154 "somewhat hollow in his convictions": Robert Barr, "RFK: Kid Who Lived to Tackle, Adult Who Lived for His Brother," *Los Angeles Times,* June 5, 1988.

155 Senator McCarthy as Kennedy family friend: "RFK's Enemies," *American Experience,* PBS.org.

155 "sharing his father's dislike of liberals": Sorensen, "RFK Assassination."

155 "politically dangerous": Evan Thomas, *Robert Kennedy: His Life* (New York: Simon & Schuster 2007), 74.

155 "Indian hand wrestling": Thomas, *Robert Kennedy,* 77.

156 "became my mortal enemy": Tye, *Bobby Kennedy,* 53.

156 "bug the little bastard": "RFK's Enemies," *American Experience,* PBS.org.

156 "the horns just blaring": Tye, *Bobby Kennedy,* 78–79.

156 "throw acid in the eyes of his six children": Tye, 78.

156 "can you fix us some lunch?": "Hickory Hill: RFK's Virginia Home," *American Experience,* PBS.org.

156 "made him a sympathetic figure": Joe Scarborough, "The Metamorphosis of the Ruthless Bobby Kennedy," *Washington Post,* July 22, 2016.

156 May 1963 Gallup poll: Lydia Saad, "Gallup Vault: A Look Back at Robert Kennedy," *Gallup,* June 5, 2018.

157 "Bobby goes a little further": *Morning Joe* staff, "An Excerpt from 'The Revolution of Robert Kennedy,'" MSNBC.com, June 6, 2017.

157 "won't be here by Christmas": Arthur M. Schlesinger Jr., *Robert Kennedy and His Times,* fortieth anniversary edition (New York: Houghton Mifflin Harcourt, 2018), 606.

157 "drink to the President of the United States": Schlesinger Jr., *Robert Kennedy and His Times,* 606.

157 Bobby gets the call about JFK: Sheila Anne Feeney, "Robert Morgenthau Was with Bobby When He Got the News," *Newsday,* November 21, 2013.

157 "shoots and kills the son of a bitch": Thurston Clarke, *The Last Campaign: Robert F. Kennedy and 82 Days that Inspired America* (New York: Henry Holt, 2008), 25.

157 "I thought something was wrong": Schlesinger Jr., *Robert Kennedy and His Times,* 608.

157 Hoover says JFK's been shot: Schlesinger Jr., *Robert Kennedy and His Times,* 608.

157 "wasn't the way": Schlesinger Jr., 629.

158 "didn't want to leave him": Feeney, "Robert Morgenthau Was with Bobby."

158 "About thirty minutes after": Schlesinger Jr., *Robert Kennedy and His Times*, 608.

158 "Jack is dead": Feeney, "Robert Morgenthau Was with Bobby."

158 "I thought they would get one of us": Peter Collier and David Horowitz, *The Kennedys: An American Drama* (New York: Summit Books, 1984), 312.

158 "Did the CIA kill my brother?" Collier and Horowitz, *The Kennedys*, 317.

158 "most wonderful life": Evan Thomas, *Robert Kennedy: His Life* (New York: Simon & Schuster 2007), 277.

158 President Lyndon Johnson: Tye, *Bobby Kennedy*, 288.

159 "Why, God?": Schlesinger Jr., *Robert Kennedy and His Times*, 611.

CHAPTER 27

160 "one of the toughest guys": Thomas Maier, *The Kennedys: America's Emerald Kings* (New York: Basic Books, 2003), 488.

160 "much left for me": Larry Tye, *Bobby Kennedy: The Making of a Liberal Icon* (New York: Random House, 2016), 291.

160 Bobby's silver cigarette case: Tye, *Bobby Kennedy*, 287.

161 "I have another brother": Arthur M. Schlesinger Jr., *Robert Kennedy and His Times,* fortieth anniversary edition (New York: Houghton Mifflin Harcourt, 2018), 613.

161 "natural for Bobby to take charge": Tye, *Bobby Kennedy*, 289.

161 "all the things that Jack started": Schlesinger Jr., *Robert Kennedy and His Times,* 612.

161 "I don't have the heart for it": Schlesinger Jr., 632.

161 "the significance of Jack's death": Maier, *The Kennedys*, 488.

161 "wild, informal mixture": "Hickory Hill: RFK's Virginia Home," *American Experience,* PBS.org.

161 "a menagerie": "Hickory Hill: RFK's Virginia Home."

162 "And if Bobby died": *Morning Joe* staff, "An Excerpt from 'The Revolution of Robert Kennedy,'" MSNBC.com, June 6, 2017.

162 Rosemary's whereabouts: Evan Thomas, "The Fierce Rebellion and Compassion of Eunice Shriver," *Washington Post,* April 13, 2018.

162 Jack's possible visit to Rosemary in 1958: Liz McNeil, "Why Rosemary

Kennedy's Siblings Didn't See Her for 20 Years After Her Lobotomy," *People,* September 2, 2015.

162 "mentally retarded sister": "Rosemary Kennedy, JFK's Sister, Dies at 86," NBCNews.com, January 8, 2005.

162 "give them a lollypop": Kirk Johnson, "Reaching the Retarded: An Old Kennedy Mission," *New York Times,* June 23, 1995.

162 "You know how Eunice is": J. Randy Taraborrelli, *After Camelot: A Personal History of the Kennedy Family 1968 to the Present* (New York: Grand Central Publishing, 2012), 37.

162 "Just give Eunice what she wants": Thomas, "The Fierce Rebellion and Compassion of Eunice Shriver."

163 Eunice's summer camp: Eunice Kennedy Shriver, "Hope for Retarded Children," *Saturday Evening Post,* September 22, 1962.

163 "they will not be the victims of our neglect": "Remarks upon Signing the Maternal and Child Health and Mental Retardation Planning Bill (434)," October 24, 1963, *Public Papers of the Presidents: John F. Kennedy, 1963.*

163 "the custodian of the Kennedy dream": Schlesinger Jr., *Robert Kennedy and His Times,* 647.

163 "came out of Dallas alive": Garrett M. Graff, "Angel Is Airborne," *Washingtonian.*

163 "Bobby should have waited": Schlesinger Jr., *Robert Kennedy and His Times,* 657.

CHAPTER 28

164 Ted's 1964 plane crash: Peter Collier and David Horowitz, *The Kennedys: An American Drama* (New York: Summit Books, 1984), 322.

164 Two of five killed: "Senator Kennedy Tells of His Rescue in Plane Crash," *New York Times,* October 20, 1964.

164 "a great year for the giggles": Collier and Horowitz, *The Kennedys,* 322.

165 "to vote not for LBJ but RFK": Rick Klein, "Jacqueline Kennedy Reveals That JFK Feared an LBJ Presidency," ABCNews.com, September 8, 2011.

165 "Robert Kennedy's activities were of special interest": Arthur M. Schlesinger Jr., *Robert Kennedy and His Times,* fortieth anniversary edition (New York: Houghton Mifflin Harcourt, 2018), 663.

165 "Kennedy wing of the party": Collier and Horowitz, *The Kennedys: An American Drama,* 322.

165 "what you can do for the Kennedys": Evan Thomas, *Robert Kennedy: His Life* (New York: Simon & Schuster, 2007), 299.

165 RFK's house in Glen Cove: "Kennedy Takes Lease on House in Glen Cove, L.I.; He Will Announce Candidacy for Senate Today—Fight Is Pledged by Stratton," *New York Times,* August 25, 1964.

165 "such strong public feeling": "Kennedy's Role as Attorney General," *New York Times,* September 4, 1964.

166 Bobby/Jackie romance rumors: Annie Wilkinson, "RFK: A Ripple of Hope," *Long Island Press,* September 4, 2018.

166 "Bobby's wife thought": J. Randy Taraborrelli, *Jackie, Ethel, Joan: Women of Camelot* (New York: Warner Books, 2000), 310.

166 "unprintable outrage": "Kennedy vs. Keating in New York."

166 "His appearance is ever modern": Kerry Kennedy, "Kerry Kennedy: What My Father, RFK, Means Today," *Time,* May 31, 2019.

166 "Too many young people": Thomas, *Robert Kennedy: His Life,* 299.

166 "like a Beatle": "Kennedy, Keating Close Campaigns; Democrat Favored to Win—Senator's Polls Show Extremely Close Race," *New York Times,* November 3, 1964.

167 "in a juke box but not in an election box": "Keating vs. Kennedy: A Near-Debate; Senator Faces Empty Seat; Democrat Tries to Sit in It," *New York Times,* October 28, 1964.

167 "Let's just go home": "Kennedy-Keating: Finally a Face-to-Face Meeting; Keating, Kennedy Meet in a Debate on Radio Program; Candidates Discuss a Wide Range of Issues for Hour on a Late-Night Show; Hoffa's Role Is Argued; Senator, on TV Earlier, Leaves Studio Door Open in Vain for Opponent," *New York Times,* October 31, 1964.

167 "He is really very shy, but he has the kindest heart in the world": Taraborrelli, *Jackie, Ethel, Joan,* 303–4.

167 The *Post* backs Bobby: "Kennedy, Keating Close Campaigns."

167 Bobby wins Senate race: Collier and Horowitz, *The Kennedys,* 324.

167 "a way-stop for this man on the run": R. C. Baker, "Bobby the K: Robert Kennedy Comes to New York," *Village Voice,* June 6, 2018.

CHAPTER 29

168 *Poverty* note: Nicolas Lemann, "The Politics of Poverty," *Atlantic* (JFK Issue), September 2013.

168 "casting a shadow on Ted": Arthur M. Schlesinger Jr., *Robert Kennedy and His Times,* fortieth anniversary edition (New York: Houghton Mifflin Harcourt, 2018), 680.

168 "in the Senate, but not *of* it": Evan Thomas, *Robert Kennedy: His Life* (New York: Simon & Schuster, 2007), 202.

168 "meteoric rise": Lydia Saad, "Gallup Vault: A Look Back at Robert Kennedy," *Gallup,* June 5, 2018.

169 George Skakel Jr. 1966 plane crash: United Press International, "Kennedy In-Law Dies in Light Plane Crash," *Desert Sun,* September 24, 1966.

169 "immediately went into seclusion," United Press International, "Kennedy In-Law Dies in Light Plane Crash."

169 "seems to be jinxed": "The Things Bobby Kennedy Said," *Esquire,* June 5, 2018.

169 "unwilling to criticize it": Schlesinger Jr., *Robert Kennedy and His Times,* 616.

170 "a big story checking out of the Holiday Inn": John Carr, "My Brush with History: With RFK in the Delta," *American Heritage* 53, no. 2 (April/May 2002).

170 "I've never seen anything like this": Larry Tye, *Bobby Kennedy: The Making of a Liberal Icon* (New York: Random House, 2016), 349.

170 "waves of the nation's poor and disinherited": Drew Dellinger, "The Last March of Martin Luther King Jr.," *Atlantic,* April 4, 2018.

170 "Mississippi's hungry children": Tye, *Bobby Kennedy,* 350.

170 "find him growing and changing": Ted Sorensen, "RFK Assassination: Aide Recalls Tragedy Repeated" and "Excerpt: 'Counselor,'" *Morning Edition,* National Public Radio, June 5, 2008.

171 "a petulant baseball player": Thurston Clarke, *The Last Campaign: Robert F. Kennedy and 82 Days That Inspired America* (New York: Henry Holt, 2008), 13.

171 "Somewhere in this man sits good": Joe Scarborough, "The Metamorphosis of the Ruthless Bobby Kennedy," *Washington Post,* July 22, 2016.

171 "chances for a Kennedy dynasty": "The Things Bobby Kennedy Said," *Esquire,* June 5, 2018.

171 "a psychic violence about him": Schlesinger Jr., *Robert Kennedy and His Times,* 804.

171 Kennedy support declining: Saad, "Gallup Vault: A Look Back at Robert Kennedy."

171 "adjectives and adverbs": Sorensen, "RFK Assassination: Aide Recalls Tragedy Repeated."

171 "there is enough to go around for all": Peter Collier and David Horowitz, *The Kennedys: An American Drama* (New York: Summit Books, 1984), 336.

172 "how I felt about Vietnam and poor people": Schlesinger Jr., *Robert Kennedy and His Times,* 825.

172 "lesson of Emerson": Jean E. Engelmayer, "The Pied Piper of Liberalism," *Crimson,* May 20, 1983.

172 "no foreseeable circumstances": Jeff Greenfield, "When Bobby Decided to Run," *Politico,* March 17, 2018.

172 "Is my Daddy going to run for President?": Schlesinger Jr., *Robert Kennedy and His Times,* 857.

172 "Santa Claus in '68": Clarke, *The Last Campaign,* 31.

173 "Bobby had so much to give": J. Randy Taraborrelli, *Jackie, Ethel, Joan: Women of Camelot* (New York: Warner Books, 2000), 316.

173 "My brother thinks I'm crazy": Clarke, *The Last Campaign,* 37.

173 "follows his own instincts": Schlesinger Jr., *Robert Kennedy and His Times,* 846.

173 "For heaven's sake, don't marry him": J. Randy Taraborrelli, *After Camelot: A Personal History of the Kennedy Family 1968 to the Present* (New York: Grand Central Publishing, 2012), 12.

174 "at least I'm at peace with myself": Clarke, *The Last Campaign,* 22.

174 "Bobby had an inferiority complex": Thomas Maier, *The Kennedys: America's Emerald Kings* (New York: Basic Books, 2003), 510.

174 "actively reassessing the possibility": Thurston Clarke, *The Last Campaign: Robert F. Kennedy and 82 Days That Inspired America* (New York: Henry Holt, 2008), 36.

174 "day before St. Patrick's Day": Maier, *The Kennedys: America's Emerald Kings,* 510.

174 "he didn't deserve to be president anyway": Evan Thomas, "The Worst Week of 1968," *Newsweek,* November 11, 2007.

174 "The same thing that happened to Jack": Schlesinger Jr., *Robert Kennedy and His Times*, 857.

CHAPTER 30

176 "I don't even think he heard the shot": Bill Hutchinson, "At 86, Andrew Young Recalls Horror of Witnessing Moment Martin Luther King Jr. Was Assassinated in Memphis," ABCNews.com, April 3, 2018.

177 "Martin, don't leave us now": Gilbert Baez, "Jesse Jackson Recalls Moment MLK Was Fatally Shot," WRAL.com, April 4, 2018.

177 "Is this faith justified?" Thurston Clarke, *The Last Campaign: Robert F. Kennedy and 82 Days That Inspired America* (New York: Henry Holt, 2008), 88.

177 "shot their spiritual leader": Arthur M. Schlesinger Jr., *Robert Kennedy and His Times*, fortieth anniversary edition (New York: Houghton Mifflin Harcourt, 2018), 874.

177 "When is this violence going to stop?" Schlesinger Jr., *Robert Kennedy and His Times*, 874.

178 "I don't want any police going with me": Clarke, *The Last Campaign*, 90.

178 "why does he have to come here?": Clarke, 92.

178 "almost like a prayer": Clarke, 90.

178 "full of anguish": Schlesinger Jr., *Robert Kennedy and His Times*, 874.

178 "nervous, self-deprecating jokes": Schlesinger, 885.

178 "I feel in my own heart": Schlesinger Jr., 874.

179 "every word out of his mouth was a balm": Mary Evans, "I Was There for Robert Kennedy's Electrifying Speech About MLK's Murder," History.com, April 20, 2018.

179 "He had empathy": Michael S. Rosenwald, "'That Stain of Bloodshed': After King's Assassination, RFK Calmed an Angry Crowd with an Unforgettable Speech," *Washington Post,* April 4, 2018.

179 "sincerity of Bobby Kennedy's words": Liam Stack, "When Robert F. Kennedy Told an Indianapolis Crowd of King's Assassination," *New York Times,* April 4, 2018.

179 "I'll help in any way I can": Schlesinger Jr., *Robert Kennedy and His Times,* 876.

179 "track down some twenty-two-year-old": David Margolick, "Book Excerpt: After MLK Death, RFK 'Poured His Heart Out,'" Reuters, March 29, 2018.

180 James Earl Ray arrest: Vincent Dowd, "When Martin Luther King Jr's Assassin Fled to London," BBC World Service, June 8, 2016.

180 "prophets get shot": Clarke, *The Last Campaign,* 126.

CHAPTER 31

181 Roy Lichtenstein's portrait of Bobby: Roy Lichtenstein, "Robert F. Kennedy," *Time,* May 24, 1968.

181 "cut off as much as you can": Arthur M. Schlesinger Jr., *Robert Kennedy and His Times,* fortieth anniversary edition (New York: Houghton Mifflin Harcourt, 2018), 857.

181 "mother of two presidents?" Rita Dallas with Jeanira Ratcliffe, *The Kennedy Case* (New York: G. P. Putnam's Sons, 1973), 303.

182 "the more you can afford, the more you spend": "How Bobby Kennedy Won the '68 Indiana Primary," *Newsweek,* May 19, 1968.

182 "much better to win": "How Bobby Kennedy Won the '68 Indiana Primary."

182 "long time until August": "How Bobby Kennedy Won the '68 Indiana Primary."

182 "I *have* to be able to win in every state": Thurston Clarke, *The Last Campaign: Robert F. Kennedy and 82 Days That Inspired America* (New York: Henry Holt, 2008), 228.

182 "Cut your hair, then we'll vote!": Douglas Perry, "Robert Kennedy, Eugene McCarthy Thrilled Young Voters During Epic Battle for 1968 Oregon Primary (Historic Photos)," *The Oregonian*/OregonLive, May 16, 2016.

182 "dramatic victory": Perry, "Robert Kennedy, Eugene McCarthy Thrilled Young Voters."

182 "I appeal best to people who have problems": Peter Collier and David Horowitz, *The Kennedys: An American Drama* (New York: Summit Books, 1984), 349.

182 "I'm going to win one for you": Collier and Horowitz, *The Kennedys,* 349.

183 "I hope Los Angeles is Resurrection City": Clarke, *The Last Campaign,* 247.

183 "Hollywood for Kennedy": Joseph A. Palermo, "Here's What RFK Did in California in 1968," *HuffPost,* May 25, 2011.

183 "Is Bobby Kennedy ready?" Clarke, *The Last Campaign,* 261.

183 "I'm planning on shooting him": David Margolick, "Book Excerpt: After MLK Death, RFK 'Poured His Heart Out,'" *Reuters,* March 29, 2018.

183 "If I'm ever elected president": Schlesinger Jr., *Robert Kennedy and His Times,* 902.

184 "We'll make a movie star of David": Collier and Horowitz, *The Kennedys,* 360.

184 "stretched out across two chairs": Palermo, "Here's what RFK Did in California in 1968."

184 "none of us will ever get over John Kennedy": Schlesinger Jr., *Robert Kennedy and His Times,* 913.

184 Frankenheimer speeding: Schlesinger Jr., *Robert Kennedy and His Times,* 913.

CHAPTER 32

185 "Do we know enough about it yet?" "Robert Kennedy Shot, Killed in Los Angeles," *Newsweek,* June 16, 1968.

185 "shaken off the shadow of my brother": Evan Thomas, *Robert Kennedy: His Life* (New York: Simon & Schuster, 2007), 388–89.

185 "Viva Kennedy!": Tim Arango, "A Campaign, A Murder, A Legacy: Robert F. Kennedy's California Story," *New York Times,* June 5, 2018.

185 "This Land Is Your Land": Richard Harwood, "With Bobby Kennedy on that Last Campaign," *Washington Post,* June 5, 1988.

185 "he didn't have any security": Arango, "A Campaign, a Murder, a Legacy."

186 "nobody special": Thurston Clarke, *The Last Campaign: Robert F. Kennedy and 82 Days That Inspired America* (New York: Henry Holt, 2008), 246–47.

186 "compassionate country": Bill Hutchinson, "50 Years After Shots Rang Out at the Ambassador Hotel, Controversy Still Surrounds RFK's Assassination," ABCNews.com, June 5, 2018.

186 "Look after Ethel": Niall O'Dowd, "Robert Kennedy's Fatal Order to His Bodyguard on Night He Was Shot That Doomed Him," *Irish Central* (UK), October 10, 2018.

186 "there's a madman in here": "Robert Kennedy Shot, Killed in Los Angeles."

187 Sirhan Bishara Sirhan: Peter Gilstrap, "What Is It Like to Be the Brother

of Robert Kennedy's Assassin? The Life of the Other Sirhan," *Washington Post*, May 31, 2018.

187 "Get this guy off in a corner": O'Dowd, "Robert Kennedy's Fatal Order."

187 Chief Reddin transports Sirhan: Associated Press, "Thomas Reddin, 88, Former Los Angeles Police Chief, Is Dead," *New York Times,* December 6, 2004.

187 "a steady stream of blood": Laurel Wamsley and Emily Sullivan, "Juan Romero, Busboy Who Cradled Dying RFK, Dies at 68," National Public Radio, October 4, 2018.

187 "Bob, Bob can you hear us?" "Robert Kennedy Shot, Killed in Los Angeles."

187 "she was overjoyed": "Robert Kennedy Shot, Killed in Los Angeles."

188 *"He's going to live"*: J. Randy Taraborrelli, *The Kennedy Heirs* (New York: St. Martin's Press, 2019), 202.

188 "I've got his shoes": Clarke, *The Last Campaign,* 8.

CHAPTER 33

189 "perfect autopsy": Seth Augustein, "Case Study: The Assassination of RFK, and 'The Perfect Autopsy,'" *Forensic Magazine,* June 19, 2018.

189 "distance of one to six inches": John M. Crewdson, "Lowenstein Says Year's Study of Evidence Shows Sirhan Was Not Assassin of Kennedy," *New York Times,* December 16, 1974.

189 "Don't look at him": Interview with John Tunney by Stephen F. Knott and James Sterling Young, *The Edward M. Kennedy Oral History Project,* Edward M. Kennedy Institute for the United States Senate in partnership with the Miller Center of Public Affairs at the University of Virginia, May 3, 2007.

189 "killing all the Kennedys": Associated Press, "Pierre Salinger Dies at 79," NBC News, October 17, 2004.

190 "same kind of disaster": Rose Fitzgerald Kennedy, *Times to Remember* (Garden City, NY: Doubleday, 1974), 475.

190 "death of the president": Peter S. Canellos, ed., *Last Lion: The Fall and Rise of Ted Kennedy* (New York: Simon & Schuster Paperbacks, 2010), 137.

190 Rumors of Joe Sr.'s death: David Margolick, "Robert F. Kennedy's Final Flight: The Storied Journey of the Ride from California to New York," *Washington Post,* June 3, 2018.

190 "Air Force jets bear the bodies": Margolick, "Robert F. Kennedy's Final Flight."

190 "three widows": Margolick.

190 Bobby's funeral: "Robert Kennedy Shot, Killed in Los Angeles," *Newsweek,* June 16, 1968.

191 "started kicking the box": Richard Harwood, "With Bobby Kennedy on That Last Campaign," *Washington Post,* June 5, 1988.

191 Bobby's funeral train: Thurston Clarke, *The Last Campaign: Robert F. Kennedy and 82 Days That Inspired America* (New York: Henry Holt, 2008), 6.

191 "He's got *it!*": Joe Keohane, "But the Dream Should Die," *Boston,* November 30, 2009.

192 "traumatized by Dr. King's assassination": Kathy Lohr, "Poor People's Campaign: A Dream Unfulfilled," *Morning Edition,* Special Series: Echoes of 1968, National Public Radio, June 19, 2008.

192 "a great white moon": Arthur M. Schlesinger, *Robert Kennedy and His Times,* fortieth anniversary edition (New York: Houghton Mifflin Harcourt, 2018), 916.

192 "the Kennedys draw the lightning": Larry Tye, *Bobby Kennedy: The Making of a Liberal Icon* (New York: Random House, 2016), 442.

CHAPTER 34

193 "crippled kids running around": Eileen McNamara, "Eunice Kennedy Shriver: The Hidden Kennedy Powerhouse," *Saturday Evening Post,* February 19, 2019.

194 "full judgment of the Kennedy legacy": Carla Baranauckas, "Eunice Kennedy Shriver, Influential Founder of Social Olympics, Dies at 88," *New York Times,* August 11, 2009.

194 "I like Teddy": Peter S. Canellos, ed., *Last Lion: The Fall and Rise of Ted Kennedy* (New York: Simon & Schuster Paperbacks, 2010), 127.

194 "I wouldn't support your brother": Transcript of Interview with Robert Healy by Stephen F. Knott, "Robert Healy Oral History, Journalist, the *Boston Globe,*" *Presidential Oral Histories—Edward M. Kennedy Histories,* Miller Center for Public Affairs at the University of Virginia, August 10, 2005.

194 "your own unique quality": Jean Kennedy Smith, *The Nine of Us: Growing Up Kennedy* (New York: HarperCollins, 2016), 109.

194 "My little pet": Larry Tye, *Bobby Kennedy: The Making of a Liberal Icon* (New York: Random House, 2016), 13.

194 "It is so very difficult": Barbara Perry, *Rose Kennedy: The Life and Times of a Political Matriarch* (New York: W.W. Norton, 2013), 299.

194 "Had Bobby lived": Tye, *Bobby Kennedy*, 442.

195 "what I had gone through five years earlier": Ted Sorensen, "RFK Assassination: Aide Recalls Tragedy Repeated," *Morning Edition*, National Public Radio, June 5, 2008.

195 "much better man for knowing him": Tye, *Bobby Kennedy*, 443.

195 "If he hadn't stopped to shake your hand": Laurel Wamsley and Emily Sullivan, "Juan Romero, Busboy Who Cradled Dying RFK, Dies at 68," National Public Radio, October 4, 2018.

195 "able to go through this awful experience with such dignity": Arthur M. Schlesinger Jr., *Robert Kennedy and His Times*, fortieth anniversary edition (New York: Houghton Mifflin Harcourt, 2018), 915.

195 "I'm telling you here and now": J. Randy Taraborrelli, *Jackie, Ethel, Joan: Women of Camelot* (New York: Warner Books, 2000), 357.

195 "if anything happens to this baby": Taraborrelli, *Jackie, Ethel, Joan*, 376.

196 "this new Kennedy can't miss": Taraborrelli, 377.

196 Bringing Rory to Bobby's grave: Taraborrelli, 378.

PART SIX
THE SENATOR: EDWARD MOORE KENNEDY

CHAPTER 35

199 "you're all we've got": Peter Collier and David Horowitz, *The Kennedys: An American Drama* (New York: Summit Books, 1984), 364.

199 Lowenstein suggesting Ted for 1968: Justin N. Feldman, recorded interview by Roberta W. Greene, February 4, 1970, Robert F. Kennedy Oral History Program of the John F. Kennedy Library.

199 "do it to that family a third time": David Oshinsky, "One Person Made a Difference," *New York Times*, November 7, 1993.

199 "no record in public life strong enough": Adam Clymer, *Edward M. Kennedy: A Biography* (New York: William Morrow, 1999), 121.

200 "My babies were rocked to political lullabies": John M. Broder, "Edward M. Kennedy, Senate Stalwart, Is Dead at 77," *New York Times,* August 26, 2009.

200 "work out plans to make people happy": Clymer, *Edward M. Kennedy,* 12.

200 "serious about serious things": Rose Fitzgerald Kennedy, *Times to Remember* (Garden City, NY: Doubleday, 1974), 111.

200 "loved his esprit": Interview with John Tunney (2007), *The Edward M. Kennedy Oral History Project,* Edward M. Kennedy Institute for the United States Senate in partnership with the Miller Center of Public Affairs at the University of Virginia, 2016.

200 "youngest and reputedly stupidest": Hendrik Hertzberg, "Ted and Harvard, 1962," *The New Yorker,* August 27, 2009.

201 "such a fatty": Peter S. Canellos, ed., *Last Lion: The Fall and Rise of Ted Kennedy* (New York: Simon & Schuster Paperbacks, 2010), 26.

201 "two boys instead of one": Canellos, *Last Lion,* 26.

201 "such a bad student": Canellos, 27.

201 "permission to paddle": Fitzgerald Kennedy, *Times to Remember,* 116.

201 "seemed fat as ever": James W. Graham, *Victura: The Kennedys, a Sailboat, and the Sea* (Lebanon, NH: University Press of New England, 2014), 183.

201 "strong as hell": Transcript of Interview with Robert Healy by Stephen F. Knott, "Robert Healy Oral History, Journalist, the *Boston Globe*," *Presidential Oral Histories—Edward M. Kennedy Histories,* Miller Center for Public Affairs at the University of Virginia, August 10, 2005.

201 "really sticky fingers": Clymer, *Edward M. Kennedy,* 17.

202 "didn't have to cheat": Canellos, *Last Lion,* 38.

202 "you're not clever enough": Canellos, 38.

202 "look at what you're signing?" Clymer, *Edward M. Kennedy,* 18.

202 "all meat and muscles": Canellos, *Last Lion,* 42.

202 "learned a lesson": Canellos, 42.

202 Ted in jersey number 88: Loren Amor, "Football '09: Kennedy: Fighter from the Start," *Harvard Crimson,* September 18. 2009.

202 "a possible Pro Prospect": John Chandler, "Ted Kennedy a Success in More Than One Contact Sport," NESN.com, August 26, 2009.

203 "never been so frightened in his life": Canellos, *Last Lion,* 42.

203 "another contact sport": Chandler, "Ted Kennedy a Success in More Than One Contact Sport."

CHAPTER 36

204 Ted and John Tunney at UVA: Interview with John Tunney (2009), *The Edward M. Kennedy Oral History Project*, Edward M. Kennedy Institute for the United States Senate in partnership with the Miller Center of Public Affairs at the University of Virginia, 2016.

204 "life of the party": Ted Strong, "Kennedy's UVA law roots remembered," *Daily Progress*, August 27, 2009.

205 "what side of the court": Adam Clymer, *Edward M. Kennedy: A Biography* (New York: William Morrow, 1999), 21.

205 "tried to outrun me": William Safire, "Prelude to the Bridge," *New York Times*, October 29, 1979.

205 "blink their lights": Peter S. Canellos, ed., *Last Lion: The Fall and Rise of Ted Kennedy* (New York: Simon & Schuster Paperbacks, 2010), 54.

205 Ted earns pilot license: Interview with John Tunney (2009).

206 "I was afraid to fly with him": Interview with John Tunney (2009).

206 "clearly wasn't running it": Interview with Lester Hyman, *The Edward M. Kennedy Oral History Project*, Edward M. Kennedy Institute for the United States Senate in partnership with the Miller Center of Public Affairs at the University of Virginia, 2016.

206 "The Kennedys go into politics and then they grow up": John M. Broder, "Edward M. Kennedy, Senate Stalwart, Is Dead at 77," *New York Times*, August 26, 2009.

206 "the most natural politician in the family": Interview with John Tunney (2007).

206 "the perfect amalgam": Interview with Lester Hyman.

207 "Ted's all heart": Transcript of Interview with Robert Healy by Stephen F. Knott, "Robert Healy Oral History, Journalist, the *Boston Globe*," *Presidential Oral Histories—Edward M. Kennedy Histories*, Miller Center for Public Affairs at the University of Virginia, August 10, 2005.

207 "run for the Senate": Interview with John Tunney (2007).

207 "Here's to 1960, Mr. President": Canellos, *Last Lion*, 59.

CHAPTER 37

208 "He was tall and he was gorgeous": Peter S. Canellos, ed., *Last Lion: The Fall and Rise of Ted Kennedy* (New York: Simon & Schuster Paperbacks, 2010), 55.

208 modeled for Revlon and Coca-Cola: Orla Healy, "The Tragic Life of a Kennedy Wife," *Independent* (UK), April 24, 2005.

208 "kind of girl anyone would want to date": J. Randy Taraborrelli, *Jackie, Ethel, Joan: Women of Camelot* (New York: Grand Central Publishing, 2012), 77.

208 "What do you think about our getting married?": Canellos, *Last Lion*, 57.

209 Joe purchases the ring: Taraborrelli, *Jackie, Ethel, Joan*, 88.

209 "From the beginning, she was in trouble": Taraborrelli, 88.

209 "Being married doesn't really mean": Clymer, *Edward M. Kennedy*, 24.

209 "A couple of such attractiveness": Healy, "The Tragic Life of a Kennedy Wife."

209 "No woman is ever enough": Taraborrelli, *Jackie, Ethel, Joan*, 80–81.

209 "He was thinking of going west": Interview with John Tunney (2007), *The Edward M. Kennedy Oral History Project*, Edward M. Kennedy Institute for the United States Senate in partnership with the Miller Center of Public Affairs at the University of Virginia, 2016.

210 Ted steadily gains weight: Canellos, *Last Lion*, 63.

210 "terrible with candy and ice cream": Interview with Lester Hyman, *The Edward M. Kennedy Oral History Project*, Edward M. Kennedy Institute for the United States Senate in partnership with the Miller Center of Public Affairs at the University of Virginia, 2016.

210 "delivered Wyoming": Transcript of Interview with Robert Healy by Stephen F. Knott, "Robert Healy Oral History, Journalist, the *Boston Globe*," *Presidential Oral Histories — Edward M. Kennedy Histories*, Miller Center for Public Affairs at the University of Virginia, August 10, 2005.

210 Jack makes Ted a dare: Clymer, *Edward M. Kennedy*, 28.

210 "carry the Western States in 1964": Canellos, *Last Lion*, 66.

211 "his father wanted him to run": Canellos, 67.

211 A room in memory of Joe Jr.: Peter Collier and David Horowitz, *The Kennedys: An American Drama* (New York: Summit Books, 1984), 287.

211 "he couldn't talk but he still called them": Transcript of Interview with Robert Healy by Stephen F. Knott.

211 "milling around, stark naked": Rita Dallas with Jeanira Ratcliffe, *The Kennedy Case* (New York: G. P. Putnam's Sons, 1973), 69.

212 "Teddy got caught cheating": Transcript of Interview with Robert Healy by Stephen F. Knott.

212 "Harvard Examination Incident": Clymer, *Edward M. Kennedy*, 36.

212 "more fucking trouble with this than I did with the Bay of Pigs": Transcript of Interview with Robert Healy by Stephen F. Knott.

212 The "Teddy-Eddie" debate: Interview with Lester Hyman.

212 "Brother of the President": Interview with Lester Hyman.

212 "Nobody's laughing": Clymer, *Edward M. Kennedy*, 40.

213 "Kennedys can do no wrong": Interview with Lester Hyman.

CHAPTER 38

214 "stiff as a billy goat at ten in the morning": Interview with Edward M. Kennedy (01/06/2007), *The Edward M. Kennedy Oral History Project,* Edward M. Kennedy Institute for the United States Senate in partnership with the Miller Center of Public Affairs at the University of Virginia, 2016.

214 "The pressure of all the others": Adam Clymer, *Edward M. Kennedy: A Biography* (New York: William Morrow, 1999), 15.

215 "an extraordinary family man": Interview with John Tunney (2007), *The Edward M. Kennedy Oral History Project,* Edward M. Kennedy Institute for the United States Senate in partnership with the Miller Center of Public Affairs at the University of Virginia, 2016.

215 "the one who most came to see the father": Interview with Lester Hyman, *The Edward M. Kennedy Oral History Project,* Edward M. Kennedy Institute for the United States Senate in partnership with the Miller Center of Public Affairs at the University of Virginia, 2016.

215 Ted breaks news of Jack's death to Joe: Peter S. Canellos, ed., *Last Lion: The Fall and Rise of Ted Kennedy* (New York: Simon & Schuster Paperbacks, 2010), 96.

215 "segregation was morally wrong": Ted Kennedy, "Standing Up for Equal-

ity and Staring Down Discrimination," floor of the United States Senate, April 8, 1964.

216 "What do you want me to do, crack up an airplane?": Canellos, *Last Lion,* 100.

216 "The fog is really rolling in": Canellos, 100.

216 "It was just like a toboggan ride": Clymer, *Edward M. Kennedy,* 58.

216 "as though a kitchen knife sliced through it": Clymer, 58.

217 "like a sack of corn under my arm": J. Taylor Rushing, "Bayh Remembers 1964 Plane Crash," *The Hill,* August 28, 2009.

217 "You don't think it's Kennedy?" Interview with Edward Martin, *The Edward M. Kennedy Oral History Project,* Edward M. Kennedy Institute for the United States Senate in partnership with the Miller Center of Public Affairs at the University of Virginia, 2016.

217 "going to be fine": J. Randy Taraborrelli, *Jackie, Ethel, Joan: Women of Camelot* (New York: Grand Central Publishing, 2012), 284.

217 "Nobody knows more about backs than you do": Interview with Ann Gargan, *The Edward M. Kennedy Oral History Project,* Edward M. Kennedy Institute for the United States Senate in partnership with the Miller Center of Public Affairs at the University of Virginia, 2016.

217 "Dad doesn't think that's a very good idea". Interview with Ann Gargan.

217 "educating himself as he was lying there": Interview with John Tunney (2007).

218 "the biggest, nicest strawberries": "Senator Bayh on Ted Kennedy," *Newsweek,* August 25, 2009.

218 "Joan became the candidate herself": Taraborrelli, *Jackie, Ethel, Joan,* 288.

218 "his wife won the campaign for him": Neil Swidey, "Turbulence and Tragedies Eclipse Early Triumphs," *Boston Globe,* February 16, 2009.

218 "Is it ever going to end for you people?" Swidey, "Turbulence and Tragedies Eclipse Early Triumphs."

218 "Can we just chalk it up to coincidence?": Taraborrelli, *Jackie, Ethel, Joan,* 285.

CHAPTER 39

219 "I think that Bobby was Teddy's best friend": Interview with John Tunney (2007), *The Edward M. Kennedy Oral History Project,* Edward M.

Kennedy Institute for the United States Senate in partnership with the Miller Center of Public Affairs at the University of Virginia, 2016.

219 "The fucking Kennedy machine rides again": Interview with Lester Hyman, *The Edward M. Kennedy Oral History Project,* Edward M. Kennedy Institute for the United States Senate in partnership with the Miller Center of Public Affairs at the University of Virginia, 2016.

220 Ted and Joan move to McLean, VA: Adam Clymer, *Edward M. Kennedy: A Biography* (New York: William Morrow, 1999), 93.

220 With Helga Wagner on night of the 1968 California Democratic presidential primary: Clymer, *Edward M. Kennedy,* 109.

220 "Days of partying": Maxine Cheshire, "The Mysterious Helga Wagner," *Washington Post,* March 13, 1980.

220 "get that plane, or your career is over": Clymer, *Edward M. Kennedy,* 109.

220 "his brain was not working": Interview with John Tunney (2007).

221 "one million dollars and a car": Michael Cooper and John M. Broder, "FBI Opens Kennedy File," *New York Times,* June 15, 2010.

221 "multiply as you watched": Lorna Luft, *Me and My Shadows: A Family Memoir* (New York: Pocket Books, 1998), 104.

221 "We need you so much": Judy Garland 1964 Telegram to Ted Kennedy (Western Union), Lot #284, Nate D. Sanders Auctions, Autographs & Memorabilia.

221 "symbolic of all my dreams and wishes": "Judy Garland, 47, Found Dead," *New York Times,* June 23, 1969.

222 "sail all night long by himself": James W. Graham, *Victura: The Kennedys, a Sailboat, and the Sea* (Lebanon, NH: University Press of New England, 2014), 192.

222 "I pick up a fallen standard": John M. Broder, "Edward M. Kennedy, Senate Stalwart, Is Dead at 77," *New York Times,* August 26, 2009.

222 "learn to fight your own battles": Peter S. Canellos, ed., *The Last Lion: The Fall and Rise of Ted Kennedy* (New York: Simon & Schuster, 2009), 25.

222 Assistant leader of the Senate: Broder, "Edward M. Kennedy."

223 "maybe I'm just not attractive enough": J. Randy Taraborrelli, *Jackie, Ethel, Joan: Women of Camelot* (New York: Grand Central Publishing, 2012), 78.

223 "how vulnerable I was": Orla Healy, "The Tragic Life of a Kennedy Wife," *Independent* (UK), April 24, 2005.

223 "as if I weren't hurt or angry": Healy, "The Tragic Life of a Kennedy Wife."

223 "fill it with vodka": Interview with Lester Hyman.

223 "his dark side appeared": Dominick Dunne, "Damage," *Vanity Fair,* October 1991.

224 "shoot my ass off the way they shot Bobby": Michael Kelly, "Ted Kennedy on the Rocks," *GQ,* April 15, 2016.

224 "And by God, it did": Interview with Lester Hyman.

CHAPTER 40

225 "never been so tired in my life": Interview with John Tunney (2007), *The Edward M. Kennedy Oral History Project,* Edward M. Kennedy Institute for the United States Senate in partnership with the Miller Center of Public Affairs at the University of Virginia, 2016.

226 "take us sailing again": "Ted Kennedy Car Accident in Chappaquiddick," *Newsweek,* August 3, 1969.

226 Twenty-eight-year-old Mary Jo Kopechne: William C. Kashatus, "Remembering Mary Jo," *Citizens' Voice* (Wilkes-Barre, PA), July 26, 2015.

226 "always the first to leave": Kashatus, "Remembering Mary Jo."

226 "unconditional loyalty and discretion": Kashatus.

226 "invaluable asset to the senator": Interview with Edward Martin, *The Edward M. Kennedy Oral History Project,* Edward M. Kennedy Institute for the United States Senate in partnership with the Miller Center of Public Affairs at the University of Virginia, 2016.

226 "Don't ride around in new cars": Transcript of Interview with Robert Healy by Stephen F. Knott, "Robert Healy Oral History, Journalist, the *Boston Globe,*" *Presidential Oral Histories—Edward M. Kennedy Histories,* Miller Center for Public Affairs at the University of Virginia, August 10, 2005.

227 When Ted gets out of the water: Robert Sherill, "A Tragedy, an Enigma, a Political Achilles Heel," *New York Times,* July 14, 1974.

227 "he was very badly advised": Interview with John Tunney (2009).

227 "so sad that he didn't have somebody": Interview with John Tunney (2009).

227 "The car has gone off the bridge": Peter S. Canellos, ed., *The Last Lion: The Fall and Rise of Ted Kennedy* (New York: Simon & Schuster, 2009), 154.

228 "You take care of the girls; I'll take care of the accident": Canellos, *The Last Lion,* 155.

228 Ted makes a number of phone calls: Canellos, 155.

228 The innkeeper, Russell Peachey: George Lardner Jr., "Chappaquiddick 1989," *Washington Post,* July 16, 1989.

228 "veritable female 007": Shaun Considine, "Helga Wagner Sells 'She Shells' and Shushes Talk That She's Teddy's or Prince Charles' Blond Bombshell," *People,* September 8, 1980.

228 "all the Kennedys": Maxine Cheshire, "The Mysterious Helga Wagner," *Washington Post,* March 13, 1980.

228 "someone arriving in a hurry, or someone leaving in a hurry": Peter Collier and David Horowitz, *The Kennedys: An American Drama* (New York: Summit Books, 1984), 371.

228 "Your best friend is in terrible trouble": Interview with John Tunney (2009).

228 "It was a terrible thing": Interview with John Tunney (2009).

229 "I thought she had gotten out": Interview with John Tunney (2009).

229 "never had any kind of sexual relationship": Interview with John Tunney (2009).

229 "I don't feel guilty": Interview with John Tunney (2009).

CHAPTER 41

230 "Something told me it was more than just a car in the water": Peter S. Canellos, ed., *The Last Lion: The Fall and Rise of Ted Kennedy* (New York: Simon & Schuster, 2009), 158.

230 The same big black car: "Senator Kennedy Is Charged with Leaving Accident," *Vineyard Gazette,* July 22, 1969.

230 "They [the Kennedys] don't drive anywhere": Canellos, *The Last Lion,* 160.

231 License plate L78207: George Lardner, Jr., "Chappaquiddick: A Tale Time Has Not Resolved," *Washington Post,* November 12, 1979.

231 Associate county medical examiner: Robert Sherill, "A Tragedy, an Enigma, a Political Achilles Heel," *New York Times,* July 14, 1974.

231 "difference between a big black car and a little white car": Lardner, "Chappaquiddick: A Tale Time Has Not Resolved."

231 "Senator Kennedy was driver": Michael Cooper and John M. Broder, "FBI Opens Kennedy File," *New York Times,* June 15, 2010

231 "working on what really happened": Jere Hester, *New York Daily News*, "Haldeman Diaries Offer Another Look at Nixon," *Seattle Times*, May 16, 1994.

231 "He had a fixation, Nixon did, on the Kennedys": Transcript of interview with Robert Healy by Stephen F. Knott, "Robert Healy Oral History, Journalist, the *Boston Globe*," *Presidential Oral Histories—Edward M. Kennedy Histories*, Miller Center for Public Affairs at the University of Virginia, August 10, 2005.

232 "Lead with the moonwalk or Chappaquiddick": Transcript of interview with Robert Healy.

232 "happening at the worst possible moment for Ted Kennedy": Lorraine Boissoneault, "Why the True Story of Chappaquiddick Is Impossible to Tell," Smithsonian.com, April 2, 2018.

232 "I tried to interview people about it. Not only Kennedy": Interview with Adam Clymer, reporter, the *New York Times*, *The Edward M. Kennedy Oral History Project*, Edward M. Kennedy Institute for the United States Senate in partnership with the Miller Center of Public Affairs at the University of Virginia, 2016.

232 "You knew you weren't going to get anything from the Kennedys": "Robert Healy Oral History, Journalist, the *Boston Globe*."

232 "I was the driver": Canellos, *The Last Lion*, 161.

232 "I'm in some trouble": Rita Dallas with Jeanira Ratcliffe, *The Kennedy Case* (New York: G. P. Putnam's Sons, 1973), 338.

233 "what he is, is just not enough": J. Randy Taraborrelli, *Jackie, Ethel, Joan: Women of Camelot* (New York: Grand Central Publishing, 2012), 390.

233 "people think I'd be trying to get their sympathy": Dallas, *The Kennedy Case*, 340–41.

233 "before he or anyone else told me what was going on": Jim Rattray, "Joan Kennedy said Thursday Her Former Secretary and Confidante, . . ." United Press International, October 18, 1985.

233 "seemed to have trouble kneeling": "Sen. Kennedy Attends Funeral of Secretary Killed in Wreck," *Desert Sun*, July 22, 1969.

234 "a degree of alcohol, but it was very well down": "Sen. Kennedy Attends Funeral of Secretary Killed in Wreck."

234 "no business in giving a Breathalyzer": "Ted Kennedy Car Accident in Chappaquiddick," *Newsweek*, August 3, 1969.

234 A misdemeanor charge: Canellos, *The Last Lion*, 168.

234 "Has already been and will continue to be punished": Canellos, 169.

234 "I think they disserved him": Interview with Lester Hyman, *The Edward M. Kennedy Oral History Project,* Edward M. Kennedy Institute for the United States Senate in partnership with the Miller Center of Public Affairs at the University of Virginia, 2016.

235 "so impaired that I should resign": Edward M. Kennedy, "Address to the People of Massachusetts on Chappaquiddick," July 25, 1969, AmericanRhetoric.com.

235 "extremely favorable" ratings drop: Canellos, *The Last Lion,* 173.

235 "satisfied with the senator's statement": Canellos, 172.

235 "looking for blood money": William Kashatus, "Remembering Mary Jo: A Promising Life Lost at Chappaquiddick 40 Years Ago," *Citizens' Voice* (Wilkes-Barre, PA), July 19, 2009.

235 "damn little, considering": George Lardner Jr., "Chappaquiddick 1989," *Washington Post,* July 16, 1989.

235 Suffers a miscarriage: United Press International, "Mrs. Joan Kennedy Goes Home After Miscarriage," *Desert Sun,* September 1, 1969.

236 "nothing to do with Mary Jo Kopechne": Interview with Lester Hyman.

236 "hang Chappaquiddick around Kennedy's neck": Michael Cooper and John M. Broder, "F.B.I. Opens Kennedy File," *New York Times,* June 15, 2010.

236 "visited Greece in August, 1968": Cooper and Broder, "F.B.I. Opens Kennedy File."

237 "brought down by a mere Polish secretary": Interview with Lester Hyman.

237 "He has nothing to fear": "Former Detective Admits Leaking Chappaquiddick Probe Info to Kennedy Lawyer," Associated Press, July 25, 1991.

237 "KENNEDY OUSTED AS WHIP": John W. Finney, "Kennedy Ousted as Whip," *New York Times,* January 22, 1971.

237 "I despise cocktail parties": Sanford J. Ungar, "The Man Who Runs the Senate," *Atlantic,* September 1975.

237 "take advantage of this opportunity": Associated Press, "Haldeman Diary Shows Nixon Was Wary of Blacks and Jews," *New York Times,* May 18, 1994.

238 "to run, to hide, to get caught, and to get away with it": William Safire, "Prelude to the Bridge," *New York Times,* October 29, 1979.

238 "fall of the House of Kennedy": "Ted Kennedy Car Accident in Chappaquiddick," *Newsweek,* August 3, 1969.

238 "People have to forgive and forget": Maxine Cheshire, "The Mysterious Helga Wagner," *Washington Post,* March 13, 1980.

CHAPTER 42

239 "My uncle stuck to whatever it is that he does": Janet Maslin, "Symptoms of Withdrawal: A Memoir of Snapshots and Redemption," *New York Times,* September 28, 2005.

239 "ailments, diseases, and near-death experiences": Jon Ward, "The Son of a Bitch is Going to Run," *Vanity Fair,* January 21, 2019.

239 "the same treatment that U.S. senators are entitled to": "Ted Kennedy and Health Care Reform," *Newsweek,* July 17, 2009.

239 "The cause of my life": "Ted Kennedy and Health Care Reform."

240 Joan "breaks down": Peter S. Canellos, ed., *The Last Lion: The Fall and Rise of Ted Kennedy* (New York: Simon & Schuster, 2009), 188.

240 wedding and surgery on same day: Canellos, *The Last Lion,* 188.

240 "We're going to climb that hill together": "Edward Kennedy Jr.'s and Patrick Kennedy's Remembrances," *New York Times,* August 29, 2009.

241 "Those thousand days are like an evening gone": Terence Smith, "Carter and Kennedy Share Stage at Library Dedication," *New York Times,* October 21, 1979.

241 "I'll whip his ass": Ken Rudin, "Holding a Grudge for Thirty Years: Jimmy Carter Against Ted Kennedy," National Public Radio, September 21, 2010.

241 "politically embarrassing incident": Roger Mudd, "What Ted Said," *New York Review of Books,* November 19, 2009.

242 "so obvious to him": Transcript of interview with Robert Healy by Stephen F. Knott, "Robert Healy Oral History, Journalist, the *Boston Globe,*" *Presidential Oral Histories—Edward M. Kennedy Histories,* Miller Center for Public Affairs at the University of Virginia, August 10, 2005.

242 "an act of political destruction" Chris Whipple, "Ted Kennedy: The Day the Presidency Was Lost," ABCNews.com, August 31, 2009.

242 "now brother drains brother": Joe McGinniss, "The End of Camelot," *Vanity Fair,* September 1993.

242 "A Pied Piper to three generations": Robert G. Kaiser, Lee Lescaze, James L. Rose Jr., T. R. Reid, and Edward Walsh, "Ex-Rep Lowenstein Fa-

tally Shot by Gunman in N.Y. Law Office," *Washington Post,* March 15, 1980.

243 "We Love Ted—But Jimmy's All Right, Too": Talk of the Town, "Farewell," *The New Yorker,* August 25, 1980.

243 "I don't dwell on the past": Glenn Collins, "The Quiet Kennedy Speaks Up," *New York Times,* May 7, 1981.

243 "go through it all again": Tom Morganthau, "Why Kennedy Withdrew from 1984 Race," *Newsweek,* December 12, 1982.

243 "The Liberal Lion": Andrew Glass, "Ted Kennedy, 'Liberal Lion of the Senate,' Dies at 77, Aug. 25, 2009," Politico.com, August 25, 2017.

243 "civil rights, health, and economic well-being": The White House, "Statement by the President on the Death of Senator Ted Kennedy," Office of the Press Secretary, August 26, 2009.

244 "inherited a legend along with his name": Ward, "The Son of a Bitch is Going to Run."

PART SEVEN
THE NEXT GENERATIONS: THE KENNEDY COUSINS

CHAPTER 43

248 Magnet for the nouveau riche: Michelle Green, "Boys' Night Out in Palm Beach," *People,* April 22, 1991.

248 "an intelligent man, a likable man": David Margolick, "Accuser in Smith Trial Tells of Fear and Rape," *New York Times,* December 5, 1991.

248 "never done anything suggestive at all": Margolick, "Accuser in Smith Trial Tells of Fear and Rape."

249 $120,000: Mike Seemuth, "Pre-auction Exhibition of Kennedy Furnishings Re-creates "Camelot" in WPB," *Real Deal South Florida Real Estate News,* January 15, 2016.

249 *Profiles in Courage*: David Foxley, "The Kennedy Winter White House Is Updated with the Unexpected," *Architectural Digest,* December 11, 2017.

249 "dark, dingy, and smelly": Dominick Dunne, "Damage," *Vanity Fair,* October 1991.

249 "Ted was very drunk": Green, "Boys' Night Out in Palm Beach."

249 "I got totally weirded out": Green.

250 "a nice night with a nice guy": Lisa Ocker, "Kennedy Smith Trial: Two Lives Collide," *Sun-Sentinel,* December 1, 1991.

250 "surreal" behavior: Margolick, "Accuser in Smith Trial Tells of Fear and Rape."

250 "running, to get away": John Taylor, "Men on Trial," *New York Magazine,* December 16, 1991.

250 Bowman will later testify: Mary Jordan, "Smith's Tearful Accuser Tells of Yelling 'Stop!'" *Washington Post,* December 5, 1991.

250 "arch my back to get him off me": Margolick, "Accuser in Smith Trial Tells of Fear and Rape."

250 "I was yelling, 'No!'": Margolick.

250 "he told me to 'Stop it, Bitch,'": Margolick.

250 "pushed my dress up and he raped me": Margolick.

250 "thought he was going to kill me": Taylor, "Men on Trial."

250 "screaming and wondering why no one": "Prosecutor in Palm Beach Rape Case Releases Police Affidavit With AM-Kennedy-Assault, Bjt," Associated Press, May 9, 1991.

251 "didn't know that the police would care or would come": Margolick, "Accuser in Smith Trial Tells of Fear and Rape."

251 "I didn't know what power they held": David Margolick, "Smith Accuser Was 'Very Shook Up' After Incident, Her Friend Testifies," *New York Times,* December 4, 1991.

251 "maybe they owned the police": Ocker, "Kennedy Smith Trial."

251 Police Affadavit: "Prosecutor in Palm Beach Rape Case Releases Police Affadavit," Associated Press.

251 "calmest, smuggest, most arrogant man": Dominick Dunne, "The Verdict," *Vanity Fair,* March 1992.

CHAPTER 44

252 "she looked messed up": David Margolick, "Smith Accuser Was 'Very Shook Up' After Incident, Her Friend Testifies," *New York Times,* December 4, 1991.

252 Items taken as proof: "Prosecutor in Palm Beach Rape Case Releases Police Affidavit with AM-Kennedy-Assault, Bjt," Associated Press, May 9, 1991.

252 "all this fear and this dirtiness": David Margolick, "Accuser in Smith Trial Tells of Fear and Rape," *New York Times,* December 5, 1991.

253 "traumatic event of some sort": Paul Richter, "Smith's Accuser Testifies to Rape at Kennedy Home: Trial: Sometimes Tearful, She Tells Her Assertion of a 'Disgusting' Crime but Says She Cannot Recall Some Events," *Los Angeles Times,* December 5, 1991.

253 "Regressive behavior is a little hard to fake": Richter, "Smith's Accuser Testifies to Rape at Kennedy Home."

253 "really whacked out": "The Day a Kennedy Was Accused of Rape at the Family's Palm Beach Mansion," *Miami Herald* archives, April 15, 2019.

253 "This is really a setup": "The Day a Kennedy was Accused of Rape at the Family's Palm Beach Mansion."

253 "she will say it is rape": "Witness Says Kennedy Spoke with Nephew About Rape Allegation," *New York Times,* September 7, 1991.

253 "don't go up to the Kennedy house unless you expect to be raucous": Michelle Green, "Boys' Night Out in Palm beach," *People,* April 22, 1991.

254 "David tapped his father's sensitivity": Peter Collier and David Horowitz, *The Kennedys: An American Drama* (New York: Summit Books, 1984), 540.

254 "throwing rocks at strangers—or LBJ": Evan Thomas, *Robert Kennedy: His Life* (New York: Simon & Schuster, 2007), 383.

254 "lost this father in a most horrible way": B. Drummond Ayres, Jr., "A Troubled Kennedy Makes Last Trip Home," *The New York Times*, April 27, 1984.

254 "saved David's life the very same day he lost his own": J. Randy Taraborrelli, *After Camelot: A Personal History of the Kennedy Family 1968 to the Present* (New York: Grand Central Publishing, 2012), 253.

254 "as if he thought God had traded his life in for his Dad's": Taraborrelli, *After Camelot,* 253.

254 "No one ever talked to me about what I was feeling": Peter Carlson, "Ethel & David: Troubled Mother, Tormented Son," *People,* May 14, 1984.

255 "not a subject I want to discuss": Collier and Horowitz, *The Kennedys,* 362.

255 "one thing led to another": Taraborrelli, *After Camelot,* 253.

255 Hitchhiking to New York City and buying heroin: Carlson, "Ethel & David."

255 "wasn't any reason to be good any more": Collier and Horowitz, *The Kennedys,* 361.

255 "His SuperKennedy act": Collier and Horowitz, 399.

255 "typical Kennedy horseplay": J. Randy Taraborrelli, *The Kennedy Heirs* (New York: St. Martin's Press, 2019), 241.

255 Receiving morphine: Carlson, "Ethel & David."

255 "pneumonia": Taraborrelli, *After Camelot,* 254.

256 "David was the Kennedy screwup, not Bobby": Taraborrelli, *After Camelot,* 262.

256 "Kennedys don't fail": Taraborrelli, 273.

256 "the same as everybody else, except better": Collier and Horowitz, *The Kennedys,* 321.

256 "She was a hindrance; I am a hindrance": Collier and Horowitz, 441.

256 staggering amounts of alcohol: Carlson, "Ethel & David."

256 "God invented alcohol to keep the Irish from ruling the world": Janet Maslin, "Symptoms of Withdrawal: A Memoir of Snapshots and Redemption," *New York Times,* September 28, 2005.

256 Unable to locate him: Associated Press, "Caroline Kennedy Tried to Reach David Before Death," *Los Angeles Times,* January 15, 1985.

257 "He's dead, isn't he?": Alison Muscatine and Mary Thornton, "David Kennedy's Body Is Flown to Virginia," *Washington Post,* April 27, 1984.

257 "my chance to be a better mother died with him": Taraborrelli, *The Kennedy Heirs,* 213.

CHAPTER 45

258 Mercer, who is paid forty thousand dollars: Sean Elder, "Tabloid Nation," Salon.com, December 8, 1999.

258 Cassone charges multiple TV talk shows: Lisa Ocker, "Photographers, Witnesses Reap Windfall from Smith Rape Case," *Sun-Sentinel,* November 3, 1991.

258 "An outrageous lie": "Kennedy Nephew Surrenders to Police, Posts Bond," United Press International, May 11, 1991.

258 "most-watched legal proceeding in American history": David A. Kaplan, "Case No. 91-5482 Comes to Trial," *Newsweek,* December 8, 1991.

259 "Courtroom Television Network": Dan Sewell, "Urgent: Judge Grants Delay in Trial of William Kennedy Smith," Associated Press, July 31, 1991.

259 "This trial was perfect for TV": Johnny Diaz, "William Kennedy Smith Rape Trial Returns to TV in New Fox News Channel Documentary," *South Florida Sun-Sentinel,* March 8, 2019.

259 "Spectators' Guide": Lisa Ocker, "Kennedy Smith Trial: Two Lives Collide," *Sun-Sentinel,* December 1, 1991.

259 Local businesses: Ocker, "Photographers, Witnesses Reap Windfall."

259 "Trial Flavors": Janet Cawley, "Smith Trial Not a '10' in Palm Beach," *Chicago Tribune,* December 13, 2019.

259 "more like a football game than a news event": Diaz, "William Kennedy Smith Rape Trial Returns to TV."

260 "quite charming": John Taylor, "Men on Trial," *New York Magazine,* December 16, 1991.

260 "tried to convince [her] that that wasn't what had happened": Taylor, "Men on Trial."

260 "Willie has a really big problem": Taylor.

260 "threw me over the couch": Taylor.

260 "just getting more and more aggressive": Janet Crowley, "Women Tell Similar Tales of Attacks," *Chicago Tribune,* July 24, 1991.

261 "That's when I kind of lost it": Taylor, "Men on Trial."

261 "consensual act of sexual intercourse": Taylor.

261 "a disastrous witness": Dominick Dunne, "The Verdict," *Vanity Fair,* March 1992.

261 "I have to thank Steve Dunleavy": Elder, "Tabloid Nation."

CHAPTER 46

262 Judge Lupo's exclusion: David A. Kaplan, "The Trial You Won't See," *Newsweek,* December 15, 1991.

262 "how this nice guy had turned": Paul Richter, "Smith's Accuser Testifies to Rape at Kennedy Home: Trial: Sometimes Tearful, She Tells Her Assertion of a 'Disgusting' Crime but Says She Cannot Recall Some Events," *Los Angeles Times,* December 5, 1991.

262 "regular guy who happens to come from this amazing family": Mary Jordan, "Willy Smith, the 'Independent' Kennedy, Anonymous No More," *Washington Post,* May 10, 1991.

262 "doesn't have any violence in him": Jordan, "Willy Smith, The 'Independent' Kennedy."

263 "gentle person": Jordan.

263 Including Meg Ryan: Jordan.

263 "done something about Willie years ago": James Ridgeway de Szigethy, affidavit via Hon. James A. Traficant, Jr., February 9, 1994, Congressional Record volume 140, number 12.

263 "stick by Willie through thick and thin": Dominick Dunne, "The Verdict," *Vanity Fair,* March 1992.

263 "You just don't understand the pressure I'm under": de Szigethy, affidavit via Hon. James A. Traficant.

263 "dating and drinking ban": David A. Kaplan, "Case No. 91-5482 Comes to Trial," *Newsweek,* December 8, 1991.

263 "strategy session every night at dinner": Dunne, "The Verdict."

264 "my family is on trial for me": Kaplan, "Case No. 91-5482 Comes to Trial."

264 "And he drinks": Dunne, "The Verdict."

264 "I wish I'd gone for a long walk on the beach": Robin Toner, "In Glare of Latest Scandal, Kennedy Defends the Dynasty," *New York Times,* December 7, 1991.

264 "I was very moved by a lot of things": Dunne, "The Verdict."

265 Willie's testimony: David Margolick, "Smith Tells Rapt Courtroom His Side of Story," *New York Times,* December 11, 1991.

265 "she got very, very upset": Margolick, "Smith Tells Rapt Courtroom His Side of Story."

265 "I've searched myself every night": Margolick.

265 "The issue here is I'm innocent": Margolick.

266 Seventy-seven minutes: David Margolick, "Smith Acquitted of Rape Charge After Brief Deliberation by Jury," *New York Times,* December 12, 1991.

266 "helping me off the floor": "Willie Smith's Accuser Fainted Upon Hearing Verdict," United Press International, December 19, 1991.

266 "Willie! Willie! Willie!": Mary Jordan, "Jury Finds Smith Not Guilty of Rape," *Washington Post,* December 12, 1991.

266 "I feel great, just great!": "Jubilant Smith Thanks Florida Jurors After Swift Not-Guilty Verdict," *Deseret News,* December 12, 1991.

266 "If there's anything good": "Jubilant Smith Thanks Florida Jurors."

266 "enormous debt to the system and to God": Jordan, "Jury Finds Smith Not Guilty of Rape."

266 "My life was in their hands": Margolick, "Smith Acquitted of Rape Charge."

266 "Nobody heard it": "Smith Juror Says First Vote Made 'Not Guilty' Obvious," *New York Times,* December 13, 1991.

266 "prayer for Patty": Dunne, "The Verdict."

267 "I do not for one moment regret the action": Margolick, "Smith Acquitted of Rape Charge."

267 "A not-guilty verdict does not equate to innocence": Margolick.

267 "To some people, this has been entertainment": "Willie Smith's Accuser Fainted Upon Hearing Verdict."

267 Roy Black and Lea Haller: Karen S. Schneider, "Love and the Law," *People,* March 6, 1995.

267 Assaulting a bouncer: Associated Press, "William Kennedy Smith Charged in Assault," *New York Times,* October 24, 1993.

267 "with his mother in Ireland for the holidays": Charles W. Hall, "William Kennedy Smith Pleads No Contest in Assault," *Washington Post,* November 23, 1993.

267 Claims of sexual harassment: Nathaniel Hernandez, "Kennedy Cousin Denies Assault, Quits Job to Fight Sex Allegations," *Herald-Review,* August 31, 2004.

267 "vulnerable to these kinds of untruths": Donal Lynch, "Nightmare in Palm Beach," *Independent* (UK), December 2, 2007.

CHAPTER 47

268 "the best public relations a trust fund can buy": Margaret Carlson, "Divorce, Kennedy-style," *Time,* May 12, 1997.

268 "more in touch with the scandals": Elizabeth Mehren, "Crisis Crosses Camelot's Moat in Massachusetts," *Los Angeles Times,* May 6, 1997.

269 "emblems of a tabloid time": Debra Rosenberg, "A Dynasty in Decline," *Newsweek,* June 22, 1997.

269 Sheila Rauch Kennedy's book *Shattered Faith*: Rosenberg, "A Dynasty in Decline."

269 "Catholic gobbledygook": Michael Shnayerson, "Bobby's Kids," *Vanity Fair,* August 1997.

270 "seen as the future of the clan": Pam Lambert, "A Betrayal in the Family," *People,* May 12, 1997.

270 "No one was jealous": J. Randy Taraborrelli, *The Kennedy Heirs* (New York: St. Martin's Press, 2019), 118.

270 "a lot like Bobby": Shnayerson, "Bobby's Kids."

270 "resemblance was so striking": Taraborrelli, *The Kennedy Heirs*, 257.

271 "neither one gets what the other does": Shnayerson, "Bobby's Kids."

CHAPTER 48

272 Vicki looks for Michael: J. Randy Taraborrelli, *The Kennedy Heirs* (New York: St. Martin's Press, 2019), 136.

272 "would call her parents": Margaret Carlson, "Divorce, Kennedy-style," *Time,* May 12, 1997.

272 Babysitter moves in: Taraborrelli, *The Kennedy Heirs,* 129.

272 Family vacations: Michael Shnayerson, "Bobby's Kids," *Vanity Fair,* August 1997.

273 Making people uncomfortable: Taraborrelli, *The Kennedy Heirs,* 129, 142.

273 Vicki finds Michael in Marisa's room: Taraborrelli, 136.

273 "straight arrow": Corky Siemaskzo, "An Accident Kills a Kennedy Promise Waned with Sex Scandal," *New York Daily News,* January 1, 1998.

273 "something snapped": Patrick Rogers, "Death in Aspen," *People,* January 19, 1998.

273 "wasn't a mean drunk, just reckless": Rogers, "Death in Aspen."

273 Family intervention: Taraborrelli, *The Kennedy Heirs,* 132.

273 "I had a dependence on alcohol": "Passages," *People,* February 27, 1995.

273 "No one has hidden behind alcoholism": Shnayerson, "Bobby's Kids."

273 "indomitable" Rose: Associated Press, "Rose Kennedy Eulogized as 'Ambitious' for Family," *SF Gate,* January 25, 1995.

273 Funeral: Phil McCombs, "Mother of the Century," *Washington Post,* January 25, 1995.

274 "kick his [ass]": Debra Rosenberg, "A Dynasty in Decline," *Newsweek,* June 22, 1997.

274 "We talk to each other a lot": Rosenberg, "A Dynasty in Decline."

274 "*This* is the girl you're going to hell for?" Taraborrelli, *The Kennedy Heirs,* 147–48.

274 "angry, hurt, sad, confused": Taraborrelli, 149.

274 *"Fucking Kennedy Curse"*: Taraborrelli, 149.

CHAPTER 49

275 "really be on the warpath": J. Randy Taraborrelli, *The Kennedy Heirs* (New York: St. Martin's Press, 2019), 150–51.

275 "sleeping with the Kennedy guy": Pam Lambert, "A Betrayal in the Family," *People*, May 12, 1997.

275 "caught in bed with him": Lambert, "A Betrayal in the Family."

276 "someone with a heart could've answered": Taraborrelli, *The Kennedy Heirs*, 234.

276 Verrochi breaks it off: Kate Zerike and Scot LeHigh, "Controversy Surrounds a Kennedy's Alleged Affair with Baby-Sitter," *Chicago Tribune*, April 25, 1997.

276 Kennedys separate: Zerike and LeHigh, "Controversy Surrounds a Kennedy's Alleged Affair."

277 "in a castle with a moat around it": Michael Shnayerson, "Bobby's Kids," *Vanity Fair*, August 1997.

277 "an embarrassment in the press": Shnayerson, "Bobby's Kids."

277 "private and personal matters": Shnayerson.

277 *Omertà*, Irish-American-style": Shnayerson.

CHAPTER 50

278 Death of Anne Skakel: "Mrs. Rushton Skakel," *New York Times*, March 7, 1973.

278 Greenwich royalty: David Van Biema, "A Crime in the Clan," *Time*, January 23, 2000.

278 "Nixon, not Jack, in the 1960 election": J. Randy Taraborrelli, *The Kennedy Heirs* (New York: St. Martin's Press, 2019), 141.

279 "throwing protocol into utter panic": William F. Buckley Jr., "His Greatness Was More Than Relative," *Stanford Daily* 150, no. 7 (October 3, 1966).

279 "more a self-made man than Joe Kennedy": Peter Collier and David Horowitz, *The Kennedys: An American Drama* (New York: Summit Books, 1984), 154.

279 Great Lakes Carbon Corporation: Van Biema, "A Crime in the Clan."

279 Death of George Skakel Sr.: "Executive, Wife Die in Air Crash; Skakel, 63, Head of Carbon Company Here, Victim in Oklahoma Disaster," *New York Times*, October 5, 1955.

279 Death of George Skakel Jr.: Buckley, "His Greatness Was More Than Relative."

279 "They didn't like discipline—the kids or the parents": Leslie Yager, "Skakel Nanny Speaks After 50 Years," Patch.com, December 22, 2013.

279 Ethel's brothers as terrors of neighborhood: Collier and Horowitz, *The Kennedys,* 154.

279 "more intense level of chaos": Susan Campbell, "The House of Skakel," *Hartford-Courant*, June 9, 2002.

279 "a coterie of priests and nuns and a series of live-in tutors": Leonard Levitt, "Michael Skakel Was Convicted of Murdering Martha Moxley, So Why Is He Free?" *Daily Beast,* April 22, 2017 (updated May 8, 2017).

279 Skakel ages in fall 1975: Campbell, "The House of Skakel."

280 "Best Personality": James Feron, "Friends and a Fund Recall the Murdered Girl in Greenwich," *New York Times*, December 23, 1975.

280 "the Moxleys were 'Leave It to Beaver'": Campbell, "The House of Skakel."

280 "bludgeoned young Martha": Feron, "Friends and a Fund Recall the Murdered Girl in Greenwich."

280 A rare Toney Penna six-iron: Van Biema, "A Crime in the Clan."

280 Decades go by without any arrests: Levitt, "Michael Skakel Was Convicted of Murdering Martha Moxley."

281 "full-blown, daily-drinking": Campbell, "The House of Skakel."

281 The Élan School: "Skakel Set to Go on Trial in 26-Year-Old Murder Case," CNN, April 1, 2002.

281 "tough love and discipline": Stevenson Swanson, "1975 Murder Case Revived," *Chicago Tribune,* January 23, 2000.

281 1992 winter Olympics: Swanson, "1975 Murder Case Revived."

281 "He helped me to get sober": Robert F. Kennedy Jr., "A Miscarriage of Justice," *Atlantic*, January/February 2003.

281 "I rarely saw the Skakel boys growing up": Kennedy Jr., "A Miscarriage of Justice."

281 "His primary passion in life is helping other alcoholics": Kennedy Jr..

281 "one of the most honest and open people I know": Patrick Rogers, "The Boy Next Door," *People,* February 7, 2000.

281 Working for the Kennedys: David Chen, "Glare of an Old Horror Intrudes on a Privileged Life," *New York Times,* January 22, 2000.

281 Known simply as "Skakel": Taraborrelli, *The Kennedy Heirs,* 141.

282 "the sweetest human being": Michael Shnayerson, "Bobby's Kids," *Vanity Fair,* August 1997.

282 Vicki calls Skakel: Taraborrelli, *The Kennedy Heirs,* 143.

282 Ethel and nephew: Taraborrelli, 145.

282 "some very disturbing news": Taraborrelli, 235.

282 "accompanied Mrs. Verrochi to the hospital": Shnayerson, "Bobby's Kids."

282 "any business telling a Kennedy what to do": Shnayerson.

282 Sets Marisa up with a therapist, Taraborrelli, *The Kennedy Heirs,* 229.

282 "not your place": Taraborrelli, 238.

282 "He's been trying to save everyone, left and right": Taraborrelli, 261.

283 "He admitted to me": Shnayerson, "Bobby's Kids."

283 "Nobody can stab you in the back": Taraborrelli, *The Kennedy Heirs*, 237.

283 "it was a bum rap": Alex Kuczynski, "For Writers, a Murder Case That Had all the Ingredients," *New York Times,* January 20, 2000.

283 William Kennedy Smith never met any Skakels except Ethel: Kennedy, "A Miscarriage of Justice."

283 "Michael Skakel is guilty of this murder": Craig Offman, "Kennedy Cousin Confesses Crush on Murdered Girl," Salon.com, November 9, 1999.

284 "Dead Man Talking": Offman, "Kennedy Cousin Confesses Crush on Murdered Girl."

284 "he has ultimately trapped himself": David M. Herszenhorn, "Prosecutors Weave a Web of Inferences," *New York Times*, June 4, 2002.

284 "the state's case is entirely circumstantial": David M. Herszenhorn, "Final Defense Witness Bolsters Skakel Alibi, Saying It Matches Victim's Hour of Death," *New York Times,* May 29, 2002.

284 "unrequited feelings": Herszenhorn, "Final Defense Witness Bolsters Skakel Alibi."

284 Marisa Verrochi for Skakel defense: Orla Healy, "Ghosts Come Back to Haunt Kennedys," *Independent* (UK), May 26, 2002.

284 "a very, very, very good case": Jessica Gresko and Dave Collins,

"Supreme Court Rejects Michael Skakel Case; Kennedy Cousin's Vacated Murder Conviction Stands," *Washington Times*, January 7, 2019.

285 "The evidence shows": Joseph Ax, "US Supreme Court Won't Reinstate Murder Conviction for Kennedy Kin," Reuters, January 7, 2019.

285 "Michael dished some pretty nasty dirt": Bill Hewitt, "The Reckoning," *People*, May 27, 2002.

CHAPTER 51

286 "potentially irreparable harm": Sara Rimer, "A Kennedy Faces the Fallout from a Scandal," *New York Times*, July 10, 1997.

286 "great pain and suffering": Michael Shnayerson, "Bobby's Kids," *Vanity Fair*, August 1997.

286 "without the willing involvement": "Mass. Prosecutor Ends Probe of Michael Kennedy," *Washington Post*, July 9, 1997.

287 "do all I can to make up": "Mass. Prosecutor Ends Probe of Michael Kennedy."

287 "easier to get an AA meeting together": Shnayerson, "Bobby's Kids."

287 "none of the RFK sisters": Shnayerson.

287 "None of the rakehell appetites": Debra Rosenberg, "A Dynasty in Decline," *Newsweek*, June 22, 1997.

287 "the best the family represents": Shnayerson, "Bobby's Kids."

287 "I should pick up the torch... er, pick up the flag": Rosenberg, "A Dynasty in Decline."

288 "walk right into the governor's office": Elizabeth Mehren, "Crisis Crosses Camelot's Moat in Massachusetts," *Los Angeles Times*, May 6, 1997.

288 "poster boys for bad behavior": Kate Storey, "'It Was Just the F*cking Coolest': The Inside Story of JFK Jr.'s 'George' Magazine," *Esquire*, April 22, 2019.

288 "apologize on television for getting divorced": Storey, "It Was Just the F*cking Coolest."

288 Joe on *Good Morning America*: Shnayerson, "Bobby's Kids."

288 "Ask not what you can do for your cousin": Leslie Doolittle, "JFK Jr.'s Tsk-Tsk Pooh-Poohed," *Orlando Sentinel*, August 12, 1997.

289 "probably wishes he hadn't written it": Thomas W. Waldron, "Moral Message Oldest Kennedy Grandchild Tries to Balance Demands of

Public Office with Life in Her Famous Family; Kathleen Kennedy Townsend," *Baltimore Sun*, August 31, 1997.

289 "the landfill of tabloid dreck": Margaret Carlson, "Divorce, Kennedy-style," *Time*, May 12, 1997.

CHAPTER 52

290 "accustomed to both controversy and criticism": Elizabeth Mehren, "Crisis Crosses Camelot's Moat in Massachusetts," *Los Angeles Times*, May 6, 1997.

290 "Never forget that you are a Kennedy": J. Randy Taraborrelli, *The Kennedy Heirs* (New York: St. Martin's Press, 2019), 170.

290 "Kennedys all take care of each other": Patrick Rogers, "Death in Aspen," *People*, January 19, 1998.

290 "overwhelming sense of a continuing commitment": Dan Dalz, "Legacy of Untimely Death Continues," *Washington Post*, January 2, 1998.

291 "You're a *Kennedy*. You have to pull it together": Taraborrelli, *The Kennedy Heirs*, 265.

291 Christmas in Colorado: Rogers, "Death in Aspen."

291 "the central thing in Michael's life": Rogers.

291 Aspen Mountain on New Year's Eve 1997: Tom Kenworthy, "Michael Kennedy Dies in Accident on Aspen Slopes," *Washington Post*, January 1, 1998.

291 "They hang at the top of the mountain": Michael Janofsky, "Favorite Game for Kennedys Took Deadly Turn on Slopes," *New York Times*, January 2, 1998.

291 Conflicting reports: Janofsky, "Favorite Game for Kennedys Took Deadly Turn on Slopes."

291 "A tremendous drive for living on the edge": Rogers, "Death in Aspen."

292 "two weeks without a visit to the emergency room": Debra Rosenberg, "A Dynasty in Decline," *Newsweek*, June 22, 1997.

292 "An unbelievably good athlete": Michael Shnayerson, "Bobby's Kids," *Vanity Fair*, August 1997.

292 "wherever he could test himself at the edge": Rebecca Mowbray, "Kennedy Family, Friends Say Farewell to Michael," *Los Angeles Times*, January 4, 1998.

292 "The greatest athlete of our generation": Taraborrelli, *The Kennedy Heirs*, 121.

292 "never seen anyone ski as beautifully": Taraborrelli, 266.

292 Olympic ski coach Bob Beattie praised Michael's talent for skiing: Rogers, "Death in Aspen."

292 "could ski downhill backwards and blindfolded": Janofsky, "Favorite Game for Kennedys Took Deadly Turn on Slopes."

292 Daughter Rory "videotaping their antics": Janofsky.

292 "death to the loser": Nancy Gibbs, "Tragedy Strikes Again," CNN, January 12, 1998.

292 "Pass me the ball": Matthew Malone, "The Kennedys in Aspen: A New Year's Tragedy," *Modern Luxury,* November 27, 2017.

293 Michael's crash: Gibbs, "Tragedy Strikes Again."

293 "blood all over the snow": "Coroner: Kennedy Death Accidental," CNN, January 1, 1998.

293 Rory administers CPR: Malone, "The Kennedys in Aspen."

293 "now is the time to fight": Gibbs, "Tragedy Strikes Again."

293 "Please help my daddy!": Gibbs.

293 "on their knees saying the Lord's Prayer": "Coroner: Kennedy Death Accidental," CNN.

293 "intensive cardiac care": Kenworthy, "Michael Kennedy Dies in Accident on Aspen Slopes."

293 Cause of death: Janofsky, "Favorite Game for Kennedys Took Deadly Turn on Slopes."

293 No drugs or alcohol found in his body: Gibbs, "Tragedy Strikes Again."

293 "Should I drop you off at Admissions or Emergency?": Malone, "The Kennedys in Aspen: A New Year's Tragedy."

293 Flown to Hyannis Port on Kevin Costner's jet: Gibbs, "Tragedy Strikes Again."

293 Buried next to his brother David: "Michael Kennedy Laid to Rest," CNN, January 3, 1998.

294 "We don't know what to make of another Kennedy death": Dalz, "Legacy of Untimely Death Continues."

294 "The Kennedys play too hard and live too hard": Rogers, "Death in Aspen."

294 "The price you pay for great glories": Dalz, "Legacy of Untimely Death Continues."

294 "the athlete dying young of A. E. Housman's verse": Fox Butterfield, "A Fearless Michael Kennedy Is Remembered at Funeral," *New York Times,* January 4, 1998.

294 "The next thing he saw was God": Taraborrelli, *The Kennedy Heirs,* 270.

294 "nugget of happy news": Nadine Brozan, "CHRONICLE," *New York Times,* May 23, 1997.

295 "couldn't understand a word he said": Kevin Cullen, "You Only Live Twice," *Independent* (UK), January 30, 1994.

295 Victim of an IRA bombing: Bernard Weinraub, "Bomb Kills a Doctor Near London Home of Caroline Kennedy," *New York Times,* October 24, 1975.

295 "I was at home": Michael Shnayerson, "Bobby's Kids," *Vanity Fair*, August 1997.

295 "sensitive and emotionally vulnerable": Shnayerson, "Bobby's Kids."

295 "suffering from depression": "Lost and Found," *Herald* (Scotland), May 10, 2002.

295 "one name too many": Deborah Sontag, "Struggling to Please the Father Who Died," *New York Times,* June 15, 1997.

295 Signing her name: Saoirse Kennedy-Hill, "Mental Illness at Deerfield," *Deerfield Scroll,* February 3, 2016.

295 "less manic" environment: "Lost and Found."

296 "very Irish": "Lost and Found."

296 "a hundred brothers and sisters": Liz McNeil, "Timothy Shriver Calls Niece Saoirse Kennedy Hill a 'Wounded Healer' in His Heartbreaking Eulogy," *People,* August 9, 2019.

296 "a hundred Kennedys": "Robert F. Kennedy, Jr. "My Eulogy to Saoirse," Medium.com, August 7, 2019.

296 "outgoing imp": Kennedy, "My Eulogy to Saoirse."

296 Personal essay: Kennedy-Hill, "Mental Illness at Deerfield."

296 Deerfield Students Against Sexual Assault: Julie Bosman, Kate Taylor, and Nicholas Bogel-Burroughs, "The Kennedy Grandchildren: Bearing the Privilege and Burden of a Family Name," *New York Times*, August 2, 2019.

296 Bill Stone: Adam Carlson, "Fearless, Fierce, Troubled, Gone: Inside the Short Life and Sudden Death of Saoirse Kennedy Hill, RFK's Granddaughter," *People,* August 2, 2019.

297 "kind, gentle spirit": Carlson, "Fearless, Fierce, Troubled, Gone."

297 "wasn't a partier": Emily Smith, "Saoirse Kennedy Hill Wasn't a Partier: Family Source," *New York Post,* August 2, 2019.

297 "woke up with God": Kennedy, "My Eulogy to Saoirse."

297 "methadone and ethanol toxicity": Joey Garrison and Leora Arnowitz,

"Robert F. Kennedy's Granddaughter, Saorise Kennedy Hill, Died of an Accidental Overdose," *USAToday.com*, November 1, 2019.

297 "God loves the Kennedys": Kennedy.

298 Taylor Swift: Rebecca Macatee, "Taylor Swift's Boyfriend: Five Things to Know about Conor Kennedy," eonline.com, April 22, 2012.

298 Braison Cyrus: Helen Regan, "Miley Cyrus and Patrick Schwarzenegger's Siblings Are Also Dating," Time.com, January 15, 2015.

298 Katherine Schwarzenegger marries actor Chris Pratt: Lauren Hubbard, "A Definitive Timeline of Chris Pratt and Katherine Schwarzenegger's Relationship," TownandCountrymag.com, June 9, 2019.

298 "case of triumph and tragedy": Bosman, Taylor, and Bogel-Burroughs, "The Kennedy Grandchildren."

298 "back to the Kennedys": Michael Levenson, "For Kennedy Grandchildren, Family Name Is a Burden and a Blessing," *Boston Globe,* August 2, 2019.

298 "federal elective office": Emilia Petrarca, "A Guide to the Very Large, Very Beautiful, and Very Connected Kennedy Family," *W Magazine,* November 25, 2018.

298 "all eyes have been on Joe": Taraborrelli, *The Kennedy Heirs,* 539.

299 "not easy psychologically": Darrell M. West, "The End of the Kennedy Dynasty?" *Brookings,* February 16, 2010.

299 "faint of heart": Taraborrelli, *The Kennedy Heirs,* 547.

PART EIGHT
THE PRINCE: JOHN FITZGERALD KENNEDY JR.

CHAPTER 53

303 "Jackie has been rushed": W. H. Lawrence, "Kennedy Alters Schedule to Stay Close to New Son, *New York Times,* November 25, 1960.

303 "never there when she needs me": Thurston Clarke, "A Death in the First Family," *Vanity Fair,* July 1, 2013.

304 Captain Dick Cramer: Lawrence, "Kennedy Alters Schedule."

304 "really something": Merriman Smith, "President Elect Proud of Son to be Named John F. Kennedy Jr.," United Press International, November 25, 1969.

304 "asked the name of his son": Smith, "President Elect Proud of Son."

304 "named him": Evan Thomas, "Living with the Myth," *Newsweek,* July 25, 1999.

304 "life more challenging": Liz McNeil, "Revealing the Real (and Very Complicated) John F. Kennedy Jr. 20 Years After His Death: 'He Was Two People,'" *People,* July 2, 2019.

304 "Isn't he sweet, Jack?": "Kennedy's Son Baptized in Hospital Chapel," special to the *New York Times,* December 9, 1960.

304 "Gift for Kennedy Baby": "Gift for Kennedy Baby," special to the *New York Times,* June 1, 1961.

304 "still has a cold": "John Jr. to Miss Party; Kennedy's Son Still Has Cold—Condition Not Serious," *New York Times,* November 25, 1961.

305 "Fauntleroy" hairstyle: Martha Brant, "Coming of Age," *Newsweek,* August 13, 1995.

305 "children tumbling": "Jackie O's Antiquated Views Horrified Grandkids," Associated Press, September 14, 2011.

305 "It was John's treat": Mark Mooney, "Jacqueline Kennedy's Audio Tapes: 'John John' Says 'He's Gone to Heaven,'" ABCNews.com, September 13, 2011.

305 "didn't like to read books to them": Jacqueline Kennedy, "In Her Voice, Jacqueline Kennedy, the White House Years," John F. Kennedy Presidential Library and Museum.

305 "President and Caroline were sailing with Franklin Roosevelt": Arthur M. Schlesinger Jr., *A Thousand Days: John F. Kennedy in the White House* (New York: Greenwich House; distributed by Crown, 1983), 668.

306 "oblique pun": Peter Collier and David Horowitz, *The Kennedys: An American Drama* (New York: Summit Books, 1984), 311.

306 "part of the yacht": Collier and Horowitz, *The Kennedys.*

306 "stories about other Presidents": Jacqueline Kennedy, "In Her Voice, Jacqueline Kennedy, The White House Years."

306 "Jackie wanted her kids": Christopher Anderson, *These Few Precious Days: The Final Year of Jack with Jackie* (New York: Gallery Books, 2013), 147.

306 "nurses and Secret Service men": Donald Spoto, *Jacqueline Bouvier Kennedy Onassis: A Life* (New York: St. Martin's Press, 2000), 146.

306 First airplane ride: Martha Sherrill, "He Speaks," *Washington Post,* September 7, 1995.

306 "put on the pilot's helmet": Maud Shaw, *White House Nannie: My Years with Caroline and John Kennedy, Jr.* (New York: New American Library, 1966), 146.

307 "one wonderful memory" Shaw, *White House Nannie*.

307 "He adored airplanes": Rita Dallas with Jeanira Ratcliffe, *The Kennedy Case* (New York: G. P. Putnam's Sons, 1973), 230.

307 "bought them by the gross": Dallas, *The Kennedy Case,* 230.

307 Photo of John Jr. dated January 21, 1963: "John F. Kennedy, Jr. (JFK, Jr.), in the President's Secretary's Office, Cecil Stoughton, White House Photographs. John F. Kennedy Presidential Library and Museum, Boston.

307 "usual pacified": Dallas, *The Kennedy Case,* 230.

307 "when I grow up": Dallas, 230.

307 "when he's old enough": Paul Bentley, "Nobody's Going to Shoot Me: How JFK Tried to Get the Secret Service to Back off," *Daily Mail* (UK), November 20, 2013.

308 "the poor Secret Service": Bentley, "Nobody's Going to Shoot."

308 AP photo dated October 3, 1963: AP wire photo (f513000tf-HWG), 1963.

308 "racing across the lawn": "Ted Kennedy Pays Tribute to His Nephew," CNN.com, July 23, 1999.

309 "Good night, Daddy": Barbara Leaming, "The Winter of Her Despair," *Vanity Fair,* September 18, 2014.

CHAPTER 54

310 "yacht of a Greek oil millionaire": "Jackie Kennedy: One of the World's Most Expensive Women," *India Today,* November 30, 1977.

310 "number one targets": Peter Collier and David Horowitz, *The Kennedys: An American Drama* (New York: Summit Books, 1984), 367.

311 "very lonely": Jessica Contrera, "'How Could You?' The Day Jackie Kennedy Became Jackie Onassis," *Washington Post,* October 20, 2018.

311 "comes as a surprise": Hilary Weaver, "The Marriage Proposal Jackie Turned Down," *Vanity Fair,* February 9, 2017.

311 "wise and kind": Weaver, "The Marriage Proposal."

311 "now that Bobby was gone": Contrera, "'How Could You?'"

311 "We are very happy": Peter Jonas, "Jackie Kennedy Marries Greek Billionaire in 1968," *New York Daily News,* November 21, 1968.

311 "Who wouldn't be": Barbara A. Perry, *Rose Kennedy: The Life and Times of a Political Matriarch.* (New York: Norton, 2013), 302.

311 "business transaction": "Jackie Kennedy: One of the World's."

311 "Jackie's glance kept turning": "Jackie Kennedy: One of the World's."

311 "the fabled vessel": Peter Mikelbank, "All About the Luxury Yacht Heidi Klum and Tom Kaulitz Will Charter for Their Wedding Celebration," *People,* August 2, 2019.

311 "Jackie, How Could You?": Collier and Horowitz, *The Kennedys,* 367.

312 "fifty years ago": Contrera, "How Could You?"

312 "engulfed in shadows": J. Randy Taraborrelli, *After Camelot: A Personal History of the Kennedy Family 1968 to the Present* (New York: Grand Central Publishing, 2012), 203.

312 "good father to John and Caroline": Contrera, "How Could You?"

312 "widow and mother": Dallas, *The Kennedy Case,* 328.

313 "profound perhaps disturbing": Spoto, *Jacqueline Kennedy Bouvier Onassis,* 75.

313 Christina's death: GCT, "November 19, 1988, Christina Onassis Sadly Passes Away Aged 37," *Greek City Times.*

313 "happy man before I married": Taraborrelli, *After Camelot,* 195.

CHAPTER 55

314 "bleeding inside": Barbara Leaming, "The Winter of Her Despair," *Vanity Fair,* September 18, 2014.

314 "Nobody can do for them": Leaming, "Winter of Her Despair."

314 "controlling and domineering mother": Maureen Callahan, "Inside Ethel Kennedy's Cruel Neglect of Her Troubled Kids," *New York Post,* September 13, 2015.

314 "moods could swing drastically": Callahan, "Inside Ethel Kennedy's Cruel Neglect."

315 "Jackie on a budget?": J. Randy Taraborrelli, *Jackie, Ethel, Joan: Women of Camelot* (New York: Grand Central Publishing, 2012), 253.

315 "If anything happens to John": Liz Cantrell, "John F. Kennedy Jr.'s Close Friend Sheds Light on the Former First Son's Final Days in New Biography," *Town & Country,* July 14, 2019.

315 "allowed to experience life": Katherine Q. Seelye, "John F. Kennedy Jr., Heir to a Formidable Dynasty," *New York Times,* July 19, 1999.

315 *"Me too":* J. Randy Taraborrelli, *The Kennedy Heirs: John, Caroline, and the New Generation — A Legacy of Tragedy and Triumph* (New York: St. Martin's Press, 2019), 318.

315 "cannot tempt fate:" Taraborrelli, *The Kennedy Heirs,* 319.

316 "never let my children fly": Taraborrelli, 319.

316 "jumping all over the place": Ronald Kessler, *The Sins of the Father: Joseph P. Kennedy and the Dynasty He Founded* (New York: Warner Books, 1996), 415.

316 "good for her son": Evan Thomas, "Living with the Myth." *Newsweek,* July 25, 1999.

316 "happy-go-lucky": Bethany Bray, "PA Teacher Remembers Life with JFK Jr.," *Andover Townsman,* December 4, 2008.

316 "incredible pressure": Michael Powell, "JFK Jr.: As Child and Man, America's Crown Prince," *Washington Post,* July 18, 1999.

316 "great boarding school mother": Bray, "PA Teacher Remembers Life with JFK Jr."

317 "push the disciplinary envelope": Evan Thomas, "An Unsettling Portrait of Four Privileged Classmates Who Met Untimely Deaths," *Washington Post,* July 25, 2019.

317 John Jr.'s undergraduate application: Emily Smith and Tashara Jones, "Jackie Worked Hard to Keep JFK from Flunking." *New York Post,* October 9, 2017.

317 "special consideration for my children": Eileen Reslen, "JFK Jr.'s College Application and Jackie Kennedy's Letters to His Professors Are for Sale," *Harper's Bazaar,* October 9, 2017.

317 "bad habits of borrowing money": Thomas, "An Unsettling Portrait."

317 "borrow a quarter every night": Martha Brant, "Coming of Age," *Newsweek,* August 13, 1995.

318 Off-off Broadway debut: "Acting Up Off-Off-Broadway, John Kennedy Jr. Auditions a New Stage for Himself," *People,* August 26, 1985.

318 "best young actors": "Acting Up Off-Off-Broadway."

318 "John's problem as an actor": Brant, "Coming of Age."

318 "only a hobby": Brant.

318 "not a legal genius." Bob Greene, "'The Hunk Flunks' and We Are Shamed," *Chicago Tribune,* May 7, 1990.

319 "difficulties for any defense": Ronald Sullivan, "Prosecutor Kennedy Wins First Trial Easily," *New York Times*, August 30, 1991.

319 "Winning is better than losing": Sullivan, "Prosecutor Kennedy Wins First Trial Easily."

CHAPTER 56

320 "steal your soul": Evan Thomas, "Living with the Myth," *Newsweek,* July 25, 1999.

320 "skating down West Broadway": Frank DiGiacomo, "John Kennedy, New Yorker," *Observer,* July 26, 1999.

320 "I was blown away": DiGiacomo, "John Kennedy, New Yorker."

321 "you're a *Kennedy*": J. Randy Taraborrelli, *After Camelot: A Personal History of the Kennedy Family 1968 to the Present* (New York: Grand Central Publishing, 2012), 312.

321 "hated his hair": "What JFK Jr. Thought of His Hair, 'Sexiest Man Alive' Title & Having Kids: His Assistant Tells All," Extra.com, July 29, 2016.

321 "best-dressed lists": Thomas, "Living with the Myth."

321 "magicians are only as good": Elizabeth Mehren, "Crisis Crosses Camelot's Moat in Massachusetts," *Los Angeles Times,* May 6, 1997.

321 "'I'm JFK'": Martha Brant, "Coming of Age," *Newsweek,* August 13, 1995.

321 "interesting to be you": Liz McNeil, "Revealing the Real (and Very Complicated) John F. Kennedy Jr. Twenty Years after His Death (He Was Two People)," *People,* July 2, 2019.

322 "legacy or a mystique," Katherine Q. Seelye, "John F. Kennedy Jr., Heir to a Formidable Dynasty, *New York Times,* July 19, 1999.

322 "obviously very close": "John F. Kennedy Jr.'s Life in the Spotlight," Oprah.com.

322 "more of a brother": Stephanie Nolasco, "John F. Kennedy Was 'Emotionally Devastated' by His Cousin Anthony Radziwill's Cancer Diagnosis, Says Pal," Fox News, July 16, 2019.

322 "Anthony had his back": Julie Miller, "Carolyn Bessette's Fraught Final Summer," *Vanity Fair*, July 16, 2019.

322 "loved John, hated John": J. Randy Taraborrelli, *The Kennedy Heirs—John, Caroline, and the Third Generation: A Legacy of Triumph and Tragedy* (New York: St. Martin's Press, 2019), 240.

323 "raised to be President": Peter Collier and David Horowitz, *The Kennedys: An American Drama* (New York: Summit Books, 1984), 346.

323 "remarkable experiment in eugenics": Collier and Horowitz, *The Kennedys*, 355–56.

323 "the most Kennedy": Barbara Matusow, "Bobby's Children Showed the Best, Worst of Family," *Sun-Sentinel*, November 17, 1988.

323 "You're not Kennedys, you're only Shrivers": Collier and Horowitz, *The Kennedys*, 341.

323 "endure as a Kennedy": William D. Cohan, "You Don't Just Wallow in Death. You Move on. You Hold it Inside": The Struggle of John F. Kennedy Jr, American Prince," *Vanity Fair,* July 7, 2019.

323 "her two miracles": R. W. Apple Jr., "Death of a First Lady: The Overview; Jacqueline Kennedy Onassis Is Buried. *New York Times,* May 24, 1994.

324 "Ultimate Beautiful Person": Cohan, "You Don't Just Wallow in Death."

324 "ordinary person": Cohan.

324 "Carolyn isn't everything": J. Randy Taraborrelli, *The Kennedy Heirs: John, Caroline, and the Third Generation—A Legacy of Triumph and Tragedy* (New York: St. Martin's Press, 2019), 40.

324 "smoke and mirrors": Taraborrelli, *The Kennedy Heirs.*

324 "definitely chased her": Sarah Grossbart, "Inside the Heartbreakingly Tragic Final Days of John F. Kennedy Jr. Family Strife Financial Woes and Talk of Divorce," *E! News,* January 4, 2019.

324 "enthralled with her": Julie Miller, "Carolyn Bessette's Fraught Final Summer."

325 "held the proposal off": Grossbart, "Inside the Heartbreakingly Tragic."

325 "What's John been doing": Thomas, "Living with the Myth."

325 "called my hotel": Kate Storey, "The Inside Story of John F. Kennedy Jr.'s *George* Magazine," *Esquire,* April 22, 2019.

325 "rollerblading with John": Storey, "The Inside Story of John F. Kennedy Jr.'s *George* Magazine."

326 "video was terrible": Glynnis MacNichol, "Who Was Carolyn Bessette Kennedy?" *Town & Country,* August 3, 2016.

326 Islanders gathered: Margo Harakas, "Preserving a Legacy," *Sun-Sentinel,* April 22, 1999.

326 "If Mr. Kennedy wanted privacy": Kevin Sack, "The Island That Kept a Wedding a Secret," *New York Times,* September 26, 1996.

326 "fooled everybody": Sack, "The Island That Kept a Wedding a Secret."

327 "more security than wedding guests": Leah Bourne, "#Throwback Thursday: Carolyn Bessette and John F. Kennedy's Jr. Truly Timeless Wedding," StyleCaster.com.

327 "mysterious and female": Ann Gerhart, "Bessette Tried to Avoid Kennedy Spotlight," *Washington Post,* July 18, 1999.

327 "any privacy or room you could give": MacNicol, "Who Was Carolyn Bessette Kennedy?"

327 "JUST LEAVE HER ALONE": MacNichol.

327 "We're used to a certain degree of being watched": "John F. Kennedy Jr.'s Life in the Spotlight," Oprah.com.

327 "invited me on your show": "John F. Kennedy Jr.'s Life in the Spotlight," Oprah.com.

327 "born famous": Nolasco, "John F. Kennedy Was 'Emotionally Devastated.'"

327 "see the paparazzi": Miller, "Carolyn Bessette's Fraught Final Summer."

CHAPTER 57

328 US government to pay the Zapruder family: Michael E. Ruane, "As He Filmed Abraham Zapruder Knew Instantly That President Kennedy Was Dead," *Washington Post,* November 21, 2013.

328 "John Cole": Stacey Singer, "Students: Kennedy Took Safety Seriously," *South Florida Sun-Sentinel,* July 19, 1999.

329 "Flight Safety Academy": Edward Klein, *The Kennedy Curse: Why America's First Family Has Been Haunted by Tragedy for 150 Years* (New York: St. Martin's Press, 2003), 216.

329 "strict with me": Singer, "Students: Kennedy Took Safety Seriously."

329 "He told me his wife didn't want him to do it": Singer.

329 Flight training: National Transportation Safety Board Aviation Accident Final Report, July 6, 2000.

329 "The only person": Evan Thomas, "Living with the Myth," *Newsweek,* July 25, 1999.

329 "I don't trust him": Thomas, "Living with the Myth."

330 "exist without John?" Carl Swanson, "*George* Magazine Loses a 'Yes' Woman as Hachette Steps In," *Observer,* January 18, 1999.

330 "content and in love": J. Randy Taraborrelli, *The Kennedy Heirs: John, Caroline, and the New Generation—A Legacy of Tragedy and Triumph* (New York: St. Martin's Press, 2019), 300.

330 "not the truth": Julie Miller, "Carolyn Bessette's Fraught Final Summer," *Vanity Fair,* July 16, 2019.

330 "not going to sugarcoat": Miller, "Carolyn Bessette's Fraught Final Summer."

330 "emotionally devastating": Stephanie Nolasco, "John F. Kennedy Was 'Emotionally Devastated' by His Cousin Anthony Radziwill's Cancer Diagnosis, Says Pal," Fox News, July 16, 2019.

331 "gone too far": "Not a Lot of Love in Camelot," *Irish News* (UK), November 13, 1999.

331 "not a priority": Sara Stewart, "Carolyn's Secret Torment," *New York Post,* January 19, 2012.

331 "will be fun": Klein, *The Kennedy Curse,* 220.

32 "enough to be dangerous": Dale Russakoff and Lynne Duke, "JFK JR. Gave Up Copilot as Ankle Healed," *Washington Post,* July 21, 1999.

333 "pilot was not ready": National Transportation Safety Board Aviation Accident Final Report, July 6, 2000.

332 "emotional ups and downs": Elizabeth Wolff, "Inside JFK Jr.'s Daze of Doom," *New York Post,* June 17, 2007.

332 Graves' disease: "John Kennedy's Medical Secrets Linger," CBC News, November 21, 2013.

332 "last I ever heard from her": Megan French, "Carole Radziwill Recalls the Night John F. Kennedy Jr. and Carolyn Bessette Died," *US Weekly,* March 7, 2017.

333 "ran into a thick haze": Rinker Buck, "Experts: JFK Flight May Have Been Illegal," *Hartford Courant,* July 21, 1999.

333 "No chance": Wolff, "Inside JFK's Jr.'s Daze of Doom."

333 "to do it alone": Matthew W. Wald, "Safety Board Blames Pilot Error in Crash of Kennedy Plane," *New York Times,* July 7, 2000.

333 "Flying at night": Wald, "Safety Board Blames."

333 "North of Teterboro": Wolff, "Inside JFK's Jr.'s Daze of Doom."

333 American Airlines Flight 128: Wolff.

333 "not in contact": National Transportation Safety Board Aviation Accident Final Report, July 6, 2000.

334 "hard to see the horizon": David Barstow, "Kennedy's Plane Lost: The Overview; John Kennedy's Plane Vanishes Off Cape Cod," *New York Times*, July 18, 1999.

334 "they're not here": French, "Carole Radziwill Recalls the Night John F. Kennedy Jr. and Carolyn Bessette Died."

334 "My cousin's missing": French.

334 "If Jackie was alive": J. Randy Taraborrelli, *After Camelot: A Personal History of the Kennedy Family 1968 to the Present* (New York: Grand Central Publishing, 2012), 3.

334 "Johnny as one of my own": Taraborrelli, *After Camelot*.

335 "family that has distinguished": Mike Allen, "The Kennedy Burial: The Overview; A Private Ceremony at Sea for the Three on Kennedy Plane," *New York Times*, July 23, 1999.

335 "very grim, very quiet": Steve Dunleavy, "Another Grim Trip to ID a Dead Loved One," *New York Post*, July 22, 1999.

335 "crashes down on Ted": Interview with Lester Hyman, *The Edward M. Kennedy Oral History Project*, Edward M. Kennedy Institute for the United States Senate in partnership with the Miller Center of Public Affairs at the University of Virginia, 2016.

335 "Catholic priests conducted": "Remains of JFK Jr., Wife, and Sister-In-Law Buried at Sea," CNN.com, July 22, 1999.

336 "protocol allows sea burials": "Remains of JFK Jr., Wife, and Sister-In-Law Buried at Sea."

336 "asked me to marry him": Sara Stewart, "Carolyn's Secret Torment," *New York Post*, January 19, 2012.

336 "flowers onto the ghosts": Isabel Vincent and Melissa Klein, "Kennedy Family Feuded Before Bodies Were Recovered in JFK Jr. Crash," *New York Post*, November 3, 2013,

336 "the American family": N. R. Kleinfield, "The Kennedy Memorial: The Service; Doors Closed, Kennedys Offer Their Farewells," *New York Times*, July 24, 1999.

336 "John's last hours": Michael Shelden, "The Deaths Brought Me to My Knees," *Telegraph* (UK), October 25, 2005.

337 "John ever fathomed": Lisa DePaulo, "John F. Kennedy Jr. and *George* Magazine: A Story of Politics, Love and Loss, Twenty Years Later," *Hollywood Reporter*, April 9, 2019.

337 "If there's a curse": J. Randy Taraborrelli, *The Kennedy Heirs: John,*

Caroline, and the New Generation—A Legacy of Tragedy and Triumph (New York: St. Martin's Press, 2019), 51.

337 "film's worth": David Johnson, "Zapruder Heirs Get $16 Million for Dallas Film," *New York Times,* August 4, 1999.

337 John's Piper Saratoga II: "NTSB: JFK Jr.'s Plane Shows No In-Flight Break-Up or Fire," CNN.com, July 30, 2019.

337 "spatial disorientation": Wald, "Safety Board Blames Pilot Error."

338 "a stupid mistake": Ed Vulliamy, "Why John Crashed," *Guardian,* July 25, 1999.

CODA

339 "My poor Joe": Rita Dallas with Jeanira Ratcliffe, *The Kennedy Case* (New York: G. P. Putnam's Sons, 1973), 344.

339 "sense the tears": Dallas, *The Kennedy Case,* 345.

339 "sound of Teddy's footsteps": Dallas, 344.

339 "best I can": Thomas Maier, *The Kennedys: America's Emerald Kings* (New York: Basic, 2003), 533.

340 "Please answer me": Dallas, *The Kennedy Case,* 346.

340 "pain of the burden": Barbara Perry, *Rose Kennedy: The Life and Times of a Political Matriarch* (New York: Norton, 2013), 308.

340 "woman in black": Ronald Kessler, *The Sins of the Father: Joseph P. Kennedy and the Dynasty He Founded* (New York: Warner Books, 1996), 422.

340 "true story of Joe Kennedy": Seymour M. Hersh, *The Dark Side of Camelot* (New York: Little, Brown, 1997), 81.

341 "needed to ask Kennedy": StoryCorps, "Busboy Who Cradled a Dying RFK Recalls Those Final Moments," *Morning Edition,* National Public Radio, June 1, 2018.

341 "men it remembers": John F. Kennedy, "Remarks at Amherst College upon Receiving an Honorary Degree (439)," *Public Papers of the Presidents: John F. Kennedy, 1963,* October 26, 1963.

ABOUT THE AUTHOR

JAMES PATTERSON is the world's bestselling author and most trusted storyteller. He has created many enduring fictional characters and series, including Alex Cross, the Women's Murder Club, Michael Bennett, Maximum Ride, Middle School, and I Funny. Among his notable literary collaborations are *The President Is Missing,* with President Bill Clinton, and the Max Einstein series, produced in partnership with the Albert Einstein Estate. Patterson's writing career is characterized by a single mission: to prove that there is no such thing as a person who "doesn't like to read," only people who haven't found the right book. He's given over three million books to schoolkids and the military, donated more than seventy million dollars to support education, and endowed over five thousand college scholarships for teachers. For his prodigious imagination and championship of literacy in America, Patterson was awarded the 2019 National Humanities Medal. The National Book Foundation presented Patterson with the Literarian Award for Outstanding Service to the American Literary Community, and he is also the recipient of an Edgar Award and nine Emmy Awards. He lives in Florida with his family.